Porous City

From Metaphor to Urban Agenda

Porous City

**From Metaphor
to Urban Agenda**

Editors:
Sophie Wolfrum
Heiner Stengel
Florian Kurbasik
Norbert Kling
Sofia Dona
Imke Mumm
Christian Zöhrer

Birkhäuser
Basel

Content

Producing Space and Acting

Urban Regulations and Planning

Urban Territoriality and Strategies

Detecting Porosity

Porous City—From Metaphor to Urban Agenda
Sophie Wolfrum

In its iridescent significance, the term *porosity* develops from a descriptive and analytically employed metaphor toward the category of urbanist agenda. This has been a process over decades, but gathering pace in recent years. The source commonly referred to is a 1925 essay on Naples by Walter Benjamin and Asja Lacis.

"As porous as this stone is the architecture. Building and action interpenetrate in the courtyards, arcades, and stairways. In everything they preserve the scope to become a theater of new, unforeseen constellations. The stamp of the definitive is avoided. No situation appears intended forever, no figure asserts its 'thus and not otherwise.'" (Benjamin and Lacis 1925, 165–66) The description of morphologic features of the natural terrain has been transferred onto the architectural characteristics of the city: "as porous as this stone" Naples is located on and built of. "The city is craggy" (Ibid., 165). But these crags are full of caves and voids and holes. Porous crags: full of the lives of people. Soon afterwards, the authors transfer this observation to the social characteristics of Naples city life, which they observe strolling through the city on their visits, while in fact living on the island of Capri nearby.

The metaphor of porosity was almost immediately picked up by Ernst Bloch in his essay "Italien und die Porosität," applying it to habits he observed in southern Italy generally. This text sounds much more stereotyped to the contemporary reader than Benjamin and Lacis's. It is full of observations and descriptions of scenes of a premodern society. "Things and people have no borders (Dinge und Menschen haben keine Ränder)" (Bloch 1925, 512). This focus on the muddle of functions, not merely an inversion of private and public, inside and outside, more its intermingling (*Durcheinander*) and the cross-references to baroque features are still of relevance today (see Eduard Bru in the present volume).

The text on Naples is a piece of literature, beautifully written. This may have supported its spread. (The English translation is unfortunately less poetic.) Moreover, the method of close observation of details differed from all contemporaneous and previous reports on Naples by German writers. In this reportage, it is the flaneur who is affected by spaces of daily life but not by the canonical monuments of art history listed in the popular Baedeker travel guide. This special viewpoint of the flaneur presages Benjamin's *Arcades Project (Passagen-Werk)*. In particular, the feature of interpenetration (*Durchdringung*) is in the focus of more contemporary reflections of different disciplinary professional origins (see Benjamin 2007; Fellmann 2014). This aspect is especially attractive for an urban agenda in the professional realm of our book, but it has also been regarded as a significant stepping stone to Benjamin's epochal essay on media theory "The Work of Art in the Age of Its Technological Reproducibility" (1936; see Fellmann 2014). Furthermore, the flaneur operates in a modest, sublimated everyday sense, as Walter Benjamin notes in this context: "Architecture has always offered the prototype of an artwork that is received in a state of distraction and through the collective" (Benjamin 1936, 40). Perception by distraction is again a line of thought which has been reflected on frequently in the theoretical architectural discourse.

"Irresistibly the festival penetrates each and every working day. Porosity is the inexhaustible law of the life of this city, reappearing everywhere. A grain of Sunday is hidden in each weekday, and how much weekday in this Sunday!" (Benjamin and Lacis 1925, 168) Interpenetration, permeability (*Durchdringung*) is described as prevalent in Naples not only in private and public urban spaces but in the temporal rhythm of city life as well. It affects the entire conduct of life. Even the cafés are "true laboratories of this great process of intermingling" (Ibid., 172). Though Benjamin did not use the notion of porosity in his later writings literally, interpenetration remains an important pattern in his thought.

In the modernist period, by contrast, the tendency has been to separate and distinguish spheres of life and activities in society: night from day, housing from working, reproduction from production, transport from traveling, etc. Cities reflect these basic distinctions; thresholds are missing. The modernist city has been characterized by homogenous zoning classifications and solidifying borders. The contemporary city in the Western world, in Western-influenced areas, and in the postsocialist world, continues to be profoundly influenced by this mind-set. "Space and opportunity at any price" ("Raum und Gelegenheit auf alle Fälle") is lost. Although Naples in the year of 1924, during the visits by Benjamin, Bloch, Adorno, and later famous German writers, might have been still a premodern city in many respects, porosity is adopted as a countermodel, a critique of the modern city. Working with the agenda of porosity opens up alternatives by focusing on interpenetration, superimposition, connectivity, and thresholds.

Porosity identifies qualities and architectural attributes that seem indispensable for the complexity and adaptability of urban spaces. As Amin Ash and Nigel Thrift put it, "porosity is what allows the city to continually fashion and refashion itself" (Ash and Thrift 2002, 10). They use the term *porosity* explicitly as a metaphor with regard to Benjamin and Lacis. Porosity is announced as one of four key metaphors with which to grasp the everydayness of cities: "transitivity, porosity, rhythm, and footprint" (Ibid., 5). However, in the text in question, porosity plays second fiddle to the term *transitivity*, though Benjamin's writings on cities remain in the focus. They never really go into depth, and at the end of the chapter they state the shortcoming of metaphors for a theory of everyday urbanism due to their lack of methodological clarity (Ibid, 26). For them the focus is on everyday life, as it comes to life in the report on Naples. The porous city might enable typical urban ambivalences: distance and proximity, exclusion and integration, heterogeneity and homogeneity, anonymity and community. This requires significant urban spaces as well as, at the same time, a dense interweaving and use of these spaces. Richard Sennett, another scholar who uses the term frequently, understands the porous city as a place of radical mixture. He puts his finger on the wound and asks: "Why don't we build them?" (Sennett 2015)

"Porosity results not only from the indolence of the Southern artisan, but also, above all, from the passion for improvisation, which demands that space and opportunity be at any price preserved. Buildings are used as a popular stage. They are all divided into innumerable, simultaneously animated theaters. Balcony, courtyard, window, gateway, staircase, roof are at the same time stage and boxes." (Benjamin and Lacis 1925, 166–67) The last sentences are especially appreciated by architects. Here the ubiquitous analogy of city and stage is expanded by a perception of urban space via its performative characteristics. Space is generated by activities induced by these very specific architectural elements. Walter Benjamin and Asja Lacis, however, observe the intertwining / interpenetration of urban spaces and the urban texture mainly from a cultural and social perspective. The layering and mélange of spaces, the perforation of borders, and the ambiguity of thresholds are perceived as specific urban qualities.

Regarding the porous city from an explicitly architectural perspective, porosity becomes a crucial spatial criterion, for Walter Benjamin and Asja Lacis convey a specific appreciation of the architecture of Naples's historical center: everything merges together, is commingled. No figure is definite. There is no allocation of private and urban functions to defined places: "Here, too, there is interpenetration of day and night, noise and peace, outer light and inner darkness, street and home" (Ibid, 172). In our perspective on performative urbanism (Wolfrum and Brandis 2015), we have underscored architecture's potential for sensation and action as equivalent and complementary characteristics of its physical presence. In this sense, we see porosity as an attribute of urban spaces of all scales.

In view of the widespread use of porosity as an urbanist urban agenda in the contemporary debate, we might notice that this adoption started earlier in Southern Europe. Paola Viganò and Bernardo Secchi were at the vanguard, inspired by the metabolism of water and soil in the dispersed landscape of the Po Plain. They frequently apply and develop this agenda in different urbanized European regions, for example in Flanders and Greater Paris. They use *porous city* almost as a general concept and spatial model, in which the "porousness of urban tissue" is only one of several desiderata target figures (Viganò 2009). Conversely, Stavros Stavrides focuses on porous borders, thresholds, passages, membranes, osmosis, and lived space. "Urban porosity may be the result of such practices that perforate a secluding perimeter, providing us with an alternative model to the modern city of urban enclaves. A city of thresholds. [...]" (Stavrides 2007, 174)

Porosity in its programmatic turn addresses both physical and social space, one of the few terms that incorporates both realms of urban space without compartmentalization (no pigeonhole thinking). Nevertheless, in the conceptual sense porosity remains rather diffuse. With the help of different approaches by authors from different backgrounds, this book attempts to explore porosity from a variety of perspectives.

· Reflections on the term—to what extent is *porosity* a useful term in architecture and urbanism? Its conceptual versatility is explored as well as the issues of working with an open metaphor.
· Urban architecture and design—related to border, membrane, threshold, intermediate space, and transparency. The focus is on elements of architecture in between which support or cause interpenetration.
· Producing space and acting—sensuality, temporary interventions, and negotiation bring performativity into focus and connects to the discourse on performative urbanism, which we initiated some years ago.
· Urban regulations and planning—related to legal frameworks, basic politics vs. tactics, exception, and tolerance—discussion of whether porosity in a programmatic sense can be achieved by urban planning. Or are conditions based on formalized urban planning inevitably contrary to porosity as a concept?
· Urban territoriality and strategies—discussion of the multiple connotations, simultaneity, complexity, diversity, and, notably, superimposition of urban landscapes in processes of suspension and/or transformation.
· Detecting porosity—this invites us to embark on in-depth analytical journeys that seek to explore the more hidden simultaneities and constellations in porous urban environments. Texts, photos, and drawings are used as research instruments that open up new perspectives on porosity.

Does this journey bring us to any defined end? The fuzziness and blurriness of the term *porosity* might just turn out to be its advantage. Clearly, it meets our desire for complexity. In this state of vagueness we may restart our exploration with Walter Benjamin (1950, 8):

"Not to find one's way in a city may well be uninteresting and banal. It requires ignorance—nothing more. But to lose oneself in a city—as one loses oneself in a forest—that calls for quite a different schooling."

("Sich in einer Stadt nicht zurechtfinden heißt nicht viel. In einer Stadt sich aber zu verirren, wie man in einem Walde sich verirrt, braucht Schulung.")

References:
Amin, A., and N. Thrift. 2002. *Cities: Reimagining the Urban*. Cambridge. | Benjamin, A. 2007. "Porosity at the Edge: Working through Benjamin's 'Naples,'" in *Moderne begreifen: Zur Paradoxie eines sozioästhetischen Deutungsmusters*, edited by C. Magerski, R. Savage, and C. Weller, 7–119. Wiesbaden. | Benjamin, W. 1936. "The Work of Art in the Age of Its Technological Reproducibility," in *The Work of Art in the Age of Its Technological Reproducibility and Other Writings on Media*, ed. M. W. Jennings, B. Doherty, and T. J. Levin, eds, 19–55. Cambridge, MA, 2008. | Benjamin, W. 1950. "A Berlin Chronicle," in *Reflections: Essays, Aphorisms, Autobiographical Writings*, edited by P. Demetz, 3–60. New York, 1978. | Benjamin, W., and A. Lacis. 1925. "Naples," in *Reflections: Essays, Aphorisms, Autobiographical Writings*, edited by P. Demetz, 163–73. New York, 1978. | Bloch, E. 1925. "Italien und die Porosität," in *Werkausgabe*, vol. 9, *Literarische Aufsätze*, 508–15. Frankfurt am Main, 1985. | Fellmann, B. 2014. *Durchdringung und Porosität: Walter Benjamins Neapel: Von der Architekturwahrnehmung zur kunstkritischen Medientheorie*. Münster. Sennett, R. 2015. "The World Wants More 'Porous' Cities—So Why Don't We Build Them?" *The Guardian*, November 27, 2015. | Stavrides, S. 2007. "Heterotopias and the Experience of Porous Urban Space," in *Loose Space: Possibility and Diversity in Urban Life*, edited by K. A. Franck and Q. Stevens, 174–93. New York. | Viganò, P. 2009. "The Metropolis of the Twenty-First Century: The Project of a Porous City," *OASE*, no. 80: 91–107. | Wolfrum, S., and N. v. Brandis, eds. 2015. Performative Urbanism. Berlin. | Wolfrum, S., and A. Janson. 2016. *Architektur der Stadt*. Stuttgart.

Reflections on the Term

Porosity—Porous City
Sophie Wolfrum

Does the term *porosity* develop from a descriptive and analytically employed metaphor toward the category of urban agenda? This chapter turns the statement "from metaphor to urban agenda" into a question in contradictory contributions. Though these articulate a multitude of contradictory arguments—not all of them approving—a tableau of elements nevertheless emerges to flesh out the term *porosity*.

The reference to Benjamin and Lacis's essay (1925) in the literature is still frequent, though in many cases the essay has simply been mined to establish a relationship to the famous thinker Walter Benjamin while often ignoring Asja Lacis. Focusing on Benjamin resonates with his reflections in the unfinished *Arcades Project (Passengen-Werk)*, with his poetic manner in writing about cities, with the flaneur as a practitioner and a figure of thought in perceiving the urban realm differently. Walter Benjamin himself did not stick literally to the term *porosity* in his further writings, as Dietrich Erben reveals in this book, criticizing the metaphor as being imprecise and its conceptual history too vague. Nevertheless, it has since taken on a life and force of its own. In the city of Naples itself, it has been unquestioningly inducted into the terminology of the urban design profession since then. Being attentive—as we editors of this book are—one cannot help but notice the frequency with which the term is now used in urbanist discourse.

Porosity invokes a panoply of interdependent connotations such as:
· interpenetration, superimposition, and multilayering of spaces
· integration, overlapping, and communication of spatial elements
· ambiguous zone, inbetween space, and threshold
· permeability, spaciousness, and ambiguity of borders
· coexistence, polyvalence, and sharing
· blurring, ambivalence, and even weakness
· provisional, incomplete, and even kaput
· openness of processes concerning coincidence, rhythm, and time
· the flaneur's perspective and a performative approach to urban architecture

The visualizing aspect of the term is its key advantage. This helps to bridge the two worlds of our profession as urban designers and of urban everyday life—architectural features and qualities of the built environment on the one side and the socially produced space of a complex urban society on the other—the material and the social. The characteristic of a *Denkbild* "in which conceptual and pictorial understanding interpenetrate" (Erben, 28) turns out to be very productive. Porosity is one of the few terms with this complexity of double-connotation yet which still opens a field of associations fit for purposeful acting and room for maneuver.

Whether *porosity* can be "considered to be a fundamental architectural phenomenon" (Janson, 100) or on the contrary as "a piece of architectural terminology" (Erben, 30) might be interpreted as an academic debate from different theoretical perspectives, architect versus art historian. However, we abide by the term as urban designers on the side of architecture exactly because it is of practical relevance, even in terms of object and space, and yet has all the iridescent connotations of openness (see Bru). It is precisely these connotations which invoke qualities our cities and their architectural urban fabric desperately lack. Qualities we as urban designers can achieve if we are attentive. This opens a field of analysis and operations which are critical of modernist planning practices and "refrains from the use of ordering regimes, thus enabling a polyvalence in design" (Koch, 20).

The contemporary city is still trapped in the modernist planning paradigm of zoning and cleaning up. If the "Naples essay is exemplary of modernism" and the figure of threshold might be paradigmatic of that (Erben, 28), we must, unfortunately, note that the modern formal urban planning system is completely unaffected by the threshold paradigm and is in fact dedicated to the contrary. It is located on the other side of the Janus-face of modernity. Following Max Horkheimer and Theodor W. Adorno (1947), we have to consider how desperately modernity is enmeshed in two opposing stances: one of efficiency and instrumentalization of reason and the other of open structures, connectivity, and transition. The legal system, however, is on the side of efficiency, it demands unambiguousness, is definite and rational. Thresholds are substituted by barriers, protection walls, and strict zoning regulations. Against this backdrop, *porosity* turns out to be a positive goal for urban design and the architectural features of urban spaces (see chapter 2, "Architecture and Urban Design"). No wonder the above list cloud of connotations refers much to the postmodern discourse, which has emphasized the multitude against efficiency. It is in this sense that Isaiah Berlin is referred to in *Collage City*: "A fox knows many things, but a hedgehog one important thing" (Rowe and Koetter 1978, 91).

At the same time, the idea of a porous city prevents us from falling back into modernist delusions of a perfect city to be achieved by urban design. "The porous city will never be completed." Maren Harnack refers to the historicity of cities and praises the "messy city" (Harnack, 41), a tack which leads to Giorgia Aquilar's contemplations on the advantages of the broken—*kaputt* (Aquilar, 42).

Stavros Stavrides contributes an explicit political position to the discourse within this chapter, bringing the mediating character of thresholds together with a political agenda of commons and the right to the city struggles. "Urban pores in principle connect and establish opportunities for exchange and communication, eliminating thus space-bound privileges" (Stavrides, 32). The double connotation of the *Denkbild* is extensively explored in terms of its social interpretation from the perspective of lived space. This line of reflection holds that a city of thresholds might contribute to a city as engine of tolerance. The porous city has already become an urban agenda in a broad political sense dedicated to an emancipating urban culture.

Paola Viganò's contribution reveals the most programmatic and practically oriented application. She assigns porosity a productive role as conceptual metaphor within several projects undertaken by her office. The planning study *Greater Paris*, for example, is centered on porosity not by transferring it abstractly via directives, but more using the term as a mirror to reflect missing spatial qualities. Conceptual fields of planning and action are derived from a deep analysis of the metropolitan spatial structure and its problematic centralized hierarchical systems: "The absence of porosity became the inspiration for a metropolitan vision which translated into five main spatial strategies" (Viganò, 52). The "project of a porous city" (Ibid.) for *Greater Paris* is again, like the other Studio Secchi-Viganò planning studies, deeply rooted in a profound observation of the respective territory and its spatial structural deficits and potential.

This brings us back to the question of whether porosity may work as an urban agenda. We are aware that the history of our discipline is trapped in a frantic search dedicated to "abstracting the phenomenon of urbanity into conceivable analogs and metaphors" (Lehnerer, 170), while "the titles of the publications seem to be poetically evoking new urban forces [...] has by now filled the libraries" (Koch, 20).

Consequently, we intend to refrain from a fixed programmatic agenda proclaiming new preconceptions or putative certainties in favor of a tableau of the above-listed connotations.

All these terms focus on uncertainties and dichotomies and yet stand for qualities the profession can foster. In this respect, the agenda of the porous city might be entangled in a dialectical opposition. Most formal planning instruments, regulated by law, are intended to be as precise and reliable as possible (see chapter 4, "Urban Regulations and Planning"); an agenda might also have the intrinsic tendency to establish new ordering regimes. But the idea of the porous city is exactly the opposite: openness, connectivity, interpenetration. This may count as a categorical contradiction and is not without risk. But we do not regard this as an opposition of paradoxical character: one can insert weakness, for example, on one's agenda without compromising one's will to act. The intrinsic dialectical opposition of porosity as urban agenda encourages the finding of new forms of spatial solution, of new kinds of tactics, and promotes action, not least because the urban profession has a method at its disposal for dealing with the oppositions, contradictions, and wicked problems: that is design.

References:
Horkheimer, M., and T. W. Adorno. 1947. *Dialectic of Enlightenment.* Translated by J. Cumming. London, 2016. | Rowe, C., and F. Koetter. 1978. *Collage City.* Cambridge, MA.

News from Naples? An Essay on Conceptual Narratives
Michael Koch

The porous city: a new concept for the revival of urban professions in view of the helplessness of urbanism? The profession has struggled with this challenge at least since the inception of postmodernism. The following essay will take up this trajectory. Sophie Wolfrum's initiative for this publication is a vigorous call for the overcoming of disciplinary boundaries and for the readjustment of professional instruments and competences (Koch 2012).

The Perforated New City

Architectural modernism claimed to take the lead in all matters concerning the city of the future, being convinced that the conditions in cities were appalling, while being motivated by an enlightened sociopolitical impetus. Furthermore, its proponents asserted that they had the necessary conceptual skills to generate the City of the Future by means of planning. Accordingly, legislative bodies provided the instruments that were understood to be required for this process. Although democratically legitimized, this may ultimately be considered a claim to omnipotent design authority. Research work that is critical of this approach has by now filled the libraries, seeking to define an appropriate relationship between social and urban reality. The titles of the publications seem to be poetically evoking new urban forces: *La ville eparpillée* by Gérard and Roux in 1976, *Métapolis* by Ascher in 1995, *La ville èmergente* by Dubois-Taine in 1997, *Zwischenstadt* by Sieverts 1997, or *Multiple City* by Wolfrum and Nerdinger in 2008 (Koch 2013, 102ff). Since the flexible intermediate planning stage (*flexible Planzwischenstufe*) was introduced to the planning frameworks in the 1970s, the search for soft and adaptable planning instruments has been a continuous issue. New and predominantly informal planning instruments have been developed to make planning more effective through increased flexibility. Also, since the 1970s, the participation of groups concerned with planning (*Betroffene*) has raised awareness of the world of actors (*Akteurslandschaft*) through and in which planning is realized and modified. Later, in the wake of the work of Michel Callon, John Law, and Bruno Latour, and their actor-network theory approaches were developed in the hope of making planning more effective.

Finally: The Porous City?

The editors of this publication suggest in the introduction that, if porosity as metaphor informs an urban agenda, "Porosity is adopted as a countermodel, a critique of the modern city" (see page 10 in this publication). Porosity of the city is here related to Walter Benjamin and understood as limiting or refraining from the use of ordering regimes, thus enabling a polyvalence in design. It is understood to produce additional scope for the new, for unexpected urban constellations and changes, as well as for spaces of resonance in which improvisations become possible. Hence, it is more about enabling urban practices and less about one-dimensional fixations on building or function.

We have to defend these theses on the porous city against being regarded as a promise of salvation in urbanism, against being misunderstood as a prescription for building the livable city of the future in view of the growing sociospatial and economic conflicts of resource allocation in our cities.

Naples for All?

What does Naples stand for? For an urban utopia—at least from a Northern European perspective? For an urban dystopia from the viewpoint of the socially disadvantaged in Naples? Or simply for a philospohical-ethnographic travel report which is rooted in the period of its origin? "During the mid-1920s the Gulf of Naples was a popular destination of German revolutionaries, nonconformists, and project makers of all couleur" (Später 2013). Reading Walter Benjamin's text, a rather unromantic perspective on the realities of Naples is revealed: dominated by church and Camorra, at times quite frightening to the visiting traveler, marked by the struggle for survival, poverty, and misery. "With the pawnshop and lotto the state holds the proletariat in a vise. [...] To exist, for the Northern European the most private of affairs, is here, as in the kraal, a collective matter." (Benjamin and Lacis 1925, 169 and 171) A faint degree of social romanticism, embedded in the spirit of the time, pervades when Walter Benjamin juxtaposes the "sober, open rooms resembling the political People's Café" and the "confined, bourgeois, literary world" of the Viennese coffeehouse (Ibid., 172–73).

Yet it would be a misunderstanding to conceive of the Naples of Walter Benjamin as the prototype of a pioneering urban design, or of a true urbanity beyond time.

The Beauty of the Big City?

There is a sense of fascination with this culturally different city in Benjamin's text on Naples. The visitor's experience of the city complements the common perception in one's own everyday life, which all too often fails to recognize the ambivalences and opportunities of the city. Literature and art have always highlighted the personal, and at times painful experience of ambivalence as the main characteristic of the city (Endell 1908, Roters and Schulz 1987, Dethier and Guiheux 1994). Urban ethnography and urban sociology seek to develop an understanding of the respective phenomena. The concept of an intrinsic logic (*Eigenlogik*) of cities opens up the possibility of reconstructing the narratives that are of relevance for the production of identity (Berking and Löw 2008).

This fascination with the empathetic view from the outside seems to be suitable for discovering—within the existing city, which in many respects is often full of conflicts—something which is worth preserving.

Jane Jacobs (1961), Wolfgang Mitscherlich (1965) and Wolf Jobst Siedler (1964) turned against the planned destruction of the existing, lived, and inherited city. The latter author, as is well known, supported postmodernism in architecture with the belief that special window dimensions and architecture, designed to the so-called human scale, would be able to reconstruct the urbanity of the beloved, bemoaned European city that had been destroyed. However, if it is difficult for architecture to achieve exactly that—can architecture still contribute toward the beautiful or urban city, through generating porosity? The kind of porosity discussed here is embedded within the cultural context of Naples in a specific way. Despite that, we may propose that the urbanity we observe and value within everyday practices in other places requires similar kinds of open microspaces, ready for appropriation, as well as similar spatial constellations.

Or Rather: The Perforated City?

This new variant of the European city emerged almost as a necessity from the processes of urban shrinking and the massive number of vacant buildings in Leipzig. In response to the physical and functional voids in the urban fabric, the concept of the perforated city was developed in 2001 (Stadtbauwelt 2001, Lütke Daldrup 2003). Once again, the task was to understand the city in a new way and to redesign it conceptually as well as in terms of process. Based on the indispensable cooperation between relevant actors numerous laboratories of a coproduced city emerged. Both terms, *perforation* as well as *porosity*, are based on the idea of a nonplanned, nonintentional ordering structure that results from the emergence of voids in urban tissue or urban morphology. While the discourse on perforation led to the reinterpretation and reconceptualization of urban interrelations, the question of porosity is rather one that engages with the preconditions of urbanity from an architectural perspective and from the perspective of urban design.

As a response to *chaotic* processes of development, both concepts, however, call for the renegotiating of the roles of architecture, urban design, as well as planning.

Professional Consequences?

Key results of the debate on the perforated city were the insights that normative rules are easily degraded to wishful thinking and that the unsystematic nature of processes of urban transformation requires a playful and creative response (Doehler 2003). The porosity observed in Naples does not follow an obvious and easily reproducible ordering principle. Can we, despite that, produce the desired urban potentialities which we associate with porosity? By means of specific (micro)architectures and/or by the way such (micro)architectures are designed and realized? Different conflicting logics of spatial production interfere with each other in the urban domain, which results in a kind of city-conglomerate if they are not, or cannot be, synchronized. Or rather in a metrozone city? The term *metrozone* was introduced for the International Building Exhibition (IBA) in Hamburg to describe spaces that have resisted rational logics of development and that emerged at the edges of functionally ordered areas (IBA Hamburg 2010). They were analyzed for their urban potentiality (*urbane Potentialräume*), with the outcome that tailored concepts and strategies can convert them into new elements of the city.

Transformative Learning

To achieve the desired qualities in the redesign or new design of city quarters along the principles of the postulated porous city, concepts and strategies are needed that are grounded in the situation and the context. To this end
1. Architecture as the art of building can contribute with innovative design proposals
2. Planning can offer appropriate concepts and processes for realization
3. Both disciplines can train specialist actors who are capable of acting and reacting in changing situations. This includes the ability to improvise.

As part of the related urban negotiating processes and collective processes of urban change the relationship of creativity and the issue of multiple authorship may be newly defined and reformulated according to the situation. Concerning the required specialist and personal skills we could speak of artistry and art, in line with the ideas of a *transformative science*. Art, in this context, is understood as being based on knowledge, experience, perception, imagination, and intuition.

The Art of Building

Architects in their professional role are commonly understood as the specialists of the physicality and atmosphere of space, concerned with its structural integrity, use, and appearance—as well as its beauty!

As part of this, the question as to what extent architecture may directly affect human behavior is shrouded in speculative mystery (Kirstgen 2018). Recent research demonstrates, however, how different architectural attitudes, different architectural languages, have produced precisely articulated settings in different morphological contexts, and how they have contributed toward an enrichment of space (Pape and Koch 2018). In doing so, architecture may contribute to the production of urban narratives and support processes in which parts of the city are collectively appropriated. Architecture's capacity to contribute to the morphology of cities is also needed in the porous city. If the production of porosity goes hand in hand with the technical and material modification and adaptation of spaces, an intensive analysis of the context is needed. Moreover, appropriation presupposes everyday knowledge, which suggests that such spaces are generated in processes of coproduction. Among the many predominantly younger practices that are engaged in such work, I refer to the collective Assemble in London, who were awarded the Turner Prize in 2015. I would also like to mention the *Universität der Nachbarschaften*, a pioneering project in joint teaching and research initiated by Bernd Kniess and his team at HCU (HafenCity University) Hamburg. To what extent the envisaged level of everyday, independent, and emancipative use of the provided non-predetermined spaces is realized depends on the financial resources and to a large measure on the legally granted scope of appropriation.

The Art of Planning

In the political process of conceiving and structuring our urban future, we also have to address the question of how to communicate the future potentiality of the "complexity and adaptability of urban spaces" (see page 10 in this publication) so that the issues involved are made available to the public, supporting debate and stimulating multiple actors in the required decision-making processes. To this art of planning belongs the convincing representation of future situations, as well as the making of proposals for process-based strategies of their implementation. In 2008 Paola Viganò and Bernardo Secchi drew up their urban development strategy for greater Paris under the title "La Ville Poreuse" as part of the "Le Grand Pari pour Grand Paris" competition, and translated their strategic proposition into sets of spatial concretizations (Secchi and Viganò 2011). Jean Nouvel and his very large team of renowned colleagues worked out their competition entry in an almost encyclopaedic manner. His key message is that concepts for a livable city have to be enabled through political decisions (Nouvel et al. 2009). The discipline of regional planning has also begun to focus more regularly on the visualization of planning intentions and the articulation of spaces, understanding that this way the connections between the spaces of everyday urban life and functionally organized spatiality become more apparent. This positioning of everyday space enables local actors to better grasp the dynamics at work and to connect to them in a productive way (Koch 2009, Thierstein and Förster 2008, Bornhorst and Schmid 2015).

Artists of Space and Planning

Spatially analogous, model-like representations of concepts in architecture and planning acquire a new significance with the digitalization of our lifeworlds. Such models for spatial and functional explorations of urban development possibilities are made by and for collaborative working processes, in what we usually refer to as *workshops* or *life laboratories* (*Reallabor*). Practical experience suggests that in many different disciplines more than specialist knowledge is required from the specialist. They can make use of their expert knowledge productively only if they have the required sensitivity and empathy, as well as communicative and social skills (Werner 2016, Disziplinaeregrenzgaenge 2016). This means, in the broadest sense, a performer—a personality who shapes and supports the collective decision-making process with the same virtuosity and creativity as she or he does with the object in question to be designed. According to the findings of the *Prozess Städtebau* research project, which is part of the Swiss national research program 65 *Neue Urbane Qualität* (New Urban Quality), a new sensitivity is needed, for it is impossible to provide a best-practice recommendation for the best design of a process (Wezemael 2014).

At the urban scale the notion of urban commons (*urbane Allmende*) embodies the necessity for public negotiation of spatio-functional frameworks (Franck 2011). The claiming of so-called new ground (*Neuland*) requires similar processes of communication and negotiation (Team E 2014, Crone 2014). On new ground projects, obstructive legislation could be experimentally removed to create a situative deregulation that can be filled with new sets of collectively established rules, which can then address the local development potential in a better way. Hence, our society should offer or allow spaces of experimentation, in which exemptions from restrictive and outdated rules can be realized to test the models of the future.

Changing Perspectives

Many new fields of urban work have now emerged in practice (Disziplinaeregrenzgaenge 2016). New curricula have begun to respond to this change. In a new understanding of urban design, the scope of design may be extended. Designing includes in the broadest sense the creative conception of participation and processes of coproduction. These are elements that are and have been relevant to courses in urban planning for some time. However, the diversity which we currently see in the urban practice of different actors, and which informs the present inquiry into a porosity of cities, may encourage us to further intensify and expand our discussion of such practices beyond disciplinary boundaries. It may also give us ideas as to how we could establish and test, in a step-by-step process, the teaching and learning programs that could generate the required skills and practical knowledge across the disciplines (Koch et al. 2018).

References:

Benjamin, W., and A. Lacis. 1925. "Naples," in *Reflections: Essays, Aphorisms, Autobiographical Writings*, edited by P. Demetz, 163–73. New York, 1978. | Berking, H., and M. Löw. 2008. *Die Eigenlogik der Städte: Neue Wege für die Stadtforschung*. Darmstadt. Bornhorst, J., and J. Schmid. 2015. "Entwürfe für die Metropole: Internationale Visionswettbewerbe als Impulsgeber für eine strategische (Regional) Planung?" *disP* 51, no. 2: 62–73. | Crone, B. 2014. "Familienplanung/Fünf Wege zur Metropole Ruhr," *Bauwelt*, no. 7: 17–25. | Dethier, J., and A. Guiheux, eds. 1994. *La Ville, art et architecture en Europe 1870–1993*. Exhibition catalogue, Centre Georges Pompidou. Paris. | Disziplinaeregrenzgaenge. 2016. *Crossing Disciplinary Boundaries: New Fields of Work in Urban Design and Urban Research*, symposium, HafenCity University, Hamburg, July 21–23, www.disziplinaeregrenzgaenge.de. | Doehler, M. 2003. "Die perforierte Start: Chaos oder Methode?" *Deutsches Architekblatt* 35, no. 4: 6–7. | Endell, A. 1908. *Die Schönheit der großen Stadt*. Stuttgart. | Franck, G. 2011. "Die urbane Allmende: Zur Herausforderung der Baukultur durch die nachhaltige Stadt," *Merkur* 65, no. 746 (July): 567–82. | IBA Hamburg. 2010. *Metrozone/Metrozones*. Metropole/Metropolis 4. Berlin. | Jacobs, J. 1961. *The Death and Life of Great American Cities*. New York. | Kirstgen, A. 2018. "RaumReiz: Zur Wirkungsweise architektonischer Räume." PhD research project, HafenCity University, Hamburg. | Koch, M. 2009. "Stadt-RegionEntwerfen?" in *Wieviel Gestaltung braucht die Stadt?*, edited by H. Bartholomäus, T. Blankenburg, K. Fleischmann, I. Schiller, and L. Wüllner, 201–12. Cottbus. | Koch, M. 2012. "Lob des Pragmatismus, oder: Zur Tauglichkeit neuer Begriffe für das städtebauliche Entwerfen und Forschen," in *Forschungslabor Raum*, Das Logbuch, edited by M. Koch, M. Neppl, W. Schönwandt, B. Scholl, A. Voigt, and U. Weilacher, 278–293. Berlin. | Koch, M. 2013. "Prolog Metrozonen: Die Entdeckung der Bausteine einer neuen Stadt?" in *Stadt neu bauen*, edited by IBA Hamburg, 102–115. Metropole/Metropolis 7. | Koch, M., et al., eds. 2018. *New Urban Professions: A Journey through Practice and Theory*. Perspectives in Metropolitan Research 5. Berlin. Lütke Daldrup, E. 2003. "Die 'perforierte Stadt': Neue Räume im Leipziger Osten," *Informationen zur Raumentwicklung* 1: 55–67. Mittelmeier, M. 2013. *Adorno in Neapel: Wie sich eine Sehnsuchtslandschaft in Philosophie verwandelt*. Munich | Mitscherlich, W. 1965. *Die Unwirtlichkeit unserer Städte: Anstiftung zum Unfrieden*. Frankfurt am Main. | Nouvel, J., et al. 2009. *Naissances et renaissances de mille et un bonheurs parisiens*. Paris. | Pape, T., and M. Koch. 2018. "Building Urban Essays of Star Architectural Languages." Morphological and architectural studies as part of an interdisciplinary DFG-funded research project, Star Architecture and Its Role in Repositioning Small and Medium-sized Cities, DFG Grant 2015–2018 Michael Koch, HCU Hamburg KO 5090/11 in cooperation with Alain Thierstein, TU München TH 1334/111 and Martina Löw, TU Berlin LO 1144/141. Roters, E., and B. Schulz, eds. 1987. *Ich und die Stadt: Mensch und GrossStadt in der deutschen Kunst des 20. Jahrhunderts*. Exhibition catalogue, Berlinische Galerie Martin Gropius Bau. Berlin. | Secchi, B., and P. Viganò. 2011. *La Ville poreuse*. Geneva. | Siedler, W. J. 1964. *Die gemordete Stadt: Abgesang auf Putte und Straße, Platz und Baum*. Berlin. | Später, J. 2013. Review of Adorno in *Neapel: Die Reisegesellschaft der Kulturkritiker, Badische Zeitung*, September 27, 2013. | Stadtbauwelt. 2001. Editorial: "Was meint das Schlagwort 'Die perforierte Stadt?'" *Stadtbauwelt* 24: 40. | Team E. 2014. "Neuland Ruhr," in *Zukunft Metropole Ruhr, Ideenwettbewerb, ruhr.impulse*. Berlin. | Thierstein, A., and A. Förster, eds. 2008. *The Image and the Region: Making Mega-City Regions Visible!* Zurich. | Werner, Y. 2016. "Von Honoraren und Luftschlössern: Eine Untersuchung der Praxis in innovativen Planungsbüros," master's thesis, HCU Hamburg. | Wezemael, J. van. 2014. "'Es braucht eine neue Sensibilität': Conversation with Joris van Wezemael," *Tec 21* 45: 22–25.

Porous—Notes on the Architectural History of the Term
Dietrich Erben

The architectural history of the word *porous* probably began as a medical history. A brochure published by the Deutsche Linoleumwerke Hansa on the occasion of the Berlin Tuberculosis Congress claimed as early as 1899 that the synthetic material linoleum had been discovered as a countermeasure to "porous" sources of danger. It bears the clumsy title *Linoleum, the Ideal Flooring for Hospitals, Clinics, Welfare Institutions, Schools, Hotels, Business and Private Spaces*. It reads: "One of linoleum's principal qualities will appear to the practical doctor as particularly valuable from the beginning: namely, the absolute impermeability to liquid and solid materials of any kind." Natural materials such as wood or stone could not "compete with the seamless linoleum floor" because they are "porous, and the many seams offer many more accumulation points for unhealthy substances than are compatible with our present ideas of proper health care and nursing" (quoted from Aschenbeck 2014, 118). The brochure signals a declaration of war by the impermeable on the porous.

Thomas Mann's novel *Der Zauberberg* (1924; *The Magic Mountain*) also leads to the porous realm of tuberculosis. Here, the term is extended from an individual building element to the entire building. Again, as with synthetic linoleum and natural material, the opposition between health and disease plays a role. Hans Castorp, the protagonist of the novel, reads an English book on ocean steamships at the beginning of his journey to the Davos tuberculosis sanatorium. On the way to the mountains, however, he lays aside the book that promises oceanic vastness and healthy sea air, "the cover soiled by the soot drifting in with the breath of the heavily chuffing locomotive." Then, in an "already faded" sunset the sanatorium confronts Castorp as "an elongated building [...], topped by a copper cupola, and arrayed with so many balconies that [...] it looked as pockmarked and porous as a sponge" (Mann 1924, 38 and 44). The use of metaphor in the description, right at the beginning of the book, gives the reader a presentiment that the patient seeking recovery will be absorbed by the sanatorium, as it were, and will remain there for long years. The keyword *porous* conjoins the sick person and the sanatorium building; or—in more general terms—individual and institution are set in relation to one another.

In order to discover the porous one did not have to travel to Naples, like Walter Benjamin and Asja Lacis, who wrote their famous essay on the city while staying on the island of Capri. The term and its architectural connotation were already in use elsewhere. They were, as the opening quotations show, in the—discomfitingly contaminated—air. But it is due to Benjamin and his traveling companion, the Latvian-born, Moscow-trained theater activist Asja Lacis, that the terminological reflections on the *porous* have become so notorious. The Naples essay was written in the autumn of 1924 and it was published in the *Frankfurter Zeitung* in August 1925. Its literary reception began immediately, after Ernst Bloch in the same year generalized the terminology to "Italy and Porosity" ("Italien und die Porosität") in direct reference to Benjamin (Bloch 1925). Today, it is gathering unprecedented momentum in various disciplines. This terminological commerce is, however, quite contrary to the tantalizingly sporadic use of the term by Benjamin himself. In his writing, it develops no systematic presence, and ekes out a lonely existence in the Naples text. In his entire œuvre, the term appears only once more, in passing, in the *Arcades Project* (*Passagen-Werk*; Mittelmeier 2015, 57). It may, therefore, well be that the notion and object of the porous, as they emerge in the thought figure (*Denkbild*) of Naples, were essentially inspired by Asja Lacis, since it is precisely the aspect of the both public and theatrical staging of the private which plays the decisive role in the porous. During his stay on the island of Capri, Benjamin devoted himself above all to his work *Der Ursprung des deutschen Trauerspiels* (1928, *The Origin of German Tragic Drama*). In it, he also addresses the allegory of the theatrical, which is reflected as contemporary experience of the cityscape of Naples.

It is essentially two aspects that constitute the poetic fascination of the Naples text—firstly, the process of introducing the metaphorical content of porous into the text itself, and subsequently the extension of the leitmotif of the porous by way of a three-step approach: from material to space to culture. Both aspects have been mapped out by research on Benjamin in the last few years (Ujma 2007; Bub 2010; Fellmann 2014; Mittelmeier 2015, esp. 38–64). In dubbing porous "the inexhaustible law of life in this city, reappearing everywhere" (Benjamin and Lacis 1925: 168), Benjamin and Lacis seek to use the linguistic style of their essay to make this reconaissance of the city comprehensible for the reader as well—indeed, they literally expose the reader to the pores, the cavities, and the interstices in the text's trains of thought. The text, in a word, is anything but systematic. The fact alone that the typewritten draft was set down as a monolithic block, uninterrupted by paragraphs, suggests a deliberate inaccessibility. It contains neither expository thesis, nor concluding synthesis. The authors' observations follow no stringent logic, nor are they concerted into a linear chain of reasoning. Rather, the material is loosely assembled. The shape of the text is as porous as the porosity of the white spaces around which it revolves.

Benjamin's and Lacis's reflections turn on these lacunae. However, they do not leave them empty but fill them with their imaginations. The space they talk about is founded on the material, and is then expanded into the structural scenery, which in turn is the stage of social activity. The porous is magnified—from a feature of the building materials via the description of the organization of architectural space to the interpretative category of urban culture: "As porous as this stone is the architecture. Building and action interpenetrate in the courtyards, arcades, and stairways. In everything they preserve the scope to become a theater of new, unforeseen constellations. The stamp of the definitive is avoided. No situation appears intended forever, no figure asserts its 'thus and not otherwise.' This is how architecture, the most binding part of the communal rhythm, comes into being here: civilized, private, and ordered only in the great hotel and warehouse buildings on the quays; anarchical, embroiled, village-like in the center, into which large networks of streets were hacked only forty years ago." (Benjamin and Lacis 1925, 165–66) And elsewhere, this idea is further modified: "Porosity results not only from the indolence of the Southern artisan, but also, above all, from the passion for improvisation, which demands that space and opportunity be at any price preserved. Buildings are used as a popular stage. They are all divided into innumerable, simultaneously animated theaters. Balcony, courtyard, window, gateway, staircase, roof are at the same time stage and boxes." (Ibid., 166–67)

According to Benjamin and Lacis, the permeability of the porous arises on all spatiotemporal levels: Thus the sacred becomes profane; profanity is transformed into transcendence; the broken, through its reutilization, is once more rendered whole; thus ensues a dissolution of the difference between holidays and weekdays, and a blurring of the oppositions between waking and sleeping, childhood and adulthood. In its topography, the buildings of the vertical city grow out of the rock caves, crypts, and catacombs; public and private spheres overlap in apartments, streets, and plazas, in domesticity and theatricality, in house and activity. The porous is permeated by the "streams of communal life" (Ibid., 171), it is a material image of the "communal rhythm" (Ibid., 166). The porous therefore forms the antithesis of the permanent and final. "What is enacted on the staircases" occurs not, however, thanks to given stage directions, but to a quasi-instinctive social creativity of the participants: "Even the most wretched pauper is sovereign in the dim, dual awareness of participating, in all his destitution, in one of the pictures of Neapolitan street life that will never return, and of enjoying in all his poverty the leisure to follow the great panorama" (Ibid., 167).

Benjamin's and Lacis's *Denkbild* is, as this particular term for the text genre suggests, a metaphorical construction in which conceptual and pictorial understanding interpenetrate. Concrete observation and terminological concepts enter into a reciprocal relationship in the attempt to capture the city in the totality of overlapping phenomena. As with a picture, there is a visual juxtaposition and temporal simultaneity of observed details. In this regard, the Naples essay is exemplary of modernism. Just as modernist authors and artists were concerned with open structures, they were also interested in the form of transitions between the individual phenomena. Thresholds, frames, and borders are the keywords in this respect. The natural sciences wrestled with the theory of relativity, prompting one of their protagonists, Arthur S. Eddington, to treat the threshold virtually as an existential metaphor. He depicts, in *The Nature of the Physical World* (1928), the crossing of a threshold as an elementary struggle against the physical conditions of atmosphere, gravity, and the Earth's rotation. In the sociopolitical sphere, the nation-state and internationalism stood in complementary opposition to one another: While the modern welfare state concerned itself with citizens only within its national borders, it was in simultaneous sympathy with the idea of supranationalism, as manifested in the establishment of the League of Nations in 1919. The ambivalence of borders and transitions was also addressed in the area of cultural theory: the French ethnologist Arnold van Gennep introduced the concept *rites of passage* in 1909 to describe ritual threshold markers in the individual life cycle. The sociologist Georg Simmel was interested in the picture frame as aesthetic border, in his eponymously titled essay (1902). Sigfried Giedion, in his photo book *Befreites Wohnen* (1929), elected "light, air, movement, opening" as the ideals befitting the modern residence.

Walter Benjamin, too, belongs to the threshold explorers and border crossers of modernism. As the tracer beam of a torchlight the search for transitional phenomena pervades his work. At times he finds enigmatic formulations in a language where conceptual reflection and visual imagination merge. In *Berlin Childhood* (*Berliner Kindheit*) loggias are the thresholds of the house: Here "they mark the outer limit of the Berliner's lodging. Berlin—the City God himself—begins in them. The god remains such a presence there that nothing transitory can hold its ground beside him. In his safekeeping, space and time come into their own and find each other. Both of them lie at his feet here." (Benjamin 1996–2003, 3:346) Elsewhere, it is a riverbank: "Every architecture worthy of the name ensures that it is the spatial sense as a whole, and not just the casual gaze, that reaps the benefits of its greatest achievements. Thus, the narrow embankment between the Landwehr Canal and Tiergarten Street exerts its charm on people in a gentle, companionable manner—hermetically and Hodegetria-like (*hermetisch und hodegetrisch*) guiding them on their way." (Ibid., 2.1:69–70) The last two terms, which mean as much as *mysterious* and *pointing the way*, are as archaic in their modern use as the content they stand for.

With Benjamin, as is known, it is the familiar figure of the flaneur to whom thresholds reveal themselves. Even before working on the *Arcades Project* (*Passagen-Werk*), there are exceedingly poetic statements to be found in a review of a novel from 1929 (Ibid., 2.1:262–67): The city appears as makeshift "mnemonic for the lonely walker," who also possesses the sensitivity "for the scent of a single weathered threshold." The flaneur, as the great threshold seeker, "is familiar with the lesser transitions" between the two poles of city and dwelling. "The primal image of *dwelling*, however, is the matrix or shell," where the concierge acts as one of "the guardians of [the] rites of passage." Elsewhere, Benjamin refers to the house as "a lap and labyrinth" (*als Schoß und Labyrinth*) (Benjamin 1980–82, 3:390) in which the fireplace also counts as a threshold (Ibid., 3:388). This mysterious world of passages and passageways, which is to say, *passages* in the literal sense, Benjamin also finds in the type of building of the same name. For the flaneur, the passage is the place of fulfillment, for the passage does not reveal its secrets, it is an "underworld" in which experience remains ambivalent (Benjamin 1927–40, 873ff).

As indicated above, Benjamin completely lost sight of the porous during these investigations. He quite simply lost the word. Benjamin's friends, his intellectual associates and his traveling companions to southern Italy, including Theodor W. Adorno, Siegfried Kracauer, and Alfred Sohn-Rethel, never went in for the porous anyhow, although they were, in their descriptions of city and landscape, as well as in their art critcism, often attending to the same phenomena as Benjamin (Mittelmeier 2015). In the Naples text, the porous therefore is a product of the exclusive temporal, spatial, and personal constellation of the journey to southern Italy. On the other hand, one can only speculate as to why Benjamin gave up on the term after the journey. Even etymologically, the word *porous* necessarily leads one to a vagueness or, more precisely, a cleft. According to its Greek origin, the word *porós* signifies as much as *passage* or *opening*. The pore, therefore, is not only an emptiness or a given lacuna, but is so in a relational function to the environment—it is there to be permeable. Its purpose is to connect a front with a back, an exterior with an interior, although it does not itself have any substantial materiality. The pore is a thin medium.

In both—the meaning as a functional concept and the thinning out—lies the intellectual appeal of its derivations, *pore, porous*, and *porosity*, but it also entails an almost inevitable blurring of the words. Its terminological history demonstrates how the lacunae of the words acquire gravity, as it were, through the incorporation of cultural meanings. As is also revealed through Benjamin's and Lacis's thought figure of Naples, the porous becomes semantically charged: *porous* is the old and the has-been. The term is associated with morbidity and mortality. The feature described with it characterizes the cultural physiognomy of the South as opposed to the rationality of the North; it is a category of experience not of knowledge.

The fact that Benjamin wavered in his conceptualization may also be gauged by the fact that, on the one hand, he identified porosity with modernity in the *Arcades Project* (*Passagen-Werk*), the sole reference apart from the Naples essay: "The twentieth century, with its porosity and transparency, its tendency toward the well-lit and airy, has put an end to dwelling in the old sense" (Benjamin 1927–40, 221). Elsewhere, however, he put the premodern city's "intoxicated interpenetration of street and residence" in opposition to the "the new architecture" which "lets this interpenetration become sober reality" (Ibid., 423). These aporias may explain why Benjamin steered clear of the concept after Naples. In addition, the notion of *constellation* opened up the prospect of a conceptual alternative, which can already be found in the passage from the Naples essay cited above. This change of terminology involves a fundamental change of perspective. While inherent in the porous is its origin in the sphere of the natural material, which ultimately represents a given static state of affairs, the astrological origin of the term *constellation* (of the planets) is widely forgotten. It signifies a dynamic principle, allowing both material and social aspects to be incorporated equally, wherein constellations tend toward open-ended functional relationships with a barely limitable number of variables. It is precisely the suitability of this concept, being more practical for social-scientific analysis, which determines that *constellation* gained ascendency over *porous* as a term with both Benjamin and his intellectual comrades-in-arms such as Adorno (Mittelmeier 2015, 57–64).

It seems that there is a balance between skepticism and sanction toward the porous in the subsequent history of the term. Occasionally, one enters the lexical field of the porous deliberately—or one consciously bypasses it. In the Naples literature of sociological and literary-scientific provenance, the porous has by now inscribed itself as a topos in the diagnosis of the present (Larcati 2001, Savonardo 2003, Anand 2016). It is usually employed with reference to Benjamin, and both the word and its use carry a risk of contentlessness and a disintegration of logic toward meaninglessness. From the outsider's perspective, one is led to formulate naively: *porous* is a passepartout which permits one to paint in the most colorful hues. Enthusiasts for the concept are opposed by the skeptics. Among them is Bernard Rudofsky, who settled in Capri in 1932 and was very familiar with Benjamin's work. The catalogue for the famous exhibition he curated, *Architecture without Architects*, concerns the guiding theme of thresholds and boundaries within habitats, as well as within the transitions to their environment, but he refrains from the porous (Rudofsky 1964). Christof Thoenes, who, as an architectural historian, has provided the most subtle interpretations of the architecture of Naples, did likewise when talking about Neapolitan stairs as public-private spaces (Thoenes 1983).

If architectural language makes the distinction between categories, technical terminology, and metaphors (see Forty 2014), one can ultimately say that *porous*, within this vocabulary, has a primarily metaphorical value with a wide frame of association. The present volume is on the trail of the concept's potential for creative stimulus from the perspective of urban design. One may however doubt, in view of the abovementioned discontinuities in its terminological history, that the porous can be considered a piece of architectural terminology or a basic concept (*Grundbegriff*) of architecture (in this sense, Janson 2016, 35). This cannot be valid if, according to the classical conceptual history (*Begriffsgeschichte*), a basic concept is understood as a category which is irreplaceable for the understanding of reality and which, precisely for this reason, must remain controversial and therefore always contains the historical potential for development (Koselleck 2006). In architectural language, a comparatively limited set of categories could be considered in this way (space, function, materiality, planning, design, etc.).

Analytical development of the term *porous*, however, is still pending, and the question of what this might involve remains open. In a continuation of the conceptual tradition so far, an elaboration of the porous within architectural anthropology would be conceivable. This methodolgical perspective concerns the comprehensive integration of architecture into the contexts of body/corporality, fellow human/society, and environment/culturality (see Erben 2017, 101–8). Such an anthropological integration already reaches back into the conceptual tradition. Ludwig Feuerbach, for example, writes in *Towards a Critique of Hegel's Philosophy* (1839), in connection with the philosophy of the subject which he drafted and directed against idealism, and in which he binds the body to the subject again: "The I is by no means 'through itself' as such 'open to the world,' but through itself as a bodily being, that is, through the body. [...] Through the body, I is not I, but object. Being-in-the-body means being-in-the-world. So many senses—so many pores, so much bareness. The body is nothing but the porous I." ("So viel Sinne— soviel Poren, soviel Blößen. Der Leib ist nichts als das poröse Ich." Quoted in Pegatzky 2002, 81) In the present, as is well known, this very conception of the subject has been deeply shaken. If, therefore, reproductive medicine is likewise used to multiply parenthood, and allow it to be distributed among up to five people, then there are "porous boundaries" between parents and child (Bernard 2014, 83), according to the findings of Andreas Bernard. Here, the institutional relationships of kinship and parental authority as well as of social intimacy and biological proximity are put to the test. Starting from such anthropological fragments of the porous, an architectural anthropology of the porous would still have to be developed. Whether the term *porous* is still plausible would then remain to be seen.

References:
Anand, J. 2016. "Die (Un)Schuld einer Stadt. Das poröse Neapel der *Certi bambini* Diego De Silvas," *PhiN: Philologie im Netz* 76: 1–19. | Aschenbeck, N. 2014. *Reformarchitektur: Die Konstituierung der Ästhetik der Moderne.* Basel. | Benjamin, W. 1927–40. *The Arcades Project.* Translated by H. Eiland and K. McLaughlin. Cambridge, MA, 1999. | Benjamin, W. 1980–82. *Gesammelte Schriften,* 5 vols. Frankfurt am Main. | Benjamin, W. 1996–2003. *Selected Writings,* 4 vols. Edited by M. Bullock, H. Eiland, M. W. Jennings, and G. Smith. Cambridge, MA. | Benjamin, W., and A. Lacis. 1925. "Naples," in *Reflections: Essays, Aphorisms, Autobiographical Writings,* edited by P. Demetz, 163–73. New York, 1978. | Bernard, A. 2014. *Kinder machen: Neue Reproduktionstechnologien und die Ordnung der Familie: Samenspender, Leihmütter, Künstliche Befruchtung.* Frankfurt am Main. | Bloch, E. 1925. "Italien und die Porosität," in *Werkausgabe,* vol. 9, *Literarische Aufsätze,* 508–15. Frankfurt am Main, 1985. | Bub, S. 2010. "Porosität und Gassengeschlinge," *KulturPoetik* 10: 48–61. | Erben, D. 2017. *Architekturtheorie: Eine Geschichte von der Antike bis zur Gegenwart.* Munich. | Fellmann, B. 2014. *Durchdringung und Porosität: Walter Benjamins Neapel: Von der Architekturwahrnehmung zur kunstkritischen Medientheorie.* Münster. | Forty, A. 2014. *Words and Buildings: A Vocabulary of Modern Architecture.* London. | Janson, A. 2016. "Porosity: Ambiguous Figure and Cloud," *Cloud-Cuckoo-Land* 21, no. 35: 35–46. | Koselleck, R. 2006. *Begriffsgeschichten: Studien zur Semantik und Pragmatik der politischen und sozialen Sprache.* Frankfurt am Main. | Larcati, A. 2001. "Neapel, die poröse Stadt: Anmerkungen zu Benjamin, Bloch, Henze," *Literatur und Kritik* 359: 68–75. | Mann, T. 1924. *The Magic Mountain,* trans. J. Woods. New York, 2005. | Mittelmeier, M. 2015. *Adorno in Neapel: Wie sich eine Sehnsuchtslandschaft in Philosophie verwandelt.* Munich. | Pegatzky, S. 2002. *Das poröse Ich: Leiblichkeit und Ästhetik von Arthur Schopenhauer bis Thomas Mann.* Würzburg. | Pisani, S. 2009. "Neapel Topoi," in *Neapel: Sechs Jahrhunderte Kulturgeschichte,* edited by S. Pisani and K. Seibenmorgen, 28–37. Berlin. | Rudofsky, B. 1964. *Architecture without Architects: A Short Introduction to Non-pedigreed Architecture.* Exhibition catalogue, Museum of Modern Art. New York. | Savonardo, L. 2003. "Il contesto della riceca: Napoli nell'era Bassolino," in *Capitale sociale e classi dirigenti a Napoli,* edited by E. Amaturo, 73–95. Rome. | Thoenes, C. 1983. "Ein spezifisches Treppenbewußtsein: Neapler Treppenhäuser des 18. Jahrhunderts/A Special Feel for Stairs: Eighteenth-Century Staircases in Naples," *Daidalos* 9: 77–85. | Ujma, C. 2007. "Zweierlei Porosität: Walter Benjamin und Ernst Bloch beschreiben italienische Städte," in *Links, Rivista di letteratura e cultura tedesca* 7: 57–64.

Urban Porosity and the Right to a Shared City
Stavros Stavrides

Urban political action is usually channeled toward demands and struggles for the redistribution of urban goods and urban services. However, urban struggles may be also or predominantly shaped by claims for the right to the city, echoing Lefebvre's emblematic phrase. In this case, the city itself, considered as the "perpetual oeuvre of the inhabitants, themselves mobile and mobilized for and by this oeuvre" (Lefebvre 1996, 173), is reclaimed by people in action.

Urban porosity can redefine the city as a network of thresholds to be crossed, thresholds that potentially mediate between differing urban cultures, which become aware of each other through mutual acts of recognition and collaboration. Urban porosity can thus be the spatiotemporal form that an emancipating urban culture may take in the process of inhabitants reclaiming the city.

Urban porosity can be approached as a potential characteristic of both the spatial arrangements and the spatial practices that constitute the experience of inhabiting shared spaces. Benjamin's seminal essay on pre–World War II Naples captures this inherent relation between the form of a city and the culture of its inhabitants as it is daily performed: "As porous as this stone is the architecture. Building and action interpenetrate in the courtyards, arcades, and stairways." (Benjamin and Lacis 1925, 165–66) For Benjamin, porosity essentially refers to a continuous exchange (spatial as well as temporal) between the so-called public and private realms and actions. We can extend this porosity effect to today's metropolitan spatial and temporal divisions if we wish to discover practices and spatial forms that perforate barriers and create osmotic spatial relations.

In such a prospect, urban porosity may become a prerequisite of a "relational politics of place" as proposed by Massey (2005, 181). By explicitly departing from the image of space considered as a container of social life, we may understand space and action as mutually constitutive and, thus, we may focus on porosity as a process rather than as a physical characteristic of specific places. Urban porosity is activated by urban struggles and can become a form of experience that activates relationality rather than separation, considered in terms of space as well as in terms of time. In urban porosity, different spaces as well as different times become related and thus compared.

Urban porosity can describe a possible alternative to the dilemma present in various urban struggles. This dilemma can be formulated thus: are we to defend a right that establishes redistribution demands of space-bound goods and services (for example, transport, health facilities, job opportunities etc.), or are we to defend the right to hold on to or to develop situated collective identities? True, "distributional issues color the politics within explicitly identity-based movements" (Ballard et al. 2006, 409). This is, for example, the case of the identity-based gay movement in South Africa which cannot but deal with "the distributional questions raised by the poverty of significant proportion of their members" (Ibid., 411). Urban porosity can indeed extend or enhance access rights by developing possibilities of urban-spatial justice or *regional democracy*, to use one of Soja's terms (2000). Urban "pores" in principle connect and establish opportunities for exchange and communication, thus eliminating space-bound privileges. At the same time, however, urban porosity can provide the means of acquiring collective identity awareness. In such a case, situated identities lose their secluding defining perimeters without, however, becoming totally amorphous or dispersed. Porosity becomes a crucial prerequisite of identity formation processes, which are necessarily constituted in and through lived spaces.

Spaces and Spatialities of Emancipation

Perhaps one of the dominant modern images of emancipated communities presents them as barricaded strongholds, always ready to defend themselves. This typical image, embedded in the collective imaginary of the oppressed, contributes to the construction of geographies of emancipation in which so-called liberated or free areas appear as clearly defined by a recognizable perimeter. Either as islands, surrounded by a hostile sea, or as continents facing other hostile continents, these areas are imagined as spatially separated and thus completely distinct.

Emancipation however, is a process not an established state, which we may differentiate from the religious notion of a happy afterlife. Emancipation is the ambiguous actuality of spatially as well as historically dispersed struggles. There may be potentially liberating practices but there can be no fixed areas of eternally guaranteed freedom.

Could we then perhaps visualize spatialities of emancipation by considering those appeals for social justice which focus on the use of urban space? Spatial justice, in this context, could indicate a distribution principle that tends to present space as a good to be enjoyed by all. Any division, separation, or partitioning of space appears, then, as obstructing this kind of justice. True, an emphasis on spatial justice may establish the importance collective decision-making has for the social as well as for the physical definition of space. This imaginary geography of emancipation, however, has to understand space as a uniform continuum to be regulated by common will rather than as an inherently discontinuous and differentiated medium that gives form to social practices. In a somewhat crude form, this imaginary geography could end up completely reducing space to a quantity to be equally distributed. We can actually connect this way of understanding spatialities of emancipation with contemporary discourses on human rights or human communicability, Habermasian ideal speech situation included (Habermas 2015). More often than not, these discourses presuppose some kind of transhistorical and transgeographical human figure. The same kind of human figure becomes the subject of a distribution-focused spatial justice visualized as the free-moving occupant of a homogeneous spatiality.

A different kind of geographical imaginary has emerged out of a criticism of this idealized vision of a just city (or a city of justice). Sometimes drawing images from contemporary city life, this geographical imaginary focuses on multiplicity and diversity, as well as on possible polymorphous and mutating spaces, as a means of describing a spatiality of emancipation. This view has deep roots. A critique of everyday life and everydayness, already put forward during the 1960s, has provided us with a new way of dealing with the social experience of space. If everyday life is not only the locus of social reproduction but also contains practices of self-differentiation or personal and collective resistance, molecular spatialities of otherness can be found scattered in the city. As de Certeau put it, "a migrational, or metaphorical, city slips into the clear text of the planned and readable city" (1984, 93).

According to this approach, spaces of otherness proliferate in the city due to diversifying or deviating practices. Spatialities of otherness thus become inherently time-bound. At the same time, space is neither reduced to a container of otherness (idealized in utopian cities) nor to a contestable and distributable good. Space is actually conceptualized as a formative element of human social interaction. Space thus becomes expressive through use or, rather, because use ("style of use" as de Certeau has it) defines users. If an idealized version of spatial justice tends to invoke common rights in order to define space as a common good, an emphasis on spatialized molecular otherness tends to posit space as dispersed and diversified, therefore not common.

Emancipating spatialities, in such a view, would be dispersed spatialities of otherness. Discontinuous and inherently differentiated space gives ground to differing social identities allowed thus to express themselves. Essentially connected with identity politics this geographical imaginary "tends to emphasize situatedness" (Harvey 1996, 363) as a prerequisite of identity formation. Identities, however, may rather be the form that social discrimination actually takes. A social inculcation of human interaction patterns is always the scope of social reproduction. Inhabited space, in societies that lack "the symbolic-product-conserving techniques associated with literacy," is, according to Bourdieu, the principal locus of this inculcation of dispositions (Bordieu 1977, 89). Inhabited space though, seems to have resumed this role in postindustrial societies, not because people have become less dependent on formalized education but because city life itself has become the educational system par excellence. A wide variety of embodied reactions are learned through using metropolitan space. Identifying oneself means being able to deal expressively with the risks and opportunities of city life. Where someone is allowed to be and how they conform to spatial instructions of use is indicative of their social identity. Space identifies and is identified through use.

The City of Thresholds

A contemporary liberating effort may indeed seek "not to emancipate an oppressed identity but [rather] to emancipate an oppressed nonidentity" (Holloway 2002, 156). If social reproduction enforces identity formation, an emancipating struggle might be better directed against those mechanisms that reduce humans to circumscribed and fixed identities. Spaces of emancipation should then differ from identity-imposing and identity-reproducing spaces. Space as identity (and identity as space) presupposes a clearly demarcated domain. Space as the locus of nonidentity (which means relational identity, multifarious identity, open identity) has to be, on the contrary, loosely determined space, space of transition.

Societies have long known the ambiguous potentialities of these spaces. Anthropologists have provided us with many examples of spaces that characterize and house periods of ritualized transition from one social position or condition to another. What Van Gennepp has described as rites of passage (Van Gennepp 1960) is ritual acts connected with spaces that symbolize those transitions (from childhood to adolescence, from single to married life, from the status of the citizen to that of the warrior or the hunter). Ritual acts aim, above all, to ensure that an intermediary experience of nonidentity (Turner 1977), necessary for the passage from one social identity to another, will not threaten social reproduction. Through the mediation of purification rites or guardian gods, societies supervise spaces of transition, because those spaces symbolically mark the possibility of deviation or transgression. Liminality, however, the experience of temporarily occupying an in-between territory as well as an in between nonidentity, can provide us with a glimpse of a spatiality of emancipation.

Creating in-between spaces might mean creating spaces of encounter between identities instead of spaces characteristic of specific identities. When Simmel elaborates on the character of door and bridge as characteristic human artifacts, he was pointing out that "the human being is the connecting creature who must always separate and cannot connect without separating" (Simmel 1909, 174).

This act of recognizing a division only to overcome it without however aiming to eliminate it, might become emblematic of an attitude that gives to differing identities the ground to negotiate and realize their interdependence. Emancipation may thus be conceived not as the establishing of a new collective identity but rather as the establishing of the means to negotiate between emergent identities without corroborating preexisting asymmetries. Emancipation is necessarily a collective process but this does not make it a process of homogenization.

In-between spaces are spaces to be crossed. Their existence is dependent upon their being crossed, actually or virtually. It is not however crossings as guarded passages to well-defined areas that should draw our attention in the search for spatialities of emancipation. Rather, it is about crossroads, thresholds connecting separated potential destinations. The spatiality of thresholds can support spatiotemporal experiences which are rooted in the possibility of connecting. A "city of thresholds" (Stavrides 2010) might be the term to describe the spatial network which provides opportunities of encounter, exchange, and mutual recognition. Such a network presents an active alternative to the predominant urban culture of barriers, a culture that defines the city as an agglomeration of identifying enclaves (Marcuse and Van Kempen 2002; Atkinson and Blandy 2005). Thresholds, by replacing checkpoints that control access through interdictions or everyday rites of passage, provide the ground for a possible solidarity between different people allowed to regain control over their lives.

Those spaces essentially differ from the nonplaces Marc Augé describes (1995). No matter how temporary or general, the identities imposed in nonplaces are effective in reducing human life to the rules of contemporary society. Transit identities are nonetheless identities. And, most importantly, these identities do not result from negotiations between equals. Intermediary spaces can be the locus of an emancipating culture only when people assume the risk of accepting otherness as a formative element of their identities and actively explore a mutually produced common ground.

A just city is a city that may contain differing cultures allowed to communicate and negotiate in conditions of equality. Through the educative experience of urban porosity, a just city becomes a city that offers people spaces of encounter and negotiation, themselves discontinuous and differentiated. Inhabiting, using, and creating spaces of encounter means accepting that those spaces belong to no one and everybody. Porosity does not only define a communicating condition that is established through a spatial arrangement. Urban pores exist as in-between places only when they are activated by inhabitants who use them.

Creating the City through Commoning

If we are to understand the right to the city as the right to collectively create the city, then urban porosity is a crucial part of this process. Building upon Lefebvre's ideas, Amin and Thrift suggest that "cities are truly multiple" (Amin and Thrift 2002, 30). By this they mean that what actually produces the power urban life has to exceed institutionalized control, and is the prospect of a continuous experimentation inherent in urban forms of sociality. "Temporal and spatial porosity" essentially provide urban life with this potentiality (Ibid., 155).

Experimentation, however, needs to be propelled by common dreams and interests, which are realized in the process of discovering common practices to demand and to create. Thus, a way to react to Lefebvre's visionary claim for the right to the city today is to connect it with the rise of struggles to redefine the common (Stavrides 2016). In those struggles people actually redefine what is to be shared and how by actually reclaiming the city both as a means of sharing and as a distinct scope of sharing. If the right to the city can today be considered as a superior form of rights it is possibly because it characterizes the rights connected to social sharing, which are severely threatened and diminished in this society of all-consuming individualism.

The process of defining and maintaining the common in and through city life is a process of collective inventiveness. Rules of sharing are tested in practice, and collective experiences are evaluated in the course of ingraining new habits. To reduce the problematics of sharing to legal problems connected to specific established or sought-for rights misses the potentialities inherent in practices of creation which test results and try out new solutions. It is not that fixing certain rules, or even elevating them to the status of a kind of widely accepted constitutions of commoning is without meaning. Fixing and supporting rules is historically important in the fight for an emancipated society as long as those rules retain a general acceptance that is not the result of domination. However, what is to be considered as just in any practice of sharing will have to promote the expanding of sharing rather than limit it: limiting sharing within a closed community is already a way of making sharing unjust. Expanding sharing, thus, established as a shaping process of the common that it produces, is a social force that potentially gestures toward an emancipated society. Exploring the conditions and rules of sharing can be connected to exploring the prospect of an emancipated society, if sharing is not limited within a group, within a community or, in terms of urban space, within an urban enclave.

The problematics of sharing depend on the dynamics of collective rule-making as well as on the dynamics of collective transformation of developed and established rules. In the end, sharing involves power, sharing happens within specific forms of social organization necessarily based on historically specific arrangements of power. Thus, sharing can only expand and tend toward equality, as long as sharing supports an equal distribution of power. Since societies are characterized by the relations of power which reproduce them, an emancipated society of sharing will have to develop mechanisms of power sharing. The sharing of power is both the propelling force of sharing and the utmost guarantee of this expansion (Stavrides 2015).

Defending urban porosity might mean defending the right to the city as the right to overcome identification through localization. Instead of identity strongholds to be defended, we need passages that may connect and separate, giving ground to encounters of mutual recognition. It is in such encounters that commoning may develop as an expanding force of collective creativity (Stavrides 2014).

Benjamin well understood the power thresholds have to compare differing adjacent areas as well as different periods in history. His liberating profane Messiah was to appear in those thresholds in historical time. And his redeeming of modernity's liberating potential was connected with the illuminating knowledge of thresholds. A redeemed potentially emancipating metropolis indeed emerges as a city of thresholds. Parisian arcades, those ambiguous spatial passages, were to become, in Benjamin's thought, emblematic of a collectively dreamt liberating future trapped in modern phantasmagoria. Indeed, emancipation, considered as an ongoing process, is potentially emerging in spaces and times in which sharing develops mutual respect for differences as well as common ground for practices of collaboration to flourish. What we need is passages to a different future. In crossing those passages, by opening those pores through which liberating air can relieve us from the suffocating nightmares of today's harshly unjust urban life, we may perhaps "disenchant the city" (Benjamin 1927–40, 422).

References:
Amin, A., and N. Thrift. 2002. *Cities: Reimagining the Urban*. Cambridge. | Atkinson, R., and S. Blandy. 2005. "Introduction: International Perspectives on the New Enclavism and the Rise of Gated Communities," *Housing Studies* 20, no. 2: 177–86. Augé, M. 1995. *Non-Places: Introduction to an Anthropology of Supermodernity*. London. | Ballard, R., et al., eds. 2006. *Voices of Protest: Social Movements in Post-Apartheid S. Africa*. Scottsville. | Benjamin, W. 1927–40. *The Arcades Project*. Translated by H. Eiland and K. McLaughlin. Cambridge, MA, 1999. | Benjamin, W., and A. Lacis. 1925. "Naples," in *Reflections: Essays, Aphorisms, Autobiographical Writings*, edited by P. Demetz, 163–73. New York, 1978. | Bourdieu, P. 1977. *Outline of a Theory of Practice*. Cambridge. | Certeau, M. de. 1984. *The Practice of Everyday Life*. Minneapolis. | Habermas, J. 2015. *Theory and Practice*. Translated by J. Viertel. New York. | Harvey, D. 1996. *Justice, Nature and the Geography of Difference*. Oxford. | Holloway, J. 2002. *Change the World without Taking Power*. London. | Lefebvre, H. 1996. *Writings on Cities*. Edited by E. Kofman and E. Lebas. Oxford. Marcuse, P., and R. Van Kempen, eds. 2002. *Of States and Cities: The Partitioning of Urban Space*. Oxford. | Massey, D. 2005. *For Space*. London. | Simmel, G. 1909. "Bridge and Door," in *Simmel on Culture*, edited by D. Frisby and M. Featherstone, 170–74. London, 1997. | Soja, E. 2000. *Postmetropolis*. Oxford. | Stavrides, S. 2010. *Towards the City of Thresholds*. Trento. | Stavrides, S. 2014. "Open Space Appropriations and the Potentialities of a 'City of Thresholds,'" in *Terrain Vague: Interstices at the Edge of Pale*, edited by M. Mariani and P. Barron, 48–61. New York. | Stavrides, S. 2015. "Common Space as Threshold Space: Urban Commoning in Struggles to Reappropriate Public Space," *Footprint* 9, no. 1: 9–19. | Stavrides, S. 2016. *Common Space: The City as Commons*. London. | Turner, V. 1977. *The Ritual Process*. Ithaka. | Van Gennepp, A. 1960. *The Rites of Passage*. London.

Parts of this text were first presented in: ISA World Congress of Sociology 2006, RC21 Sociology of Urban and Regional Development, The Quality of Social Existence in a Globalizing World, Durban, South Africa, July 23–29, and also used in the book *Towards the City of Thresholds* (Stavrides 2010).

Drifting Clouds: Porosity as a Paradigm
Maren Harnack

From a technical perspective we may distinguish two types of porosity: open and closed porosity. Their difference is in the nature of voids: open porosity is defined by voids that are connected with one another, allowing gases and liquids to move relatively freely through the material, while closed porosity is defined by voids that are not connected, resulting in the gases and liquids remaining fully enclosed, provided the porous material is not damaged. For the city, this is of significance insofar as open porous material may absorb very different substances through which it may completely change its overall composition over and over again, although the basic raw material remains unchanged.

If we conceive of urban space as being porous, we have, on the one hand, a strong physical component, which describes the type of and connection between urban spaces, and on the other hand a process of absorbing (of people, memories, energy), which is indispensable for urban life. Porosity in this sense means that cities may assimilate and accommodate contents and ideas, without necessarily having to change their physical form. This last aspect of porosity highlights the cultural and social aspects of urban space, which is continuously constituted and produced by people. Urban change, therefore, is not just a question of planning and building, but also one of social and cultural constellations, which may develop independently from physical space.

Porous Space

Evidently, urban space can never be completely of the closed type of porosity, for it would make any movement between the spatial voids impossible. Despite this, it would still seem to make sense to inquire into the physical spatiality of porosity to develop an understanding of urban space. There have been, and still are, urban spaces almost completely disconnected from their physical environment, having subjected their transactions to high levels of control. Monasteries and ghettos, as well as prisons, army barracks, and factories belong to this category. The prevalent idea of the European City, for example, assumes a porosity that is relatively closed, featuring clearly defined spaces and the correspondingly unambiguous thresholds between them.

Historically cities themselves were closed cells which exercised strict control of access and which limited access to a few points. Conversely, the open city is one that has, in a military sense, abandoned the idea of resistance, for it grants access to the enemy with the intention of avoiding further disruption.

In this context, the current debate on the European City could be conceived as a debate on porosity. The idea of urban spaces based on clearly defined form and clearly defined connections, the clear distinction between public and private, are all properties of the closed type of porosity. They go hand in hand with specific concepts of control and security, hygiene, and order.

Porosity and Meaning: Sociocultural Porosity

However, there could be a much broader framing of porous urban space if we shift our focus from the physical voids in the built environment to their changing contents, a relation that is comparable to the Newtonian idea of space as a container versus the notion of socially produced space. Martina Löw's (2001) concept of relational space could be understood as an attempt to resolve the contradiction between them; on this view, *Spacing* is defined as the arrangement—*(An)Ordnung* (Ibid., 106)—of living bodies and goods in space, while the operation of *Syntheseleistung* (synthesis) produces ever-changing interpretations of the arrangement and assigns to it a meaning (Ibid., 134ff.). This enables completely different relational spaces to evolve in the same physical space. They may be present simultaneously, being related to different individuals or groups; also, they may change over time (Ibid.). The potential inherent in physical urban space to make possible new operations of synthesis and interpretation could be understood as sociocultural porosity.

Sociocultural Porosity and Time

There are many examples of urban spaces and constellations that have changed their meaning over time, having experienced depreciation and appreciation of certain forms of urbanity while not having necessarily been accompanied by physical changes. A prime example are city quarters of the late nineteenth century in Germany (*Gründerzeitviertel*), which, until the 1970s, had been in danger of demolition, and which today are often sought-after residential areas. The buildings and apartments in these quarters had to be refurbished to comply with modern residential standards, of course, but without the preceding reinterpretation of these quarters—from unhealthy slums to lively urban quarters—the massive investments, in particular the grants funded by tax money, would have been unthinkable.

Conversely, housing developments of the reconstruction period have been affected by a negative change in meaning for a long time now, although they were considered beacons of urban progress when they were built. Despite many of them still being in a good state of repair, offering attractive external spaces through their meanwhile lush vegetation, they are referred to as concrete jungles and breeding grounds for many social ills—irrespective of whether they are being much liked by their actual residents.

The concept of sociocultural porosity, however, goes beyond such findings, anticipating possible changes in the future. The completed valorization of late-nineteenth-century housing (The floor-to-ceiling height! The stucco! The wooden floors!), seems evident from today's perspective, to the extent that we find it difficult to imagine that modernist urban landscapes could be rediscovered with similar enthusiasm (The greenery! The clarity of lines! The pebbledash!). Porosity does not mean that we know in advance who will reinterpret these spaces and in what way, but that there is in principle a possibility this might happen, even if it seems unlikely at the present. Talking about the revival of brutalism twenty years ago would have almost certainly attracted ridicule outside a narrow specialist context.

Sociocultural Porosity and Multiplicity

Just as urban space may accommodate different meanings, interpretations, and operations of synthesis over time, they can coexist in the same space simultaneously. For instance, before it became widely accepted that late-nineteenth-century housing stock constitute valuable urban spaces that are worth preserving, different interpretations competed with one another: for many planners these quarters were speculatively built, unhealthy slums, which had to be demolished for the benefit of the local neighborhood; for investors and contractors they represented potential areas for profitable new developments; to those for whom they had been homes they were full of memories, which they did not wish to lose—or which they wanted to finally leave behind; and many young people saw in them the promise of a life that could be far more interesting than that which the practical and sanitized new residential developments could ever offer.

The many examples of urban renewal schemes (*Flächensanierung*) confirm that "orthodox city planning" (Jacobs 1961, 16) then was the dominant interpretation. Evidently, the new, and later dominant, perspective did not emerge instantly, but coexisted along with many others, in parallel with prevailing common sense. Conversely, there cannot be a single, unquestioned interpretation, synthesis, or reading of urban space today. The periods during which the prevailing common sense is retrospectively identified as having shifted are therefore of particular interest because they tell us something about changes in social constellations, for example, about the end of postwar optimism or in the future perhaps about the ending dominance of the city centers. The porous nature of urban space is often overlooked where development schemes, legal requirements, and uses are in question; very rarely is porosity seen as a quality that could enable the unexpected or innovative to emerge. Hence, orthodox urban planning is well-advised to search for deviating interpretations, too.

Paradox Porosity

The concept of porous urbanity produces different paradoxes, which could be useful for understanding the ambiguous nature of cities and urban spaces, and for overcoming the restricting power of unquestioned common sense. Common sense, in this context, is understood as a state in which, according to Richard Rorty (1989), the languages used to understand and describe the world remain unquestioned and are seen as being without alternative. This state goes hand in hand with the view that there could be an ultimate truth out there, however defined, or in the context of the issue under discussion, about the city or about urban space—a view vigorously rejected by Rorty. Porosity is a paradoxical characteristic of urban spaces, for they have a physicality that can be measured, but beyond that they can never be fully described. This paradox has different dimensions, about which I will raise a few, but by no means concluding thoughts.

The recursive city. Meanings and interpretations ascribed to the city leave traces and change the physical environment. This results in a process of recursive change, which effectively does not come to a halt. The physical adjustment of spaces to shifting interpretations produces by necessity space for new, deviant interpretations, which again permeate and affect physical space. This exemplifies how absurd it seems to restructure today's cities according to models of the past in such a way as to approximate urban situations of 1840 or 1910, without understanding that the achievements of our democratic, liberal, and secular society then also have to be questioned. This does not mean that every building and every space inevitably has to be available for modification, or that everybody always has to be able to realize their ideas. The paradox of the recursive city is, however, the fact that the preservation of urban structures in the long term, for example, with the assistance of conservation authorities, is always the result of negotiations and never of common sense as such.

The ambiguous city. The porous city, therefore, has to be ambiguous, although a single interpretation could still be dominant. In order to exploit the potential of porosity strategically, ambiguity needs to be encouraged or even included in planning processes; it is also means realizing over and over again that places and spaces could have fundamentally different meanings for other people and other groups. That writers like David Foster Wallace (Wallace 2005) and philosophers like Thomas Nagel (Nagel 1974) have closely scrutinized the fundamental subjectivity of human thought and perception shows the extent to which the limits of one's personal perception are far from obvious to us.

If urban space is approached as a physical phenomenon, such individual differences in perception do not seem to be of great significance. Regulations, provisions, and legislation, clearly defined in writing, relate to properties that are measurable: roadway width, curve radius, emission controls, building density, uses, speed limits, material properties, and so forth. However, it is individual perception and interpretation that ascribes meaning to spaces, and it is through their fundamental individuality that a porosity of meaning is established—a porosity which cannot be undone without repressive means. Acknowledging the reality of a subjectively experienced unambiguity of space, therefore, means rejecting the idea of its universal application, with the intention of not losing the qualities of urbanity.

The messy city. In the end, the porous city is always a messy city. Continuous processes of change, the emergence of new constellations, *(An)Ordnungen,* and operations of synthesis result in the production of ever newly emerging ruptures, at which different orderings intersect. Ruptures could be understood as specific sites of porosity, which are more in need of new interpretations than other spaces, syntheses, or readings. Hence they are porous and generate new porosity at the same time. Conversely, we could say of spaces that cannot be related to a single ordering system and a clearly defined interpretation, that they have the capacity to offer the kind of social or cultural innovations that are the precondition of real urbanity. The subjectivity inherent in the perception of space, which always places personal experience and norms at the center of perception, becomes useful in the recognition of such ruptures in that it allows ambiguous interpretations to be disorderly. Not immediately tidying it up, and understanding disorder as a sign of openness is an urban task that is seriously threatened by the growing pressure of economic exploitation in today's cities.

Uses of Porosity

The strength of porosity as a paradigm is based on its terminological ability to describe urban space as physical construct in the Newtonian sense, as well as the product of the processes that are characteristic of the urban condition. If urbanity is understood as being porous, questions of historical authenticity, of unambiguous ascriptions and of an ideal condition that could be achieved in the distant future and that could bring the production of urban space to completion become meaningless. The porous city will never be completed. This will keep it alive and should be seen, through the lens of porosity, as a real advantage.

References:
Jacobs, J. 1961. *The Death and Life of Great American Cities.* New York. | Löw, M. 2001. *The Sociology of Space: Materiality, Social Structures, and Action.* Translated by D. Goodwin. New York, 2016. | Nagel, T. 1974. "What Is It Like to Be a Bat?" *The Philosophical Review* 83, no. 4: 435–50. | Rorty, R. 1989. *Contingency, Irony, and Solidarity.* Cambridge. | Wallace, D. F. 2005. "This Is Water," accessed September 9, 2017, https://www.1843magazine.com/story/david-foster-wallace-in-his-own-words.

The Ideal of the Broken-down: Porous States of Disrepair

Giorgia Aquilar

In Naples, technical devices are, as a rule, broken: it is only under exceptional circumstances and due to some aston-
ishing accident that something will be found to be intact. [...] Not, however, that they do not function because they
are broken: for the Neapolitan it is only when things are broken that they begin to work. (Sohn-Rethel 1926, 33–34)

At around the same time as Walter Benjamin and Asja Lacis were describing Naples's architecture as
"porous as stone" (Benjamin and Lacis 1925, 169), Alfred Sohn-Rethel wrote "Das Ideal des Kaputten—
über neapolitanische Technik" (The Ideal of the Broken-Down: On Neapolitan Technology), published in
the *Frankfurter Zeitung* in 1926. At that time, Benjamin and Sohn-Rethel were both living near the southern Italian city, in close proximity to a German colony of the *Frankfurt School*, and in their respective
reports both suggest a paradigm for Naples—at the same time specific of the peculiar context and trans-
latable to urban space in broad terms. Both the notions of porosity and the broken-down—in which the
two dissections of the city are grounded—resist any well-defined function, combat static configurations
of potentially redeemed space, and expound the simultaneity of past and present.

 "Naples with closed doors would be like Berlin without roofs on the houses"—writes Sohn-Rethel
(1926, 33) in his essay, depicting a city where mechanical appliances are broken as a point of principle
and the functioning of a device itself only really begins when it breaks down. Porosity connotes intermingling, it allows the permeation and mediation of uses, visual and spatial transitions, interpenetrations and superimpositions, erosion of the city fabric to create social space; the broken-down questions
architecture temporality, rereads the relationship between permanent and impermanent parts, works
right into the chiastic space resulting from the coexistence of a more or less premeditated city on the one
side and its dark doppelgänger on the other. Translated to architecture—and recalling the Deleuzian
desiring-machines, working "only when they break down, and by continually breaking down" (Deleuze
and Guattari 1972, 8)—the philosophy of the *Kaputt* triggers a third way to overcoming the embalmment
perpetrated by the opposition between permanence and transformation, integrity and disintegration,
catastrophe and redemption, allowing change to be neither resisted nor wholesale, to find space for
achieving "unforeseen constellations" (Benjamin and Lacis 1925, 166) where "conclusive repairs are
anathema" (Sohn-Rethel 1926, 34).

Looking at a city where repair and maintenance are a ritual practice, "Das Ideal des Kaputten" introduces
the notion of chance (*Zufall*), which embodies a functional dysfunctionality—or dysfunctional functionality—that "tends to come to the rescue at just the right moment" (Ibid., 35), to provide a tool for a reinterpretation of porosity as a generative principle for the construction, deconstruction, and reconstruction of materials and meanings. The doors only rarely left shut in Sohn-Rethel's account—with their
missing or broken handles, existing only "for symbolic purposes" (Ibid., 33)—embody a peculiar sort of
Durchdringung: an interpenetration made possible by cracks and lacks, losses and malfunctionings,
through an endless "tinkering" process, able to turn "defects" into "advantages" (Ibid., 34).

 The broken-down is thus porous to the extent that it triggers a mutual transformation between
the object to be repaired and the subject who repairs it, shifting the focus from form to use, misuse, and
disuse. Through this commodification—taking place by means of acceptation of a state of purposeless-
ness—the notion of the broken-down can contribute to reenacting porosity by investigating its ethics
and aesthetics as inextricably interwoven through its spatial unfolding.

In the manipulation of objects, the role of disrepairs takes the form of a renunciation to any possible purity, finiteness, or integrity, thus shifting its focus from the formal to the conceptual, so requiring a profound revision of the very idea of the whole thing. What is still missing, however, is a meaningful and strategic way for the *Kaputt* to act on the urban level. And it is precisely in this lack that porosity can come to rescue: in an age in which the rhetoric of order and completeness is blatantly in crisis, the broken-down represents an inherent datum of the processes of urban genesis and constant spatial transformation; reread as a porous process it may even turn into a principle for subversion of strategic intervention mechanisms. From this perspective, reenacting porosity through the ideal of the broken-down implies passing beyond the logic of completion that conditions every concept of lack (Agamben 1990), out-lining cities that renounce the constant impulse toward forms of perfection. Intersecting architectural discourses, design practice, and urban form, the porous and the broken-down encourage a productive dialogue about their ambiguous positions—as combinations of imposition and yielding, autonomy and contingency, concealment and revelation. And this coexistence of the hidden and the apparent—which should be the prerequisite for porosity itself—may lead us to explore which narratives can be disrupted if applied critically, not only to work on traditional dualities but rather to identify processes of decomposition and recomposition of complex identities, in which function and malfunction, proper and improper, truth and lie, fact and fiction, failure and success intertwine both social and economic relations with the concrete dimension of spatial urban structures.

Drawn from Naples—where the dissolution of dualistic codifications is implicit and any restrictive dichotomy collapses—and then transferred to the wider realm of the city, the relation between porosity and the broken-down is by no means antinomic, but rather it recalls the ratio between loss—be it a loss of meaning, direction, or even matter—and survivorship (Emery 2011). In the quick and continuous oscillation of effectiveness and defect, mirrored by processes of recurrence or reincarnation (Link 2011, 325), the search for permeability inside urban tissues meets the acceptation of their rotten status as a fertile condition.

A polarized space emerges between the terms *Porosität* and *das Ideal des Kaputten*, where a set of interpretative categories may arise: incorporation, inoperativity, and reenactment may allow us to find—in the cracks of wrecked tissues—a porous room for maneuver, a malleable space for transfigurations, a paradigm for comprehending and managing change, which is not only nominal but implies new per-spectives on the use of urban spaces.

What follows can be read as a plea for a state of disrepair, but also as the pretext for reasoning on strategic directions: the broken-down is irreversible, it implies a state beyond repair.

Incorporation

To begin with, he [the Neapolitan] has destroyed the misanthropic magic of intact mechanical functions, but he then installs himself in the unmasked monster and its artless soul and enjoys this literal incorporation: ownership which gives him limitless power, the power of utopian existential omnipotence. He now shuns the technical presumptuousness of the instruments thus incorporated; with his incorruptible gaze he has seen through the illusion and deception of their mere appearance. [...] Of course, the violence of incorporation has to be acted out every hour in a victorious crash. (Sohn-Rethel 1926, 36–37)

A first line of reasoning derives from the interpretation of *kaputt* as "worn out": to make a device practical and working means to trigger a process of corruption of its integrity, able to "unmask" (Ibid., 36) the machine, to take it over. In Sohn-Rethel's words, this process leads to an incorporation (*Einverleiben*), where the interaction subject-object unfolds its porosity: "where man makes use of his veto against the closed and hostile automatism of machines and plunges himself into their world" (Ibid.), he discovers "his own body inside the machine" (Ibid., 37). The profanation introduced through the act of making something not working work again is even a "brutal" one, but the "violence of incorporation" (Ibid.) appears as necessary and fertile: through the domestication of the chance, the unpractical becomes practical again. In this regard, "Das Ideal des Kaputten" speaks of a sovereignty: "[i]n the handling of defunct mechanisms [the Neapolitan] is admittedly sovereign over all technology, and far beyond" (Ibid., 34). What emerges is not only a form of irrationality caused by an unfortunate fate, but also a real means for survival: alteration, removal, subtraction emerge as counterstrategies to preserve while changing, potential sources for triggering new life-cycles from the rubble of cities and forecasting new afterlives. The paradox of the incorporative process stands in the profound significance of the conceptual shift it triggers: incorporation bends from a limit into a point of inflection, toward the liberation of urban tissues from a state of embalmment, as a prelude to resurrection, a strategic device toward evolution, a tool for a transformational preservation of social and urban structures. Applied to the realm of architecture and the city, the process leading to incorporation could guide the clash between the quest for repair and the acceptance of the "irreparable" (Agamben 1990), where the tangible and intangible matter of artifacts and cities is asked to learn to become "neither fixed nor broken" (Ibid., 102). Paradoxically, it is perhaps precisely through corruptions, alterations, profanations—not meant as pure ideas but rather as the way the idea plays—that objects and tissues may not only be saved, but even trigger a multiplication of choices. In the space of the city, this implies a work on manipulative strategies—transfer and translation, reuse and mimicry, replication and substitution—able to question time and temporality, to turn objects of permanence and stability into ephemeral, fugitive, processual entities. It is an exercise in blurring boundaries between the original and the counterfeit, acting on the identity by "seeing through" (*durchschauen*) (Sohn-Rethel 1926, 36) its "illusion and deception" (*Schein und Trug*) (Ibid., 36), to shift from the collective and cohesive to the ambivalent, contested, and plural.

Inoperativity

One never really owns something until it has really been knocked around, otherwise it is just not worth it; it has to be used and abused, run down until there's practically nothing left of it. [...] Freed, for the better part, from the limits imposed by their intended purposes, technical devices take the most extraordinary diversions and, with an effect as surprising as it is convincing, assume entirely new raisons d'être. (Sohn-Rethel 1926, 37)

In the transition from use to abuse lies a second line of reasoning, connected to the reading of *kaput*, meaning "rendered useless" or "unable to function, become unnecessary". Chance and improvisation, caducity and obsolescence, will and domestication interweave in the interpretation of a city grounded upon improbable transformations, misuse, and false appropriations. Although Sohn-Rethel does not use a specific word to describe this phenomenon, the portrayal provided by Giorgio Agamben on "Das Ideal des Kaputten" finds in that essay a higher paradigm in the way in which opposing the automatism of the machines allows one to "learn how to move them into unforeseen territories and uses" (Agamben 2009, 99). Thus derives a form not based on action and property, but on new possibility of use. Building on this account, a second reasoning may start with the possibilities of the nonfunctional, with an explicit and incomplete reference to what Agamben describes as inoperativity.

Both Benjamin and Lacis and Sohn-Rethel depict Naples as a paradigm of misuse, referring to the intermingling of sacred-confessional and informal-illegal dimensions. Moreover, Sohn-Rethel particularly insists on the technical level of misuse: the city of unusual technologies, Naples turns the ideal of the broken-down into a paradigm for objects that are so damaged they develop the charm of being useless, finding in "the fact that things do eventually break down" (Sohn-Rethel 1926, 35) something that "makes them all the more enchanting" (Ibid., 35). The process is described in terms of a liberation (*in keiner Weise mehr gebunden*) (Ibid., 37), which passes through a diversion, a deviation (*Ablenkung*) that acts as Agamben's "destituting" or "abolishing force" (Agamben 2014a and 2014b), being as destructive as it is effective: it implies a will to abuse, a will to run down, which turns into a revelation in its ability to generate entirely new raisons d'être (*völlig fremden Lebensgrund*) (Sohn-Rethel 1926, 37). This may seem an odd move, but it is fitting in this paradoxical nonpractical and abusive practicality that the role of connection and assembly can be subverted toward the rediscovery of disconnection and disassembly (Graham and Thrift 2007, 7) in the system of things and spaces.

Transposed to architecture, the notion of inoperativity introduces the need to deactivate the old use to make space for new possible uses, new possibilities. In this "profanation" (Agamben 2005)— borrowing Agamben's words again—exclusionary logics would be discarded, and counterpractices could move in the space of contrahegemonic projects. Recalling the concept elaborated by Peter and Alison Smithson about the conglomerate ordering, a further subversion could thus be triggered: "if a thing is well achieved but its uses die, its qualities bring other things to it for which it is suitable" (Smithson 2005, 49).

Reenactment
Mechanisms cannot, in this city, function as civilization's continuum, the role for which they are predestined: Naples turns everything on its head. [...] This is how, in this city, the most complex technical creations are united to perform the simplest tasks, hitherto considered inconceivable. To this end they are, against their will, completely remodeled; they completely fail to perform according to their proper purposes. (Sohn-Rethel 1926, 38)

A third line of reasoning is introduced by the controversial etymological interpretation of the term *kaputt* in relation to the French *capoter*, meaning "to capsize", "to overturn". This additional reading allows the repair work to unfold its transformative power against a solely conservative one, sparking off a subversion of the state of being out of order—not through the imposition of a new order, but rather through the acceptation of a state of disorder. Hence a sequence emerges: incorporated and made inoperative, the impractical turns to be practical again by virtue of a reenactment.

Sohn-Rethel speaks of completely remodeled (*umgemodelt*) creations; Adorno finds in profanations the grounds for a reappropriation; the choice of the term *reenactment* implies the will to reinscribe the *kaputt* objects in the *acta*, in the events and in their records, in the ways they are transmitted (Otero-Pailos 2012). Applied to the city, the reenactement appears as an emancipatory gesture (Agnew 2004, 3) that questions whose authorship and whose ownership are at stake, triggering a further stage of the destructive-reconstructive cycle: in the process of survival that passes through an annihilation, the broken-down acts on the continuing life of objects by manipulating questions of authority, subverting its purposes.

Going back to porosity, through the reenactment, the focus is shifted again from the solid parts to the voids, from the pores back to the matter: the incorporation triggered by the subject entrusts each inoperative element with a new strength, through the coexistence of the old and new meaning, as a double bottom, at the same time object of negation and prelude (Debord 1959). Through porosity, Benjamin and Lacis describe Naples as a city dominated by unusual forms of governance; through the broken-down, Sohn-Rethel's object taken over to be repaired is equal to the end of the author, authority, and authoritarianism. This passage recalls the famous statement by Giuseppe Samonà, describing Naples as one of the most complex and interesting cases "because it rejects the plans" (Samonà 1959, 36), and the well-known retrieval of this concept—more than thirty years later—by Massimo Cacciari, depicting a city that does not develop through macroprojects, "based on a logocentric ratio, which does not reduce the complexity of tensions, conflicts, which does not tend to override them, but rather to assimilate them and almost to feed upon them" (Cacciari 1992, 164). Recalling Benjamin's definition, and identifying porosity as a "model of social relations" (Ibid., 163), Cacciari depicts a city constantly torn between extraordinariness and shambles, between the opportunity to catch a glimpse of potential oases, the constant danger of desertification (Ibid., 188), and the risk of being crystallized as a tourist attraction. Naples, the antimechanical city par excellence, which has always consolidated figures created by subversion of order, becomes the paradigm of a chaotic and labyrinthine urban space, constantly facing the "big challenge" of "combining the Southern porosity with the intrinsic characters of the rule of law, of the European ratio" (Ibid., 163). Against this background, the broken-down turns into a medium for rediscovering an unplanned porosity in the mutable, destructible, corruptible tissues of the city, a way to find porosity in the errors, by focusing on failure and breakdown inherent to artifacts and systems, bringing their vital contribution to the fore. Thus, maybe only by accepting use as a real form of project (Marini 2016), is it possible to fight the anathema that abides in every remedy that claims to be definite, to counterstrike the eschatological perspective of a misdeed completely, to contrast the apocalyptic destiny prefigured by Superstudio for Naples (Superstudio 1972, 116)—here assumed again as a paradigm for the city—to be preserved from reality at all costs.

References:

Agamben, G. 1990. *The Coming Community*. Translated by M. Hardt. Minneapolis, 1993. | Agamben, G. 2005. *Profanations*. Translated by J. Fort. New York, 2007. | Agamben, G. 2009. *Nudities*. Translated by D. Kishik and S. Pedatella. Stanford, 2010. Agamben, G. 2014a. *The Use of Bodies*. Translated by A. Kotsko. Stanford, 2016. | Agamben, G. 2014b. "What Is a Destituent Power?" *Environment and Planning D: Society and Space* 32, no. 1: 65–74. | Agnew, V. 2004. "Introduction: What Is Reenactment?" *Criticism* 46, no. 3: 327–39. | Benjamin, W., and A. Lacis. 1925. "Naples," in *Reflections: Essays, Aphorisms, Autobiographical Writings*, edited by P. Demetz, 163–73. New York, 1978. | Cacciari, M. 1992. "Non potete massacrarmi Napoli! Conversazione con Massimo Cacciari," in *La città porosa : Conversazioni su Napoli*, edited by C. Velardi, 157–90. Naples. | Debord, G. 1959. "Détournement as Negation and Prelude," in *The Situationist Anthology*, edited by K. Knabb, 55–56. Berkeley, 1981. | Deleuze. G., and F. Guattari. 1972. *Anti-Oedipus: Capitalism and Schizophrenia*. Translated by R. Hurley, M. Seem, and H. Lane. Minneapolis, 1983. | Emery, N. 2011. *Distruzione e progetto: L'architettura promessa*. Milan. | Graham, S., and N. Thrift. 2007. "Out of Order: Understanding Repair and Maintenance," *Theory, Culture & Society* 24, no. 3: 1–25. | Link, D. 2011. "Enigma Rebus: Prolegomena to an Archaeology of Algorithmic Artefacts," *Interdisciplinary Science Reviews* 36, no. 1: 3–23. | Marini, S. 2016. "L'uso come forma di progetto," in *Patrimoni: Il futuro della memoria*, edited by S. Marini and M. Roversi Monaco, 17–27. Milan. Otero-Pailos, J. 2012. "Reenactment," *Abitare*, no. 525: 74. | Samonà, G. 1959. "Considerazioni sulla città di Napoli," *Casabella*, no. 231: 35–36. | Smithson, P. 2005. *Peter Smithson: Conversation with Students*. Edited by C. Spellman and K. Unglaub. New York. | Sohn-Rethel, A. 1926. "Das Ideal des Kaputten: Über neapolitanische Technik," in *Das Ideal des Kaputten*, edited by C. Freytag, 33–38. Bremen, 1990. | Superstudio. 1972. "Salvages of Italian City Centers," translated by L. Allais, *Log*, no. 22 (2011): 114–24.

Porous Iridescences
Eduard Bru

1. One of the qualities I like most in scary movies is when someone (usually a villain) is able to disappear in front of our eyes. The emotion we experience does not come simply from the realization that the hero or antihero can magically slip away from us. We also understand that they are able to live a different life simultaneously with an ordinary one, and can move from one narrative to the other just as they want. Somehow, they have acquired the power to be here and there, moving themselves by peculiar means. In another words: they exist in multilevel frames; their life develops an iridescent and porous nature.

2. We know we are in a real city, not in a village—it is not at all a question of size—precisely when we know we can decide at any time the path we want to take. And we know we too have the ability to disappear, to be "lost" whenever we want to; we can provide ourselves with immediate privacy, just by obeying the laws of our desire. Without this vital condition, this freedom, we can build gigantic residential villages but never cities. Yes, I am talking about a quality that is a kind of porosity.

3. Let us say that this porous nature is, in terms of shape and order, the defining quality—not only, for instance, of Naples and other age-old cities, but for any real city. Sometimes we build gigantic villages, not cities. Think of the city as a kind of brain. To work well, it needs to be not only solid, clear, secure, and flexible: it must also be porous. The village, the countryside scenarios, imply permanence: permanence of place, permanence of social roles, permanent and standard ways of life, and so on. The Rossi scenarios, for instance, are not urban: they are instead illuminist villages and, obviously, cemeteries in every sense of the word. Permanence entails repetition, such as the repetition of social relationships. The most important repetition of all is the one that ensures the permanence of our identity.
But when a hero, a Dostoyevsky protagonist, for instance, arrives in the city, any city, after having suffered or enjoyed so much pain, love, violence, we can only imagine that something new, decisive, and definitive is going to happen. At that point the hero's identity will disappear, for a while, in the porous city, and he will be able once more to reinvent himself. Everything is possible because the big cities of the nineteenth century and their inhabitants frequently constituted a porous reality.
Ironically, the multiplicity of hypersophisticated gadgets that the contemporary city provides—supposedly to make life more exciting and informed and, from there, free, open-ended, and interesting—becomes a huge incentive to avoid any porosity. There are, apparently, no more open ways to be explored, right now, in the megaexposed, overwhelming city. Every option, even with a large budget, and with risk included in the budget, is already predetermined: procrastinated, also presettled in our minds, and, if doubts arise, described carefully in our highly intelligent mobile phones or in our laptops.

4. The shape and structures of modern cities work efficiently to make our movements, and therefore feelings and sensations, predictable. Just recall the final images of so many films: the protagonists start walking toward the infinite horizon of their improbable happiness. This horizon is no longer dramatic because it is predictable. We can feel it is, in every sense, not porous.

5. What does *porous city* mean? The possibility of being understood easily? The capacity, and opportunity, of any given city, to absorb you, then modify you? Or, perhaps, just the possibility of being modified by you?

Turning to my own environment, in the Mediterranean cities the complexity of their history/geography (they go together) frequently gives us a porous order, a porous framework able to offer a diversity of physical havens, ways of life, platforms of meaning and understanding. Yes, in the Mediterranean cities the way of life makes time our partner in creating complexity. Remember, for instance, the marvellous Naples, among many others cities and places.

6. What is new about porosity does not come from abstractions, or any kind of dominant universal formula. The "new" in porosity comes from an unusual approach: paying attention to the situation without the regimentation of a predetermined language. The architectural language decisions will depend on our sense of the situation: place, program, people's experiences and feelings: everything counts.
Porosity goes beyond an educated, clean, prudent relationship with reality. Porosity comes when works, and their authors too, are modified by the reality they have manipulated/created/modified.
Picasso was, undoubtedly, porous, extremely so, as was Raymond Chandler in the field of popular literature, and Doris Lessing in the domain of high culture.

7. Will porosity, finally, be just a neo-pop phenomenon? Was Venturi porous? Is Pop porous? Let's see. All of them, Venturi of course, like Pop, are rich in irony. But there is no irony, in my view, in the domain, milieu, and concept of porosity. Not exactly. Pop enjoys showing reality as a collage/contradiction. Like Venturi, it moves the door away from its central axis because the road refuses to coincide with it any more. But porosity does not take pleasure in these contradictions. It takes no pleasure in the contextualist's fictions. So, in other words, it is not concerned with tension, it is not concerned with politesse. Porosity is about being together: It is about complex harmonies.

8. So, it is just a question of form? Of the city's form? Please take a look at the megarationalist order of many of the neighborhoods constructed, for instance, on the periphery of Barcelona (or Rome, or Milan, Marseille, El Cairo…) in the 1960s to 1980s. There you will encounter, repeated hundreds of times, Hilberseimers (without his pathos). There you will encounter the antiporous idea of the city par excellence made finally porous by the spleen of the vital, intense, unexpected use of the public space, in every sense. See Ferdinand Pouillon's ensembles and experience the most rigid architecture in existence, and, at the same time, the most porous one.

9. The Postmodern was not the real end of Modern architecture, as it pretended to be. We are just now at the very end of the Modern Movement. In a world without utopias, we have no more need for its clarity, which it owes to abstraction and reduction. By now, sensuality, particularities, and exceptions, have taken over the whole screen.
In a world without new ways let us be capable of reinventing our relationship with the old gadgets, shapes, and ambiances that are still alive in the present.
Let us express the sadness, and also the complexity, diversity, and sensuality of the moment. Let us discover new feelings by baroque—I mean inclusive—methods: because their nature participates in everything. So, in other words, let's be porous.

Porosity: Why This Figure Is Still Useful
Paola Viganò

To reflect on porosity is a challenge and remains highly motivating for several reasons. The first concerns the actuality of such a concept in the field of urban design and urban studies: we are still discussing the presence or absence of porosity in cities and territories, as this book makes explicit. The second reason is that porosity continues to be a fertile instrument in nourishing ideas, interpretations, and projects for the city and the territory. Having dedicated much time and effort to this conceptual metaphor, in the following, I reconsider its constructive role within three main planning and design experiences in terms of their capacity to produce original knowledge (Viganò 2010).

Conceptual Metaphors and Concrete Qualities: On Porosity

In August 1925 Walter Benjamin and Asja Lacis published an article in the *Frankfurter Zeitung* on Naples. The gray city where only forms can be read, the craggy city grown into the rock, is defined as porous. Porosity is a gaze guiding the description, but also an interpretation of the Mediterranean city: "As porous as this stone is the architecture. Building and action interpenetrate in the courtyards, arcades and stairways. In everything, they preserve the scope to become the theater of new unforeseen constellations." (Benjamin and Lacis 1925, 163–64)

Porosity is the space of opportunities and improvisation. Through intermingling and interpenetration, the concept of porosity as transitiveness emblematizes the confrontation among Northern and Southern ways of life, cultures, and habitats. It is important to read Benjamin's and Lacis's interpretation as a perspective from the North, where Southern porosity is opposed to Northern compactness, which defines straight and rigid borders between public and private space, interior and exterior, family and community, individual and society. In opposition to the North, everything seems to blur: the South is intergenerational, without the notion of privacy so important in shaping the space and the life of the North. Ernst Bloch in "Italy and Porosity," an article of 1925 quoting Benjamin and Lacis, insists on the inability of those traditionally traveling to Italy to see this porosity, only interested in balanced landscapes and demarcations: "Looking for a totally clear, perfectly concluded life, the opposite of the crepuscular vagueness at home" (Bloch 1925, 175). In search of a perfect and atemporal country where antiquity has tamed chaos. This is the dream and myth of the classical Mediterranean space. In Bloch's words, porosity goes beyond it and reveals another South where the baroque forms and folds, later investigated by Deleuze (1988), dissolve the sharp demarcations of classical architecture into infinite continuity of space.

For some time now I have been thinking about the conceptual metaphor of porosity (Secchi 2000; Viganò 2005, 2006, 2007 and 2009) and its relevance as a tool for understanding urban dynamics and for developing a set of instruments to describe and design space. The concept of porosity derives from the natural sciences, mathematics, the earth sciences, and physics and concerns movement and resistance to movement. Following its scientific definition and its philosophical and metaphorical conception by Benjamin and Bloch in the 1920s, the investigation of porosity structures an original set of representations and design strategies to address the contemporary urban and territorial issues. It provides a means of apprehending concrete spatial, social, and environmental qualities.

Territories and Cities Which Are or Which Might Be Porous

In our first explorations of the concept, porosity was revealed by intense fieldwork and survey, by cartographic interpretation and design tests. In the case of the territorial plan for the Province of Lecce, in the south of Italy (1999–2001), the porous nature of the urban and rural organization of Salento—a dense network of roads, artifacts, agricultural production, small and medium enterprises, rich but fragmented ecological dynamics—supported the vision of a territory whose different components, heterogeneous, stratified, and superimposed, defined multiple opportunities for its populations. Its organization showed low levels of urban concentration, no development poles or big industry, no heavy infrastructure. Minimal hierarchy and geographical marginality were not absolute limitations to the emergence of a situated form of modernization, a new modernity not complying with an orthodox and generic development model. In other words, the vision proposed by the plan for the provincial territory of Lecce* (Viganò 2001) was to enhance and strengthen the in situ appearance of an alternative path to the traditional modernization process, applied in many world peripheral contexts and subsequent failures and disruption in many places. The porous Salento territory, offering a diffuse spatial capital supporting settlements, multiple ecologies, and agricultural productivity, a high quality of landscape and life, through incremental, low, and decentralized investments, seemed to us to project a process of modernization containing an innovative vision for its future. The plan was a far-reaching and complex attempt to reinforce and make explicit the possibility of a new trajectory, considering possible conflicts and contradictions, without opposing city and countryside, but stressing new coexistences, contextualizing, and reinterpreting ongoing dynamics at the prism of ecological awareness: namely, these urban densification processes in the rural territories, or the expansion of nature beyond the traditional and static frame of planning. Through an exploration of a set of conflictual scenarios (expansion of nature in relation to the growth of specialized agriculture, such as the vineyards, or of low-density settlements; superimposition of dispersed economic activities and agriculture; diffuse urbanization and groundwater pollution or extraction) reversing them into coherent and sustainable strategies, the richness of coexistences between human and nonhuman agencies, between different types of production, between cultural and natural landscapes, was revealed as an essential quality of a porous territory.

In the case of Antwerp, a city that was trying to overcome, at the beginning of 2000, a period of decline and where social conflicts among its different social, ethnic, and religious groups had exploded, the construction of the Structural plan** (Secchi and Viganò 2009) unlocked a different perspective on porosity. In this case, porosity was to be recognized in the openings within a fabric/layer where former activities or populations had fled away, in search of different living conditions in the suburban areas, or looking for new spaces outside the city for technological reasons and rising intolerance toward the mix of industrial and residential activities. Two types of porosity were considered: the porosity of a material and the porosity of fracture. The metaphor of geological material porosity, which differs greatly in the different rocks, can be translated into urban typomorphological considerations on the adaptability of the urban fabric, its resistance or flexibility to new lifestyles, practices, and spatial modifications. The second concept, porosity of fracture, has to do with the appearance of discontinuities, breaks, interruptions, and fractures in the city as well as in the geological history. It can exemplify the changes, often abrupt, at the social, economic, or technological level, which create new voids, opening and closing life cycles. New categories of wasted space appear to be evaluated and are open to reinterpretation. In both cases, the nineteenth-century belt in Antwerp, a mixed-use, working-class, dense and porous fabric/layer, with many vacant spaces and recent immigration, was an extraordinary field of porosity investigation. Weak signals of change and reappropriation (going back to live in the denser part of the city,

50
51

transforming an old warehouse into a new house, refurbishing a street with light interventions), embryonic, but visible to close reading, were followed and described (Viganò 2005). The Structural plan integrates these movements and flows without attempting to design and control them, but constructing a larger frame around the material porosity of the city in relation to the different turban tissues and their sociodemographic dynamics. Top-down and bottom-up initiatives, collective as well as individual, have both a role in the amelioration of the urban space and social cohesion: without this double relation, larger urban projects tackling the porosity of fracture, such as Spoornoord Park***, realized in the same period, would not have been able to act as a lever for larger and diffuse actions of amelioration and, vice versa, the scattered initiatives of individuals and young families coming back to live in the city would have been unable to contrast the hard confrontation with the other, in the absence of the structured mediation of a new important public space, the latter being an investment necessary to guarantee basic general conditions for living together.

Finally, for the purpose of this text, it was in the elaboration of a vision for Greater Paris**** (Secchi and Viganò 2011) and following research inside the Atelier International du Grand Paris, that porosity emerged as a missing characteristic of the great Parisian agglomeration. An original set of maps highlighted spatial injustice in Greater Paris, selecting physical elements reinforcing separation and deepening distances and enclaves. Leading onsite workshops and design experiments in Greater Paris, the absence of porosity became the inspiration for a metropolitan vision which translated into five main spatial strategies. The first addressed the problem of an unbalanced representation of the multiple cultures and meaningful places for the different social groups in Greater Paris. The maps of the porous city showed the spatial, functional, and symbolical richness of the *banlieue*, once it is redefined out of the traditional centrality of Paris, with the new nodes of an isotropic public transport system to connect them in the highly discontinuous and fragmented urban space which lies beyond the *Périphérique*.

The second strategy insisted on reinforcing biotic relations inside the metropolis, permeability of space and the ground, in a metropolitan area where water management, flooding risk, and biodiversity issues are still highly underestimated. The radical transformations occurring along the main rivers are here problematized: the Seine in particular, where former industrial areas are being transformed into new densely inhabited city areas, thus raising the risk (hazard plus damages and costs) of a higher number of people and without fundamental modifications of the current riverbank traffic flows. Going deeper into the study along the Seine river, upstream (Seine Amont) and downstream Paris (Arc en Seine municipalities), we were able to measure the shortsightedness of politicians, who tend to avoid discussion about the long term, especially when dealing with disasters. Confronting the inertia of collective imagery generates problems of choice and the need for a selection of priorities (should one save infrastructure by dismantling it prior to flooding, or sacrifice it in order to manage the population's flight to safer conditions?). The need for a new balance between resilient, newly designed neighborhoods and older areas to be protected by resistant systems to avoid the flooding of roads and guarantee accessibility in all situations was the outcome of our reflection which, unfortunately, was not openly discussed.

The third strategy for the project of a porous city was related to biodiversity and enlarged to sociodiversity, considering the unsatisfactory relationship between open and built spaces in Greater Paris, where open space often legitimizes and reinforces separations and lack of continuities among different urban areas and social groups. Instead of being a connective communal ground, parks, gardens, and cultivated areas are often delimited by exclusive or excluding borders, which stifle porosity and reduce permeability and connectivity. Attention to those borders could lead to "antiparks," spaces which announce the "park" and invite one to cross and enter, where spaces of requalification and valorization of marginal areas integrate new facilities, public access, and episodic urban densification.

The fourth strategy brought focused attention on a fundamental aspect of a porous city, its palimpsest character being the result of the use and reuse of the same surface (Corboz 1983). On the palimpsest, erasure and addition negotiate their action within the existing fabric, opening and closing porosities. This aspect takes on even greater importance nowadays when connected with the necessity to upgrade the performance and livability of the existing fabrics/layers, to contain and reduce energy consumption, valorizing the gray energy stored in urban materials and infrastructures. The "100 percent recycle scenario" later also developed in other contexts, offers a new way of regarding urban processes, seen through the lens of life cycles, embodied energy, and spatial inclusion (Viganò 2012). Here again, the two porosities of fracture and of the material were crucial to understanding and disclosing the spatial potentialities of the urban space.

The last strategy considered the weak connectivity of the Parisian centralized infrastructural model as a crucial issue for the project of a porous city, where generalized and isotropic accessibility (by public transport and alternative mobility) has to be guaranteed. The not-yet-official presidential project, a new Metro system in the form of a double eight today in progress, was not, from our perspective, able to achieve this ambition. We proposed considering isotropy at different scales (a TGV mesh is different from a network of cycle paths) together with the quality of space in relation to the different speeds, abandoning hierarchical, centralized structures in favor of acentered, decentralized, minimally hierarchical structures, such as a mesh of tramways or BRT, and slow mobility, to achieve a denser isotropic mesh.

All together, the five strategies offered a new frame in which to insert projects, new hypotheses, reinforcing the emerging horizontal relations between *banlieue* and *banlieue*, crossing them as fundamental parts of the metropolis and not only as servant territories of the big city. The radicalism of the porous city project appears in the Grand Paris crossings (*traversées*), a bundle of multiple connections and spaces which might undo the rigid organization of a capital city imagined as the center of a vast, subservient periphery: uniting, transforming along, finally reaching a new state, as in Bill Viola's *The Crossing* video installation (1996).

Conclusion: The Problem of Porosity

Too few people enter Italy from the South, Ernst Bloch complains in "Italy and Porosity" (1925). After describing the persisting Byzantine and Arab influence, and the baroque (a form that does not eject chaos, unlike classicism), Ernst Bloch concludes by indicating in the problem of porosity the interest in Italy, a place where one can learn about this problem (which we can extend to the whole Mediterranean area). Bloch's argument remains crucial. Porosity is a problem in many senses: urban porosity involves the *intérieur* and the public dimension, bodies' relations and their frictions in space, their constant and often conflictual transformations. In the city, porosity is always ambiguous and dependent, in its interpretation and projection, on perspectives which confront systems of values operating in the selection or erasure of the urban palimpsest, in the consideration of the physical, functional, social connectivity, and permeability of the urban realm. Starting with an investigation into the form of porosity, we are confronted with the ideological rigidity of all centered and hierarchical visions, which often fly in the face of common sense. This is why, I believe, the problem of porosity is still relevant in the design of the urban and territorial space and as a figure of the discourse we construct about it.

References:
Amin, A., and N. Thrift. 2001. *Cities: Reimagining the Urban.* Cambridge. | Anfione e Zeto. 2014. "Bernardo Secchi, Paola Viganò: Opere recenti: Porosità, isotropia," *Anfione e Zeto,* no. 25. | Benjamin, W., and A. Lacis. 1925. "Naples," in *Reflections: Essays, Aphorisms, Autobiographical Writings,* edited by P. Demetz, 163–73. New York, 1978. | Bloch, E. 1925. "Italien und die Porosität," in *Werkausgabe,* vol. 9, *Literarische Aufsätze,* 508–15. Frankfurt am Main, 1985. | Corboz, A. 1983. "Le Territoire comme palimpseste," *Diogène* 121 (January–March): 14–35. | Cacciari, M. 1992. "Non potete massacrarmi Napoli! Conversazione con Massimo Cacciari," in *La città porosa: Conversazioni su Napoli,* edited by C. Velardi, 157–90. Naples. | Deleuze, G. 1988. *The Fold: Leibniz and the Baroque.* Translated by T. Conley. London, 1992. | Mantia, G. 2005. "Lo spazio poroso," PhD diss., Università IUAV, Venice. | Secchi, B. 2000. *Prima lezione di urbanistica.* Rome. | Secchi, B., and P. Viganò. 2009. *Antwerp: Territory of a New Modernity.* Amsterdam. | Secchi, B., and P. Viganò. 2011. *La Ville poreuse.* Geneva. | Viganò, P. 2005. "No Vision?" in *MStadt/M city, European Cityscapes,* edited by M. De Michelis and P. Pakesch. Exhibition catalogue, Kunsthaus Graz. Graz. Viganò, P. 2006. "The Porous City: Prototypes of Idiorhythmical Conglomerates," in *Comment vivre ensemble,* edited by P. Pellegrini and P. Viganò, 335–355. Rome. | Viganò, P. 2007. "On Porosity," in *PermaCity,* edited by J. Rosemann, 163–172. Delft. Viganò, P. 2009. "The Metropolis of the 21st Century: The Project of a Porous City," *OASE* 80: 91–107. | Viganò, P. 2010. *Territories of Urbanism: The Project as Knowledge Producer.* Translated by S. Piccolo. Lausanne, 2016. | Viganò, P. 2012. "Elements for a Theory of the City as Renewable Resource," in *Recycling City,* edited by L. Fabian, E. Giannotti, and P. Viganò, 12–24. Pordenone. | Viganò, P., ed. 2001. *Territories of a New Modernity.* Naples.

Project Information:
* P. Viganò (project), B. Secchi (scientific consultant), S. Mininanni (coordinator StudioLeccePtcp: S. Alonzi, L. Capurso, A. F. Gagliardi, A. D'Angelo, L. Fabian, R. Imperato, F. Pisanò, M. D'Ambros, R. Miglietta); C. Bianchetti with P. De Stefano, G. Pasqui, L. Vettoretto (local development policy); M. Mininni with S. Carbonara, P. Mairota, N. Martinelli, G. Carlone, G. Marzano, L. Scarpina, P. Medagli, L. Rositani, M. Lamacchia, D. Sallustro (ecology); A. Tomei (geology); A. De Giorgi (energy).
** Studio Bernardo Secchi, Paola Viganò has been external consultant of the City of Antwerp.
*** The project of Spoornoord is the result of an international competition and is today realized (winning team: Studio Bernardo Secchi, Paola Viganò, Pieter Kromwjik, Rob Cuyvers, Iris Consulting)
**** STUDIO 09 Bernardo Secchi, Paola Viganò with A. Calò, D. Ming Chang, T. Cos, N. Fonty, A.Pagnacco; L. Fabian, E. Giannotti, P. Pellegrini, IUAV; Ingenieurbüro Hausladen GMBH (G. Hausladen, J. Bauer, C. Jacobsen , C. Bonnet, R. Fröhler; MIT and P-REX/ Clemson and P-REX, A. Berger, C. Brown; MOX, A. Quarteroni, P. Secchi, C. D'Angelo, F. Nobile, F. Della Rossa; PTV France, F. Reutenauer, F. Prybyla, M. Lenz; European Master in Urbanism (EMU), Fall semester Design Studio, 2008–2009, Università IUAV di Venezia, coordinated by B. Secchi, P. Viganò.

Architecture and Urban Design

Exploring the Unforeseen—Porosity as a Concept
Christian Zöhrer

Porosity is a prolific concept for architects and urban designers in addressing the principle challenges of urban space. As designing urban space means dealing with wicked problems (Rittel and Webber 1973) there is an urgent need for tools that are precise in description and at the same time allow for the appearance of unforeseen aspects within the process of planning and designing. This chapter illustrates how a metaphor can be made productive as a concept for architecture and urban design.

"Designers use the metaphor as an instrument of thought that serves the function of clarity and vividness antedating or bypassing logical processes" (Ungers 1982, 11). This is of fundamental importance for the protagonists of the discipline in overcoming the hermetic boundaries of modernist zoning in urban planning, and to avoid designing buildings as isolated objects. Instead they need to be understood as relational spaces creating specific qualities and atmospheres within their individual urban context. Thus the special emphasis on porosity is not so much concerned with its function as a purely descriptive metaphor, but as a *Denkbild* that combines conceptual power with imagination. This concept focuses on architecturally designed urban spaces with its main interests in openness, ambiguousness, and interpenetration on all scales.

For this, the complementarity of spatial form and physical form is important to the concept of porous city. The volumes of buildings always have to be perceived in relation to the (urban) spaces in between them. Alban Janson points out the importance of these dialectics of mass and pores in the urban tissue when he talks about the "Ambiguous Figure and Cloud." Gianbattista Nolli's Rome-Plan of 1748 is the perfect illustration of this figure-ground-illusion of urban space. But this aspect also appears on other scales of the urban tissue. From the metropolitan area, as shown in the large-scale figure-ground-plans of different European metropolitan regions in Xaveer DeGeyter's *After-Sprawl* (DeGeyter 2002) down to the ground-floor plans of Venice, drawn by Saverio Muratori's morphological school in 1959.

The wall as a double edge in this dichotomy of mass and hollow acquires a different meaning within the concept of porosity. It is no longer the abstract line or solid surface that draws boundaries around enclosed objects, buildings, or areas. The porous edge creates a communicative relationship between different spaces of the city in the form of thresholds. "The architecture of the city, could, in fact be conceived as the art of thresholds" Sophie Wolfrum argues (Wolfrum, 63). Stephen Bates and Bruno Krucker show some fascinating examples of deep thresholds they have explored with their students, focusing on the emotive and atmospheric aspects of these as-found situations.

A recent publication on baroque staircases in Naples illustrates the porous qualities of the various vertical thresholds which Benjamin and Lacis were so enthusiastic about (De Meyer 2017). The ambiguity of hiding and seeking, being inside or outside, appearing and disappearing at the same time as entering or leaving a building contains so much dramaturgical potential that this architectural space transforms the street or the courtyard into a stage and the people into actors. We have forgotten the great potential and the specific qualities these transitional spaces offer to the city. Thus, Francesca Fornasier uses Georges Perec's request that "We should learn to live more on staircases" as an opportunity to point out the richness and diversity of these ambiguous spaces of vertical access in an urban context (Fornasier, 79).

With the aim of enabling communication, interaction, and improvisation, the concept of the porous city provides architecturally designed elements of pervasion and multiple-coded spaces on all different levels and scales. These elements are not buildings, objects, or architectural artifacts but rather thresholds or transitions, created as relational spaces connecting the inside with the outside or the private with the public. There seems to be a contradiction within this space in-between, which Doris Zoller is focused on. These situations have to be designed very precisely in form, material, scale, atmosphere, and cultural context to create an ambiguity and openness, which enables a both rich and situated spatial practice. The concept of a porous city, resolves this apparent contradiction.

In terms of large-scale urban phenomena, the blurring of conceptual borders between the architectural object, landscape, and infrastructure could be a possible approach to generating typological ambiguity and openness, as Rita Pinto de Freitas outlines in her definition of hybrid architecture (Pinto de Freitas, 76). This fluid understanding of disciplines and typologies offers potential to the design process and it forces all the disciplines involved to overcome their particular and limiting preconceptions to see the bigger picture.

While Gunther Laux identifies a loss of porosity within the present practice of transforming urban space and highlights his arguments by using the example of the Stuttgart21 project, Margitta Buchert unfolds the qualities of another large-scale architectural project, De Rotterdam, finished in 2013 by AMO. She shows that a public space within the volume of a big building can create a porous space by means of architectural design alone. This demand for porous space as an architecturally designed open situation can be transferred from the large scale of a whole city to an individual private apartment. As urban space not only offers thresholds and openness in terms of built spaces, but also includes specific spatial practices and cultural techniques to create spatial structures, the concept of a porous city suggests permeability to the process of designing, too. This means participation and negotiations are crucial to the production of porous urban space (see also chapter 4, "Urban Regulations and Planning"). When Christoph Heinemann argues that in architectural design he is more interested in articulating a problem than providing ultimate solutions to pregiven tasks, the productive use of conflicts becomes graspable as an integral part of design processes.

The concept of a porous city avoids simple solutions to problems in binary categories of right or wrong. It seeks to create urban space as an open system but with a specific and architecturally designed spatial structure, which allows for future rearrangements and reappropriations. As Richard Sennett (2013, 14) puts it: "All good narrative has the property of exploring the unforeseen, of discovery; the novelist's art is to shape the process of that exploration. The Urban designer's art is akin."

References:
DeGeyter, X., ed. 2002. *After-Sprawl: Research for the Contemporary City*. Rotterdam. | De Meyer, D. 2017. *Showpiece and Utility: Eighteenth-century Neapolitan Staircases*. Ghent. | Rittel, H., and M. Webber. 1973. "Dilemmas in a General Theory of Planning," *Policy Sciences* 4: 155–69. | Sennett, R. 2013. "The Open City," accessed October 27, 2017, https://www.richardsennett.com/site/senn/UploadedResources/The%20Open%20City.pdf. | Ungers, O. 1982. *Morphology, City Metaphors*. Cologne.

Still Here while Being There—About Boundaries and Thresholds
Sophie Wolfrum

Humans draw spatial boundaries to structure their world, to establish conditions of stability, to differentiate between social spheres, to demarcate territories, to exercise power. Georg Simmel speaks of the "incomparable solidity and lucidity that the processes of social boundary-making obtain through their spatialization," suggesting that "every boundary is a mental, more exactly, a sociological occurrence; however, by its investment in a border in space the mutual relationship acquires, from its positive and negative sides, a clarity and security—indeed also often a rigidity—that tends to remain denied to it as long as the encountering and partitioning of powers and rights is not yet projected into a physical form, and thus always persists, so to speak, in the *status nascens*" (Simmel 1908, 552). The city abounds with such hidden boundaries between social spaces, spheres of dominance and resistance, social distinctions and rituals. As they unfold their communicative effects they become recognizable to the attentive mind. Similarly, Walter Siebel suggests that social conventions have always produced restrictions that understand public spaces as fields of exclusion, and that they continue to do so (Siebel and Wehrheim 2003, 4). All these spaces are superimposed upon one another; their borders are in a state of instability and have the tendency to drift. In many instances they are not articulated in an architectural sense, even though their delicate traces might have materialized, over time, as engravings in the urban fabric.

Then again, territories are clearly demarcated in many other instances to emphasize their solidity and lucidity. Their borders are organized according to legally, economically, and socially induced requirements of inclusion or exclusion. Property rights are defined through entries in land registers and fixed in place by means of survey points; built structures stabilize territorial boundaries, produce cohesive inner spaces, and exert control over access to space. Private spheres are shielded and claims to property asserted by emphasizing their enclosures. This is the visible world of boundaries, markings in space that are constructed to deny or limit access in the service of a regulated exclusivity: walls, fences, hedges, signs, posts, barriers, doors and gates, front gardens, legal separation distances, infrastructure corridors. Some boundaries are extensive, so that they establish territories in their own rights, others could be as thin as a line, which become effective as a barrier tape or as a curb that makes it impossible for wheelchair users to pass. The Berlin wall, the other end of the scale again, conceived as the ultimate instrument of exclusion, surrounded West Berlin as a wide and inaccessible belt for almost thirty years. Nicosia continues to have what is referred to as a territorial buffer zone: an extreme kind of hermetically sealed border architecture, devoid of any porosity or permeability.

Drawing from the writings of Gerd Held, Helmuth Berking suggests that "territory as a spatiostructural principle is based on exclusion, the city on inclusion. The former needs the boundary and in this way increases interior homogeneity, the latter negates the boundary and increases density and heterogeneity." (Berking 2008, 19) Based on these spatiostructural conceptualizations of the modern condition, the city could be conceived as spatial entity of density and heterogeneity that does not exclude strangeness. In being open to strangeness and otherness, as something that, for some, might initially be associated with the external, the external becomes internalized and vice versa. However, even if we were to follow this notion through, the principles of territorial and urban spatiality would still interfere with each other. Boundary conditions on these premises are also architectural problems, for they need to organize and articulate situations of enclosure, exclusion, deferment, in-betweenness, and communication in multiple ways.

Boundaries

August Schmarsow suggests that the marking of a border could be seen as the first step toward the architectural articulation of space: "Traces of footprints in the sand or a shallow groove drawn with a stick are further stages in the representation of continuous boundaries" (Schmarsow 1894, 287). Architecture is always concerned, if we understand the shielding of an inner space from an outer space as one of its basic tasks, with the physical articulation of territorial borders that we establish around dwellings, buildings, and city quarters. Architecture makes borders tangible, and, in so doing, makes them accessible to practical human experience. In contrast to the previous sociological definition, we may understand the architecture of the city as one of boundaries and boundary spaces. If these assume the form of edges, they constitute one of five elements in the mental maps we construct of the built environment, as proposed by Kevin Lynch in his research on the image of the city (Lynch 1960, 47; Lynch 1981).

The boundary is a membrane, skin, shared interface, an intersection through which exchange can be intensified. Understanding the boundary as an active spatial medium means to conceive of architecture as an active membrane (Teyssot 2008). Yet the production of physical distance and of dedicated buffer zones between potentially conflicting uses is still regarded as a viable way to deal with urban conflicts; in colonial cities, an empty space, euphemistically defined as *cordon sanitaire*, separated the residential quarter of the colonizers from the colonized local population. While these and other motives have disappeared from planning thought, new borders have been established, for instance through the construction of sound-barrier systems, which then separate different parts of the city from one another. Segregation continues to be effective in zoning legislation as a standard in functionalist urban planning practice. Though we are very critical of these buffer zones of modernist planning, abandoning the concept of boundaries does not seem to be an option. For if we replace the production of emptiness and leftover spaces with processes that actively engage with the condition of boundaries, is it not the in–between spaces that have the greatest urban potential in cities?

Enclosure and exclusion, between defining what is internal as opposed to what is external, stand in a mutually ambivalent relation to one another. The need for a complete protection of private areas, boundaries as defensive bulwarks are nowadays also to be found within cities. Advanced security systems, the boundary walls of gated communities, or barricaded residential buildings have replaced the former city walls. The act of projecting individual needs for security beyond the confines of the private home into the public realm raises new questions. Where do spheres of private influence and control begin? For changes that are located outside, but close enough to residential properties may result in feelings that private boundaries are violated, even if the changes are comparatively small. The wall erected in Munich in between a newly constructed home for refugees and a row of single-family homes gained notoriety during spring 2017, and was the outcome of a legal dispute between the homeowners and the municipality. On the one hand, every boundary is malleable and vulnerable, insofar as it may be overcome by the media, by environmental influences, or by violation; on the other, there is a tendency to reinforcement. Even if the dwelling is understood as spatial immune system (Sloterdijk 2004, 501–67), intended to provide complete isolation, it still has to allow for communication with the outside world. Establishing the necessary balance between isolation and integration, between protective measures and intentional transit, between closure and controlled opening is one of the tasks of architecture.

Architecture has the capacity to articulate the ambivalent relations between shielding and contact, enclosure and opening, separation and connection.

Thresholds

Based on the example of bridge and door, Georg Simmel explains how fundamental the mutual relationship between dividing and connecting as concepts of thought and action actually is, suggesting that humans "must first conceive intellectually of the merely indifferent existence of two river banks as something separated in order to connect them by means of a bridge" (Simmel 1909, 174). The bridge illustrates the task of connecting in an immediate way, which is fundamental to our understanding of its aesthetic value. "And a human being is likewise a bordering creature who has no border. The enclosure of their domestic being by the door means, to be sure, that they have separated out a piece from the uninterrupted unity of natural being. But just as the formless limitation takes on a shape, its limitedness finds its significance and dignity only in that which the mobility of the door illustrates: in the possibility at any moment of stepping out of this limitation into freedom." (Ibid.)

Thresholds make bearable the presence of borders, and, moreover, assign to them a positive connotation through architecturally defining a space that belongs to two spheres simultaneously. The door to the house acts as the threshold to the city—passing through the door means to be, for a brief moment, still inside the house while breathing the air of the city. The street is public, but we perceive it as *my street*, in which we feel at home while relating to the city. This typology of ambivalence lends itself easily to other scales in the city. Even though we do not enter the city through defensive gates anymore, train stations and airports continue to fulfill the role of transit spaces. The Mediterranean is seen as one of the gateways to Europe, and could thus be interpreted as a vast threshold space.

The moment of passage enters our experience as a situation. Thresholds control, prolong, and ritualize the acts of exiting and entering. The communicative relationship between inside and outside may be articulated in such a way that they slow down the movement while we leave a space, or make leaving a sequence; or they raise our expectations upon entering a space. The passage between two different urban spaces becomes recognizable by means of its articulation; it is thresholds to which we may connect our mental maps. Thresholds are spaces of discontinuity, and, at the same time, connecting spaces and spaces of communication; they are "simultaneously symbols and mediators of passage" (Bollnow 1963, 158). This has contributed to the word *Schwelle*'s having many different connotations in the German language. It is a meaningful act to pass across a threshold. Sometimes borders are unrecognizable unless we cross them.

Hence, thresholds are spaces of passage—we are still here while being already there; we participate in two different spheres, but their relationship and presence shifts with each step we take. At the same time, we are within a space in its own right: we are neither still here, nor are we there yet. Situations of this kind have a performative power; sometimes they make us feel uneasy, sometimes they are desirable places to be. The feelings evoked when crossing a threshold are consequential in that they directly translate into our actions: when we feel intimidated we may choose not to enter a public building, a restaurant, or a park; or we make a detour around an urban district through which we do not wish to pass. Some buildings are deliberately designed to minimize feelings of uneasiness as much as possible. Solid walls are replaced by glass, everything appears as if it is fully accessible to our gaze; instead of doors they feature strips of hot air. They abandon the distinction between inside and outside and reduce architecture to a climatic envelope that is hardly visible. Therewith, the idea that the threshold could be architecturally articulated is lost, and with it the possibility that it could offer moments of deceleration and in-betweenness that are of a unique quality.

An architecture of thresholds is indispensable for the spatial quality of cities, for thresholds are privileged and special places in the city. Their ambivalence is their strength, beginning with a cushion on a windowsill, a conversation in the front garden, or a farewell in the doorway. Sitting on walls, hanging around underneath sheltered canopies or on verandas, resting in street cafés and observing the scenery, sitting on stairs in front of entrances, sunbathing on balconies, lingering in foyers or entrance halls of stations—it is here that consequential encounters take place, for they occur unexpectedly. Urban corridors, broad promenades, plazas and squares, edges, boundaries and membranes—ambivalent places seem to be necessary at every scale. The architecture of the city could, in fact, be conceived as the art of thresholds.

References:
Berking, H. 2008. "Städte lassen sich an ihrem Gang erkennen wie Menschen," in *Die Eigenlogik der Städte: Neue Wege für die Stadtforschung*, edited by H. Berking and M. Löw, 15–33. Frankfurt am Main. | Bollnow, O. F. 1963. *Mensch und Raum*. Stuttgart. Lynch, K. 1960. *The Image of the City*. Cambridge, MA. | Lynch, K. 1981. *Good City Form*. Cambridge, MA. | Schmarsow, A. 1894. "The Essence of Architectural Creation," in *Empathy, Form, and Space: Problems in German Aesthetics 1873–1893*, edited and translated by H. F. Mallgrave and E. Ikonomou, 281–97. Santa Monica, 1994. | Siebel, W., and J. Wehrheim. 2003. "Öffentlichkeit und Privatheit in der überwachten Stadt," *disP* 153: 4–12. | Simmel, G. 1908. "Space and the Spatial Ordering of Society," in *Sociology: Inquiries into the Construction of Social Forms*, translated by A. J. Blasi et al., 2:543–620. Leiden, 2009. | Simmel, G. 1909. "Bridge and Door," in *Simmel on Culture*, edited by D. Frisby and M. Featherstone, 170–74. London, 1997. | Sloterdijk, P. 2004. *Spheres*, vol. 3, *Foams: Plural Spherology*, translated by W. Hoban. Los Angeles, 2016. | Teyssot, G. 2008. "Architecture as Membrane," in *Explorations in Architecture. Teaching, Design, Research*, edited by R. Geiser, 166–75. Basel. | Wolfrum, S., and A. Janson. 2016. *Architektur der Stadt*. Stuttgart.

Negotiating Porosity
Christoph Heinemann

Porosity is usually explored in retrospect. The scope, permeability, and flexibility of the city emerges through appropriation and transformation, system change and rupture, through constant questioning and negotiating original assignments. This is what we call urbanity—and the quality planners want to learn from in order to be able to create instantly a complexity which is usually the product of centuries.

Porosity is much more than a diagnosis. To allow for openness and participation means to create urban and architectural structures in such way that adaptations and transformations can take place. The set of problems and issues involved extends to questions of land policy, development strategies, and planning procedures, financial models, rights of ownership, tenancy, and use.

Urban structures are built according to changing economic and societal needs. They not only address the requirements prevailing during the period of construction—they are intentionally equipped with the capacity to expand and adapt in the future. Modernity broke this principle temporarily but then recognized and confirmed that adaptability is key for the vitality of cities.

The relation between planning and development processes, forms of everyday use, and change of use can be understood by studying Michel Écochards planning for Casablanca and what became of it: Casablanca would grow, that much was certain and the immigrating population needed to be addressed. The planners around Écochard, from GAMMA (Groupe d'Architectes modernes Marocains) and ATBAT (Atelier des bâtisseurs) studied, anthropologically in particular, the *bidonvilles*, the informal settlements emerging everywhere around and translated the found qualities, orders, and forms into prototypical architectural designs of horizontal and vertical densification (Écochard 1955, 103ff). Prototypical dwellings were raised on the Carrières Centrales site, among them the famous *Nid d'abeilles* by the architects Bodiansky, Candilis, and Woods.

The ATBAT projects were advanced developments and corrections of the existing CIAM dogmas of the time and became important references for Team 10. They reoriented architecture toward the everyday and relativized the importance of functional assignments. Today the images of the transformed buildings rather than the initially realized projects gain the most attention—the visible conversion is constantly discussed and interpreted. This is certainly due to the fact that the obvious questions raised cannot be answered easily. Is it possible to stimulate this appropriation by design? Did architecture fail or did it enable the transformation?

Écochard points out that the newly planned urban grid was scaled to implement different typologies—informal, horizontal, and vertical housing types to allow for different stages of evolution, and thus to deal with transformation. Evolution was to be enabled on the basis of communal property. At the end of the book Écochard claims: "It is needless to continue to govern and organize the cities as long as the urban terrain is a matter of commerce" (Ibid., 135). The massive conversion of the proper houses was probably not anticipated, but the floor plans were designed as spaces open for appropriation by different forms of dwelling (Candilis, Josic, and Woods 1968, 118). In any case, evolution from built to appropriated porosity is readable here and an icon of twentieth-century modernity is today again an icon (just google "*nid d'abeilles* architecture"). Why is this the case?

The right to the city (Lefebvre 1968)—roughly speaking, the right to avail oneself of all the possibilities and commodities the city has to offer—is today a crucial basis for making a living. The fascination with informal building structures, transformation, and appropriation, and the desire to facilitate and trigger those qualities in western planning culture is most likely linked to that fact. Modernism tried to procure access and participation through utopian and class-conscious top-down planning, welfare, and advocacy. The tools have been corrupted. The practice of well-intended interventions has led to segregation and masked speculation. By contrast informality holds out the (maybe romantic) promise of a potentially self-determined but certainly alternatively organized urban empowerment.

Porosity is fundamental to enabling participation in the city—to provide this quality structurally and socially is more important than ever (if we think this claim through to the end, the classic differentiation between public and private realm would have to disappear for the benefit of an urban structure inhabited as a whole). At the same time, we live in a society where every niche is instantly identified, filmed, posted, and commercialized. Pop-up stores and street food markets wherever you look, squats converted to coworking spaces—down to the pores. Polydimensional access to places and modes of use is also becoming a problem as it may virtually prevent self-determining action (meanwhile there still is not much to negotiate away from densely mixed-use and diverse urban quarters).

A degree of protection would help. Society has changed and simple top-down planning strategies often enough just secure capitalist and consumerist claims. Resisting this means enabling participation on all levels from planning to build to use. Integrative concepts involving local actors and global players, future users and inhabitants can help to mirror and enact urban diversity. Thus it is not only about indifferent openness and accessibility but rather about spaces open to control by occupation, ownership, and use—spaces of negotiation.

In the following short stories about some aspects of our projects, we hope to show how building structures, participatory processes, and urban politics relate to one another, and also to make clear that providing these options and making these relations work are problems that architecture has to address, thus changing the way we conceive of architecture.

Negotiations

We understand architecture as a site of everyday actions and negotiations, and develop spaces open for appropriation, allowing for multiple forms of interpretation and patterns of use. Hermetic and specialized programs are rejected in favor of flexible configurations and deliberately indeterminate proposals of use. The architectural design does not figure as an ultimate solution, but is rather understood as a detailed articulation of a problem. Intentionally introduced complications and superimpositions are to provoke the expression of conflicts in a productive way. Consequently, integrated forms of appropriation and practices of the everyday construct relationships to urban reality by constantly questioning the social relevance and political competence of architecture.

According to this understanding and aspiration, spaces have to provide the capacity for negotiation and this is set as a key question and starting point for the development of our projects. Several issues are in play—participation, appropriation, transformability, adaptability, sustainability. The question of negotiation thus extends to several working spheres—from a distinct claim and design approach up to process-oriented development strategies.

Appropriation and Intervention

In 2008 we were asked to design a project space for the Goethe Institut in New York (ifau and Jesko Fezer 2011). The main building right over the street from the Metropolitan Museum of Art was shut down for not complying with fire regulations, and the strategy was to open satellites throughout the city with the idea of coming into closer contact with the young urban public at the "frontlines of gentrification," as Stephan Wackwitz, the program director who initiated this guerrilla tactic, used to put it. The space was to host readings, screenings, seminars, performances, and is located in the deep and narrow ground floor of the Wyoming Building on Third Street next to the Bowery.

Which part of the space would be used by whom and for what purpose and what needs to be provided for in a functional or spatial sense were the lesser problems here. It was much more important to consider the type of relation with the public and the visitors, as well as the formats and the constellations in which the institutional daily routines and public events would take place in this new and temporary institution. The design intentionally includes openness and thresholds, uncertainties and complications, indications and flexibilities for the intended forms of use.

The space is left almost untouched, as robust as possible, and is furnished with standard features like chairs, tables, canopies—common things for common use and misuse. A small entrance space serves as a foyer along with a counter and bar. This room, which is open to the street, is basically able to host any format and can be separated from the rest of the venue. A passage leads to a bigger backspace, where a steel ring is installed. The ring at first view obstructs—it encircles and excludes at the same time. People can gather within its demarcation or, from the outside, lean on the railing to contemplate works on the adjacent walls; on the other hand it allows users to attach panels, or to group tables and chairs as if it were not there, the tabletops being a bit lower than the railing.

One sentence from the director of the Goethe Institut (skeptical about this intervention) still resonates: "I give you three months: if the ring doesn't function then—we will cut it off." This was a big compliment for us at the time. The space was instantly open for use and different performances took place on the building site as a test bed for future activities; while developing and discussing the final project parallel to that, the meaning of *function* had changed. The ring works as a permanent provocation and constantly questions the forms of use of the space. To install this object, this permanent conflict, ensures the constant negotiation of the space.

The conversion of Palais Thinnfeld in Graz, which we had just accomplished previously, was conceived on a larger scale but with the same approach (Kleilein 2008; Bogensberger et al. 2009). The project is based on a sociospatial reinterpretation of the structure of the existing baroque palais, which was to be used by three different cultural institutions. The brief asked for highly specified markers of identity for the respective institutions, which were renounced in favor of spaces open for appropriation by everyday routines and adjustable to further programmatic shifts and conversions.

An old passage was reactivated, cutting right through the ground floor and creating an intermediate space providing access and institutional floor space at the same time. A stairwell leads to a social foyer on the first floor, installed there as a meeting point for the three different users and their visitors. From there, the stairs lead to a grand open space under the roof—one user group per floor, one entrance, permanent disturbance, interaction, negotiation of space.

What happened is that one of the institution's directors decided to move into the first floor along with his secretary instead of his team of fourteen young staff members. This had a huge impact on the use of the building and shows that porosity, morphologically present, reactivated, or newly enacted doesn't prevent grandiosity.

Situative Standards

The negotiation of space is fundamental for the everyday work of cultural institutions—one inherent aspect of exhibition-making is to examine its own social function and to permanently redefine its use of space. This applies to housing as well if we understand habitation as a place open for adaptive changes and alterations of use by the inhabitant—"a natural relationship," as N. John Habraken calls it (Habraken 1961, 18ff).

R50 in Berlin-Kreuzberg is a cohousing project we developed with the future inhabitants (formally as a joint building venture) (ifau und Jesko Fezer and Heide & von Beckerath 2011; Fundació Mies van der Rohe 2015; Vitra Design Museum et al. 2017). The city had launched a small program, where *Baugruppen* (German for joint building venture) were able to apply for several inner-city plots which would be sold at a fixed market price—thus outside of the bidding market. This indirect but decisive subvention was linked to the condition of self-use and led to a concept-bound allocation procedure. Having formed a core group of future inhabitants, one could provide a concept for a communal housing project, which was evaluated by a jury designating a winning project.

The city's interest was to stimulate new forms of urban living and to benefit from surplus values generated by this form of participatory development. The group was given a year to elaborate the project and therefore had to buy the land only weeks before building started—which took away a lot of financial pressure in the development phase. The project was initiated by the architects and a project developer specialized in joint building ventures, and was based on premises which were not negotiable. Cost effectiveness was a main goal in order to open the project to as large a clientele as possible, and it was also agreed to build with standard materials only and for everybody. Shared spaces as communal spaces and extensions to the apartments were implemented and calculated in the budget from the start. This concept was communicated to friends and interested parties, and from there the group formed.

As a building, R50 basically works as a support structure for different forms of spatial negotiation—the construction is robust and permits multiple forms of adaption. Apartment sizes were fixed according to specific needs—they can be resized in the future. Individual floor plans were designed with each party resulting in nineteen different apartments. Size and function of the shared spaces were discussed leading finally to a space giving onto the street and garden open for different activities, serving as a guest room and venue also open for third parties. Some planning tasks were postponed—the design of the surrounding garden was conceived when everybody had moved in, as well as the communal kitchen.

So it is the architectural setting initially enabling participation in all phases—planning, use, transformation. You could also say that the premise of allowing for participation was the strongest parameter for the initial architectural design (see questions raised above). While the basic design and planning procedures were predetermined, others were just framed—like playgrounds open for action and intervention. To us a major interest was to show that using standard constructions, materials, and procedures does not contradict involving all parties and including their needs and ideas in the development process. On the contrary—the participation in decisions leads to sound solutions as opposed to bratty individualism. We would like to call this interference and synergy of knowledge situative standards—common knowledge creates a solution for a specific situation at a specific moment (for a long-term use).

The process as a whole is thereby strongly connected to questions of urban politics. For all parties, the strongest motivation to realize this project was to secure their center of (urban) life in Berlin. In 2011, when the project started it was quite obvious that land prices and housing rents would rise, and that soon many would have to leave the inner circle. To seize the opportunity of owning a part of the city meant getting rid of this pressure. Ownership versus rent is a much discussed and hotly debated topic—especially in Berlin, where housing is mostly based on rent. Without elaborating on the matter, it may be interesting to mention that the housing estate (2300 apartments) adjacent to the cohousing project has meanwhile been sold two times. Rents are increasing and the tenants are meeting frequently in R50's common room to organize their resistance.

Participatory Planning and Urban Development Strategies

To enable participation on all layers is key to meeting today's urban challenges. "The city is no longer" or "world=city" (Koolhaas 1995 and 2000), however we may put it—this is the urban age. Everybody is a part of it and wants a part of it. To answer today's need for a diverse and maybe fragmented society, synergies have to be created and organized in such a way that the claims of the different actors can be met. There can't be an overall solution and this is why it is so important to allow for processes and procedures to meet particular situations—specific problems, conflicts, potentials. It's about control and an urbanism for good and joint causes.

Since 2015, we have been involved in a project in Hamburg at Spielbudenplatz on the site of the former ESSO-Häuser, a housing project named after a petrol station open 24/7. The plot had been sold to real estate developers and the inhabitants had to move out of the existing buildings after these had been declared in danger of collapse. Resistance had already formed to save the houses and was at the base of the following negotiations with borough and city about the future planning process. The Planbude—a collective of local actors, artists, and planners—was commissioned to organize a participatory process to collect wishes, ideas, and register claims. This resulted in the so-called St. Pauli code, a kind of white paper for the future programming and design of the city block. The code calls for diversity, adaptability, originality—a mix of clubs and commerce integrating existing local venues and start-ups from the neighborhood, small apartments for rent only, with a high percentage of subsidized housing. The developer now worked closely with the Planbude and this resulted in a brief for an urban design competition (Planbude 2017).

Our answer to the brief was disappointing for the clients (as we did not interpret the code as expected). Starting from the idea of small units for commerce and apartments which we had already developed for a proposal in Berlin (Ring 2015), we suggested a robust structure, which would be differentiated during a cooperative planning process and furthermore by use, adaptation, and transformation. Small apartments as a base for affordable housing in the long-term could be connected by shared spaces and thus integrate numerous different communities, lifestyles, and live/work combinations. Permanent process, big house, small units—what we had in mind was diversity formed out of informality not formality (see top of the article to close the circle).

The winning proposal by BeL & NL Architects chose to create clearly differentiated houses and thus to formally express the diversity asked for. The concept mirrored the ethics and aesthetics of the code and was acclaimed by all involved parties. The houses would host different communities of inhabitants taking control of their part and mixing in the public and part-public spaces. This structure was taken as a base for the following architectural competition where every invited team had to design several houses to allow for a mix generated out of a wide range of entries. We fully accepted this turn and designed our buildings elaborating on BeL & NL's preliminary studies. It felt like designing an old town— so why do this? Because the story leads to this and the motives are credible outcomes of the process.

References:
Bogensberger, M., et al. 2009. "Palais Thinnfeld Graz," in *Of People and Houses: Architecture from Styria*, edited by I. Ruby and A. Ruby, 200–27. Graz. | Candilis, G., A. Josic, and S. Woods. 1968. *Candilis-Josic-Woods: A Decade of Architecture and Urban Design*. Edited by J. Joedicke. Stuttgart. | Écochard, M. 1955. *Casablanca: Le roman d'une ville*. Paris. | Fundació Mies van der Rohe. 2015. "R50Cohousing," in *Mies van der Rohe Award, European Union Prize for Contemporary Architecture, 420, Shortlisted and nominees*, 64–67. | Habraken, N. J. 1961. *Supports: An Alternative to Mass Housing*. Translated by B. Valkenburg. London, 1972. | ifau und Jesko Fezer. 2011. "12 Arbeitsthesen," *Disko* 25, edited by A. Brandlhuber and S. Linden. Nürnberg. | ifau und Jesko Fezer and Heide & von Beckerath. 2011. "R50," *ARCH+ features* 4, *ARCH+* 201/202. | Kleilein, D. 2008. "New Scenes and Partial Publics, Graz: Revitalisierung Palais Thinnfeld," in *Public Spheres: Who Says That Public Space Functions? A Europan Discussion*, edited by K. Geipel and U. Poeverlein, 288–91. Berlin. | Koolhaas, R. 1995. "The Generic City," in *SMLXL*, by R. Koolhaas and B. Mau, 1239–64. Rotterdam. | Koolhaas, R. 2000. *Mutations: Harvard Project on the City*. Barcelona. | Lefebvre, H. 1968. *Le Droit à la ville*. Paris. | Planbude. 2017. "Spielbudenplatz Projects," accessed November 10, 2017, http://planbude.de. | Ring, K., ed. 2015. *Urban Living: Strategien für das Zukünftige Wohnen/Strategies for the Future*. Berlin. | Vitra Design Museum, et al. 2017. "R50," in *Together: Die neue Architektur der Gemeinschaft*, edited by I. Ruby and A. Ruby, 306–7. Berlin.

Project Information:
ifau – institute for applied urbanism are: Christoph Heinemann, Susanne Heiß and Christoph Schmidt. | Goethe Institut Wyoming Building, New York: ifau und Jesko Fezer with common room, completed 2009. | Palais Thinnfeld, Graz: Ein radikaler Kompromiss – Revitalisierung Palais Thinnfeld, ifau und Jesko Fezer, completed 2008. | R50 cohousing, Ritterstraße Berlin: ifau und Jesko Fezer, Heide & von Beckerath, completed 2013.

Deep Threshold
Stephen Bates, Bruno Krucker

Over the last eight years at the Chair of Urbanism and Housing at TU München we have been exploring the European city, believing wholeheartedly that its density and intensity, consistency and decorum remain relevant for the future. We have been encouraging our students to develop a greater understanding of the emotive aspects of the city as much as of structure and typology.

The atmosphere of European cities is characterized by a strong connection between the urban residential typology and the street. There is a resonance between buildings and the spaces between them. In the best examples, the public character of urban space infiltrates residential buildings through deep thresholds, courts, and arcades. The buildings themselves offer something back to the city in the form of porches, loggias, and canopies. In this way, the private domain and the public character of urban spaces that surround it are locked together in a beautiful way. These spatial relationships are at the heart of the European city.

In a series of design studios, we have been exploring how it may be possible to integrate the shared moments we experience in the city in the organization of a building by designing proposals that ensure that semipublic space infiltrates the building. At the early stages of the semester, the students undertake an exercise we call *found moments*, which invites them to speculate about the possible atmospheric character of these interstitial spaces. They are asked to consider potential spatial moments that could be incorporated in their future design, spaces that feel familiar to them from their own experience of living in a European city: places of interaction with neighbors, off-street semiprivate spaces, places which offer views of the streets below. The only proviso is that they must be able to gain access to the space they select.

Having made their choice, students survey the space and photograph it very carefully, paying attention to the light level and composition. They are then asked to produce a model of the space at a scale of 1:10 based on a print of the photograph they took. The purpose of the exercise is to accurately re-create everything that can be seen in the print. A variety of materials and finishes are employed to accurately represent the space, and this necessitates sampling and testing to ensure that the scale of materials, their texture, and the lighting conditions result in an accurate equivalent of the space originally selected. They then photograph the model from the exact viewpoint the first photograph was taken from. Forensic care is taken to re-create the lighting levels and atmosphere captured in the initial photograph. The results, some of which are presented here, are powerfully evocative images poised on the edge of reality, with an emphatic focus on the atmospheric quality of these threshold spaces.

By this disciplined attention to looking, making, matching, and representing the students are brought into an intimate exchange with the powerful potential of these transitional spaces. These scenographies describe the inhabited spaces and thresholds that witness and enrich our everyday existence—courtyards, passages, stoops, porches, lobbies, porticoes, arcades, projecting canopies, and hovering balconies mediate between the public and private realms—they belong to the structural envelope of private buildings and are at the same time part of the public face of the city. They help define the character of the city, its scale and material, and enrich the lives of its inhabitants.

By selecting existing spaces which comply with conventions of urbanity and decorum, students are prompted to reflect on the status of these spaces when they were originally created. The dramatic shift that has taken place since the 1970s, with the public realm being privately appropriated as a cautionary tale and we deliberately focus attention on semiprivate, semipublic spaces that should be designed with care and given material and spatial richness that reflects their importance.

The relevance of such in-between spaces is both in their seeming ordinariness and in their deep significance. The images that follow lack any overt authorship, suggesting modesty, though that is far from what is experienced when one has direct contact with these spaces. The images are staged and emotionally charged, with an implicit narrative that emerges from an understanding of conventional codes of place-making, whether domestic or institutional. They also display aspects of the picturesque in that they are constructed and charged with emotion by a narrative mise-en-scène.

Through this exercise, students are then prompted to consider how these images could influence their own work in designing spaces. In contrast with the received image of architectural practice as an incessant series of experimentations whose value lies in abstract novelty and technical virtuosity, these images refer to the historical experience of architecture and to the elements that define its specificity as a practical activity, a cultural specialization and an atmospheric experience. We hope such a sceno-graphic approach will hone each student's personal craft, but also encourage them to give something back to the city as a gift, placing urbanity and generosity at the center of architectural discourse.

pp. 72–75: Models of threshold spaces in Munich at 1:10 scale
by students of Studio Krucker Bates at the Technical University of Munich

Porous and Hybrid: Conditions for the Complex City
Rita Pinto de Freitas

Conscious of the impotence of contemporary urban design to provide built environments that contribute to a satisfactory development of the human condition and strengthen the social life and exchange in cities, this reflection aims to offer an exploratory introduction to the potential of hybridization in urban design in the contemporary production of cities, as a way to unfold its potential and better fulfill its social commitment. "Architecture should be conceived as a configuration of intermediate [...] sites that facilitate the simultaneous knowledge of what is significant on the other side. An intermediate space in this sense proportions the common territory where the conflicting polarities may be twin phenomena." (Van Eyck 1962, 560)

Artificial Living Environments
As a consequence of the world's population growth and the expected exponential increase in the population living in massive urbanized regions—usually referred to as megacities—completely artificial environments shaped by humans are hosting an increasing proportion of the planet's population in developing regions and converting the "management of urban areas is one of the most important development challenges of the twenty-first century" (Wilmoth 2016). On one side the power and impact of city shaping is inducing, conditioning, and determining to an absolute and previously unknown level, the form, dynamics, and qualities of human life and interaction.

On the other side, the impotence of urban design as a discipline seems to have an increasingly meaningless role in the configuration of these urbanized regions, which cannot leave us indifferent. That architecture and urban design by themselves are not able to offer an effective and satisfactory model for life in cities is part of our common professional consciousness. But that architects and urban designers are not assuming, or able to assume and effectively communicate the social responsibility of the discipline is maybe less obvious. "Architecture can never be passive and there is a strong intolerance for our profession when we cannot provide any answers—and perhaps worse, when we do not even claim any answers" (Koolhaas 2010, 322). "In London, for example, [...] the public sector has almost aggressively taken the initiative and has proven successful in imposing that initiative. Our absence of manifestos, or absence of being able to claim a degree of newness, is dangerous." (Ibid.)

Lost in the social irrelevance of architecture, movements related to urban design give signs, and announce real-world needs.

The increasingly vaunted role of participation strategies in the design of spaces in cities, open source urbanism, appropriation strategies, etc., constitute marginal scenarios that aim to activate the presence of a wide number of neglected elements within the system that together configure life in cities.

Marginal, but also meaningful, they converge as critical acts claiming to introduce users as important agents who should contribute to shaping and determining the form of the space and claim in a very direct way consideration toward those actually inhabiting the space, and toward "core issues [that] are respect for people, dignity, zest for life, and the city as meeting place" (Gehl 2010, 225). "To a far greater extent than we know it today, city planning must start with people in the future. It is cheap, simple, healthy, and sustainable to build cities for people—as well as an obvious policy for meeting the challenges of the twenty-first century." (Ibid., 225) This is certainly a core value, but probably not enough.

On the one hand, and beyond the users, the dialogue with all stakeholders should be widened. From technicians to investors, via dialogue with politicians, architecture and urban design should recover the integrative and leading role of the architect, showing how all affected areas can benefit from very specific and unique architectural skills, to visualize and anticipate the global qualities of newly shaped living environments and their impact on human life, and coordinate processes toward their implementation. On the other hand, and beyond a more effective and coordinated intervention of stakeholders in the production of cities, there is also a need within our discipline to widen the priority elements that constitute the city. Public space (social space) and nature are elements which urgently need to be included as core elements with an equivalent level in the hierarchy as built masses, landmarks, and traffic infrastructures.

This contamination of design processes, the hybridization of architecture and urban design with elements from other disciplines, and with new urban elements often considered as secondary elements within architecture, may offer a possible way of introducing life in cities.

Hybrid Architecture

As an architecture which beyond its objectual condition is simultaneously landscape and infrastructure, hybrid architecture will be briefly examined in the exploration of porosities between architecture, urban design, and landscape. Hybrid architecture transcends the formal condition of architecture to explore its responsibility and impact on the configuration of systems and production of life in cities (Pinto de Freitas 2011).

Any hybridization process pursues the generation of the new as differentiated and autonomous from its parents that "ascends to a richer and more elemental totality, invigorated by a poetic union of its minor parts" (Kaplan 1985, 5). In architecture, in the words of Federico Soriano, hybridization is a "mighty instrument for revitalizing or producing something new" (Soriano 1997, 126).

When architecture is simultaneously object, landscape, and infrastructure, the borders between these areas disappear to achieve a common architectural reality. Conscious of its own power to transform urban and social realities, hybrid architecture becomes context through a careful, selective, and intentioned reading of the context that hosts it, incorporating generative laws of the context as generative laws of design. Instead of submitting to the context, hybrid architecture becomes context, contributing in this way to its redefinition. Being infrastructure, landscape, and context, hybrid architecture "blurs the contours (into) fluid spaces between exterior and interior, and a communion with nature is produced precisely by these new elastic and flexible spaces of transition" (Kaplan 1985, 5). This dissolution of borders not only allows the inclusion of nature but also allows the inclusion of public space in architecture. Architecture expands to include and transform social space, becoming through this expansion an agent of transformation in the urban reality.

In becoming infrastructure, becoming context, and becoming public, architecture has to be able to absorb the infrastructural flows as well as the human flows that characterize the use of public spaces. This continuity requires physical continuity, circulation without interruption, and a continuous ground. The design, instead of taking the ground as a neutral horizontal surface, needs to reformulate the ground and obliquely unfold its surfaces to develop vertically. This happens through the inclusion of oblique surfaces that connect interior with exterior, ground floor with roof, different plans on different levels. Ramps are surfaces with the same value as horizontal surfaces and allow displacement between levels without the physical discontinuity introduced by stairs or elevators.

This fact may have an important impact on shaping and developing spaces that have to be able to host spaces for increased circulation, but has an even bigger impact on the programmatic level: Spaces for circulation leave the realm of secondary spaces of service to become primary spaces, flexible spaces that serve simultaneously static and dynamic activities.

Hybrid architecture is a reflection on scale: The scale of architecture is not the size of architecture. The multiple scales of architecture that coexist in the same intervention are the scales of the context that generates them and the scales of the context upon which they impact. Hybrid architecture is also a reflection on city: Hybrid architecture not only dissolves distances between the architectural project, urbanism, and landscape design, but conscious of its inevitable impact on physical reality—beyond the limit of its area of intervention—hybrid architecture maximizes its commitment to urban reality. Hybrid architecture assumes its responsibility in the configuration of the qualities of the common space, as well as its potential for urban transformation and reconfiguration of the landscape.

By contaminating architecture with city we get more city, and architecture becomes more urban. Through hybridization with elements of public life, hybrid architecture becomes more public. In an analogous way, through incorporating living natures in hybrid urban design we can increase the "living nature" of cities. Public spaces (or social spaces) and nature are the principal sources of life in cities. Public spaces and nature are only two examples on a long list of neglected realities in the configuration of emerging cities. Social spaces and nature are living features of urban environments. Active commitment from the discipline of urban design and active commitment from governments to the common space are neglected realities in the configuration of emerging cities.

References:
Gehl, J. 2010. *Cities for People.* Washington, DC. | Kaplan, K. 1985. "Heterotic Architecture," in *Hybrid Buildings,* edited by J. Fenton, 4–7. 4. Pamphlet Architecture 11. New York. | Koolhaas, R. 2010. "In Search of Authenticity," in *The Endless City,* edited by R. Burdett and D. Sudjic, 320–23. London. | Pinto de Freitas, R. 2011. "Hybrid Architecture: Context, Scale, Order," PhD diss., Technical University of Catalonia, Barcelona. | Soriano, F. 1997. "Artículos hipermínimos-Manifiesto injertista," *Fisuras* 4, no. 3: 124–27. | Van Eyck, A. 1962. "Dutch Forum on Children's Home," *Architectural Design* 32, no. 12: 560. | Wilmoth J. 2014. Director of UN DESA's Population Division in press conference held at United Nations headquarters in New York on July 10, 2014, http://www.un.org/apps/news/story.asp?NewsID=48240.

Thinking about Staircases: Circulation Spaces in Residential Housing
Francesca Fornasier

Demand for affordable, instantly available residential space is constantly increasing in large cities. The housing sector therefore pays great attention to efficient use of space and the optimization of construction and running costs. Consequently, the goal is to achieve the maximum net floor area per gross floor area, while service and circulation areas are reduced to the required minimum. The quality of semipublic spaces in housing is increasingly under threat as a result. From an architectural as well as from a sociocultural perspective, this development may be considered a loss. The shared circulation area is a characteristic and significant semipublic space in every apartment block. In the German technical language terminology of DIN 277 it is defined as *Verkehrsfläche* (literally "traffic zone"). However, between the main entrance and the door to the apartment there is more than a just a distance that needs to be bridged. The route leading from the street, passing through the entrance area and into the single dwelling, at times enriched by means of programs of collective external and internal uses, forms a threshold between city and private sphere: it is here that residents and strangers engage in random encounters, that communication is possible in a casual and yet anonymous way, just as it is in the public space of the street. Circulation areas in apartment blocks may thus be understood as interfaces between the city and the social—they can be seen as porous spaces on a small scale.

"We don't think enough about staircases. [...] We should learn to live more on staircases. But how?" (Perec 1974, 38)

The extent to which circulation areas really become potential spaces for encounter and interaction, for loitering and proximity in addition to the primary function of circulation, is closely related to their articulation. This, however, is not the sole responsibility of the architects who design them, for it depends on the willingness of the client to commission communal areas that are designed to high spatial standards, that is, areas which cannot be directly rented out and converted to profit. If circulation areas in building projects are defined as spaces with a specific potential, then their profitability is realized in the long term, namely when the spatial quality facilitates interactions that produce a sense of community and an identity for the building.

"Making buildings more porous will be one of the great challenges of twenty-first-century architecture; porosity could make buildings more truly urban." (Sennett 2008)

This raises the question of by what means we can create porous spaces in residential buildings, that is, well-designed communal spaces and circulation areas for residents, the local community, and therefore for the city and for society, despite the pressures exerted by profitability and efficiency. The location and size of the project, in terms of the number of residential units, are significant in this respect. Furthermore, the setup of the project needs to be considered. It seems that private housing associations and cohousing groups, with their agenda for including future residents at an early stage in the planning process of the project, are one step ahead when it comes to porosity, for they have been frontrunners in identifying circulation areas as spaces with distinct potentiality. Many projects by cohousing groups and housing associations are characterized by generous circulation areas, which exceed the minimum requirements for escape routes as defined by building regulations. A reason for this might be that future residents are in a position to collectively define and negotiate the quality standards that are to be met, and to agree on (most frequently financial) compromises which allow them to make savings in some areas in return for more flexibility in others. Another aspect that needs to be considered is urban planning instruments, ideally defined at an early stage in binding land-use plans, which encourage high levels of porosity and a given level of space efficiency simultaneously. A regulation of this kind was in place for the *Kabelwerk* residential project in Vienna: the so-called bonus cubature (*Bonuskubatur*) allowed buildings to exceed the maximum building volume by 20 percent, provided that this extra volume was designed according to the following parameters:

1. increased floor-to-ceiling heights
2. additional communal spaces
3. additional space for circulation areas (Pamer 2012)

The provisions resulted in the production of spaces with an urban quality—despite the rather peripheral location of the projects—to the benefit of the entire new-built quarter.

Generally we can distinguish between three different categories of porosity in housing. Drawing from the terminology of materials technology we can talk of the microporous, mesoporous, and macroporous (Wikipedia 2017). For the purpose of comparability, the selection of projects is based on contemporary housing schemes realized in Germany and Switzerland.

Microporous

e3, offices (ground floor), 7 residential units (floors 1–6) for private Baugruppe, Kaden Klingbeil Architekten, Berlin, Prenzlauer Berg 2008

This project falls into the category of the microporous because the interface between city and residents is articulated in a very reduced way, and not because of the small number of units. Here, the interaction of city and residents is limited to the visual-acoustic-climatic level without making a programmatic contribution to the surrounding urban space, for this space is already rich in different programs and is well established in the city center. The semipublic platforms which are attached to the externally located stairwell, however, facilitate communication and interaction within the community and between residents. The individual dwelling units are accessed by means of a small bridge which acts as interface and creates a distance between the generous platforms and private space.

Mesoporous

wagnisART, 138 residential units, ateliers, and workshops, surgery and office space, art- and culture café which includes exhibition spaces for Wohnbaugenossenschaft, bogevischs buero architekten und stadtplaner GmbH / shag / udo schindler / walter hable architekten gbr, Munich, Schwabing North 2016

The wagnisART project is part of the new DomagkPark residential development, which is currently under construction on an inner periphery site between the A9 motorway and Frankfurter Ring. The large number of residential units is carefully divided between five polygonal buildings, for which the generous circulation spaces are characteristic. Some of them are connected by bridges which are up to 6 meters wide. These areas are exclusively for the residents, while the open courtyard and a range of different uses at ground-floor level are accessible to everyone in the neighborhood. Throughout the design process the group of residents emphasized its preference for wide circulation areas as elements of specific architectural and programmatic quality, and rejected, for example, more cost-intensive detailing as compensation.

Macroporous

Kalkbreite, 88 residential units comprising up to 9.5 rooms, 9 rentable extension-rooms *Jokerräume*, a mix of communal areas as well as 20 spaces for cultural uses, gastronomy, retail, and services, which can be used by 256 residents respectively accommodate 200 work spaces for Genossenschaft Kalkbreite, Müller Sigrist Architekten, Zurich 2014

The Kalkbreite project is a residential project constructed on a tram depot site. In terms of typological form it could be thought of as a conglomerate. Characteristic of the design is the *rue intérieure*, which connects different residential typologies along its route through the building. It offers views into the project as well as into the surrounding urban space and creates a link to the urban context through the community roof garden, where the route terminates. In order to finance the generous circulation areas (corridor widths of 2.5 meters, double-height extensions to create spaces that can be inhabited, light wells to bring daylight deep into the building plan) while ensuring affordable rents, residents have agreed on reducing the areas that serve personal dwelling needs: the average residential floor area per person is 6 square meters less than the average in Zurich. The cluster apartments in the project contribute toward the optimization of floor area. The project features a strong interface to the city, which makes the circulation areas appear as though they are extensions to the external public space, and signals that the building has a range of uses that serve the public in addition to its residential use.

References:
Pamer, V. 2012. "Kabelwerk: Ein städtebauliches Modell," accessed August 1, 2014, https://www.raumberg-gumpenstein.at/cm4/de/forschung/publikationen/downloadsveranstaltungen/viewdownload/563-nachhaltiges-flaechenmanagement/12271-kabelwerk-ein-staedtebauliches-modell.html.| Pamer, V., R. Kohoutek, and H. Buchner. 2004. *Kabelwerk: Entwurfsprozess als Modell. A Development Process as a Model*, https://www.wien.gv.at/stadtentwicklung/studien/pdf/b007566.pdf. | Perec, G. 1974. *Species of Spaces and Other Pieces.* Translated by J. Sturrock. London, 2008. | Sennett, R. 2008. "The Public Realm," accessed August 21, 2016, http://richardsennett.com/site/SENN/Templates/General2.aspx?pageid=16. | Wikipedia. 2017. "Porosität," accessed September 17, 2017, https://de.wikipedia.org/wiki/Porosit%C3%A4t.

Porosity of the Monolithic

Uta Graff

Concrete reliefs, format 40 x 60 cm, students of Technical University Munich,
Chair of Architectural Design and Conception, 2017

Bigness and Porosity
Margitta Buchert

If it increasingly becomes a challenge for the future of cities to create a greater compactness of the urban fabric, then the linkage of the idea of porosity to concepts of bigness might show some interesting operating areas. How does the effect of bigness change when porosity is a part of its concept? What kind of urban qualities might emerge? How can design components potentially recovered strengthen the generation of new forms of urbanity? Taking some theories and actual architectural projects of the urban thinker and architect Rem Koolhaas and the OMA in Rotterdam as a focus and starting point enables us to identify and reveal some specific features.

Bigness
For many years, the internationally renowned architect Rem Koolhaas has worked with the idea of bigness and related concepts (Buchert 2008). From his early studies on the history of Manhattan's sky-scrapers and urban life in *Delirious New York* (Koolhaas 1978) up to his most recent texts and lectures, the concept of bigness has shaped his and the OMA's work, and subsequently that of many others. His dedi-cation to Downtown New York and the relationship between metropolitan culture and skyscrapers, together with an interest in the works of architects like Raymond Hood, Wallace Harrison, and Mies van der Rohe, were not the only triggers for this subject. It is also part of a wide-ranging critique of the con-temporary city. The unchecked urban sprawl and the formless horizontal growth of cities as well as the inattentive lifestyles of the consumer society, for example, induced him repeatedly to suggest bigness as a conceptual tool for enhancing the qualities of urban life and architecture.

Often interpreted one-sidedly as sheer polemic, Koolhaas's manifesto-like radical involvement with bigness is linked to questions as to how bigness can be used to structure and give meaning to dis-persed territories, as well as formulating the specific place or encouraging the encounter of various activities through juxtaposition and intertwining of programs. Also, the relations of inside and outside and the performance and meaning of thresholds come to the fore. These notions show that there are some analogies to the concepts of porosity and the porous city (Ellin 2006). In the context of neoliberal policies and against the impositions of eroding tendencies, the attraction of bigness for Rem Koolhaas lies in its potential to densify and to "reconstruct the whole, to resurrect the real" (Koolhaas 1995, 510). Thus, he also tries to redefine the role and meaning of architecture and activate architectural thinking.

Coincidences
In recent years, Rotterdam's agenda has been to become a driving force of globalization and to set the stage for economic, cultural and social innovation and modern living supported by urban design and architecture. Inner city districts around the Lijnbaan and old inner city harbors on both sides of the river Maas should therefore be developed as well as some more peripheral harbor areas. One prominent project, initiated in the 1980s, is Kop van Zuid, an area near the inner city and part of the former port industries in the south (van Bout and Pasveer 1994). Social housing complexes and the programmatically vacant and partly devastated structures of the passenger harbor waited there for renewal. The planning condi-tions and features are linked with goals for better infrastructure, public transport, and quality buildings, as well as for open space design and social return, a pressing need in these socially troubled neighbor-hoods. A new metro station and a huge bridge, the Erasmusbridge, were built with the aim of uniting this southern area with central urban quarters in the north of Rotterdam and thus enhancing everyday life.

As a further step, a combination of public buildings, cultural facilities, and several educational institutions have been located here in new or renovated buildings alongside diverse housing schemes and open space facilities.

As an urban activator, the Wilheminapier, a peninsula of land with excellent river views, was conceived as a high-end high-rise quarter with the aim of generating an international hub with positive social and economic effects. This still ongoing transformation process is characterized by collaboration. Diverse municipal departments, the government, private partners, and citizens work together with architects and urban planners inspiring a multifaceted generation of development, which can itself be characterized as administratively porous.

De Rotterdam, a large buiding at the Wilhelminapier designed by Rem Koolhaas and the OMA, could serve as a model for the combination of bigness and porosity in architecture. Since the destruction of World War II the city of Rotterdam has mainly fostered new and modern architecture, taking New York as an example because of its modernity and the vigor of its skyscrapers. Consequently, bigness has been on the agenda, in parallel with Koolhaas's fascination. In addition to this obvious correlation, the pier and the site of the OMA building in the nineteenth and early twentieth centuries have been the passenger port for thousands of emigrants with New York their destination.

The density of New York, especially of Manhattan, is a reference point also for Norman Foster, who with his office designed the Wilheminapiers' master plan and a framework with simple components—with lines of sight, public quays, and covered public colonnades along the street and urban functions at ground floor levels (Weston 2004). Not only by these means, but also by quality architecture the designs should be created. Three zones have been conceived to structure the pier longitudinally. An adaptive reuse of the existing brick buildings of the shipping trade is planned as a lower-middle zone, providing light and ventilation and smaller programmatic components. In addition, two waterfront zones of large-scale residential towers at the south side of the pier and offices and mixed-use spaces at the north side have been submitted. A number of cross connections for visibility and passage at right angles to the rivers enable the experience of waterscapes and the city neighborhoods, and create a continuity of public areas through crossways as well as highlighting the site's specificity as a pier. With the interrelation of old and new, hidden and apparent, mass and void as well as interstitial spaces at ground-floor level, some components have been incorporated which could embody the qualities of porous cities. In combination with the tower concept, they potentially form a meshing of bigness and porosity, and, as conceived, these simple guidelines can function as a breeding ground.

Ambiguous Spaces

De Rotterdam was finished in 2013 and reaches a height of 150 meters (OMA 2017). A slightly irregular stacking of square volumes on a plinth forms the building's shape. The rectangular overlapping blocks make up three towers. They are partly interconnected and partly encompass vertical interspaces providing frames for vistas, air, and light. Thus, a rhythm is produced between mass and void which creates both a lighter, more adaptable, and memorable whole and various impressions from different perspectives of the city. The effect of this, together with some slight recesses and cantilevers, is to combine this extremely compact building's monumental urban presence with a voluminous and ambiguous appearance. The non-load-bearing glass curtain walls, which maximize usable floor space in the interior by improving external light penetration, reinforce this feature due to the changing impact of the facades. Depending on outside atmospheres they reflect the formations of the sky and the sunlight, either visible as part of the structure or seeming to disappear in foggy weather. Last but not least, the regular facade structure corresponds to that of the huge ocean liners nearby and harmonizes with the modern character Rotterdam chose for the rebuilding of the inner city after its destruction in World War II and for the new constructions of the following decades.

The density of the De Rotterdam complex is combined with a diversity in the buildings' program. Offices, apartments, a hotel with conference rooms, restaurants, bars, leisure facilities, and parking spaces for cars and bicycles, organized into distinct blocks and areas, generate an ensemble of multiple uses. Some of them are loosely suggested by the facades, showing cautious differentiations in the structure, the openings, and variations in transparency. Between the apartment blocks of the west tower, which additionally have balconies, and the others, the heights vary slightly. Also, the interior public and semi-public spaces are only partially indentifiable as such. At street level in the plinth due to the colonnade and through the use of double- and triple-height plateglass surfaces, spatial depth is perceptible. Above these floors, we see a more closed, horizontally structured frontage for the parking lots; and at the next level up in the east tower, the huge terrace of the public bar-restaurant urban 8, with its waterfront panorama provides an additional setback and variation of the volume.

All these features carry qualities of porosity. But there is also another strong connection with the character of the porous city. In addition to restaurants, bars, and lobbies on the ground floor, there is a huge hall situated in the plinth, called the Rotterdam Square. It is a superelevated passageway-like hall and atrium open to the public. One can pass through or linger for a while or interact. Elevators and esca-lators, which allow you to discover the building, are reached through it, and it also contains entrances to the hotel, the public bar-restaurants, offices, and parking areas as well as an open-air espresso bar, mail-boxes, and lounge furniture ensembles. In this way, a generic hub is offered with performative potentials for diverse actions and interchange, a feature which could be seen as belonging to porous cities and, on the material side with its transparency and brightness, it also represents physical porosity. At the same time bigness liberates us from the world out there, enabling a kind of freedom and introducing nuances in the distinction between public and private. In contrast to the often hegemonic closed forms of global capitalism bigness, the longing for a richness of experience led the design of this architecture to provide a mixture of simplification and determination. A kind of neutral in-between is reached, a kind of porous border to enhance urban vitality. By its physical presence and by shaping the perception and adaption of the integrated and the adjacent spaces, De Rotterdam contributes to both the overarching character of the city and the surrounding public exterior space, and modulates the outside-inside relations as ambiguous in-between spaces.

Unique Urban Scape: Timmerhuis

Another model of bigness could evolve from punctual extension and reuse of the already built. By its massing of cuboidal units, the 2015 building, Timmerhuis, designed by OMA, creates a densification of downtown Rotterdam (Ibid.). It is characterized by the way it merges with and accommodates the con-text of the surrounding area and the existing fabric. The volumetric totality of this new building for the city hall, which houses municipal services, offices, and residential units of various size as well as a local history museum and a public passageway, café, restaurant, and forum can only be perceived from an aerial view. While the volume blends in on two sides with the existing buildings from the 1950s, thus forming a block-like structure at ground level, the stacking of identical prefabricated modules is gradually set back from the street and moves up into two irregular peaks. This makes the building appear smaller than it actually is and provides a means to balance small scale and large scale. The rhythm of the carefully detailed glass facade and fenestration patterns appear as relatively homogenous in a context where the state of exception has become the norm for new buildings. This architecture appears lightweight, cautious, and dynamic.

With its concept of flexible use of the units as either housing or office space, and the possibility of adding or removing according to changing demands over time, the core structure has a porous quality. Moreover: What the building especially offers are roof gardens for the apartments and a larger communal garden. In addition to this interplay of inside and outside spaces on the upper areas, there are two large atriums, which act as lungs and light catchers. One of them is extended as a passageway, which blends into the surrounding urban texture by corresponding to open spaces and axes and through its material analogies. It is cut out of the volume to a double to triple height as an interstitial area, forming a threshold with undulated plateglass membranes to the exterior and the adjacent interiors, and can be opened to the public. Thus, accessibility and intimacy are combined in a space for dynamic coexistence of activities and open engagement with the city. With this penetration of the building with a public and with semipublic spaces as well as with the manifold but minimalist upper zones, qualities were added, which create a unique urban landscape. Again, porosity can be seen as part of the concept and built environment.

New Urban Architecture

If we look at the subtle interaction of scales, spaces, programs, and effects, the potentials and limitations of the interplay of bigness and porosity and of the relationship between architecture and the city are revealed in the concepts and projects presented here. Where a balance between openness and closure form threshold conditions and ambiguous spaces, where unique urban scapes are generated by convertible spaces in a physical and anthropological sense, new urban architecture and new forms of urbanity can arise. This may differ from the ideals of the "old" European city as well as from familiar modern urban design models. However, in reflecting the nature of contemporary states of integration and disintegration through the combinations of bigness and porosity, the emergence of creative urban performance environments may be stimulated.

References:
Buchert, M. 2008. "Activating: Koolhaas's Urban Aesthetics," in *Aesthetics Bridging Cultures*, edited by the International Association for Aesthetics and J. N. Erzen, 33–39. Ankara. | Ellin, N. 2006. *Integral Urbanism*. New York. | Koolhaas, R. 1978. *Delirious New York: A Retroactive Manifesto for Manhattan*. New York. | Koolhaas, R. 1995. "Bigness or the Problem of the Large," in SMLXL, by R. Koolhaas and B. Mau, 494–516. Rotterdam. | OMA. 2017. "De Rotterdam," accessed August 8, 2017, http://oma.eu/projects/de-rotterdam. | van Bout, J., and E. Pasveer, eds. 1994. *Kop van Zuid*. Rotterdam. | Weston, R. 2004. "A Sense of Place," in *Norman Foster: Works 4*, edited by D. Jenkins, 194–203. Munich. | Wolfrum, S., and A. Janson. 2016. *Architektur der Stadt*. Stuttgart.

Reintroducing Porosity
Gunther Laux

Firmitas, Utilitas, Venustas. According to Vitruvius the counteracting of the natural entropy inherent to all things is at the core of classical architectural design, with the purpose of generating order. Spaces have to be stable and useful as well as beautiful. In this sense Giambattista Nolli's plan of Rome perforates the compact body of the city with semiprivate uses and formulates a homogenous balance between inside and outside, public and private, and the in-between.

Unlike perforation which means drilling through or piercing, porosity is more closely connected to density. The relation of solid to void is defined by the position, number, and size of pores within a volume. While perforations of the solid base of the city are useful connectors in the network of space, now as in the past, they may be problematic on the structural level of cities in that they have the potential to make the cohesion of the urban fabric disintegrate.

Urban design and architecture continue to represent spatial manifestations of contemporary tendencies and effects. Cities grow, cities shrink; urban places change and are increasingly subjected to dynamic processes. At some places nothing happens at all. Furthermore, the contemporary city is no longer an ideal, hermetical object, but an intersection, permeation, and juxtaposition of a multitude of aspects and lifeworlds which exist spatially, culturally and socially. The planned separation of uses is often confronted with unprogrammed multiple coding, when a lack of ambiguity meets situations of higher interpretative scope.

If Richard Sennett claims that "The world wants more 'porous' cities—so why don't we build them?" (Sennett 2015), and if he describes New Delhi's Nehru Place as "every urbanist's dream: intense, mixed, complex" (Ibid.), we may ask how far this "porous city" could be applied to a different context. Can we really build, design, install, and enable porosity, or is it rather the result of a situative dynamic? To begin with, porosity has a positive connotation in line with Sennett's description. It is an urban concept that is characterized by density, diversity, and permeability, as well as by the multiplicity and ambiguity of urban spaces and their uses. Conversely, porous structures may have negative connotations, depending on the dimension, distribution, and scale of the pores.

The ambivalent relationship between these two positions becomes apparent when we analyze existing urban phenomena. For this purpose we take a brief look at Stuttgart, a city which is currently experiencing extreme change. Being located within a multiple core urban agglomeration of 2.7 million inhabitants, the city of Stuttgart is a federal capital city and the center of the metropolitan region. Porosity is ubiquitous in Stuttgart, not least because of its topographical situation. The slopes surrounding the center are steep and the area in the central basin is very limited. Hence the classicist urban layout is more favorable for the fragmented structure of open perimeter blocks with gaps between buildings, rather than for closed perimeter blocks. The permeable passages to the yards are publicly accessible, compact, and used intensively. The pores produce a permeability in the sense of a positive porosity, through a very fine degree of microperforation, despite or because of the high building density and intensive mix of uses.

Stuttgart's urban postwar reconstruction efforts adhered to the modernist concept of the car-friendly city, resulting in an increased level of fragmentation of the already compact-porous urban structure, through the spatial effects of dominant traffic infrastructures. Urban squares were converted into infrastructure nodes, and urban spaces became major traffic routes, which changed the proportion of the pores in the city.

The resulting fragility of Stuttgart is further increased through a zoning practice that is based on a strict separation of uses. Since the modernist period, the zoning organization of the city has hardly changed. There is a concentration of workplaces in central locations, residential areas on the hills, housing estates at the urban periphery or in the urbanized region. All cultural, administrative, and educational services are in the heart of the city; leisure and recreation take place in the green surrounding areas. However, the grain size of these monofunctional conglomerates has increased significantly, most evidently in the building complexes in the finance sector, in the massing of retail uses, and in corporate headquarters. The mixing and superimposition of different uses are replaced by dominant infrastructure links, whereby the close-knit fabric of relations is abandoned in favor of large-scale corridors.

It seems as if urban space will struggle to cope with the meanings, tasks, and burdens assigned to it, because new challenges will create further deformations in the urban fabric. The new central station is relocated in a spectacular way belowground, track beds are reorganized, hills are tunneled through, traffic infrastructure adjusted, new urban quarters projected, while the mix of uses and small-scale spatial structures are further abandoned as a result. This is a familiar prospect for Stuttgart, as the city has been shaped by the processes of expansion and urban linking with the region since the reconstruction period. The design of spaces is currently losing its distinctness, however, because solitary mega-projects line up along extensive infrastructures, while newly constructed quarters are increasingly monofunctional. Even though traffic volume has now by far exceeded the acceptable limit, the central area continues to attract new residents from the region. The pressure on the urban area is further increased. The formerly porous structure is getting more and more fragile.

The urban restructuring resulting from the Stuttgart 21 railway project will have the greatest impact: new urban quarters and residential areas will be constructed on former railway land, comprising an area of 100 hectares in a central location next to Schlossgarten, and marketed as nice and green. The persistent insistence on an object-based urban design approach, which has been typical for Stuttgart since the reconstruction period, makes it impossible to reinstate a positively connoted porosity due to the scale of the proposed urban elements. The clustering of large volumes dominates, instead of creating a balanced relationship of solid and void, mixing and superimposing of different uses, multiple coding and ambiguity.

Can we create porosity in the sense of Sennett's descriptions at all? Is the concept just the romantic idea of a sociologist? Or is porosity produced at best autonomously? The example of Stuttgart shows, at least, that porosity may have different connotations. Pores have to be fine-grained and permeable to enable porosity. This is not necessarily intrinsic to the built environment. The ensuing problem of fragility in Stuttgart may only be stabilized through the retrofitting of a small-scale, porous fabric of open spaces. Structures of open spaces are required which assemble spaces which connect different cells or foam-like structures to foster the production of niches and in-between spaces instead of perforating the city in a fragmenting way. It is not the object-like building that produces architectural form in the city. Solids and the spaces in-between have to be seen as parameters that in their reciprocal relationship constitute urban space. Porosity needs an inverted architecture.

Reference:
Sennett, R. 2015. "The World Wants More 'Porous' Cities—So Why Don't We Build Them?" *The Guardian,* November 27, 2015.

Space In-between
Doris Zoller

1. The space in-between (Van Eyck 1962) is not confined to just one usage. The space in-between allows more than one use, and the appropriation of space is caused by its ambiguity. The project Sluseholmen in Copenhagen by Arkitema and Sjoerd Soeters is characterized by canals and small bridges. At the bridges, overlaps between the blocks create open spaces that, to a certain extent, are appropriated as private outdoor spaces by the ground-floor residents of the corner buildings.

2. Ambiguity and openness are not equivalent to randomness. On the contrary, the in-between spaces are precisely formed and designed with their own specific identity—they become spaces of transition. In the project Eden Bio in Paris by Maison Edouard François, threshold elements from the street are formed by accesses to the alleys. All around there are some alleys that can be opened and closed by gates in various buildings. The gates at Eden Bio use different materials and have varying degrees of transparency toward the street, but they are only accessible to the residents.

3. The spaces in-between, created by architectural elements, articulate the transition between inside and outside the building. Aspects like proportion ranging from details to the whole, dimension and volume of the space and the architectonic elements, materiality and surface properties, robustness in use and the inclusion of daytimes and seasons are equally important. In the project Urban Housing and Créche in Geneva by Sergison Bates architects, the building is offset on the ground level within the arcade space, forming various entrance niches. Delimited by the interior space and the columns of the arcade, the ground level is connected to the somewhat lower-lying ground floor by means of small slopes.

4. The space in-between exists also between objects such as architectural elements such as stairs, entrances, parapets, and railings. These zones under stairs, next to entrances, on top of parapets, between pillars, and so on remain unnoticed, but in fact vitally contribute to the specific character of a place. The architect and designer create through the precise design of these elements different qualities for additional use. The project Nuovo Portelloin in Milan by CZA Cino Zucchi Architetti creates thresholds and niches in the public space that merge with the arcade and the transitions into the building. A low wall runs along the diagonal pathway and then connects onto the inner facade layer under the arcade on the ground floor. A difference in height of two steps below the wide columns forms small niches, which are used as recreational areas, adding a special feature to the project.

5. It is more the precise design of the necessary means, rather than adding additional objects, that determines the "capacity" (Janson and Wolfrum 2006) to trigger various uses. In the project NonProfit Apartments by Cesta v Goricein Ljubljana by bevk perović arhitekti, the smaller courtyard opens up toward the parking area by means of wide steps, providing a communal area, which is not just for children, with its gravel surfaces, concrete platforms that are also seating, and its playground equipment. On the outside toward the parking area there are mailboxes, a bulletin board for news and internal matters, and a bench integrated into a wooden structure that provides a niche for children and young people out of sight of the adults.

References:
Janson, A., and S. Wolfrum. 2006. "Kapazität: Spielraum und Prägnanz," *der architect*, no. 5/6: 50–54. | Van Eyck, A. 1962. "The In-between Realm," in *Aldo Van Eyck: Writings*, vol.1, *The Child, the City and the Artist*, edited by V. Ligtelijn and F. Strauven, 53–71. Amsterdam, 2008. | Wüstenrot Stiftung, ed. 2014. *Herausforderung Erdgeschoss—Ground Floor Interface*. Berlin. | Zoller, D. 2016. *Schnittstelle Erdgeschoss*. Münster.

1

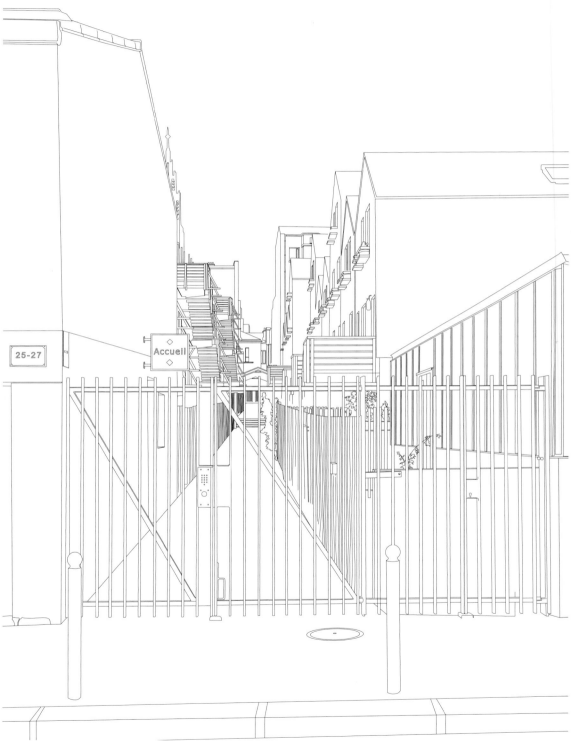

Accueil

25-27

2

Theodor Fischer, Urban Spaces Munich
Markus Lanz

crossing the intersection

Munich, Neuhausen-Nymphenburg, March 13, 2012
Dom-Pedro-Straße, Merianstraße, Hübnerstraße
Building alignment plan, Theodor Fischer, August 1898

a look back

along the street

Munich, Neuhausen-Nymphenburg, March 13, 2012
Gudrunstraße, Nibelungenstraße, Winthirstraße
Building alignment plan, Theodor Fischer, August 1898

then to the left

Ambiguous Figure and Cloud
Alban Janson

In this essay porosity will be addressed in a very elemental, concrete, material sense, thus considered to be a fundamental architectural phenomenon.

Distinguishing between inside and outside is commonly regarded as the essential distinction in architecture. That is, in any case, how the system theorist Dirk Baecker defines it: "It is architecture if you can go in and come back out again, and when the relationships change with this going-in-and-coming-back-out" (Baecker 1990, 83). What I would like to show, by contrast, is that another basic distinction is at least as fundamental for architecture, even if it tends to be underrated: the difference between filled and hollow, mass and void, volume and space. We gain our experiences with architectural space in the interaction between bodily elements and spatial figures or between spatial form and physical form. In what follows, I would like to consider this interaction, the complementarity and continuity or, if you will, the mixture of filled and hollow, mass and void, volume and space from the standpoint of porosity.

Porosity—that is to say, the manifold integration of hollow spaces with physical mass—gives us a specific experience when translated to the scale of architecture. Porosity in architecture does not limit our spatial latitude with a solid boundary but rather gives us the feeling that we can follow the infiltrating gaze in order to penetrate different forms and depths spatially as well.

I would like to approach the question of what that could mean in detail for architecture along two different paths: first, the path of oversimplification, the keyword for which is *figure-ground illusion*, and, second, the path of refinement or analysis, for which the keyword is *cloud* (see Soeder, Schmitz-Hübsch, and Janson 2015).

Ambiguous Figure

Let's begin with the scale of a single building and its immediate vicinity. In his *Handbuch der Architektur* of 1926, Fritz Schumacher, the municipal architect of Hamburg, pointed out "that architectonic corporeality is a doubled producer of space. This physical manifestation functions as a demarcation of space in two ways: namely, of the interior space and of the exterior space. [...] In the interior, the physical shell of the building represents the entire spatial termination; in the exterior, it is, as a rule, just one element of this termination, which is only completed by other elements of architectural or scenic character. [...] Thus when characterizing the essence of architecture we have to be aware that it is about designing subordinated spaces by means of designing the solid volumes in relation to superordinated spaces." (Schumacher 1926, 27–28)

According to Schumacher, therefore, the "essence of architecture" is based not necessarily on a mixture but certainly on an interweaving of solid volume and space. "In the brief form of a definition of terms," he thus formulated it as follows: "Architecture is the art of doubled design of space by means of designing solid volumes" (Ibid., 28).

The relationship of object and space, of full and empty, was discussed extensively in *Collage City* by Colin Rowe and Fred Koetter in their comparison of the modern city and the traditional city: "the one [is] an accumulation of solids in largely unmanipulated void, the other an accumulation of voids in largely unmanipulated solid; and, in both cases, the fundamental ground promotes an entirely different category of figure—in the one object, in the other space" (Rowe and Koetter 1978, 62). For the authors of *Collage City*, the advantage of the traditional city is that it forms "the solid and continuous matrix or texture giving energy to its reciprocal condition, the specific space" (Ibid.). But they believe that "the situation to be hoped for should be recognized as one in which both buildings and spaces exist in an equality of sustained debate" (Ibid., 83).

This debate is based on an ambiguity which the book illustrates by citing Edgar Rubin's figure-ground illusion. In this ambiguous figure, black and white areas interweave in such a way that the decision on what is figure and what is ground becomes uncertain, depending on whether it is interpreted as a vase or as two faces in profile. In fact, every porous shape raises the question: Is it a mass with holes in it or holes with a mass around them?

The figure-ground ambiguity of architectural masses and (urban) spaces, which in the graphic design of a figure-ground plan is represented by black and white areas, should be imagined as a kind of opposed relationship "in which victory consists in each component emerging undefeated. [...] It is a condition of alerted equilibrium which is envisaged." (Ibid.)

But can an interweaving of full and hollow go so far that a building is both object and space and fluctuates between the two, suddenly turning from the one to the other? The architect Peter Eisenman refers to Plato's dialogue *Timaeus*, in which that which is called *chora* in Greek is described as a premorphous force that, still undecided between solid and space, makes it possible for both to become reality. To make it concrete, he proposed the shape of an angled element, in his words "something between place and object, between container and contained." He employed this element in a design project and said of it: "It breaks the notion of figure/frame, because it is figure and frame simultaneously. [...] [T]he material of this house [is] unlike a traditional structure of outside and inside, neither contains nor is contained." (Eisenman 1989, n.p.)

If we move from the scale of the house to the scale of the city, we find the interweaving of enclosing and being enclosed when we take into account the fact that the mass (in the black of the figure-ground plan) in turn contains interiors, as the map of Rome by Giambattista Nolli from 1748 shows. The "continuous matrix or texture giving energy to its reciprocal condition, the specific space" mentioned in *Collage City* (Rowe and Koetter 1978, 62) can be regarded as a "habitable *poché*" (Ibid., 79), as they call it. This ambiguous assignment of black and white in Nolli's map corresponds to the fundamental possibility of locating oneself in a position that is at once surrounded by mass and lies inside mass.

We thus encounter once again the phenomenon of the dovetailing of spaces within architectural volumes and spaces between architectural volumes: the "doubled design of space by means of designing solid volumes" (Schumacher 1926, 28). However, we experience this intertwining of architectural mass and space concretely in a kind of sudden switching between the two that we have to seek not in a graphic figure-ground illusion, such as the image of the vase, but in an architectural form of reversal.

This process of architectural switching was described by Fritz Schumacher. The crucial thing is that it is not about merely visual perception or the consideration of form; instead, we perceive this process as a living situation, just as architecture is never solely about objects and forms but always about constellations of entire situations. And thus Schumacher goes on to say: "We explore the organic structure of space not only with our eyes, which breaks it down into images, but also by moving our physicality. By doing so we are living in the organism; we become part of it, so to speak. The sensory impressions we experience are doubled, an enriching conjunction that in this form is unique to architecture." (Ibid., 30)

Here he describes the movement in detail, such as circulation on a public square, which as a concave figure is framed by several architectural volumes. The individual architectural body can, by contrast, be walked around as a convex figure, while inside the building one is ultimately moving in the concave space again. Where the architectural body is part of the wall of the square, however, both processes coincide, and the concave effect and the convex effect can switch from one to the other, and one form of movement into another.

It is clear that this switching is a dovetailing in which the difference between full and hollow is preserved, rather than a blurring. The tension experienced through movement is preserved only if the difference between solid volume and space is not blurred. The real work is the switching.

Even though architecture should always be understood as a constellation of spatial situations, it is always designed with material and experienced through our confrontation with mass and materiality. The masses that shape the space affect our senses through their material. Its surfaces and textures feed on the contrast between massiveness and porousness, between light and shadow. They become permeable in joints and openings and open up spatial depth.

For the perception of the interplay between mass and hollow space, one peculiarity of human perception is crucial; it can be defined as the "spatial extension" of our personal sphere of space. The anthropologist Helmuth Plessner remarks of it: "nestling in, going with, probing, being filled up, the thousand ways of living in attitudes and through attitudes giving the silent image of spaces and areas an immediate relationship to myself are the ways to understand architecture" (Plessner 1923, 249–50). We project our bodies into the architectural forms before us, so to speak, into their recessions, projections, and openings. The diverse interactions between surface and depth, the dovetailing of architectural volumes, of hollow and interim spaces include the back and forth of resistance and close contact, pressure and suction, rejection and seduction. Building masses press themselves toward us or recede from us into depth, compel us and let us loose. Do we not also extend the antennae of our personal spatial sphere into tight hollow spaces, into small pores? (see Janson 2013)

Cloud

In this second approach, the observations should move in the opposite direction of progressive refinement, dissection, or dissolution. Starting out from the compact mass of a building, porosity can result, on the one hand, from eating away at the mass from inside, for example in the form of niches and hollow spaces carved out of the thick walls of medieval buildings. Working from the outside in, porosity can, as the historian of the city Paul Hofer expressed it, erode "the Cartesian rational, sharp-edged city model of the contrast between hollow and full. (Hofer 1979, 24; in the 1970s Hofer advocated the theoretical approach of *Collage City*, along with Bernhard Hoesli at the ETH Zürich). In the model he advocated of a "densely interwoven, layered city of the dovetailing of architectural mass and spatial design," he argues that "the building volumes are not armored but rather staggered, permeable, layered. The boundary between hollow and full is no longer the planar wall with perforated openings but rather contains space, a zone of interpenetration. The building and the open space interlock." (Ibid.)

Passages or arcades, verandas, galleries, and courtyards are interim spaces within building volumes and can be categorized in various ways: spatial intersections that are not terminated sharply by an exterior wall but only partially surrounded, built over, or partly closed off, semipublic, semiprivate, half inside, half outside. They break down the strict division by which the exterior space is located outside the building volumes and the interior space within them. In this way, compact architectural masses become perforated, dissected, they become increasingly porous. The tendency to break down is first revealed in the building shell. What happens, however, when the masses and hollow spaces are broken down further and begin to be distributed as individual elements within the overall volume of the building? Elements of mass that form architectural space no longer have to appear as compact volumes but can also contribute to the shaping of space in a quasi-dispersed form.

Walls may be dissolved into a field of columns or thin supports. Several particular observations can be made here, for example, in relation to the conditions of sight and movement. Otto Friedrich Bollnow made comparable observations about the forest: "It is rather the obstruction of vision by the things themselves, [...] which enclose us in their own realm, almost as if in a kind of inner space. The gaze penetrates only so far into the forest and then loses itself among the tree trunks. [...] Man is enclosed in a narrow space, though this has no firm, assignable boundary. He can to a certain extent move freely. He can walk through the forest. But as soon as he enters it on one side, he finds no escape from the imprisonment of his gaze, and he does not gain freedom, for the narrow, observable area moves with him, like his shadow; he cannot get rid of his constriction, but remains enclosed in it." (Bollnow 1963, 218)

What at first seems like an obstacle turns out to be a condition of a specific state. It is the characteristic form of movement in such dispersed distributions of masses, a drifting movement that is not steered in directions determined by the architecture but in which one can allow oneself to be swept about or can adopt an individual rhythm of movement and thus create spatial connections solely from their own movement.

When the material of voluminous masses is broken down further, it changes its character again. The Japanese architect Kengo Kuma, for example, sees here atmospheric effects that building materials and architectural elements do not otherwise have; emphasizing: "No matter how rich the tactile qualities of materials are, if they appear as single masses, then to me they are not vivid, because they do not change their expression. If materials are thoroughly particlized, they are transient, like rainbows. At times they strongly appear as objects, but with a momentary change of light, or with regard to the observer's movement, they instantly disperse like clouds and dissolve like mist." (Kuma 2000, 222)

It is the atmospheric character that lends its identity and unmistakable character to a cloud-like spatial structure. Dispersions of elements of mass do not have sharp boundaries. At first, they appear before you like a kind of diffuse swarm. Suddenly, you end up inside and then unexpectedly are outside it again. They may perhaps permit architecture to dispense with boundaries or spatial partitions. Depending on the density of the dispersion, the entrance can also offer a certain resistance, for example, in undergrowth or a shrub. On entering, you have to confront the resistance it offers, to eat your way in or through, so to speak. But once you have penetrated or plunged into the interior, such a form of shaping space permits continuously variable hybrid forms between separation and connection or of different states of spatial density.

On the one hand, such structures can be perceived as a "noise" (*Rauschen*); on the other, they can also produce a "buzz" (*Rausch*). Being exposed on all sides to the diffuse rush of countless small and tiny elements can have a confusing effect, much like that of a snow flurry. In the story *Bergkristall* (Rock Crystal), Adalbert Stifter described such a situation from the perspective of two children wandering about:

"In the meantime, while they kept on, the snow became so thick they could see only the nearest trees. [...] But on every side was nothing but a blinding whiteness, white everywhere that nonetheless drew its ever narrowing circle about them, paling beyond into fog that came down in waves, devouring and shrouding everything till there was nothing but the voracious snow. [...] After a time rocks suddenly loomed up dark and indistinct in the white luminescence. [...] After a time the children left them behind and could not see them any more. As unexpectedly as they had come in among them, as unexpectedly they came out. Again there was nothing about them but whiteness, with no dark interruptions looming up. It seemed just one vast fullness of light and yet one could not see three feet ahead; everything was closed in, so to speak, by a single white obscurity, and since there were no shadows it was impossible to judge the size of objects." (Stifter 1852, 40 and 46)

The blurriness of such noise can lead to hazy configurations or structures of uncertain value whose reality appears and disappears involuntarily. Leonardo da Vinci famously spoke of how such confused mixtures could stimulate the imagination when he said: "[W]hen you look at a wall spotted with stains or at rocks of diverse mixture, if you are about to devise some scene, you will be able to see in it a resemblance to various landscapes. [...] [I]t should not be hard for you to stop sometimes and look into the stains of walls, ashes from a fire, or clouds, or mud or like places, in which, if you consider them well, you may find really marvellous ideas. [...] [B]y indistinct and uncertain things the mind is stimulated to new inventions." (Klinger 2013, 58)

Finally, a state of most delicate atomization of the mass has been achieved with the cloud. In this case, the architecture, as a quasi-structural system, does not break down into the duality of mass and void but rather exists in an interim state of nearly homogeneous mixture. It is perhaps a qualitative jump, since while thus far we could design architectural space almost exclusively indirectly, by arranging architectural masses accordingly, now we can work with the substance of spatiality itself. The architect Philippe Rahm, for example, has claimed "to work directly on space itself and to design its atmosphere by shaping temperature, vapor, or light" (Rahm 2013).

I will leave it open whether porosity in the extreme form of the most delicate atomization and mixture of the tiniest particles of solid volume and space does not perhaps open up for architecture new possibilities, such as creating atmospheric conditions of their very own, possibly poetic quality.

References:
Baecker, D. 1990. "Die Dekonstruktion der Schachtel: Innen und außen in der Architektur," in *Unbeobachtbare Welt: Über Kunst und Architektur*, edited by N. Luhmann, F. Bunsen, and D. Baecker, 67–104. Bielefeld. | Bollnow, O. F. 1963. *Mensch und Raum*. Stuttgart. | Eisenman, P. 1989. *Guardiola House*. Berlin. | Hofer, P. 1979. "Materialien eines dialogischen Stadtentwurfs: 1. Anti-urbane und urbane Stadtgestalt," *Werk-Archithese* 79, no. 3334: 23–27. | Janson, A. 2013. "Räumliche Erstrecktheit," *Cloud-Cuckoo-Land* 18, no. 31: 239–249. | Klinger, F. 2013. *Theorie der Form: Gerhard Richter und die Kunst des pragmatischen Zeitalters*. Munich. | Janson, A., and F. Tigges. 2014. *Fundamental Concepts of Architecture: The Vocabulary of Spatial Situations*. Basel. | Kuma, K. 2000. "The Relativity of Materials," in *Kengo Kuma: Works and Projects*, edited by L. Alini, 222–23. Milan, 2005. | Plessner, H. 1923. *Die Einheit der Sinne: Grundlinien einer Ästhesiologie des Geistes*. Bonn, 1965. | Rahm, P. 2013. "Constructed Atmospheres," *ARCH+*, accessed February 13, 2016, http://www.archplus.net/home/news/7,1-10067,14,0.html. | Rowe, C., and F. Koetter. 1978. *Collage City*. Cambridge, MA. | Schumacher, F. 1926. "Das bauliche Gestalten," in *Handbuch der Architektur*, edited by E. Schmitt, 4.1:5–63. Leipzig. | Soeder, A., K. Schmitz-Hübsch, and A. Janson, eds. 2015. *Unerkannte Räume: Sechs Experimente im Grenzbereich der Architektur*. Berlin. | Stifter, A. 1852. *Bergkristall*. Stuttgart, 1961. | Wolfrum, S., and A. Janson. 2016. *Architektur der Stadt*. Stuttgart.

Producing Space and Acting

Performativity, Sensuality, Temporary Interventions, Negotiation
Heiner Stengel

A multiplicity of actors including architects and urban designers, local authorities, developers, citizens, activists, artists, curators as well as public institutions such as museums, libraries and theaters, are engaged in the making of urban spaces.

How can porosity be understood as a strategy to act in urban environments? How can porosity inform the production of urban spaces? How can porosity become a spur to action? How can porosity enable constantly changing performativity of urban spaces?

In June 2015 the German government passed a law defining a ceiling for rents (*Mietpreisbremse*) to cope with the continual increase, especially in prosperous and growing city regions in Germany. A price comparison defines the local rent index. But the law offers many exceptions—"room for improvisation"—one could argue. The rent index does not, for example, apply to new buildings. Another niche, currently used by real estate agents to sidestep the ceiling for new lettings is to rent out apartments as fully furnished. This allows them to ignore the ceiling, which due to the absence of affordable options is frequently accepted, even if new tenants eventually move in with their own furniture. Is *porosity* the right term to describe this practice in today's urban real estate market in Germany? Certainly not! In-between spaces, which can be appropriated, are not to be confused with the spaces of neoliberal deregulation.

The permeability (*Durchlässigkeit*) of complex systems that organize and regulate urban environments certainly includes the potential for exploitation of porous loopholes, and thus has the capacity to enable alternative ways to act. Increasingly processes and actions shaping the urban body seem to be conducted merely to increase market value, branding, or a particular interest. As we understand the concept, porosity differs from this. A wide range of motivations impact the way urban transformations, interventions, and negotiations are influencing urban societies today. Where can the niches that supply the freedom to realize porous initiatives be detected? The contributions to this chapter show examples that use permeabilities to create interpenetrations which impact urban body and urban society in a way intended to foster common goods.

Today, however, even performative actions that per se have an improvisational character—take street music in the city of Munich as an example—are being legalized and licensed, must pass a curatorial board and follow certain rules of the game (*Spielregeln*). Since the 1970s, artists have put the focus of their work on the public space "as places for autonomous action and communication" (Rung, 114). Hanne Rung argues that ideally a "curated city" with all the contradictions that are inherent in the practice of curation itself could enable spaces for the unexpected which are able to "expand and continuously refresh the public discussion about urban space" (Ibid.). Porosity is in this sense understood both as an indispensable precondition as well as a result. Conventional ideas of curating, however, seek to generate qualities through control, which ultimately might take away room for improvisation.

Within an overcurated, overplanned, overregulated, overcapitalized, and overdigitalized contemporary urban environment, public institutions may offer room for maneuver not to be found on the open market, which leaves very limited opportunities to create ambiguous constellations. Public institutions are by definition dedicated to the interest of a wider common good rather than to market-driven private interests. The protected, supposedly conservative and dusty spaces of public institutions—due to a certain independence from neoliberal market principles that currently dominate the fate of urban societies—offer opportunities and freedom to act in unorthodox ways and produce spaces outside the box. In this sense, cultural institutions like public libraries, theaters, and museums are beginning to understand their role in urban societies not only as making knowledge accessible or to staging plays or exhibitions but as creating spaces of openness, "of social exchange, and coproduction" (Fitz, 112) where culture, conflict, and correlation are addressed within a public space.

Institutions nowadays are bringing their respective content and actors out of institutionalized space into open space, "to discover, to improvise, and to learn from new experiences" (Matton, 126), to impact the built environment by "enabling modes of play in research and practice" (Dell, Kniess, Peck, and Richter, 122), or to attract a broader, more multifaceted audience within the protected spaces. Institutions redefine their thresholds, giving up elitist ideas of former periods to create a lively discourse about urban spaces and society and simultaneously find niches to impact the production of space. What significantly distinguishes institutional spaces from commercial facilities or commercially motivated cultural activities is that, by definition as public, they are open and penetrable to everybody—porous within and to the outside. The minimization of the various borders to these institutions, such as entrance fees, education gaps or accessibility, is a key task for public institutions if they are to impact the urban realm (Merk, 174), hence we could say that porosity found in specific cultural environments is in many cases enabled by an institutional base. However, one does not have to be a professor at university or a director at a public theater or museum. Even without the privilege of working from within the safe environment of public institutions there are ways to take the initiative.

The interplay of specific cultural practices and urban spaces, from narratives like Salsa Urbana in Columbia (Diesch) to the tradition of protest culture, negotiations, and bottom-up participation in Hamburg (Stengel), as well as the role of architects and urban designers in the process (Heinemann, 64) visualize the different ways in which urban societies cope with the specifics of ongoing transformations.

Power to the people! During the 1960s, this phrase was a clarion call to rebellion against what young people then perceived as a repression by the older generation, and in particular to what they understood as the establishment. In the city of today, individuals are joining forces and forming collectives and groups that have become an integral part of the urban discourse and impact both cultural and architectural practice. As formations of heterogeneous personal perspectives, some of these groups have become a melting pot of ideas and represent a fusion of citizens with differing backgrounds collaborating to become powerful actors, whether the common goal is to fight gentrification, engage in cultural and spatial practice, or simply form housing collectives to be able to secure a place to live in their cities. The ideas, processes, and the spatial production resulting from these collaborative discourses impact the mainstream and sometimes become institutionalized or part of a brand themselves—culturally, architecturally, socially. Resistance produces new forms of participation that have become an integral part of urban transformation processes in Hamburg (Stengel). Experimental architecture groups like ConstructLab are invited to produce temporary interventions at arts museums (Römer). At the same time this group is collaborating with university students in an open-build process for the realization of the Poppenbüttel 43 community building, in the effort to combine a theoretical approach with a practical impact on the built environment and the local community (Dell, Kniess, Peck, and Richter). Processes and discourses initiated and supported by multifaceted groups have the power to change conventional institutional approaches and routines.

What Can Architecture Do? Blueprint for a Porous Architecture Museum
Angelika Fitz

The question of porosity arises not only in the design, construction, and appropriation of architecture and city, but also in the mediation of architecture. How can an architecture museum offer "space and opportunity at any price"? When I started my work as director of the Architekturzentrum Wien (Az W), I was repeatedly asked whether I would initiate a program for an architecture museum that would also be of interest to nonarchitects. Have the practice and theory of architecture really become so far removed from everyday life? Are their vocabulary and concerns completely incomprehensible, their discourses impermeable? In my experience, architecture is only widely discussed when it disturbs, or when it upsets, as for example when architects are accused of incompetence or self-indulgence. This is even more true of urban development. Beyond the individual tourist moment, urban spaces usually remain in the background of perception.

I would therefore like to investigate the question of how an architecture museum can succeed in creating a permeability between everyday experience and expert discourse. My proposal is a shift of perspective: from a focus on the question What is architecture? to What can architecture do? Thus *is* becomes *can*. This small change—it is only two verbs—opens up new possibilities.

I would like to begin by saying that *can* refers to the willingness and ability of its grammatical subject to act. Readiness to act and the ability to act seem to me to be central in a time when "crisis" has long since left specialist discourse and has become the all-consuming topic of the day. Witness stagnation in climate policy, demographic change, the suffering of refugees, unbridled capitalism, lack of prospects for young people, privatization of public space, social polarization. Given the number and scale of these crises, one could easily fall into a kind of paralysis. This understandable feeling of powerlessness also extends to architects: the building industrial complex seems too overwhelming, the system is too overregulated at the level of detail, and at the same time too deregulated at the structural level, and many decision-makers seem to be disinterested in quality and architectural culture.

At the same time, I can see strong social reactions to the everyday experience of crisis in recent years: On the one hand, anxious individuals who often look toward right-wing populists—not only in Austria, but also in many European countries and beyond. And on the other, the outraged who want to reclaim their ability to act. The indignant people of Occupy Wall Street, Puerta del Sol, Syntagma Square or Gezi Park, for example, inspired a great deal of hope and, in its wake, a commensurate number of critics. The inability or lack of willingness to institutionalize as a political movement was criticized as a postpolitical stance that is reneging on its potential for change. Perhaps the resistance to new "-isms," however, is precisely the strength of these actors. Perhaps it is exactly this that makes it possible for criticism, protest, and change to interact closely. Not only was there a rebellion, people actually lived on city squares. Objects, content, and relationships were created, new spaces were tested, bodies were supplied and cared for. And many of these practices have left the squares and been diffused into urban spaces.

What can an architecture museum learn from this? There are in fact many things I have learned in my curatorial work in Southern European cities in recent years. Such as the nerve to ask fundamental questions. What began as a questioning of the austerity policy in the European Union quickly led to questions about society as a whole. In the years following the economic and financial crisis of 2008, the focus was soon on nothing less than the question of what constitutes "the good life." The architecture museum I envisage places architecture and urban development on the horizon of central social issues, knowing that "the good life" will be the subject of ongoing negotiations.

What else can an architecture museum learn from the outraged? I see another lesson in the relationship between informal and formal knowledge. Many city dwellers no longer wait to be invited to participate, and young architects do not wait until they win competitions. Both have begun to take matters into their own hands. Together they are working on the transition from investor-led to user-driven urban development. But how can this new form of concern for the city bear fruit and not lead directly to a neoliberal substitution of public services or to a commercialized version of the sharing economy? For this purpose, new interfaces between public institutions and small-scale constellations of actors are needed. The institution of the museum could be one of the platforms that mediates between bottom-up and top-down. This means that in the future, the museum will not only impart knowledge, but also increasingly share it.

What instruments does a museum need to share knowledge with different social groups? This would have to include new formats for coauthorship and coproduction, needless to say, the combination of digital and hands-on strategies along with the formation of new alliances beyond one's own community. Whether and how a museum can involve the anxious populace mentioned at the beginning of this article remains the biggest challenge. What a museum, or rather what an individual exhibition can do, is to create a common space where change is both represented and produced. Not all visitors to exhibitions can be expected to become coproducers. That would end up being either a hopelessly romantic gesture or a fundamentalist creative imperative. Nevertheless, in this sort of working exhibition, the visitors—whether looking, speaking, or making—may share a common semantic space in which it is once again acceptable to ask societal questions.

Being able means not only being ready, but—and I am therefore proposing a second shift, which triggers the word *can*—being able also means having the appropriate skill, methods, and knowledge. What can the material do? What can the form do? How does coproduction work? And what can solidarity do? Since the 1960s, we have witnessed the trend toward collective formation in several waves, sometimes in the style of rock bands, sometimes as smart diversified start-ups. I am currently observing a generation of architects and urban planners who, like the outraged, not only have their own collective in mind, but are capable of forming alliances with other groups. Their way of acting combines research, analysis, and change, and they look beyond the boundaries of their discipline. In the best-case scenario, the results are projects that offer socially diverse, ecologically and economically resilient, and highly poetic spaces—good reasons for an architecture museum to be a stage for totally novel practices.

And what can architecture do in terms of exhibiting architecture? What skills can it contribute? First and foremost, architecture stands in its own way. Its products are too large and too immobile, rarely can they be conveyed 1:1 into a museum. Architecture usually has to remain outside and the museum is confined to presenting representations, substitutions, and traces. At the same time, we should not forget that the objects in the collections of architectural museums, such as drawings, renderings, or models, are much more than empirical evidence of a discipline. Planning instruments aim to invent a piece of the future and at the same time have to find buyers for this projection in the present and convince all manner of players of their worth: clients, competitors, investors, authorities, politicians, neighbors. One could also add that they both show and hide.

The epistemic objects of an architecture museum do not simply report on past and possible realities. They tell us about the intentions of their authors and the conditions of their creation. In order to exploit this complex knowledge potential, the architecture museum will have to expand its skills in the future and go beyond classical architectural history research. Analogously to artistic research or design-related research, I would like to explore the possibilities of curatorial research more closely. This demands knowledge and exhibition formats that do not deconstruct and catalogue the investigated object but use curatorial means to reconceive it in new ways.

The performative interplay between thinking and acting, between examining, producing, and showing leads to the curatorial work not primarily concerned with a cumulative show of projects, but with the production of new content. This applies both to the museum workspace and the city workspace, where I intend to be increasingly active with the Az W. As part of the Care + Repair project, which I curate together with Elke Krasny, for the first time, the Az W opened a public workspace in a current urban development area, namely in a former warehouse for tropical fruits at Vienna's Nordbahnhof. It is not only the formats—from exhibitions, discussions, and walks to hands-on formats—which are permeable here, but also the assembled constellations of actors, ranging from developers and master planners to international architectural offices and universities to neighbors and civil society initiatives. This is in line with the conviction that cultural institutions must increasingly become places of social exchange and coproduction, that is, places where knowledge is not only made accessible but produced and shared. The architecture museum is at the center of the negotiation between architecture and society, with all its opportunities and adversities.

This brings me to a third level of meaning for the word *can*. *Can* also means having the right or permission to do something. This inevitably leads to the question: What can or may architecture not do? And this question seems to me to be extremely exciting in relation to the work of an architecture museum. Popular media, from TV thrillers to lifestyle magazines, continue to show the architect as the almighty creator of the world, always on the lookout for the ingenious design, for which they—in some thrillers—even step over dead bodies. The reality of architectural production is usually quite different. Planning and building are embedded in a multitude of social negotiation processes, economic, legal, political, and technological. These processes are already part of designing and all the more so as cocreators of the built environment. The architect seldom enjoys unlimited freedom to act.

But what do architectural museums do to communicate the vast complexity and contradiction of planning and construction? In the age of digital search engines, WikiLeaks, and Internet forums, many of us are used to having broad access to information. Previously undisturbed expert positions face new challenges because they are increasingly confronted by everyday experts. Just think of the problems of doctors with so-called Google patients, who suddenly question everything instead of just taking their medication. Looking behind the scenes has become a sport. An architecture museum can take advantage of this curiosity by taking visitors on a tour behind the scenes of architectural and urban production. Perhaps the demystification of architecture, the overcoming of the beautiful image, the questioning of the role and power of the architect, may occasionally lead to a greater understanding and interest in the ways our built environment is shaped.

On the one hand, the role of the architect is unraveling, but on the other, architects are burdened with ever more tasks and responsibilities. All in all, this seems to me to be a good time to question how architecture is mediated. How do we circumvent the technical jargon and create connections between expert discussions and everyday life? One way forward could be to include user perspectives. And by this I don't mean the abstract category of "the user," as it has haunted architectural history for decades, but rather individual experience in the habitation and appropriation of architecture. How do buildings develop after the glossy promotional photos have been shot? In my experience, architects rarely receive feedback from the users of their buildings; communication is usually limited to the elimination of technical defects. What can architecture do? An architecture museum cannot answer this question without involving all stakeholders.

Finally, and this brings me to the fourth and perhaps most important aspect of that small word: *can* means possible, conceivable, and feasible. This opens up a speculative relationship with reality. What if? How can architecture and urbanism change reality? How can they exceed the expected? How can they create spaces and opportunities? A porous architecture museum is a place where spaces and opportunities are coproduced, negotiated, and reviewed, with diverse alliances, publics, and types of knowledge.

The "Curated" City—Art in Public Space

Hanne Rung

The freedom to make and remake ourselves and our cities is, I want to argue, one of the most precious yet most neglected of our human rights. (Harvey 2012, 4)

"In the past, young people wanted to become a DJ. Nowadays the trendy job is: curator" (Reichert 2011), a *Tagesspiegel* headline stated. In 2017 Stefan Heidenreich aggressively demanded: "No more curators!" (Heidenreich 2017) in an article in *Die Zeit*. The activities of the curator, that is, to curate, are in the public interest and are viewed very critically. If we speak in positive terms of agents, networkers, and connectors, then the curator brings together things, people, space, and discussions that have not been connected before. But how can the curator of a city initiate "the passion for improvisation," as specified by Walter Benjamin and Asja Lacis, which is needed to enable the best possible "space and opportunity at any price" (Benjamin and Lacis 1925, 166–67)?

An increasing dissolution of the links between social and spatial structures, along with the fragmentation and increasing heterogeneity of urban space and its surroundings, took place during the twentieth century. Since the 1970s, this has led to artists focusing more on the city and its public spaces—for instance, Gordon Matta-Clark's cuttings or Trisha Brown's performance of *Roof Piece* on the roofs of Manhattan. In these works, the city served both as the raw material and as a resource. The new site-specificity of art sought to counteract the nondiversification of urban space that followed from functionalist principles of urban design and the implementation of major infrastructural developments. It was related closely to the wish to make public space facilities—as places for autonomous action and communication—accessible to urban society.

During the 1980s, the opportunities for artistic practice to go beyond the institutionalized context of museums and galleries gained greater prominence. The "art as public space" movement took a critical look at the newest political and social themes. It was not only concerned with the aesthetic experience of a location, but also about an overall improvement in urban living conditions, along with the creation of new communication arenas. Innovative exhibition practices were called for and the curator's brief expanded; originally an archivist and collector, (s)he became an agent of the artists, a location scout, and mediator. Jessica Cusick's *Messages to the Public*, for example, formed a key part of the Public Art Fund's long-term commitment to media-based artworks. Running from 1982 to 1990, the show featured a series of artists' projects created specifically for the Spectacolor light board at Times Square. Every month, a different artist, such as Jenny Holzer or Lorna Simpson, presented a thirty-second animation.

Artistic interest in sociopolitical questions increased in the 1990s. According to Suzanne Lacy's anthology *Mapping the Terrain*, New Genre Public Art (NGPA), or art in the public interest, emerged then. The focal point here was not so much the identity of the city but rather the importance of putting citizens at the forefront. Criticism of the art institution included criticism of urban design. The "White Cube" should have been open to an alternative critical publicity and to other social groups, thus enabling a collective experience (Hildebrandt 2012, 727–28).

But who are the actors, protagonists, or makers of the curated city? At present, planners and architects are discussing the interactions between "appropriation, planning, everyday use, and protest" (Hauck, Hennecke, and Körner 2017, 11). Today the search for the right level of supervision, organization, and administration is the main task undertaken by curators of public space. Referring to the examples of

Munich, Münster, and Hamburg, time and space gaps in the city will be examined and the perspectives of various actors will be captured. What is needed to curate a city alive?

Is curating always associated with an exhibition, created by an abstract idea, and presented temporarily? What does this mean for public space in our cities? Does the city expose herself? Does the city expose? Is the city a stage? A display? A forum? An exhibition site? Probably it is a bit of all of these— and even more. It is not only about displaying yourself but rather about the need and wish to expand and continuously refresh the public discussion about urban space.

Munich

As early as the 1970s, a pedestrian underpass below Munich's famous Maximilianstraße and Altstadtring was used as an exhibition space by private initiators. The location was institutionalized by the Städtische Galerie in the Lenbachhaus under the name of Kunstforum for almost twenty years. More than 150 exhibitions, performances, and concerts were held, such as the 1976 Joseph Beuys installation *Show your wound*. With the opening of the Kunstbau in the direct neighborhood of Lenbachhaus, the underpass became a cultural wasteland. Following a city council decree in the late 1990s, architect Peter Haimerl was put in charge of redesigning the space. His room-high wing doors with display windows enable the creation of different space layouts—without hindering the original function as a passage.

The conception behind what is now named the Maximiliansforum is to display art in public space with a focus on media art. From 2004 to 2009 the Center for Art and Media Technology in Karlsruhe used the place as ZKMax to present a continuous, high-quality program. Since then, the host (the Department of Arts and Culture of the City of Munich) has invited several curators to revitalize the forum through site-specific exhibitions and discussion—seeking to make the location visible to a wider audience.

Through the series Public Art Munich, the City of Munich met the challenge of its public space being viewed from outside by international curators and artists—with all its sociocultural and historical coordinates. The aim of the series was to deal with the city and its inhabitants and also with utopias for urban life. *A Space Called Public / Hoffentlich Öffentlich* was curated by the artist duo Elmgreen & Dragset (2013). Through sculptures, performances, and installations, seventeen international artists dealt with the question: What is public space today?

In 2018 the Polish curator Joanna Warsza will pick up the torch. Her project is to explore the status of democracy at a time when the political situation in Germany is calling it into question, and life is more publicly monitored than ever. In collaboration with local actors, fifteen international artists' performances will be developed for the Munich city center, addressing freedom of expression, transparency, privacy, monitoring, and social mobilization.

Münster

The Münster *Skulptur Projekte* have long ceased to be an insider tip. Since 1977, every ten years, work by established stars such as Donald Judd, Bruce Naumann, or Rosemarie Trockel, along with young visual artists, has been exhibited almost casually and naturally in the urban space of the city. In 2017 the project generated a large number of headlines and media coverage surrounding the nearby, world-famous competition event: documenta 14. In the end it was the exhibition in Münster rather than the one in Kassel which was more convincing to both visitors and the critics. The curational team stated that, "a public should be created not only with art, but also for art," convinced that "art in the urban realm is capable of activating historical, architectural, social, political, and aesthetic contexts." The team see "its potential not in the occupation, but rather in the creation of spaces" (LWL—Museum für Kunst und Kultur 2017).

In 1973 public outrage followed the installation of George Rickey's kinetic sculpture *Three Squares Gyratory*. Klaus Bußmann, the custodian at that time, initiated an "aesthetic self-awareness program" with Kasper König [artistic director], to enable a wider public to engage in an everyday exploration of modern sculpture. Since then, the exhibition has become a unique feature of Münster. This is not only due to the recurring high quality of the temporary sculptures. The generous implementation cycle—a whole decade—and continuous curation over decades have generated a growing reputation for a great sense of responsibility. The City of Münster, a reliable cooperation partner and permanent venue, offers the curatorial team a great deal of freedom, including at the financial level, and rectitude. Exhibition development is based on proposals by invited artists.

But art in public space is not just a matter of pleasure. For example, the work of New York artist Nicole Eisenman, *Sketch for a Fountain*, was beheaded by strangers at the very beginning of the exhibition, which attracted international attention. Together with the curatorial team, the artist decided not to reconstruct the damaged figure.

In any case, the great success of the exhibition even led to a call to hold it more frequently: just as in Kassel, some said the *Skulptur Projekte* should be renewed every five years. This proposal was categorically rejected by Kasper König, artistic director of all five previous exhibitions. Moreover, he asked: "Is it even necessary to continue this long-term project, or will the next generation have to come up with a completely different one?" and instead demanded "a new eleven-year gap to preserve the *Skulptur Projekte* from permanent comparison with other exhibitions" (Loy 2017).

In an interview with the newspaper *Westfälische Nachrichten*, Kasper König aired another criticism: "public space in Münster is already saturated and there is a lack of perspective and development opportunity." This would require "removing some works of art here and there" (Loy and Speckmann 2017).

Nonetheless, in 2017 the curatorial team recommended to the Regional Council and the City of Münster purchasing some sculptures—for the purpose of continually changing the cityscape. At the closing event, citizens could participate in the selection decision and in the discussion of the question: Who do the *Skulptur Projekte* belong to?

Hamburg

In 1981 Hamburg replaced the Art in Buildings program with the Art in Public Space program. This was a response to cultural and societal transition, including the changing requirements of the city as a living and interactive space for the urban public. Urban space was opened for free art projects. In 2013 the cultural board initiated the pilot project City Curator Hamburg with Sophie Goltz in order to assess the relevance and timeliness of the Art in Public Space program, to question its orientation and objectives, and to resume public discussion. After successful completion of the three-year project, it was decided to continue the program in 2018 and 2019. The Task Force on Perspectives of the Hamburg Art Commission called for an extension of the program in its evaluation of 2017. They proposed establishing an open institution as a center for management accountancy, as an intermediary and service point for all facets of the program.

"Contrary to the apparently outmoded notion of the city as a stage with its theatrical and self-observing flaneurs and tourists, the idea of a city as a factory focuses on the production of a local urban everyday life, with its diversity and connectivity, by the citizens. Cohabitation within global urban society relies on urban self-organization and civic engagement. Both practices are informal processes of active participation and codetermination, which is an integral part of the urban culture of Hamburg. Facing enormous challenges, one might wonder how civic politics and administration will be capable of generating, again and again, free spaces for multidimensional and multiple-coded acting enabling the creation of new forms of transparency and inclusion management." (Arbeitsgruppe Perspektiven der Hamburger Kunstkommission 2017, 2)

How to Curate a City Alive

So what are the specific tasks of a curator in terms of art in public space? It is not just a matter of showing high-level art with an international flair within the urban space, but rather it is about communal work that integrates cultural education into different urban milieus, thus enabling urban development and a lively social discourse on urban arts.

But let us turn back to the question: who are the makers and who is the audience?

"The city is everything and what remains is the individual experience, the discourse on social topicality" according to Philipp Messner (2016), artist and curator. Thus it is all about perception and participation. There are plenty of requirements and opportunities for curated urban space. Nevertheless, many good intentions have been unsuccessful in terms of public utility, the legal context of public space, historical connotations of places, or even political conditions. It is not surprising that all the efforts directed at the city, temporary places, and their neighborhoods can only be worthwhile if the specific needs of these places and their inhabitants are precisely analyzed and explored, and if participation is ensured through sensitive interventions resisting the temptation of commercialization and staging events.

This is where the city curator comes into play: as a researcher, evaluator, networker, and, last but not least, as a mediator between the city, urban space, art, and citizenship. The need for political will is beyond question. An open, participatory process in which all stakeholders can be an active part is of equally great importance. The task of the curators is to moderate and coordinate this process, to test new structures in a playful way, and to make them effective both in urban and political terms.

In the best sense, curators challenge traditional institutions and inspire cultural policy to create new, multifunctional, transdisciplinary interventions, which are socially, economically, and environmentally relevant, and are designed to reach an urban public composed of all age groups, social statuses, and educational backgrounds—"For nothing is concluded" (Benjamin and Lacis 1925, 166).

References:

Arbeitsgruppe Perspektiven der Hamburger Kunstkommission. 2017. "Gutachten zur Neuausrichtung des Hamburger Programms 'Kunst im öffentlichen Raum' und zur Einrichtung einer Modellinstitution für Kunst im urbanen Raum Hamburg," accessed January 3, 2018, http://www.hamburg.de/contentblob/8718414/792d82396c28df2ce1870322f995d06f/data/konzept-urbane-kunst.pdf. | Benjamin, W., and A. Lacis. 1925. "Naples," in *Reflections: Essays, Aphorisms, Autobiographical Writings*, edited by P. Demetz, 163–73. New York, 1978. | Elmgreen, M., and I. Dragset. 2013. "A Space Called Public," accessed September 28, 2017, www.aspacecalledpublic.de. | Harvey, D. 2012. *Rebel Cities: From the Right to the City to the Urban Revolution.* London. | Hauck, T., S. Hennecke, and S. Körner. 2017. *Aneignung urbaner Freiräume—Ein Diskurs über städtischen Raum.* Bielefeld. | Heidenreich, S. 2017. "Schafft die Kuratoren ab!" *Die Zeit*, June 21, 2017. | Hildebrandt, P. M. 2012. "Urbane Kunst," in *Handbuch Stadtsoziologie*, edited by F. Eckardt, 721–44. Wiesbaden. | Loy, J. 2017. "Auf Wiedersehen—in elf Jahren?" *Westfälische Nachrichten*, September 28, 2017. | Loy, J., and L. Speckmann. 2017. "Die Kunst nimmt Abschied: Welche Skulpturen sollen bleiben?" *Westfälische Nachrichten*, September 27, 2017. | LWL–Museum für Kunst und Kultur. 2017. "Skulptur Projekte," accessed September 28, 2017, https://www.skulptur-projekte.de/#/De/Information. | Messner, P. 2016. Transcribed conversation with the author. | Reichert, K. 2011. "Stell die Verbindung her: Traumjob Kurator," *Der Tagesspiegel*, July 14, 2011.

Building Vibrant Environments
Alex Römer

Experimental architectures, constructions, and narratives are at the center of the concepts that Construct-Lab develops for its interventions. For members of the collective ConstructLab, the idea of a porous city means turning sites into places of porosity, understood here as a condition of dissolved spatial and social conventions that make room for a kind of togetherness that can generate unforeseen dynamics.

While ConstructLab projects are intended to make cityscapes more porous, porosity is often already inherent in spaces the team appropriates, such as industrial wastelands, infrastructural residues, or neglected spaces in general, which are often disregarded from the urban planning perspective and therefore not subject to restrictive urban regulatory systems. That said, porosity is often a vital precondition in ConstructLab projects, which is then further enhanced through spatial and social interventions. Whenever porosity is not found as a precondition, for example, if the space is less marginal and rather institutional, ConstructLab develops ways of puncturing it through spatial, performative, and participatory action. In between most of the actual projects stories become real!

The Arch / ZomerwerfGenk (Genk, Belgium) 2017

The project developed from an invitation by the city of Genk, which asked for an intervention in the industrial landscape of a former coal mine. With quite a number of these sites in the region, maintaining and transforming them into something promising for current and future generations is an important and often challenging task for the cities in this region. In Genk, the area on top of the former coal mine, Waterscheid, is to become Thor Park, a place for the development of innovative and sustainable technologies. In connection with the research activities already happening or to be established at Thor Park, ConstructLab proposed an applied public research laboratory, an in-between of artistic experimentation and public action research. This low-tech and hands-on laboratory offers a complementary approach to academic scientific models, aimed at dealing with new technologies in an accessible and associative way.

For this purpose, The Arch, a three-story wooden structure, 26 meters long and 8 meters tall was developed, which would house the research laboratory at its very heart. The structure, which was set up at the beginning of summer 2017, was conceptualized as an inhabited support structure open to welcome the public. A support structure is a building tool that stabilizes a construction during its installation and is also used in mines to create extremely deep tunnels. Metaphorically, it can also be applied as a social, artistic, and community-shaping tool to be a support and catalyst in a first phase of appropriation. Including publicly accessible areas and private zones under one roof, the structure generated different thresholds from the surrounding open public space to the intimate living zones of the residents. The ground floor's entire facade was mobile, creating a literally porous shield between the publicly accessible research lab and the surrounding industrial wasteland. When opened in the mornings, the facade turned into a roof welcoming visitors and even enlarging the publicly accessible space with its workshop, stage, bar, and sanitary facilities. When closed at night, it became a protective shield. The first and second floors represented a level of privacy, where on average ten people from ConstructLab lived and worked together throughout the summer.

Once the structure was up, there were a variety of residencies and public workshops, which were mostly concerned with plastic waste and different ways of creating building material out of it. Others focused on the social dynamics of the project. Sometimes they were led by residents, sometimes by experts from further afield. This participatory research approach became a means of creating an environment that engaged all kinds of different individuals, including members from nearly all social groups in Genk and beyond. People worked on bricks or made tiles by using plastic waste that they themselves could bring in, for instance the caps of bottles. ConstructLab paraded through the city with a miniature version of The Arch, which was used to collect plastic caps. The aim was not only to create awareness of the project The Arch, but also to create awareness of plastic waste as a material which could be reused.

As a result of this collective effort, a monumental arch made from these recycled materials was raised at a building festival. The arch symbolizes a paradigm shift from the faith in efficiency and large-scale productivity of former times when Genk's local and regional economy thrived on huge industries such as Ford and the coal mines toward a smaller, transparent production in the city, which incorporates deviation and allows change.

Van Abbemuseum / Museum of ArteUtil (Eindhoven, The Netherlands)

The Museum of Arte Útil, for which ConstructLab worked together with the collectives Bureau d'Etudes (artists) and Collective Works (graphic designers), was a project initiated by Tania Brugera and Eindhoven's museum for contemporary art, the Van Abbemuseum. The original Van Abbemuseum was built in 1936. It is a listed brick building with a square floor plan and a rather closed monumental facade. Combined with its 2003 extension, the museum covers an area of more than 9,829 m². From December 2013 to March 2014 this conventional exhibition space was to be turned into the Museum of ArteÚtil, which can be translated as "useful art" in the sense of believing in art as a driver for social change. The Van Abbemuseum was temporarily converted into a "social power plant" where art's use value and its social function could be tested and experimented with.

For the exhibition design ConstructLab decided to introduce a new form to the old square building: a perfect circular wooden wall that went through the white-cube exhibition rooms. The wooden circle generated an inside and outside in the existing spaces in order to move the otherwise unshakable brick walls of the Van Abbemuseum. Coming out of the building at its entrance facade into the public space, the circle created a new entrance area, which drew the attention of all kinds of passersby and made the experience of entering a museum space less daunting than it is often perceived to be.

The ring was not only an architectural proposition but also a tool for creating social porosity and an atmosphere of participatory action in a space usually subject to the interpretational sovereignty of specialist art curators. With the design-built process, ConstructLab provided the opportunity to collaboratively design the Museum of ArteÚtil by working with students from the local Design Academy and the team from the Van Abbemuseum. All the participants were asked to build and experience the design of the different spaces in the exhibition related to the curatorial themes, resulting in a playful translation into an exhibition design that made the visitor become the actual user. The circle's center was designated for the archive of the Arte Útil movement. The case studies that were presented in this exhibition were examples of how to discover tactics, strategies, and uses that could activate the different spaces along the wooden wall. During the time of the exhibition the archive space was meant to be used as the display for all the activities within the Museum of ArteÚtil. In this way, ConstructLab proposed a first test-run for the activation of the Museum of ArteÚtil, thereby providing one of the many answers to the central question of what may happen with a socially engaged art project when it is taken out of its cultural context and presented in a museum, as well as what may happen to the museum itself.

Introducing a layer of puncturing is a frequently used architectural gesture within ConstructLab projects, since ways of entering and leaving an installation are usually of central importance, whether in a neglected space such as the industrial wasteland of the Waterscheid coal mine in Genk or an institutional space such as the Van Abbemuseum in Eindhoven. Other common characteristics of ConstructLab projects are the self-initiative, an often-limited budget, temporary buildings or a relatively short construction time, all of which play a vital role in creating conditions that favor experimentation. For these experiments, ConstructLab invites people to gather and make a huge, combined effort in a self-building process. In these temporary interventions resulting from joint effort, constructed simply and cheaply, essential concerns that lie between architectural form and political action become visible and tangible!

When this method and the described preconditions come together, the places ConstructLab appropriates turn into porous environments that have the potential to empower people and generate a long-term dynamic! It is the interplay of both spatial and social porosity found in all ConstructLab initiatives which creates an environment of local empowerment to fulfill the social, cultural, and at times also political interests and aspirations of such projects. Thus, porosity here can be seen as a means to an end, not an end in itself.

Porosity and Open Form

Christopher Dell, Bernd Kniess, Dominique Peck, Anna Richter

The Cooperative Review Process Building a Proposition for Future Activities Suggests How Urban Design Will Eventually Enable Modes of Play in Research as Practice on the City.

Momoyo Kaijima points her finger at a projected image of a group of people sitting around a table. She hands her MacBook to her assistant Tamotsu Ito, gets up from an armchair, walks toward the projection wall, stops in front of it, tightens her upper body for a moment, walks back, sits back down, and continues her talk on what it means to live in postdisaster Tohoku, a region of Japan's Honshu island, devastated by an earthquake, a tsunami, and a nuclear meltdown in 2011. Her bodily gestures highlight her talk about the physique of some of the men and women sitting around the table. Some of the Tohoku long-term residents in the image are fishermen, some are new residents aspiring to learn about becoming fishermen. The situation captured in the photo occurred during an early project stage of Atelier Bow-Wow's work in the area, which is about enabling potentialities to develop and sustain secure livelihoods for old and new residents in the region's uncertain and contingent postdisaster environment. The projected image is part of a fifteen-minute talk during the cooperative review process Building a Proposition for Future Activities in Poppenbüttel, Hamburg, organized by the stakeholders of the project Begegnungshaus Poppelbüttel 43, a community building to be realized in an open-build process with old and new neighbors in the city-wide program "refugee accommodation with dwelling in perspective." Both Atelier Bow-Wow's project in Japan and the project in Poppenbüttel, Germany, challenge the conventional notion of how knowledge of the city comes about in planning and architectural production, and how this process interplays with the aspect of porosity. In this article, we take on the theme of representation. Although the cooperative review process Building a Proposition for Future Activities is intended as a performative setting with an open-build mode of architectural production, this production has to be translated into representation to make it accessible for further project(ion)s (for details about the research and teaching program refer to the references section below).

Is Representation Everything?

One can argue that there is no architectural practice without representation today. This confronts us with a dilemma, which, we argue, must be tackled at its conceptual level: As long as space was understood as a fixed container in which actions unfolded, traditional and established architectural modes of representation proved productive. However, if we consider space as socially produced, the representation of a fixed situation gets in its own way. For us, being openly propositional in architectural production calls for an understanding of architecture and the city through use and ultimately requires a different mode of representation. In particular when we open up urban potentialities the chosen modes of representation must be able to capture performativity in its indeterminacy—as open form. How can this be achieved? Here we would like to focus on two aspects of architectural production: (a) its redesign of the specifics, the concrete situation, and its modes of use; and (b) the interplay of potential relations between human and nonhuman actors in order to make intersubjective negotiations and thus future potentialities available to those actors.

Since the middle of the nineteenth century, the problematization of representation has seen a well-established line of semiotic thinking ranging from Charles Sanders Peirce (1839–1914), Ferdinand de Saussure (1857–1913), Louis Hjelmslev (1899–1965), to Charles William Morris (1901–1979). For Urban Design, the pragmatist approach to semiotics plays a particularly important role as it considers semiotics as a mode of practice. One key aspect is the notion that a sign only exists in relation to the act of inter-pretation and thus involves a motive. The meaning of a sign is evident solely in the interpretation that affects sign users. In this process, the interpreter acts as the active medium between what is represented and how it is represented. Stressing the relevance of the active process of interpretation implies rejecting the equation of content and meaning. In relation to use, this act also emphasizes the user and the process of sense-making. The meaning of a sign is not a given in the sense that it is contained within it. Instead, meaning arises in the sign's interpretation. Insofar as the function of the interpreter must be accounted for, propositions about uses and users of signs or referents are always embedded in a relational context.

If Representations Are Motivated, We Must Ask to What End

Transposing this model of semiotics to urban research for us implies a research mode that not only aims at understanding representation as sign and at what representation signifies, but also at the actions and actors that are involved in the process of interpreting the urban as a system of signs in use. This emphasis of use has two implications. First, the researcher never acts as a neutral observer but is enrolled as user. It is in this context that the model frees the observation of the urban from a dyadic model of representa-tion and built structure and thus makes it possible to view the human and nonhuman actors as being related to the city by action on specific sites. Second, meaning goes further than use. Analogous to the sign, use is not a given form, but comes about in practice.

One can argue that one of the main goals of the cooperative review process Building a Proposition for Future Activities was to show that the Community Building Poppenbüttel 43 (CBP43) is a doable project. Let's focus on how this goal was projected. Again, two aspects appear of key importance in this mode of architectural production: (a) to pursue an open form depends on a minimal structure that keeps the process of the form open—stabilizing action without closing it; (b) the open form needs a represen-tational layer that instigates reflection while the action is taking place. The closing day of the summer school Building a Proposition for Future Activities 2016 proves to be a prolific firsthand account here. Challenged by the project's active players to come up with a rendering of the future CBP43 as a means of collecting funds from philanthropists, the research and teaching program Urban Design proposed, organized, and succeeded with a performative plan. After two weeks working on the project's motif in the form of three different, yet related takes, the participants of the summer school invited public officials, old and new neighbors, and active players in the project to discuss pertinent aspects of the struggle to project what CBP43 is meant to become. Several modes of representation were hybridized into one conclusive yet open setting that laid out the minimal structure of the future project(ion)s. It was about two weeks later that Hamburgische Bürgerschaft agreed to pay for the cost of construction of CBP43 (EUR 600,000) and all the active participants enrolled in the summer school and the planning leading up to it have now reassembled under new auspices for the upcoming phases of the realization and uses of CBP43 (a detailed account and thick description of the closing ceremony can be found in Kniess, Dell, Peck, and Richter [2017], 140–59).

But What Does It Mean to Make Potentialities Available?

Taking the semiotic problem into account—representations are motivated, rather than discrete—we propose to interpret potentialities as structurally ingrained in given urban situations. They are there, yet not there, visible and not visible, provide hope, yet if you expect something specific, you expect too much. Potential is a void, a porosity. To be structurally ingrained means being located in its underlying principle or a logic of an arrangement that can be defined by the spatial attribute of being habitable (Barthes 2002, 47). What does that mean? It means that potentialities are relations in the same way as existing situations are. Making potentialities available means making existing situations accessible in the unrelational modes of emergence. Concerning the production of space and thus the urban, the means of architectural production can help one to visualize and render the complexity of spatial production accessible as a pivot to open up the urban form for future modes of activities and underlying minimal structures. They are ingrained in modes of recombining, rearranging, reordering, and recomposing. At the same time, we suggest that this recombining only becomes possible when it is accompanied with a certain perspective on the urban, a certain way of looking at, reading, making sense of—and representing it.

We take a sentence literally that common sense has supplied us with: "When you smile at the world, it smiles back at you." Not only does every new mode of looking at the world change the way the world—here the city—looks back at us, it also changes us as well as our always relational mode of looking at the world—the city. If one is to understand this new mode of looking as a new perspective, one must also come up with a new mode of seeing that is appropriate to this perspective. Considering potentialities and open form we suggest a mode of representation that integrates the perspectivism of any new mode of seeing as a changing process in itself. This integration challenges the notion of a fixed meaning in representation. We aim for a representation of open form as open form, a representation of the unrepresentable, of a potentiality that is conditioned by porosity. Alongside Charles Sanders Peirce (1903) one could argue that while every new way of seeing provokes an epistemological situation in which the seeing subject and the world change at the same time, a third layer is involved: the interpreter of representation—that is, generative rather than passive. To put it succinctly: all that it takes to design the city is reading, interpreting, and representing it according to its generative potentialities. Let's remind ourselves: interpretation is nothing more than the intellectual act of translating one's own motif into a moving, cultural construct.

This mode of play in research as practice on the city was put to the test during the project days of the cooperative review process Building a Proposition for Future Activities. Over two days at the beginning of September 2017, participants—old and new neighbors, international students enrolled in curricula concerned with the urban, and industrial school students from different construction trades—enacted the future CBP43 in their encounter. This took place on the actual construction footprint of the building measuring 20 x 20 meters in the northeastern part of the site on which the city-wide program refugee accommodation with dwelling in perspective is being built. The play was structured in the form of takes—a series of detailed instructions in composition with everyday objects and luxurious things. Each take allowed participants to collaboratively enact a single or hybridized aspect of the future program. A camera crew recorded actions taking place. These recordings went through postproduction and provided one set of material for understanding the play in the form of a participatory project archaeology (PPA). This PPA was presented as part of the kick-off colloquium on the first day of the cooperative review process and thus became part of the tender documents. The participants of the project days were joined by five architecture project leaders and formed project offices on site in order to pick up work with an altered reading of what the future community building is meant to be.

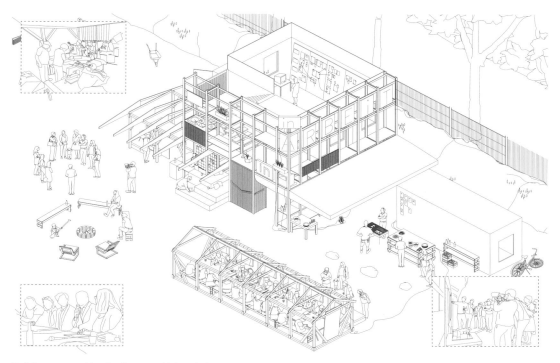

Building a proposition for future activities, closing ceremony

Play

By concentrating on the analysis of the city's use or the use of the signs of the city, we are not suggesting that the analysis should be reduced to a pragmatism that is guided by function, realization, or success. That a building has been or is used in a certain way, or a sign of the city is used in a certain way does not determine the potentialities of their uses alone. The making of the city as well as the sense-making of the city is founded on contingency and therefore depends on the facticity as well as the potentiality and generativity of the creative process itself. We resist any hierarchy between and conflation of agency and structure: yes, structure enables agency. But agency can also produce structure (Dell 2012). This explains why we play when we research: we want to find out how we use action as topology of knowledge and how the topology of knowledge instigates use (Kneiss, Dell, Peck, and Richter 2017). Play constitutes a framed field of experience which renders represented processes of interpretation possible that go beyond closed representations. These representations are neither solely based on similarity (which would exclude contingency, that is, potentialities) nor on arbitrariness (which would exclude the making of the representation), but on the porosity of permanent experimentation as research on and making of the city.

References:
Barthes, R. 2002. *A Lover's Discourse*. London. | Dell, C. 2012. *Die improvisierende Organisation: Management nach dem Ende der Planbarkeit*. Bielefeld. | Dell, C., B. Kniess, D. Peck, and A. Richter. eds. Tom Paints the Fence, in preparation. Berlin. | Kniess, B., C. Dell, D. Peck, and A. Richter. 2017. "Disciplined Disturbance," in *Science and the City: Hamburg's Path into an Academic Built Environment Education*, edited by W. Pelka and F. Kasting, 140–59. Berlin. | Peirce, C. S. 1903. "Harvard Lectures on Pragmatism," in *The Essential Peirce*, edited by The Peirce Edition Project, 2: 133–257. Bloomington, 1998.

WandererUni around the World

Ton Matton

Space and design strategists of the University of Art and Design Linz (Austria) researched the pores of Austrian Mountains, German cities, an African village, and a small Austrian town in an educational hiking tour: a nonlinear geographic journey to discover, to improvise, and to learn from new experiences. This is the essence of performative urbanism. Through new confrontations with reality, students subjectivize the circumstances, attach new meanings to them, and thus improvise their way through the world. This is what space and design practice is about.

The idea of pores, as developed by Walter Benjamin and picked up by Sophie Wolfrum in this research, serves as the guiding reference in this article. The journey is described as a search for new and practical philosophies in space and design strategies. The key lies in quick changes and confrontations that focus on in situ local conditions and on responsive and improvised actions. These actions can be globally inspired, as the contrast between European and African locations shows.

Identity, Space, and Design Strategies

In 2017 the faculty of space and design strategies moves across the Danube. From the laboratories in Linz Urfahr in the South the department moves to the main square in the center of Linz. The direct route over the Danube bridge would be 950 meters. We decided to go in the opposite direction: instead of crossing the bridge, we would circumnavigate the world to arrive at the new ateliers via Halle, Freiburg, Cologne (Germany), Charleroi (Belgium), South Africa, Totope (Ghana), Milan (Italy) and Marchtrenk (Austria) in the middle of Europe, at the Hauptplatz in Linz. This is a detailed summary of the journey.

On our way, we developed a view of the identity of space and strategies. The main goal is clear: a design, based on research, for a better world. This cannot be a theoretical and abstract vision: faced with the local circumstances, we adopted flexibility and applied our talent for improvisation, and we also developed strategies based on doubt and critical thinking.

Beforehand, it is good to be aware of the following; we are not urban planners who generally work in terms of structures and organization rather than in terms of daily life and personal experiences. We are not architects who often develop designs according to concepts which we adhere to even when the building does not fit the concepts anymore. We are not interior architects or designers either. We start from feelings and emotions, and designs often end up in the waste bin because they are not beautiful or do not fit in with these feelings and emotions. Are we artists? Artists work more personally, in a more autobiographical way and are therefore more like activists. They base their work on direct experiences and local conditions, and much more on the ever-changing present. The preliminary conclusion on identity politics is that probably space and design strategies can be found somewhere in between shaping society, ecological planning, and artists' activism. This can only be experienced through action on location.

The Fragility of Mankind

4–6 October 2016, Austrian mountains, Snow, stormy, and very cold

37 space and design strategists feel the power of nature and the fragility of humans and human culture. We are neither in the classic modernist category of recreation nor in a mode of mobility.

At the start of the semester, we walked into the Austrian mountains. Some students were familiar with the territory and sprang like goats over the rocks and stones. Others had less experience and wore in linen summer shoes. After a restful night in a shelter (*Berghut*), we headed for the mountaintop next morning. Quite soon, though, we were caught up in a snowstorm. After four hours' climbing, in ever-heavier snow, we arrived at a cable car station. Unfortunately, it was closed because of the unexpectedly heavy weather. This meant we had to go on to the next station on the other side of the mountain, another three hours on foot, as the men at the station informed us without a trace of sympathy.

Then Waleed, one of our master's degree students, stood up. The year before he had come to Europe as a refugee on foot and over the Mediterranean in a rubber boat. "If this is the biggest problem," he said, strapping one backpack to his stomach, another backpack to his back, and the Chinese student who it belonged to under his arm, "let's go!" And the group went on: freezing, exhausted, and some in tears, but we made it.

This event was a significant distillation of the essence of WandererUni. It became clear that our society, our culture, acquired a different meaning high up in the mountains, where we could feel the power of the mountains, the fragility of mankind, the thinness of our cultural layer. No longer were we in the classical modernist category of recreation, nor were we in a mobility mode.

We were on our own in a porous mountain chain. Order and disorder no longer existed. In contrast to the cybernetic understanding of systems by Cedric Price and Archigram, insecurity is not calculable. The world is a process and it is not under our control, but there are pores to be discovered and improvised upon with design or Gestaltung.

Design Deconstructs Old Meanings

5–9 November 2016, Freiburg, Germany, rain, cold

7 space and design strategists invented an instrument to view the city in a different way and from a different angle and to dismantle conventional ways of urban planning where democratic rules and laws prohibit/deny entrance to certain citizens, and to develop new enriching views and interpretations.

When we passed Freiburg, we got involved in the preparations for the Dietenbacher Festspiele. A new suburb is being planned in a classical modernist style, arguments about living, working, recreation, and transport, but based on investors' money and sales arguments of comfort. The theater wanted to research both of the neighborhoods, Rieselfeld and Weingarten, to generate a program for the new area of Dietenbach. While making these preparations, some students were considering how to research the city in another way rather than taking the capitalist urban planning machine for granted. It seems as if urban planning is still following this functional order, as if Jane Jacobs had not asked more than half a century ago what is actually happening in our cities. We wanted to find new mapping forms to show, like Kevin Lynch, that functionalism fails adequately to take account of the city. We follow the Chicago school system using participative observations.

It is amazing what happens in our minds when our view is redirected with mirrors as shown in the work of Ayan. Suddenly the concepts of a frog's perspective or a bird's-eye view are realized in front of your eyes and immediately adapted by your brain. To observe the city from the perspective of a mole, an ant, a cat, a giraffe, or a drone opens another dimension of perception. The incredible volume of rules and regulations, which of course are imposed in a new suburb, are questioned in Romy's Neulandteppich; a Euclidean space in a tabula rasa mind, which shows how quickly the pores of the city are filled with a rash of regulations: where to (not) park the cars, how high the fence adjoining the neighbors' garden should be, how far the trees should be from the facade so the branches will not touch the windows, (whereupon a worker has to come with a ladder to trim them), and the roots of the tree should not grow into the ditch and clog the drains, when to dispose of the empty green bottles and when the brown. The Neulandteppich is a Lefebvrian attempt to make contact with the inhabitants and to understand everyday life in relation to freedom, rules, and utopia. The fear is expressed that the suburb of Dietenbach and many others are accessible only for a certain clientele, for those who can afford it, who shield themselves with democratic rules and regulations that automatically deny access to others.

Rich Empty Spaces
24–26 November 2016, Halle / Leipzig, Sun, chilly Christmas atmosphere
9 space and design strategists need friends with a power generator and some beers to improvise within the luxury of empty buildings.
The luxury of emptiness is our next research task: what is the potential of deserted buildings? Both cities, Halle and Leipzig, are literally porous. They are full of *Baulücken, Brachflächen und Bruchbuden* ("empty lots, brownfield sites, and derelict buildings"). For example, behind the station, where the infrastructure is badly connected and the derelict slaughterhouse attracts attention, there is no bakery, no supermarket, but there is the old former GDR *Eisdiele* (ice cream parlor) with the best reputation in town. Here you see the potential of pores in their urban quality, as Walter Benjamin wrote in his notes on Naples. However sad it may seem, the potential is enormous.

You only need a few friends with an electricity generator and a 6-pack of beer, and the party in some deserted building kicks off, says a philosophy student from Leipzig with a passion for improvisation. A great deal has been restored in the historic center; the city administration has sold its stock of low-budget dwellings, which are much sought-after by artists and low-to-no-income groups, to affluent young families who indulge in their pricy chai lattes with soy milk. It is here that pores are not only converted into party spaces, but also clogged by investors.

Niches, Biotopes, and Pioneers
24–30 June 2017, Cologne Mülheim, Extensive rain showers, windy and cold
29 space and design strategists have doubts about regulations, neoliberal market behavior and the disappearance of social cultures.
How is it that theater directors have to be concerned with the future of life in the cities? Is that not the job of urban planners? Our performative, urbanistic research project in 2015 in the village of Gottsbüren, where for a month we squatted in some empty houses along with forty students, brought us an invitation from two theaters to do some research with them. Both the Theatre Freiburg and the Schauspiel Köln invited us to participate in the festival *Die Stadt von Morgen* (The City of Tomorrow).

Two more requests from other small villages stalled in the first round of talks, because of planning formalities. Do traditional urban planning departments have more problems with informality and improvisation? Do they still see the city as a piece of work (*Werk*) in the Heideggerian sense? Or are they more sensitive to the interests of investors and their lobbyists?

Under the bridge, in the pouring rain, we have a lot of time to express our doubts about the city of tomorrow. And, as at the university, expressing doubt is exactly what we should be doing. That is our task in contemporary society, where too much commissioned research is done with the only goal being to prove the hypotheses, instead of questioning them through research.

Some students attend a course on hygiene—otherwise cooking in a public space is not allowed—and learn that you should wash your hands before dinner. There was a time, back when the bridge was being rebuilt after the bombing, when no laws were needed, and washing your hands before dinner and cooking was obvious. Today, you have to install an extra washbasin. The law does not say that hands must be washed, but insists on the technical neoliberal requirement that you have to be able to wash your hands. The possibility of using one of the 97 washbasins in the houses around is not part of this regulation. We could even say it is suppressed. To have it yourself, rather than approaching someone to use theirs, is the mantra of neoliberalism.

Despite the demand for transparency, we buy rotten meat (*Gammelfleisch*), clothes made by modern slaves, coffee in plastic paper cups, manipulated VW diesels, stocks and shares of dubious origin, and so on. So contemporary politics is based on a falsehood, which Alan Greenspan, the author of neolioberal-ism, acknowledged was a lie as early as 2008, and for which he publicly made an apology: neoliberalism is, in the end, a utopian thought; the consumer being ready to buy everything, including the goods they do not want. Today you start a company instead of starting a revolution, a company of your own, finding a gap in the market (*Marktlücke*), an empty pore, and try to create the right life in the wrong one (*Es gibt kein richtiges Leben im falschen*. Theodor W. Adorno 1951).

A pore has to function as a niche, which delivers the requirements for a protected biotope and so delivers the freedom for the pioneers. So a city needs pores like under the Mülheimer Bridge, where you can kiss secretly (bild yue) or smoke your first cigarette. Or a niche behind the Turkish curtains in the Keupstraße, where you can withdraw from everything . The pores have to be discovered and recognized, for example, like the empty office buildings at night that long for human attention.

In the work Botschaft (Embassy) thousands of rules structure the 12-square-meter representative embassy and guide visitors properly through the collection of pictures of the city. The collection changes one's perceptions continually by repeatedly resorting the pictures. It makes it immediately clear that it is subjectively based. The point of view changes continuously.

The embassy exposes the construct of efficiency, of categorization and regulation as a question-able attempt to bring order to the city. It is a perception of the city, no more, no less. It is helpful for a few things but blind to many others. (*Hilfreich für einiges, aber blind für vieles.*) With the instrumentalization everything is, perhaps, under control (*im Griff*), but you are working inside your own constructed system, a point of view that is blind to the city and its inhabitants and its subjective experiences.

But what happens when we go under the skin and catch the city in flagrante? By continuous reinterpretation, the reality changes constantly. We should recognize this de facto as a design.

What if subjectification is so important that you have to do subjective research in a real situation? "How could we make this subjectivity accessible in a general way, without resorting to closure?" "*Welche Möglichkeiten gibt es, diese zu vermittelnde Subjektivität wieder allgemeingültig zu machen, ohne sie abzu-schließen?*" asks the urban philosopher and improvisational musician Christopher Dell, who we meet in a lecture in Cologne. How to achieve a fluid subjectivity is a question that we will engage with in the coming semester.

City of the Future

13–30 April 2017, Totope, Ghana, Sun, warmth, heat, and more heat

5 space and design strategists, their skin full of dust, meet the chief and the elders of the village, Totope. Climate change threatens the village through the rising sea level. Finding solutions for the city of the future acquires quite a different meaning here.

The porosity of the asphalted roads on our way to the village of Totope is to be taken literally. Maintaining the asphalt roads is much more complicated compared to sand roads. The holes are more jagged. The problem of how to slalom around them can be applied metaphorically to society. Almost everything takes place in public space; actually you only go inside the hut to sleep. Cooking, washing, and eating happen in public space. It feels like a mixture of living, working, recreation, and mobility, without it being possible to differentiate between them. Also shops and workshops are open to the street or directly situated on the roadside.

Every product offered in our supermarkets is presented on the street here, piled on the side of the road, in baskets and plates on the head or on market stalls. The saleswomen and men offer their articles in quick succession: deodorants, biscuits, facial tissues, meatballs, soap, towels, toothbrushes, cotton buds, skipping ropes, cookies, curry powder, jewelry, skirts, maize, apples, sugar cane, more biscuits, medicine, toothpaste, bread, combs, malt beer, more deodorants, more biscuits again, kitchen rolls, body spray, headphones, shoes, ice cream, dresses, prepaid phone cards, warning triangles, eggs, coconuts, ropes, Chinese bags, shirts, avocados, sat nav holders, chewing gum, maps, Koran introductions, crisps, torches, bananas, caps, radios, steering wheel covers, sunglasses, socks, belts, high-visibility vests, black Adidas sneakers, flip-flops, women's hats, magic trees, library books, exercise books for English grammar, toilet rolls.

The pores of the city are full of sweat and dust, like the pores of our skin. It is impossible to look at what is taking place; a clear vision of Ghanaian society seems impossible. All these global problems in one small village alone are too much to deal with, and we from space and design strategists are overwhelmed at first. It feels like a continuing blur, everything is fuzzy. Here we baulk at the externalization of the modern world. All the world's waste seems to have been deposited here.

Our first idea, to lift the village on a pedestal like in a museum, is received with great applause at the meeting of the elderly men. But that maybe just shows the despair of the villagers and not that the idea is convincing. The proposal to explain this idea to Kofi Annan at a local dinner is received with enthusiasm. The elderly women start to immediately list what they would offer Kofi Annan for the dinner. Make Fufu not War, is printed on the T-shirt which our student Lukas bought in Ghana. We will try to do precisely this in our next semester.

The Comfort Society

1–9 July 2017, Festival der Regionen (Festival of Regions), Marchtrenk, Sun, warmth, heat, rain showers

All space and design strategists meet in the small Austrian town of Marchtrenk in an attempt to research local conditions, which seem to be characterized by new levels of comfort.

Finally we arrive in Marchtrenk, where the summer festival of the regions took place. Urbanization there has, as in every city, reached a new level. In performative urbanism, the students not only try to discover the city of Marchtrenk in an acupunctural way, but also seek to explore its performative realities. We enter this so deeply that we not only use the toothbrushes of the inhabitants and discover the odd socks in the wash basket but even suck the bacteria out of their dirty carpets. We hawk goods on our cart with our baldachin through the streets. We collect old television sets, expired medicine, and Glücksbringer. We take photos of every house, every fence, and categorize them. We look for black-and-white pictures, interview the garden gnomes (*Gartenzwerge*), and analyze the character of the occupants based on the ringtones of their doorbells. We literally take the first step into a new life.

Conclusion and Discussion

The cell phones of the Ghanaians are the same as those of the Marchtrenkers, Kölners, or Linzers. We agree with Henri Lefebvre's thesis that urbanization of the city and of the countryside is the same, as he writes in his book *The Production of Space*. Maybe we want to push it one step further and place it in the globalized world. The haircuts, the clothes are the same in a European city as in an African village. Only the amount of odd socks differs in Europe from Africa. What does this mean for our future? What will our lives be like? How will our society function? We are practiced in performative urbanism, we can discover and even improvise thanks to Sophie Wolfrum's invitation to research this term. Pertaining to porosity, the pores of the city, we will drill some more holes to make it possible to have distance and closeness, exclusion and integration, heterogeneity and homogeneity, anonymity and community at our university, too. The task is, as ever, to ensure that our university does not replicate all the problems in the world; so please no nuclear power, clean drinking water, no plastic waste (not in our blood either), a good sewage system, healthy food, printers without dirty ink, clothes not made by modern (child) slaves, and so on. How does a university function in a broad welfare economy? We will watch and observe this from our vantage point next semester.

Reference:
Adorno, T. W. 1951. *Minima Moralia: Reflexionen aus dem beschädigten Leben.* Berlin.

Note:
The text is an expanded version of my contribution to M. Koch et.al., eds., *New Urban Professions: A Journey through Practice and Theory.* Perspectives in Metropolitan Research 5, Berlin, 2018.

Improvised City
Dimitris Theodoropoulos

The four projects described here represent an in situ examination of the porosity of the Greek urban land-scape. In these instances, porosity expresses itself as the scope for autonomous, improvised intervention; for adopting alternate solutions, slipping through the gaps of urban systems, creatively exploiting their nonfunctional aspects, and can be observed as a kind of criticism on anything established.

Summer Ladders is a project about an annual practice of the inhabitants of the Epidaurus area, who every summer install metal ladders that provide them with access to the rocky coastline. They construct the ladders on well-prepared concrete bases among the rocks of the coast. In winter, the ladders are taken down and laid out on the ground and covered with transparent plastic sheets. In their plastic shrouds the ladders evoke for visitors the improvised nature of this practice, the participation of local inhabitants in the formation of public space, and the seasonal manifestation of private concerns in the public realm. The Errands group documented the project using video interviews with local residents and printed postcards.

Local Dispute is a project about a special construction discovered by the Errands group in Mani Peninsula in a list of sights worth seeing put together by local schoolchildren. The house was built following a property dispute between two neighbors. Their disagreement was about the right of one of them to erect a building on a very small lot which would stand in front of the view of the other. It was built in 1998, with planning permission, on a triangular base. The narrowest side of this two-story residential building measures just 1.10m. After a long dispute in the courts, the house was demolished in 2009. Mani is a peninsula in Greece where similar disputes often occur. The house could be characterized as a contemporary monument in an area where the practice of vendetta was common, a reminder of the old towers of Mani, built for battles between families.

Errands collected information about the house while it still existed. The material collected from the research was presented in the form of interviews printed as posters, a video installation of the demolition, photographs, and postcards.

p. 133: Summer ladders, Epidavros
below: Local dispute, Mani
p. 135: Freattyda, Piraeus
below: Air conditioners, Athens

Freattyda. Along the rocky coast of Piraeus the sea restructures and reshapes the ruins of neoclassical Piraeus that were thrown away during the 1960s and the 1970s and dumped were the debris landfills once used as public spaces, parks, cafés and sport fields. The sea exposes objects such as stairs, tiles, marble corbels, metal structures, and concrete foundations and creates a new landscape together with the rocks and other natural elements. The newly created landscape is a small hidden beach with marginal inhabitants. The area above is fenced off by the city's archaeological department, which is excavating the 1960s debris to uncover the ancient Kononeio wall of Piraeus buried below. Errands interviewed the people who live there and catalogued the objects that have been revealed.

Air conditioners is a research project about the largely unnoticed and unofficial practice of the residents of certain neighborhoods in Athens, who collect the water that drains from air conditioners on nearby buildings to water the trees on the street. To do this, they attach pipes to the air conditioners on the upper floors—which would otherwise drip water on pedestrians as a form of artificial rain—and connect them to the trunks and bases of the trees. The emergence of a small private movement that contributes in an entirety of a chaotic urban functional behavior can be seen as a synergy between the constructed and the natural. Errands interviewed the people involved and documented their practice.

Does the City Blur All Its Traces?
Heiner Stengel

The 1990s was an extraordinarily productive period for subcultural do-it-yourself music movements. In Hamburg's Schanzenviertel and St. Pauli quarters, a movement known today as Hamburger Schule (Hamburg School) arose—a new genre of popular music—Diskursrock, critically reflecting urban society using German lyrics. Illegal bars and informal spaces were the first venues of this new scene. A private basement of eight rooms at Licolnstraße 19 on St. Pauli formed the original Pudel-Club, where there was also a secondhand shop named Boutique Pudel. The original Pudel was limited to a small group of people, who were updated on coming events via an informal network—a telephone list, later using a dictaphone for efficiency. Porous inside and impermeable to the outside, within this protected space everything seemed to be possible. What urban conditions enabled the emergence of the genre? What traces of Hamburger Schule are still to be found in the city of Hamburg? What examples of interplay between urban space, urban society, and urban culture exist today?

The name and the concept Pudel (poodle) have become an enduring part of Hamburg's subcultural scene, and is well established today. A poodle, a breed even more ostentatious than a sausage dog, although trendy—is a peculiar name for a venue, which was meant as a rebellion against all things conventional, against philistinism, in particular German popular music. "German hits are essentially the bastardized version of bourgeois music, so to say, the operatic aria. The best metaphor for it are the sheds in the eastern part of the city, where in allotment gardens the palaces found in the western part of the city, in Blankenese, are replicated in a kind of miniature format." (Spilker 2017)

The storyline of the Hamburger Schule—the name was initially used by Thomas Groß, editor of the *taz* daily newspaper, correlating the creative process of the bands and the philosopher-sociologist Frankfurter Schule (Frankfurt School) around Max Horkheimer and Theodor W. Adorno—is one of open spaces, urban wastelands, and rural exodus. Many of the protagonists came into the city from the countryside to tap into new freedoms. "At the time we moved to the city, the last German economic-miracle-generation-phenomena, we came there with our ragged biographies, out of the countryside, or wherever we came from—to the city. This was still possible at the time." (Kamerun 2017)

In 1925 Walter Benjamin and Asja Lacis described the city of Naples as a porous city, characterized by multicoded spaces. "In everything they preserve the scope to become a theater of new, unforeseen constellations. The stamp of the definitive is avoided. No situation appears intended forever, no figure asserts its 'thus and not otherwise'. [...] For nothing is concluded. Porosity results [...] from the passion for improvisation." (Benjamin and Lacis 1925, 166) This description also provides an apposite description of the places the artists of the Hamburger Schule could make their own. "I think that in our approach, this is exactly what we were aiming for, and that this is ultimately what we still yearn for today. In those days we started something, out of an impulse like an emotion, out of a naivety. To some extent there was a longing, to maybe somehow create a contrast with where you came from. Today we describe our resistance or our clashes in this way." (Kamerun 2017)

"Benjamin and Lacis's description reflects an atmosphere that I experienced in Hamburg during the early 90s, because space there was open, playable. All those bars on St. Pauli—today one of the most desirable quarters of the city, part of the ongoing real estate speculation and gentrification—at the time no one wanted to be there. Everything was pretty run-down with all those brothel-like private single-room bars. My generation caught on to this and we created our own bars. At some point, the whole Bernhard-

Nocht-Straße was just one bar after the other—all of them somehow temporary setups. Freedom like that is of course very inviting. A new subculture developed in its slipstream. Of course this has a lot to do with a certain group of people, with discourses." (Spilker 2017)

Out of an initially small subcultural elite, bands like Tocotronic, Die Sterne, Kante and Die Goldenen Zitronen emerged and are still around today. Their members have expanded their artistic, social, and political impact in further fields of experimentation.

The Pudel Club, Schanzenstraße 46/48 corner of Kampstraße was an illegal venue operated, among others, by Schorsch Kamerun, where concerts, parties, readings, and all kinds of subversive performances—and of course the freedom of the big city—were celebrated. "The first Pudel was just an empty space. We asked if we could use it as a bike shelter. Permission was granted. The space was not needed anyway. If you find something where you don't have to make too much of an effort, you don't look at it too critically. At the time we found something no one wanted. There was a lot of space, which had huge creative potential, which provided opportunities that no longer exist—there's been a 180-degree turnaround. Today this part of the city—Schanzenviertel—is the center of gentrification. In St. Pauli it actually began with the musical *Cats*. There people could discover something—not the forbidden, not the red-light, but a disparate area, that had something sleazy, dirty, something exotic. Something thrilling. It's still like that today. People still move to St. Pauli because they find it exciting. Today everything here is orderly and sanitized, even if the walls are distressed and covered with stickers." (Kamerun 2017)

What traces of the Hamburger Schule can be found in the urban spaces of the city of Hamburg today? What happened to the places that enabled the development of Diskursrock? Of course, those places have been transformed over the last twenty-five years. The clubs and bars on St. Pauli, adjacent to the Reeperbahn, are still watering holes today, although no longer secret. They have become tourist attractions, sited next to musical theaters, the landmark building Tanzende Türme (Dancing Towers) and Spielbudenplatz, a square hosting public events—the scene has changed out of all recognition. At the same time, erstwhile informal, secret places have disappeared. Lincolnstraße 19, where once the original Pudel Club stood is today a fallow wasteland. The corner of Kampstraße and Schanzenstraße, former venue of the second Pudel, has been developed as market-oriented investor-driven architecture boasting ground-floor shops and apartments on the upper levels. Simon-von-Utrecht-Straße, where Heinz Karmers Tanzcafe was located, is now a speculators' wasteland. The former dance café, although a simple shack on a street corner, across the road from Heiligengeistfeld—a huge open space that hosts Hamburg's biggest people's fair—was one of the central gathering places of the Hamburger Schule. As Spilker remarks: "At the end of the 90s, the area was vacated, the barracks were torn down, and we supposed that redevelopment would begin immediately. Nothing has happened. This is an absurd process. These spaces today are worth more as question marks—as wasteland. This seems to be part and parcel of contemporary free-market shenanigans." (Spilker 2017)

Cities worldwide, and the city of Hamburg in particular, are currently experiencing a revitalization and a boom in urban culture, while urban society is suffering from straitened economic conditions, global tourism, AirBnBization, and a constantly widening socioeconomic gap. Today the number of people aspiring to live in inner cities outnumbers the housing stock available. Where in the big cities of today, and in Hamburg in particular, can we discover what Walter Benjamin and Asja Lacis describe in the Naples essay?: "Building and action interpenetrate. [...] This is how architecture, the most binding part of the communal rhythm, comes into being here: civilized, private, and ordered only in the great hotel and warehouse buildings on the quays; anarchic, embroiled, village-like in the center. [...]" (Benjamin and Lacis 1925, 165) "Today there is a distinct contrast to the countryside. Anarchic structures in the city center—yes that's what it was in the early 90s. Today you might still find such constellations in Beijing, in the hutongs, which unfortunately are also about to disappear. Walter Benjamin wrote the [Naples] text before fascism and before the Nazis in Germany. They [the Nazis] carried out a sort of urban cleansing— in Hamburg, too, for example, in the Gängeviertel quarter. The point was to eradicate the anarchy, the direct communication they could not control. Such things have preserved somehow. Naples, the Gänge-viertel, the Beijing hutongs aren't necessarily things you want to re-create, because they were ghettoes somehow. The problem today is not the architecture, because you can come up with things that inspire community spirit. But that requires the political will to do it. But the contrary is the case. It's still all about controlling and containing people. If the right political will is lacking, you're going to end up sorely frustrated." (Spilker 2017)

Today, cities compete in a globalized market, selling themselves as locations for investment, living space, education, business, and the creative milieus form an important aspect of this urban brand culture. "Subcultures and their venues play an ambiguous role in the process of gentrification and urban planning upgrades. On the one hand, they are pioneers, on the other hand, troublemakers." (Twickel 2003, 8) Could a subcultural movement like the Hamburger Schule develop in the overplanned, overreg-ulated, overcurated, overcapitalized, and overdigitalized city of today? Or is there a lack of space for such possibilities? Where can we find the interpenetrations and permeability that allows the juxtaposition of very contradictory structures " which has its source in the heart of the city itself" (Benjamin and Lacis 1925, 163). "Of course we have the extreme problem of land speculation. If interest rates are so low that everybody puts their money into bricks and mortar. Nevertheless, I think that Hamburg and also Berlin do offer enough freedom, which is still waiting to be claimed. This is a luxury people in London or New York don't enjoy. That's why they all come to Berlin. By comparison, Berlin is still a big playground. The main problem is the availability of livable and playable space, but above all the problem is the market." (Spilker 2017)

"Is do-it-yourself urbanization of any interest anymore? If it's even a possibility at all. If it's not just images. It's the same with other factors related to popular culture, because they have all been some-how appropriated by marketing and advertising. I think this whole process is somehow over. The idea of self-defined urbanization, taking over spaces is somehow over. The things I refer to as exotic, I didn't perceive as such at the time. If we were to try this approach today, it would seem ersatz, artificial—just another of those images. I'm always on the lookout for that otherness, originality, because it's gone, and I don't think it's feasible anymore. The ubiquitous camera of the mainstream has absorbed everything. The idea, the desire for a kind of rough-and-ready improvisation seems somehow obsolete. The codes are known, transcribed, subsumed to marketing." (Kamerun 2017)

Even pop-up-stores, in themselves a sign of future transformative processes, are being marketed digitally today and have become a part of the city portfolio.
Increasingly, the protagonists of Hamburger Schule find the freedom for a creative process thematically still concerned with the correlation of cites and urban society in high culture.

Within the supposedly conservative, subsidized, protected world of institutions, a different freedom than in pop culture seems to exist, and offers some kind of market independence. Frank Spilker has written a novel about the urban creative precariat and is currently working on an audio drama for a public broadcasting service. This way he is also able to record new music. In 2007, the band Kante provided musical accompaniment for the revue *Rhythmus Berlin* at the Friedrichstadt-Palast theater in Berlin, drawing its inspiration from Walter Ruttmann's 1927 silent movie *Die Sinfonie der Großstadt*. The lyrics written for orchestra by Peter Thiessen focus on the city of Berlin and were shortly afterward published as a rock album with different music. "A whirlwind of the present, of poverty, power and capital, architecture of the dreams and desires, the city blurring all its traces." ("Ein Wirbelsturm aus Gegenwart, aus Armut, Macht und Kapital, aus Traum- und Wunscharchitektur, die Stadt verwischt all ihre Spuren.") Schorsch Kamerun directs stage plays interrogating concepts of urbanity at the most well established theaters in German-speaking countries. In the search for "otherness" he deals with areas far removed from the city centers. *MünchenKomplett* (Munich Complete), a collaboration between the Münchner Kammerspiele and the Bayerische Staatsoper (Bavarian state opera) was an experimental performance in the urban periphery of Munich in 2012. Currently he is working on a project for the Ruhrtriennale arts festival in Bochum. "I want to temporarily gentrify a city quarter, Cool Stahlhausen. From the perspective of the gentrifier, which of course is my own, I will stroll through the area together with a thousand people: It deserves gentrification, you only need to install a cup of coffee and you're away. These are playful things which I feel comfortable with, and I am able to think and reflect and I can actually and practically do something. And this applies also to the band as well as to the Pudel Club." (Kamerun 2017)

Since 1994 the Golden Pudel has existed as a center of counterculture at Hamburg's Fischmarkt 27, "where readings, concerts and all sorts of useful and useless sessions take place" (www.verfuege.de). The space for improvisation described by Benjamin and Lacis (1925, 166–67), an indispensable necessity for urban spaces, is something that is still fought for and defended in Hamburg today. Beyond the new images and symbols of the city, like the Elbphilharmonie by Herzog & de Meuron, the Tanzende Türme by Hadi Teherani on Reeperbahn or the Riverside Empire Hotel by David Chipperfield at Bernhard-Nocht-Straße, spaces emerge which, underpinned by protest culture, manage to slow down the mechanisms of repression, to preserve traditional social milieus and simultaneously to implement new forms of participation, generating autonomous architectural and urban qualities of spaces which could be understood as the "true laboratories of this great process of intermingling" (Benjamin and Lacis 1925, 172).

The Golden Pudel Club is situated in the vicinity of the squatted houses at Hafenstraße and Park Fiction. This open public space has been developed collaboratively, involving among others, the artists Margit Czenki and Christoph Schäfer. Park Fiction "is one of the few realized examples of participative planned urban art" (www.parkfiction.de) which was initiated as a reaction to gentrification and large-scale development in the area in 1997, and subsidized by the local authorities within the program Kunst im öffentlichen Raum (Arts in Public Space). Guided Walkman tours, lectures on parks and politics, exhibitions, workshops and discussion, and a *Planungscontainer* (planning container) formed the framework for a "collective production of desire, a planning process as a play. Construction of the park started years later, after Park Fiction was invited to documenta xi. The Park was inaugurated in 2005 with a Picnic Against Gentrification." (www.parkfiction.net) "The project is pretty radical. The process differentiates definitively from the curated participation of today." (Kamerun 2017) "Park Fiction is the best description.

It's an example: an experiment to visualize with artistic means what would be possible, if there might be another political will to understand participation of the neighborhood, which also equips the residents with a certain aspiration, not only the landowners, but also the residents." (Spilker 2017)

In spite of, or maybe even due to deteriorating socioeconomic conditions, the joy of discourse, of political self-determination and protest seems to be consolidated in Hamburg's urban society and might serve as an example when discussing the issue "For whom do we build our cities?" "We've cut our teeth on and have extensive experience in dealing with the city. We are very solidary in that respect." (Kamerun 2017) As early as 1989 the so-called Rote Flora was occupied in the fight against and finally prevent the musical project *Phantom of the Opera*. Rote Flora still exists as a self-administered political and cultural center. Most recently, the center made headlines in connection with the protest against the G20 summit in Hamburg in 2017. Like Park Fiction and Rote Flora the recent discourse on the so-called former Esso-houses illustrates how a culture of protest and resistance can influence the way our cities are designed collaboratively. The Esso—a social housing project from the 1960s, very near to the Tanzende Türme on Hamburg's Reeperbahn, which aside from social housing units incorporated, among others, the music club Molotov as well as the eponymous petrol station Esso. The Esso petrol station provided visitors to Hamburg's Reeperbahn with (almost) everything needed and gained national attention due to intense media coverage. In 2009 the entire Esso-complex was bought by an investor. After various contrasting expert assessments and a lengthy legal dispute between the investor and the Esso-Initiative, the complex was evacuated and torn down in 2014 despite massive protest. Local residents together with artists, scientists, architects, and other activists organized multiple protests, in conjunction with artistic interventions like *Verschöner your local Bauzaun* (Beautify your local site fence). Images of the former residents adorned the fence and folding removals crates mounted to the fence supplied space for expressions of support. The concept of planning container adopted successfully in Park Fiction was developed further in the so-called Planbude (planning shack), where former residents, affected neighbors and local business people were able to voice their ideas in a participatory process to crack the "St. Pauli Code". Once again Margit Czenki and Christoph Schäfer played a decisive role in the process. "There is the term of collaboration in the sense of a study by the social-philosopher Mark Terkessidis [2015]. Within a negative term you can impose your objectives up to 100 percent. Esso is a great example of that. The planning shack that puts itself in there and says you won't get us out of here otherwise there will be social unrest. Also the developer had to learn that he couldn't do anything without the citizens. And that's something new. A collaboration on both sides." (Kamerun 2017) Despite demolition and new construction, the results of the participatory process will allow all former residents of the social housing estate to move back into the new complex Paloma-Viertel (Paloma-Quarter). The project design, by Bel Architekten, ifau mit Jesko Fezer, and NL Architects is characterized by a very detailed mixture of living, working, small businesses and entertainment, and—depending on its outcome—could potentially be another example of how urban dwellers negotiate the city of today.

The Golden Pudel Club at Fischmarkt 27, "from the start an integral part of the artistic concept of Park Fiction" (park-fiction.net) burnt down almost completely in mysterious circumstances in February 2016. After a lengthy legal battle, a solution was reached to preserve the space in its well-established conditions and reinventing it at the same time. As the Elbphilharmonie der Herzen (Elbphilharmonie of hearts) the club, overlooking Hamburg's harbor with its splendid view of Hamburg's new landmark Elbphilharmonie, is scheduled to undergo reconstruction. Until this happens, the club reopened as a fragment, operated by a collective, in August 2017. Currently, there is a little shed on the stairs above the remaining concrete base, the Pudel Salon, a protest building that housed the archive of Park Fiction, which was also affected by the fire in the so-called Park-Fiction-Archiv-Exil. This is a prior notice of what is going to happen here in the near future. "There will be a house on top of it. I would have wished that an architecture will arise that says: I am architectural froth, total antiarchitecture. Now it will be, I believe, pretty interesting. The Arts School is involved. It's going to be a bit experimental for sure and supposedly makes more sense than froth. But wouldn't that be beautiful—nonsensical architecture? What is nonsensical? Purposeless! Of course we have somehow become part of the brand. Of course the tourists parade through Hafenstraße and Park Fiction. We receive money, not only from the city, but also from a foundation. We are a collective and the group has decided to do it this way. But absolutely no one can tell us what we have to do. There are no constraints. The Pudel Club has its concepts, and I think they work well. We celebrate the experiment; there is a system of interchange. You could say that, within this cosmos, this protected space, we are still free." (Kamerun 2017)

References:
Benjamin, W., and A. Lacis. 1925. "Naples," in *Reflections: Essays, Aphorisms, Autobiographical Writings*, edited by P. Demetz, 163–73. New York, 1978. | Kamerun, S. 2017. Author interview with Schorsch Kamerun, August 31. | Spilker, F. 2017. Author interview with Frank Spilker, September 6. | Terkessidis, M. 2015. *Kollaboration*. Frankfurt. | Twickel, C., ed. 2003. *Läden, Schuppen Kaschemmen: Eine Hamburger Pop Kultur Geschichte*, Hamburg.

Open Leipzig, 2009
Sofia Dona

The public installation "Open Leipzig" consists of a minor intervention and an event. The installation involved attaching hinges to the base of the wooden panels that sealed the ground-floor windows of the abandoned buildings on Ludwigstr., so that they folded down into tables on the pavement. The gradient of the street resulted in different heights of the improvised furniture. A flexible construction meant the panels could be closed and opened again, transforming the street into an open public space for the inhabitants to activate. The action and event involved rethinking the future of the city of Leipzig together with the inhabitants in this in-between space. Leipzig has been changing very rapidly in the last few years, from a shrinking city into so-called Hypezig.

pp. 142–43: Open Leipzig, installation, Leipzig

Salsa Urbana
Alissa Diesch

Manuel de Solà-Morales (1997) describes urbanism as a dance, a play of space and time. For this purpose, he defines three elements of urban growth: urbanization, parceling, and construction. *Urbanization* here is understood as the utilization of land and the installation of infrastructure; *parceling* relates to the subdivision of the former rural sites into developable plots, and *construction* is concerned with the buildings. These elements may arise with their own independent rhythms in different phases and represent, according to the Catalan architect, different forms of urban growth including newly established villages, designed suburbs, and informal settlements among others. The way Solà-Morales connects the time factor to the spatial aspects of the evolution of a city as dance is very poetic, although it leaves out another important aspect: the dynamic dialogue of the built environment with its inhabitants and users. "People and places script each other" (Amin and Thrift 2002, 23): this steady interaction can be understood as a constantly transforming dance as well.

In Bogotá, it is easy to detect a huge variety of patterns, logics, and origins in its built portions, as the city has expanded rapidly from around 200,000 inhabitants in the 1920s to the current population of 8 to 9 million. This illustrates the changing ideals, purposes, and needs of a century of urban growth, traced in its built fabric. These extensions, in most cases, have been built up in fragment-like barrios (Borsdorf and Hidalgo 2010). In their contours, they often make visible ancient rural landownership or former geographic features; in the inner subdivision—the parceling—they exhibit their sociocultural status and the urban uses they were originally planned for.

However, the dance goes on and the city is changing continuously in uses, actors, and, on a physical level, adapting itself and its barrios to new challenges and realities. These transformations of formal and nonformal character are executed by different stakeholders, like the city administration, private investors, and the community itself. Moreover, Bogotá is powerfully and steadily shaped by sociocultural interaction, pop cultural expressions, and manifold imaginaries.

When we talk about rhythm and dance in Colombia, the comparison to salsa as music, dance, and cultural practice is almost self-evident. Based on Caribbean rhythms that derive from diverse African themes, salsa is a mixture, a spicy sauce of different ingredients that emerged in the 1970s in an enduring act of fusion. Urban encounters have played a vital role in its evolution. In the New York of the 1960s, big bands with musicians of Latin-American, mainly Puerto Rican, background, performed sounds like mambo and cha-cha, based on traditional Afro-Cuban rhythms, at regular dance events. These bands constantly felt the urge to incorporate new sounds. One important source of inspiration came from jam sessions, where big band members met jazz musicians and started mixing musical influences. New instrumentations, band configurations, and representations were set up and allowed improvisation and a more dynamic and flexible performance. In the 1970s the successful productions of Fania Records coined the term *salsa* for this new kind of music, and it spread through vinyl albums and radio stations beyond the borders of New York City.

At the same time, urbanization in Colombia had picked up speed, gathering people from the countryside in the quickly growing sprawl of the bigger cities, uniting diverse cultural influences in single neighborhoods. In the seaports on the Pacific and Caribbean coasts, working-class communities started popping up, bringing together people from local rural origins. The population of Afro-Colombians in urbanized regions grew and through that, the presence of their traditional music, with similar rhythms to salsa, due to the same roots. The harbor cities became hotbeds for the emerging sound: the new vinyl records from abroad arrived there, festivals like Barranquilla's carnival were the perfect setting for the new sound and the increased Afro-Colombian presence helped the new music to establish roots as local musicians adopted the New York salsa tunes to the traditional music of the coasts (Betancourt 2011). Radio stations began to play salsa even after the festival season and local interpreters started conquering the local music scene. The trend swept over to Bogotá, where immigrants from the coast settled in working-class neighborhoods, opened the first *salsotecas*, and played the music live at diverse occasions. Furthermore, radio stations and records helped to increase its popularity in the Colombian capital, too.

Since then salsa has become a cultural expression that is used to articulate social and urban matters; simultaneously, the music itself characterizes events, venues, barrios, cities, and nations through concerts and songs that are dedicated to these places. This produces and reshapes clichés and imaginaries. It is the least common denominator of a nation with such social extremes, but salsa is unquestionably present in all social classes. This cultural glue joins together contrary forces. The sound and practice of salsa is possibly the best reflection of the national identity and is a powerful and highly democratic instrument for forming images of people and places and bringing them together. Salsa is simultaneously: commercial, handmade, private, public, posh, and common.

The mixture of encounters, local and international roots, the unifying power of festivals like the carnival, and its rapid appropriation by local musicians, made salsa a widely spread phenomenon, even among the Colombian upper classes, and through the process of cultural anthropophagy (De Andrade 1929) the music is now seen as something authentically Colombian. Precisely this moment permitted the fusion of the physical space of music venues and the abstract space of music traditions and radio transmissions with the flow of goods and people. It's an excellent example of how most Latin American culture is based on diverse origins, merging and reinterpreting traditional and contemporary patterns to new porous hybridizations (Garcia Canclini 1989) that successfully support a particular identity.

It's now curious to see that the same dynamics—immigration, inherent and imported patterns, the mixture of contemporaneity and tradition, the urban reality in Bogotá—is widely considered chaotic and backward. Salsa could be seen as a metaphor and vision for trans-national urbanism, representing high transitivity and combining manifold rhythms of different footprints (Amin and Thrift 2002) that describe an energetic city that continually reinvents itself. A simple 4/4 time with the clave-rhythm, the typical salsa on-beat-off-beat, is the framework for a multiplicity of polyrhythmic themes. The same is true for the typical Bogotan regular perimeter block development of colonial origin, filled with diverse and alterable constructions, uses, and rhythms. The inherent openness to improvisation is not a lack of perfection but a vital factor in creating resilience and an expression of the city's capacity to adapt to new challenges (Dell 2017).

Instead, the constant inner alteration of the city's barrios is usually divided into good improvements of barrios of informal origin and bad downturns, the latter often accompanied by nostalgia, always following a static, immaculate ideal. Gentrification of already existing neighborhoods is a growing phenomenon, but mainly understood as demolition of existing structures followed by a completely new construction driven by real estate speculation (Yunda and Sletto 2017). This is presumably due to an urban lifestyle that celebrates a perfect, clean, bourgeois world, inhabited exclusively by white people, supposedly only attainable in recently built condominiums or shopping malls. The urban reality is in stark contrast to the dream many aspire to. This market driven urban redevelopment abruptly puts a stop to the ongoing dance and leaves the original population in dissonance, while implementing a completely different tune, without any transitions or opportunity to build on existing rhythms, patterns, or footprints. Also, the new inhabitants do not have the possibility of making themselves part of the history of a place, and getting in tune with an already established neighborhood. This kind of planning ignores and negates the existing capacity of the city to incorporate new inhabitants, lifestyles, uses, and architectural forms harmoniously.

A widely discussed case (Ibid.) of gentrification in Bogotá is the Los Olivos barrio of informal origin and built in the 1970s, in the form of humble houses on the foothills of the eastern mountain chain. With the growth of the city, it became a central place and is well connected to the infrastructure by a city highway built in the 1980s. After the neighborhood was officially recognized in the 1990s, and in the 2000s, new zoning regulations permitted a larger maximum building height in this area and as a result further increased the land value. This eventually led to acquisition of single plots by investors who planned luxury high-rise residential towers in the area. For the people who lived there, a struggle began over whether to stay united or individually take advantage of the rising prices, sell their homes and get bigger estates with better equipped homes in a less central area of the city. Naturally, this conflict threatened the peace of the tight-knit social tissue of the original barrio and caused mistrust and suspicion among the community. In 2013 developers started to demolish the houses they had acquired, leaving the rubble between the homes of the remaining residents to discourage them from staying, while the community received support from university student groups and churches. At this point, diverse stakeholders of spatial proximity were already on the scene, but the struggle that took place had nothing to do with dance. To make the case even more complex, the district council intervened by declaring the whole zone an Area of Urban Renewal, making use of the expropriation law. First, the properties that had been purchased by the developers were expropriated and then the remaining inhabitants were persuaded to sell their properties in exchange for an apartment in a nearby socially mixed housing development. The city district did this with best intentions to support the community in an attempt to mitigate the effects of an urban process that was clearly shaped by economic forces and utterly unequal negotiating parties. However, the community refused their proposal, as the city offered them significantly lower prices for their property than the investors had proposed before. The proposal to convert the former working-class barrio into a residential neighborhood for different social classes—by making available land for public space and new housing typologies—could have been a good response to the rise in property prices, but came too late. In this prominent case, the administration missed the entry to conduct the delicate concert, leaving everyone involved in the dispute disappointed. Without doubt it is challenging to meld so many diverse interests into a well-sounding theme, but the lessons that salsa has teaches that it is possible to bring together seemingly opposing actors and make them dance to the same tune.

Salsa is music composed and played for dancing, which makes it extremely performative, as the audience itself is an active performer, interpreting and claiming the sound for its moves. The Los Olivos example suggests that the same is true for urbanism: every action causes an often unforeseen reaction, and pulls new actors onto the stage. The direct dialogue between musicians and dancers during the salsa get-together provokes constant adjustments and creative improvisation on both sides. The predisposition for these adjustments allows apparently incompatible patterns or situations to merge and helps us to understand urbanism not as something static or following a rigid program but as structural work on an open form (Dell 2017). The performative aspect of staging salsa that respects the audience not as a mere consumer of the music but as an active partner in the performance, generating a unique production, can be a useful analogy for the project of establishing a formal urbanism guided by principles that are deeply rooted in the city, respecting and including all of its stakeholders.

References:
Amin, A., and N. Thrift. 2002. *Cities: Reimagining the Urban.* Cambridge. | Betancourt, F. 2011. "Historia de la Música Postmoderna Colombiana," thesis, Pontificia Universidad Javeriana, Bogotá. | Borsdorf, A., and R. Hidalgo. 2010. "From Polarization to Fragmentation: Recent Changes in Latin American Urbanization," in *Decentralized Development in Latin America: Experiences in Local Governance and Local Development*, edited by P. Lindert and O. Verkoren, 23–34. Dortrecht. | De Andrade, O. 1928. "Cannibalist Manifesto, Sao Paulo," translated by L. Bary, *Latin American Literary Review* 19, no. 38 (1991): 38–47. | Dell, C. 2017. "Organisation musikalisch denken," in *Improvisation und Organisation: Muster zur Innovation sozialer Syteme*, edited by W. Stark, D. Vossebrecher, C. Dell, and H. Schmidhuber, 31–46. Bielefeld. | García Canclini, N. 1989. *Culturas híbridas: Estrategías para entrar y salir de la modernidad.* Mexico DF. | Solà-Morales, M. 1997. *Las formas del crecimiento.* Barcelona. | Yunda, J., and B. Sletto. 2017. "Property Rights, Urban Land Markets and the Contradictions of Redevelopment in Centrally Located Informal Settlements in Bogotá, Colombia, and Buenos Aires, Argentina," *Planning Perspectives* 32, no. 4: 601–21.

Many thanks to Melissa Pinto, Marco Fajardo, and Amin Mokdad for their support and help to capture the structure, essence and history of salsa.

Beyond the Wall
The Tentative Collective

In response to Karachi's increasingly privatized, securitized, and segregated public spaces, the Tentative Collective organized a group gathering on top of the boundary wall around Shaheed Benazir Bhutto Park. This is one of the city's most beloved parks, where public access has now been restricted with a boundary wall and the imposition of an entry fee. Some fifty people from different parts of the city, including the nearby migrant colony (Shirin Jinnah), joined us at 4:00 pm on a Sunday to drink chai and hang out in an unusual gathering place.

p. 148: Composite of gathering
p. 149: Scaling the wall

Urban Regulations and Planning

About Legal Frameworks, Basic Politics, and Tactics
Imke Mumm

There is a material side to legislation! All disciplines engaged with the practice of planning and building are familiar with the fact that land law (*Bodenrecht*) and ownership law (*Eigentumsrecht*) are consequential for architecture and the city in the same way as environmental and building laws are. Hence, a serious debate about urban porosity cannot take place without an inquiry into the legal frameworks and basic politics of cities.

In this chapter, the postulate of the porous city as bearer of specific qualities is scrutinized while taking into consideration the realities of urban production. According to the *Gabler Wirtschaftslexikon*, modern urban planning seeks to balance the conflicting interests of private land use on the one hand and their social and economical effects on the other for the purpose of advancing general public welfare. It defines urban planning as an instrument through which space is regulated and structured in the interest of the public (Gabler Wirtschaftslexikon 2017). However, Michael Koch suggests that a porous city does not follow a clearly defined and easily reproducible ordering structure (Koch, 20). All articles in this chapter share the view that control mechanisms, being embedded in different legal frameworks, materialize in built structures and affect everyday practices in the city. The common view that legislation acts as a limiting factor to the unfolding of creativity and the unforeseen in cities, is here complemented by asking how a different, more flexible, more open and actor-oriented production of space could be achieved. In this extended view, the difficult relationship between porosity and regulation is not reduced to one side unilaterally restricting the other.

For example, authors observe and seek to understand the effects of creative powers (*Gestaltungs-kräfte*) that operate unintentionally as the by-products of other processes (Dona, 167). In these cases, existing regulations have even triggered the creation of spatial and social structures to which there is a porous quality. Florian Hertweck's inquiry into the specific legal history of German land law made him demand a reform of the law in view of the current urban challenges (Hertweck, 154). The recent changes to the Federal Building Code, in which a new land category *Urbanes Gebiet* (urban area) was established as part of the Land Utilization Ordinance, demonstrates how tightly the limits for reform are set by legislation (Wolfrum, 158).

To merely perceive regulations as an inevitable obstacle is to neglect their creative capacity and the need to constantly adjust them so that they meet our changing requirements. Consequently, the design of rules and regulations should always be seen as an integral part of the work done in planning and architectural practice (Mumm, 162). With the title "Just *Design* It," Nicolai von Brandis calls for an understanding of the design process as the opportunity to engage with regulations in a creative and active way, whereby creativity becomes effective within the regulations themselves, rather than working around them. Every kind of regulation requires a multitude of negotiations to take place between the actors involved. Based on the example of everyday neighborhood relations, Alex Lehnerer argues that living together in the city cannot be realized without rules, but that a set of relative rules would be preferable to a strict plan (Lehnerer, 170). Marc Angélil and Cary Siress's analysis shows how within informal processes of development specific rules emerge which are adapted to the situation. Systems that regulate themselves seem to have the ability to develop sets of rules within a short period of time (Angélil and Siress, 182). Michael Koch urges that we should not mistake the idea of a porous city for urban salvation, or as a kind of prescription through which we could build the livable city in view of increasingly fierce allocation conflicts over spatiosocial and economic resources (Koch, 20).

The authors of this chapter seek to identify the scope within existing regulatory constructs, the kind of regulations that could facilitate porosity, or ways of doing without strict rules. The planning disciplines tend to perceive legal frameworks as being external, as defining restrictions for practice, and as preventing good design from being realized. Understanding legal frameworks as being imposed from the outside means being caught up in the tradition of authoritarian thinking, which provides two alternatives to act: either to stick strictly to the statutory requirements, or else to apply them flexibly and creatively, but for the sole purpose of pushing one's own ideas through the perceived obstacle. Both attitudes are apolitical and difficult to reconcile with the idea of urban and regional planning counterbalancing the forces of the free market (Kamleithner 2008, 6). Contemporary planning addresses the plurality of economic and social powers and makes use of legal frameworks, providing them with a certain structuring order and responding to their requirements. But this is just one task among many others. Only if the structuring aspect is framed by the freedom of interpretation and the possibility of changing the rules might the porous city become a reality. Planners and architects are asked to get involved actively with the frameworks that define their practice. They should sketch out the idea of a self-reflective city which questions the status quo and which acts as the catalyst for the renegotiation of the rules on which it is based.

During the last few decades, the economic and political situation has changed along with the belief in the knowledge and the authority of planning. In the years following the civil protest in the 1960s and 1970s, people spoke of the retreat of politics and of market dominance. The challenging of the self-image of planning required the disciplines to develop new processes and forms of cooperation that included new actors. At first sight, this seems to indicate that there has been a general loss in regulative power. Sociologist Christian Kamleithner argues that this development is accompanied not by a loss of regulation but by a shift toward a different kind of regulation, based on "a regulatory framework, in which planning and freedom are interlocked." However, this is not a new phenomenon. Kamleithner suggests that Foucault's concepts of governmentality could provide answers to the question of how the planning disciplines could perceive and position themselves (Ibid., 9).

Relating planning and freedom to each other to form an ordering system is clearly a design task which requires the involvement of the planning disciplines. Florian Hertweck is not alone in his appeal to the profession to participate in political discourse, for it is precisely a political attitude that is needed. The immanent significance of societal regulatory frameworks for the physicality of our cities has to be recognized so that we do not leave their creative power (*Gestaltungskraft*) to chance, and instead place it in the service of positive change.

References:
Gabler Wirtschaftslexikon. 2017. "Stadtplanung," accessed October 22, 2017, http://wirtschaftslexikon.gabler.de/Definition/stadtplanung.html. | Kamleithner, C. 2008. "Planung und Liberalismus," *dérive*, no. 3: 5–9.

Toward a New Land Reform
Florian Hertweck

In his governmental address of January 18, 1973, federal chancellor Willy Brandt defined the reform of the land law (*Bodenrecht*) as one of the main tasks for the legislative period ahead. The coalition of liberals and social democrats planned to introduce a land value tax (*Bodenwertzuwachssteuer*) whose purpose was to "inhibit the scandalous and irresponsible speculation with land" ("das Ärgernis der verantwortungslosen Bodenspekulation zurück[zu]drängen") (Brandt 1973, 25). Brandt asserted that in the same way as private property is protected, "this government would ensure that its social obligation requirements are in good hands." Although Brandt did not explicitly mention the reform of the land law, Oscar Schneider, a member of the conservative party CSU, pointed out the connection between this statement and the reform bill which had been introduced to the parliament by the social democrats SPD in July of the same year (Deutscher Bundestag 1973, 3103). The newly appointed minister of Regional Planning, Construction and Urban Development Hans-Jochen Vogel, former major of Munich who had firsthand experience with problems of market-led valorizations of property, was the driving force behind the reform of the law. Brandt's commitment to the concept of social obligation (*Sozialbindung*) did indeed anticipate Vogel's project for a social obligation in relation to land and property. In support of his agenda he was able to refer to a 1967 decision by the Federal Constitutional Court, which rejected the idea of a purely market-led valorization of land and property: "The fact that land is both limited and indispensable means that we cannot leave its use to free market forces or to the will of individuals; our legal and social obligations, which are based on justice, mean that in this case we need to consider public interests to an extent far greater than this is required for other financial goods" (Bundesverfassungsgericht 1967). Vogel sought to overcome the seeming contradiction between the right to property and the idea of a social obligation in relation to property, which is also mirrored in the formation of the parliamentary coalition between social democrats and the liberals—appropriately addressed by Brandt in his governmental address in a dialogic way—by means of treating land and buildings as separate entities. The land should be in public or communal ownership and control (*Verfügungseigentum*), while buildings and their uses should remain in private ownership (*Nutzungseigentum*) (Führer 2015, 3–84).

While the concept of land value tax is based on the ideas of Henry George, who—only six years after Friedrich Engels had raised the question of housing—demanded in his 1879 publication *Progress and Poverty* that the valorization of property values should be highly taxed, the distinction between control and use of property is based on historical precedents, as found, for example, in Germany. During the twelfth century a leasehold system emerged in cities, through which landowners were able to let a plot of land in return for an annuity, which granted the lessee the right to unrestricted use of the plot. According to land reformer Rudolf Eberstadt, the German real estate legislation of medieval times was aimed at the "treatment of land and built structure as two fully separate entities"; the values "produced by capital and labor were not allowed to mix with the property rights of the landholder" (Eberstadt 1920, 44). Vogel's concept bears a close similarity to the *Freiland* theory of German social reformer Silvio Gesell. Like George did Gesell refer to the medieval "doxa" and put into question the unearned income generated through ground rents; he proposed to convert all landholding rights into public or communal property on the basis of compensation, while, in contrast to Engels, buildings were to remain with the private rental and leasehold market (Gesell 1916).

The common land theory was subsequently developed further, most notably by Swiss architect Hans Bernoulli. In his publication *Die Stadt und Ihr Boden* Bernoulli draws on the feudalist concept of treating landholding rights and the ownership of buildings as separate entities, but he criticizes the granting of leaseholds for indefinite periods, for this would undermine the intended separateness. He observes that toward the end of the eighteenth century, when ground rents were abolished in the aftermath of the French Revolution, "the city had been almost sold out" (Bernoulli 1949, 24 and 449). In view of the overwhelming task of postwar reconstruction, Bernoulli advocated the complete transfer of landholding rights into public ownership, for he understood that the art of urban design could only come to full fruition "if the city can decide freely on the land as its owner; [...] if private buildings can be constructed on communal land by means of granting building rights." He suggests the lease period should match the expected service life of the constructed buildings instead of a period of multiple generations. In accordance with the common land theory ground rents are to be calculated on the basis of the potential usability of the site—"higher in advantaged locations, lower in modest locations" (Bernoulli 1949, 109 and 115). Bernoulli's commitment went far beyond the writing of critical and solution-oriented texts in that he took initiative for a corresponding parliamentary bill in his function as member of the national council, which ultimately failed to pass (Kästli 1981, 32).

That this system was put into practice in the GDR (German Democratic Republic), with an arrangement in which the state was defined as the global owner of land granting land use permissions (Dieterich and Dieterich 1997, 65), making it possible for the state to expropriate landholdings that exceeded 100 hectares without compensation from 1945 onward, explains why the debate on Vogel's land law reform bill was so ideologically heated in parliament. The liberals FDP, in coalition with the social democrats SPD, supported the project of a land value tax for counteracting rising property prices and land speculation referring to the Freiburg proclamation (*Freiburger Thesen*), but rejected the socialization and communalization of land. Representatives of the conservative CDU/CSU party claimed that they, too, wished to fight speculation, while emphasizing that they would not touch the right of ownership. Addressing Vogel, Schneider asserted that whoever took that direction "will say good-bye to the free social market economy." The conservative politician went on to suggest that "the abolition of private property is the beginning of dictatorship" (Deutscher Bundestag 1973, 3105–8).

Following the failure of the reform proposal, the federal government of Helmut Schmidt made another attempt to reform the land law in 1974. This time, rather than insisting on a system based on public landownership and private utilization, the plan was to target surplus value generated through planning permissions, and introduce a compensatory instrument through which 50 percent of privately made valorization profits be redistributed to the municipalities (Deutscher Bundestag 1974, 8036f). The Minister of Regional Planning, Construction and Urban Development then in office, Karl Ravens, stated in the first reading of the bill, that "if the goal is to have citizens participating early in the planning process, then speculation resulting from the municipalities' early announcement of their development plans must be avoided" (Ibid.). Again, the opposition rejected the bill, arguing that the value of land and property could not be determined with sufficient accuracy (Ibid., 8041). Bernoulli's solution to this problem was the Tax and Buy model, which the Liberal Land Committee of the British parliament had demanded for their case as early as 1923 and 1925. According to this model landowners prepare their own estimate, on which either taxation or, if the municipality acquires the land, the purchase price are based. Schneider, who followed Minister Ravens in office, introduced as an alternative to the taxation of valorization profits the policy of mobilizing additional building land, with the aim of stabilizing rents and land prices (Ibid., 8042). In this policy, urban land uses and agricultural uses are seen as competing with each other.

The most recent attempt to reform the land law, for the time being, was made in 1996, again on the basis of a valorization taxation. The federal state of North Rhine-Westphalia introduced the initiative to the Federal Council. The federal state's Minister of Building and Housing, Michael Vesper, member of the green party (Bündnis 90/Die Grünen) and head of the initiative, added to the social argument of previous justifications an ecological agenda in line with the spirit of the time: "We need new and equitable regulations in land use. Regulations that allow the economically disadvantaged to satisfy their housing needs in places where, from the perspective of ecology, urban design, regional planning, and national economy, this seems to be most sensible: in the core areas of residential urban development." (Vesper 1997, 11) Like the previous attempts at a reform of the land law the initiative did not succeed; in 1987 more than 50 percent of all privately owned apartments in the Federal Republic were not owner-occupied, and were purchased for investment or tax-saving purposes.

Today the question of land ownership is again on the agenda through its relatedness to the housing problem. The issue is critically discussed in many exhibitions and publications, while alternatives to the standard investment-driven approach are tested in experimental dwelling arrangements, new designs, and modes of housing construction; also, there is an open discussion about how land and property could be better controlled in the public interest. This trend could be seen as a response to the urban development policies of the last thirty years. With the ascendancy of market-oriented politics, according to which the state should increasingly withdraw from the urban development and housing sector, based on the assumption that, first, the market operates more economically, and second, that a free market regulates itself, European cities have developed into pyramidal entities whereby the dominant centers are increasingly shifting beyond the reach of many. In Munich the cost of building land increased by 16 percent in the last year alone, while the value of building land earmarked for residential development increased by 31 percent (Hoben 2017). The rent for a 60-square-meter apartment increased by 50 percent in the last five years, and by more than 70 percent in Berlin over the same period. While the nationwide average for the rent of an apartment of this size increased by 30 percent, gross incomes increased by 13.5 percent. In Luxembourg 92 percent of the land with building potential is in private hands. For decades the political policy in Berlin has been to leave the provision of new housing to the private market; furthermore, the city has sold publicly owned property to the highest bidder and has done so on a grand scale, particularly with the aim of balancing the municipal budget that had been devastated by the banking crisis. The resulting real estate economy has failed to satisfy the urban housing needs of all social strata, for it has instead concentrated on affluent new Berliners (*Neuberliner*) who are more readily prepared to pay the highest rents and house prices in the most central locations. While the housing shortage is, like the logics of location, at the root of the real estate economy, it gives also rise to "poverty, social segregation, and a growing concern, even in the so-called middle class, about the very foundations of future livelihood" (Fezer et al. 2017). It seems that cities are increasingly becoming unporous, if one understands porosity, with Richard Sennett and the editors of this publication, as a radically diversified and mixed city—a city in which all social strata have access to housing, including the central areas. Based on this perspective, the question of porosity may not be primarily a question of architecture and urban design, but rather a socioeconomic and political problematic. Nevertheless, architects and urban designers could make contributions in different ways by engaging directly with the political discourse as Hans Bernoulli or Peter Conradi have done or by addressing the problematic in their works so far as it is possible, as architects as different as Ildefons Cerdà, Hannes Meyer, Louis Kahn, or Frei Otto have tried in the past.

References:

Bernoulli, H. 1949. *Die Stadt und ihr Boden.* Erlenbach. | Brandt, W. 1973. "Regierungserklärung des zweiten Kabinetts Brandt/ Scheel," January 18, Presse und Informationsamt der Bundesregierung. | Bundesverfassungsgericht. 1967. Decision of the Federal Constitutional Court BVerfG, 12.01.1967—1 BvR 169/63, https://opinioiuris.de/entscheidung/1436. | Deutscher Bundestag. 1973. Minutes of the 54th plenary session, 7th legislative period, held on October 4, 1973, http://dipbt.bundestag.de/doc/ btp/07/07054.pdf. | Deutscher Bundestag. 1974. Minutes of the 120th plenary session, 7th legislative period, held on September 27, 1974, http://dipbt.bundestag.de/doc/btp/07/07120.pdf. | Dieterich, B., and H. Dieterich. 1997. "Einführung," in idem., *Boden—Wem nutzt er? Wen stützt er? Neue Perspektiven des Bodenrechts*, 64–77. Braunschweig. | Eberstadt, R. 1920. *Handbuch des Wohnungswesens und der Wohnungsfrage.* Jena. | Fezer, J., C. Hiller, N. Hirsch, W. Kuehn, and H. Peleg, eds. 2017. *Wohnungsfrage.* Berlin. | Führer, K. C. 2015. *Die Stadt, das Geld und der Markt: Immobilienspekulation in der Bundesrepublik 1960–1985.* Berlin. Gesell, S. 1916. *Die natürliche Wirtschaftsordnung durch Freiland und Freigeld.* Les Hauts-Geneveys. | Göllner, W., and T. Finkbeiner. 1997. "Die Bodenrechtsdebatte in Deutschland nach der Verabschiedung des Städtebauförderungsgesetzes 1972 bis 1996," in *Boden—Wem nutzt er? Wen stützt er? Neue Perspektiven des Bodenrechts*, edited by B. Dieterich and H. Dieterich, 138–61. Braunschweig. | Hoben, A. 2017. "Studie zum Münchner Immobilienmarkt: In allen Bereichen explodieren die Preise," *Sueddeutsche Zeitung*, May 31, 2017. | Kästli, T. 1981. "Hans Bernoulli und die Freiland-Freigeldlehre," *Archithese* 11, no. 6: 31–32. | Lepsius, O. 2002. *Besitz und Sachherrschaft im öffentlichen Recht.* Tübingen. | Lienhard, R. 1971. "Erneuerung der Städte ohne Bodenreform?" *Sozialdemokratische Zeitschrift für Politik, Wirtschaft und Kultur* 50, nos. 8–9: 204–8. | Vesper, M. 1997. "Auf dem Weg zu einer sozialverträglichen Bodenordnung," in: *Boden—Wem nutzt er? Wen stützt er? Neue Perspektiven des Bodenrechts*, edited by B. Dieterich and H. Dieterich, 9–12. Braunschweig.

Urbanes Gebiet
Sophie Wolfrum

Zoning

The *Athens Charter* is the pithy title of Le Corbusier's manifesto-like treatment of the issues dealt with at the fourth Congress of International Modern Architecture CIAM 1933. It has widely been used as representative of a practice that is still widespread: the spatial separation of urban areas according to their types of use. Internationally, this is known as *zoning*. Reduction of the diversity of a city to social functions that are to be physically separated from each other—a mind-set that favors tidiness, boundaries, and purity—has permeated urban design and planning until today. This form of functionalist modernist thought has become deeply embedded in contemporary everyday life.

Working, housing, recreation, and traffic are said to be the four basic functions of urban life and spatial organization, and were still taught in the newly established spatial planning studies in the 1970s, even though there had already been massive criticism of the functional city for a long time. As early as the 9th CIAM 1953, Alison and Peter Smithson presented an Urban Re-Identification Grid whose categories were no longer based on functions but instead put the spotlight on spatial connectivity as it exists in people's lives: "the more existentialist or phenomenological notions of house, street, district, and city— four overlapping yet distinct levels of 'human association'" as they called it (Risselada and Heuvel 2005, 30). Even though a short time later they dismissed these categories because they were "too loaded with historical overtones" (Smithson 2005, 30), interest focused on community, spatial clusters, social relationships, and cross-linking by the time of the *Doorn Manifesto* 1954, or at the tenth CIAM 1956, when TEAM 10 became clearly established. Beyond the early internal debate among specialists, a heated discursive critique of new modern cities developed with a slight delay. Edgar Salin's *Urbanität* (Urbanity), Jane Jacobs's *The Death and Life of Great American Cities*, Hans Paul Bahrdt's *Die moderne Großstadt* (The Modern Metropolis), Wolf Jobst Siedler, Elisabeth Niggemeyer and Gina Angreß *Die gemordete Stadt* (The Murdered City), along with Alexander Mitscherlich's *Die Unwirtlichkeit unserer Städte* (The Inhospitality of Our Cities) were published between 1960 and 1965 in Germany alone. Criticism had an international reach, and it was loud and clear. The demand was that cities must do more than fulfill basic functions since they were also specific, cultural places. Urbanity was reclaimed. The term *porosity* was not yet currency, but many of its ingredients were already in circulation.

Zoning Still Exists

However, these earlier conflicts between thinking and acting, and between theory and practice, would not occupy our attention if it were not for the fact that this division has now existed for more than half a century. Indeed, at the same time in the early 1960s, spatial planning law came into being in Germany; it is still in place today, having been updated through a succession of amendments but never fundamentally modified. The German Town and Country Planning Code (which came into force as the Bundesbaugesetz in 1960), together with the Land Use Ordinance (BauNVO), is imbued with the spirit of the modern, classifying urban surface areas according to their uses. Zoning provides the basic pattern that enables spatial conflicts to be resolved and social considerations to be incorporated. German legislation distinguishes between nine types of area, which allow a finely balanced and refined ratio between the old, familiar functions: housing, working and social purposes. Type 10 includes recreation and Type 11, called "special area," isolates everything else in, once again, homogeneously used spatial areas.

Environmental law has been added to planning law. In the 1970s and 1980s, a new, complex body of law took shape not only in Germany, but across most European countries. As a consequence, the principle of separation and division received further impetus. The historical background is easily understood if we retrace the development of institutionalized urban planning. When it came into being toward the end of the nineteenth century, it was above all devoted to the city's hygiene and the health of urban dwellers. It was indispensable in fighting cholera epidemics and rickets, as well as protecting people from industrial emissions. The primary task of early building regulations, as well as later construction and planning legislation, was to manage chaos in order to ensure healthy living and working conditions. The industrialization of European cities led to their growth, and the adverse effects of production plants had to be contained.

The fundamental objective of environmental law today is still to provide legal protection from emissions. If emissions (for example noise or exhaust fumes) cannot be prevented at source, which is the intention of policy measures under the basic polluter-pays principle, then at least exposure (that is, their effects on people concerned and on natural resources) ought to be checked through planning policy for physical separation. Since then, the separation principle has been structurally imprinted in the body of building, planning, and environmental legislation as a legally codified paradigm. Today, wherever formal planning exists and has been implemented, zoning is the prevalent management and legal practice (see ISoCaRP 2008).

A Critique of the Modernist City

In contrast, theoretical discourse in the fields of urban development and urban design reflects a different world. The ideology based on a functional separation of spheres of life has been rejected in the academic discourse within urban studies since the inception of the postmodern and its early theoretical texts on architecture. In their programmatic publication, *Collage City* (1978), Colin Rowe and Fred Koetter named the key concepts which still hold sway today: mixed use, superposition, ambiguity, urban diversity, potential spaces, and collage. With the proclaimed demise of the modern, the uniform, all-encompassing plan is just as obsolete as the grand narrative. Contradiction and incompatibility, contingency and difference, heterogeneity, and event density are regarded as constitutive of the city. And these terms are adjacent to what is currently under discussion in respect of porosity.

Policy practice within cities and local authorities has also attempted, repeatedly, to establish new planning principles by issuing new manifestos that seek to emulate the significance of the Athens Charter. The *Venice Charter* (1964) dealt with historical building structures and monuments in reaction to modernism's obliviousness to history. The *Aalborg Charter* (1994) committed the signatory cities primarily to objectives related to environmental protection, sustainability, and public participation. Compactness and mixed-use were explicitly named as objectives in order to minimize transport and energy use—a weak and at heart still a functionalist rationale. The *Leipzig Charter* (2007) wished to reformulate the idea of the European city, taking a stand against monotony, one-sidedness, and isolation. But these political manifestos were toothless.

In spite of a paradigm shift in the theoretical debate, functional separation has been firmly in place in spatial-administrative land-use practice since the inception of modernism. It remains closely attached to functionalist thinking. Our codified planning law was shaped at the apex of modernism, continues to serve as the basis of the jurisdiction, and thus hampers the potential for local or any innova-tive planning. It remains the legal instrument urban planners are bound to. The Land Use Ordinance in Germany has had only four amendments up to 2017. This jurisdiction perpetuates itself in such a way that the postmodern paradigm shift hardly registers. Only great political pressure could set a commensurate change in motion.

Urbanes Gebiet 2017

Given the lack of housing space in German cities, has the time, perhaps, come at last? An amendment to planning law "for the strengthening of the new coexistence in the city," which was adopted by the German Parliament and came into force in May 2017, gives grounds for hope. Under the amendment, a new category of the Land Use Ordinance (BauNVO), Urbanes Gebiet (MU), ought to provide more flexible options for mixing and allow higher densities. The name alone is promising.

This new category should, at last, allow urban structures similar to those found—and well-liked—in historical city quarters. The following points are explicitly named:
· High densities of GRZ 0.8 (site occupancy ratio) and GFZ 3.0 (floor space index) will be allowed.
· A mixture of housing, businesses, and social, cultural, and other amenities that do not substantially disturb residential use, will be allowed.
· The mixture of uses will not have to be evenly balanced (until now this was a problem on mixed-use sites).
· Facing the street, residential use on the ground floor may be excluded.
· Above a certain floor, designated in the development plan, permission may be reserved for housing.
· A certain proportion of the allowed floor space, or a certain amount of allowed floor space, may be assigned to residential or to business use.
· In the Technical Instructions on Noise Protection (TA Lärm) that have been changed in parallel, construction zone–related emission reference values higher than those currently used in mixed-use sites have been set: 63 dB(A) in daytime and 48 dB(A) at night.

During the legislative procedure, there was much disagreement on the last point. How much noise may be inflicted on urban dwellers? The ministry in charge—rearranged after the last federal elections—is first of all an environment ministry, and in the second instance an urban development ministry. It was therefore prejudiced.

Issues related to protection from emissions have been particularly controversial during the legislation process. It would also be a paradigm shift to weaken the secure protection level that has been achieved and this is leading to a real conflict of interests, not least within planning circles. Although today the main problem is traffic noise, the emissions protection paradigm is still closely connected with experiences associated with the industrial city. This is why the adjustment of TA Lärm (Technical Instructions on Noise Protection) constitutes the largest political and technical conflict of interests. It is not simply lawyers and politicians on one side and planners on the other. The conflict is splitting the planning profession right down the middle. In particular, colleagues from cities and regions with a strong industrial character view the achievements of the modernist city above all in terms of the environmental quality that has been reached now. (see Reuther in Wolfrum 2017)

From the legislators' perspective the polluter-pays principle should not be softened up in any way. The "green" German states were against a generous interpretation of the noise protection standards. That was the decisive point of contention. Sites undergoing subsequent densification are usually mixed-use sites where housing moves closer to businesses, but the official concern is that business should not be driven away. The pressure to build residential flats in growing cities is colliding with the need to likewise protect businesses within the city. The polluter-pays principle is placing the burden on business as the principal source of emissions. From a historical point of view, this is an achievement; today, however, this generally no longer concerns the emissions of industrial plants but traffic noise. And it has to be measured at a distance of 0.5 meters from a residential window, not inside the dwelling. If the polluter-pays principle had been redefined so that the advancing residential development was viewed as the originator of the conflict in the new mixed-use zone, then the so-called Hamburg window would have been the solution (see Merk in Wolfrum 2017). This window has been developed for HafenCity Hamburg and provides interior sound insulation while allowing fresh air to enter. The Senatsverwaltung für Stadtentwicklung Berlin (Senate Department for Urban Development of Berlin) also argued for noise emission values measured within buildings as the reference value, because raising emission values in a single zone goes against social justice. However, the inside measurement model was rejected by the Federal Assembly during the legislative procedure to secure the polluter-pays principle. It will continue to be a decisive handicap (Wolfrum 2017).

The topic of high density and enablement of any form of mixed uses has been of particularly great interest for large cities. The whole process has therefore been initiated by the larger German cities, and was referred to as the "Large Cities Paper" during the process. Initiated by Hamburg, Berlin, Bremen, Munich, the German Academy for Urban Design and Land Use Planning, and the Association of German Cities, it was even more ambitious at its inception. Now the chief planners of these cities do not agree on whether or not it represents a paradigm shift which overcomes zoning. At least it opens the door. With this amendment, it will become easier legally to implement dense and mixed-used urban quarters, at least as far as the modernist restrictions of German Planning Law are concerned. Hitherto the legal system is still predominant in practice.

What porosity stands for is in total contradiction to zoning. On the other hand, it is not identical with mixed-used high density. This is just an option. Nevertheless, Urbanes Gebiet will greatly facilitate the work of planners in German cities.

References:
ISoCaRP. 2008. *International Manual of Planning Practice*. The Hague. | Risselada, M., and D. van den Heuvel. 2005. *TEAM 10, in Search of a Utopia of the Present*. Rotterdam. | Rowe, C., and F. Koetter. 1978. *Collage City*. Cambridge, MA. | Smithson, A., and P. Smithson. 2005. *The Charged Void: Urbanism*. New York. | Wolfrum, S. 2017. "Interview with Regula Lüscher, Secretary of State, State of Berlin; Elisabeth Merk, Stadtbaurätin, Landeshauptstadt München; Iris Reuther, Senatsbaudirektorin, Free Hanseatic City of Bremen; and Jörn Walter, Oberbaudirektor, Hanseatic City of Hamburg," in *Yearbook, Faculty of Architecture TU Munich*, 118–24. Munich.

The Porous City Cannot Be Planned!

Imke Mumm

Hence everything is a plan, but not a plan of the whole. Karl Jaspers (1932, 32)

"The world wants more porous cities—so why don't we build them?" is the headline of an article published by sociologist Richard Sennett in *The Guardian* in 2015 (Sennett 2015), in which he presents Delhi's Nehru Place as "every urbanist's dream: intense, mixed, complex" (Ibid.). If these are the qualities we aspire to, he goes on to ask, why do the cities constructed around us look so different? This article will discuss the question of the extent to which urban porosity may be created by means of formal planning processes. Thomas Adams suggests the multiple tasks of urban planning be defined by three categories: "City and town planning is a science, an art, and a movement of policy concerned with the shaping and guiding of a physical growth and arrangement of towns in harmony with their social and economic needs" (Adams 1936, 21). Based on this proposition, we could well imagine that the scientific element in planning could at some stage confirm the significance of porosity in evaluating the quality of physical and social space. We could also imagine that design processes could deliver visions of intrinsic porous situations and places. However, the crucial issue seems to be the realization of porous qualities within the existing legal frameworks dominating the production of urban space.

The physical form of our built environment is determined by numerous norms, regulations, and laws. They establish the framework in which the interests of the individual and the general public are meant to be balanced with each other. The legal foundations for the production of space define, on the one hand, the external conditions for urban development, and on the other hand the basic and binding instruments for planning and third parties alike. During the full length of a planning process these legally defined realities cover a wide field while adhering to their own specific rationale. The technical language of jurisdiction seeks to establish the democratically legitimized regulatory requirements of complex matters in an accurate and preferably unambiguous way in contrast to the design proposal, which often describes spatial qualities, possible uses, and urban life in an evocative and imaginative way.

Porosity and Planning Law

Looking at spaces and situations, we associate the concept of porosity with a series of different properties. There is no precise definition of the term when it comes to the city. The concept of porosity contains properties such as indeterminacy, blurredness, permeability, ambiguity, contingency, or adaptability, which contrast with the legal requirement of the precise allocation of building use categories and building densities. Porosity and planning law contradict each other in a fundamental way.

Pragmatism of Planning Law

The German Städtebaurecht (Urban Development Law) of 1960 brought together all existing and debated urban regulations into a single and universally applicable legal framework for the first time. In this respect, we could say that the basic premises of the Urban Development Law were influenced by the ideas of modernism that prevailed during this period. Since its first enactment in 1960, the body of law has grown consistently. Taken together, the different planning acts reflect the changing expectations associated with Urban Development Law (Krautzberger 2010, 45). Planning legislation has responded to the specific tasks of each period, ensuring that the most urgent planning problems are managed by the instruments provided by the law. In this sense, the changes to the Baugesetzbuch (Federal Building Code) of

2014 and 2015 have to be understood as the products of a "crisis management strategy," which is also reflected in the fact that, for the first time, their period of validity is limited. Neither these pragmatically induced adaptations nor the amendments of 2017 were accompanied by a fundamental debate about issues relating to the qualities of spaces produced through the Baugesetzbuch. The only exception is the adding of a new land use category, Urbanes Gebiet (Urban Area), to the Baunutzungsverordnung (Land Utilization Ordinance).

From Design Project to Binding Land-Use Plan

As a response to the problem of working within a field of urban contradictions (Siebel 2006) planning tends to apply a kind of task management to its process. It identifies problems, defines the goals, and seeks to resolve the problems within the planning frameworks. This approach operates on the basis of a static plan which conveys a completed image of the city. Its main characteristic is its capacity to create order and the idea of producing a functioning city which ideally is free of conflicts.

There are many proposals for departing from this pragmatic and solution-oriented approach. Some projects have been implemented with promising results. In informal planning, for instance, urban development projects are conceived as step-by-step processes. The extensively conducted processes of informal participation, in which planning goals are developed together with local actors, have also changed the idea of planning within the profession. Projects have emerged that address the issue of spatial and social qualities as well as the ability of the plan to adapt to changing conditions. However, the stage of formalization preceding the stage of realization requires the reduction of content and the committing to a specific plan, just as in the formal planning process.

As early as 1965, only shortly after the adoption of the Urban Development Law, the urbanist Gerd Albers bemoaned the difficulties raised by static planning—respectively by static thinking, and the rigidifying effects of its codification (Albers 1965, 26). The need to adopt a fixed development plan continues to be a legal requirement despite the awareness of the problem of static planning. It ensures that landowners are entitled to use and build on their plots, that adequate infrastructure is provided for each plot, and that potential conflicts are resolved at the planning stage rather than at a later stage. This goes hand in hand with establishing sharp-edged demarcations and clear definitions. It seems that in the process of providing a legal framework for development, the text of the initial urban vision, full of promises and possibilities, is inevitably translated into a reduced and precise description, in the style of a manual for a technical device that has a specific function.

Habermas suggested that the main problem of urban planning is not one of design, but of managing the process in an anticipatory way and of keeping at bay the anonymous system of imperatives which interfere with urban processes and urban life and threaten to consume their intrinsic substance (Habermas 1985, 24–26).

Invisible Boundaries

The freedom to access and make use of space is limited by a multitude of regulations. Their main focus is on balancing public and private interests, the safeguarding of the public, and the provision of all that is needed for a functioning city. The rules have to be of sufficient precision while being applicable to very different situations. Hence, there is a certain degree of universality to them. The clear definition of properties such as densities, mass, or type of use, as well as the precise definition of area boundaries and spatial boundaries preclude any permeability and blurred transitional zones. Jurisdiction interprets legal provisions and defines what is deemed an appropriate implementation. Future projects are often influenced by precedents as planners act in anticipatory obedience. Aspects of spatial quality tend to be sidelined in this process.

The applicability of legal provisions always has to be sufficiently concrete and safeguarded against misinterpretation. Ambiguity or unclear provisions are considered problematic from a legal point of view. In Germany, the legal enforcement of personal rights or complaining about legally non-permissible behavior has become increasingly popular in the private as well as the public domains. However, areas and spaces intended to be used without the restrictions of predefined rules and the permission of higher authorities require different processes of negotiation. Drawing on his experience with the Französisches Viertel in Tübingen, Andreas Feldtkeller observes that "the multiplicity of uses also means [...] that the public domain cannot be associated with the pleasant, entertaining, and enriching alone, for it also requires us to respond to [...] the unpleasant [...] disturbing, ugly, and agonizing aspects of everyday life in the city" (Feldtkeller 1995, 59).

Due to the far-reaching regulation of the city the range of spaces which permit or even encourage porosity is very limited. In addition to the conditions analyzed above, other factors seem to influence the way we make use of space, which mean we hardly notice them and take them for granted. The question of where we can do what is often implicitly reproduced in our behavior. Only when we encounter unexpected practices of spatial appropriation of people who, due to their different cultural backgrounds, do not adhere to these implicit rules, are we reminded of their operative effect.

Present legislation seeks to define and arrange spaces according to their function and use. A simultaneity of uses and a blurring of boundaries, however, cannot be achieved through drawing limits and imposing rigid regulations. For instance, an area in which different uses occur requires negotiating about who may use the place at which time; it requires negotiating the state in which users may hope to find the place and in which they should leave it.

Scope of Action versus Rules

It is the in-between spaces, the spaces in which not everything is clarified and fixed, where porosity unfolds—in temporary uses, threshold spaces, and phases of transition; where there is neither claimant nor judge, where no authority feels responsible for restricting uses and user groups on grounds of legal regulations. The city has to be given the opportunity to develop and establish its permeability across all scales. The qualities of a city cannot be reduced to its mere functionality, for which the binding land-use plan is conceived. For the purpose of creating in-betweenness a degree of flexibility has to be established within the regulations. But is this extra scope of action possible in view of the constraints imposed by the system?

Exceptions, Derogations, and Exemptions

The production of spaces through appropriation and informal use has in many cases a playful, temporal, and somewhat accidental character. Conversely, formal planning has to be sufficiently defined in order to withstand legally and socially induced contestation. Once the binding land-use plan is authorized and published, opportunities to make changes are very limited. If regulations and provisions cannot be met, application for exception, derogation, and exemption can be made according to the respective building regulations of the federal state. However, these instruments neither result in a more flexible implementation of the binding land-use plan, nor do they enable the generation of in-between spaces. For the accumulation of exceptions or exemptions is nothing more than the establishing of another set of rules. Authorities then talk of the switching of a land-use category through which the criteria established by the exceptions and exemptions begin to define the new standard for granting planning permissions. At which stage a limit is reached or the basic intent of a plan is breached produces problems of arbitrariness in legal interpretation. This leaves us with the unanswered question as to whether we can regulate flexible ranges of action at all.

Formal Production of Space
One of the basic problems of the body of legal instruments is its requirement to be universally applicable. If seen from the perspective of planning, the way of thinking within the legal domain often seems to lose sight of the initial goals. Although the consideration of individual cases is backed by the Federal Building Code, the actual scope of changes is understood to be very narrow, in keeping with the democratic principles of appropriateness, equality, and transparency. From a legal point of view, no single question should be left open. The practice of clarifying gaps in the regulatory framework on the local level has given way to the forwarding of the issue to the next higher regulatory level. Ultimately, a court decision gives rise to new regulatory requirements and defines a precedent, which needs to be taken into account in future planning projects. The rules defined by the Federal Building Code follow the logic of legislative thinking. Decades of urban practice have established specific ways of working with the regulating instruments, which have inscribed themselves into the materiality of the city. The Federal Building Code has made itself indispensable through its practical application.

Spaces of Experimentation
Complaints about decades of lack of experimentation in the field of legal regulations have been raised in recent public debate (Feldtkeller 2017, 65; Sieverts 2017, 32). But how would such an experiment look?
        One possibility could be the establishing and toleration of zones that are not fully defined so that they can truly develop in the process; sites for which there is no completed image yet, which take their character from the negotiation of different interests and that are void of predefined and compulsory uses and regulatory frameworks. In a recent interview, Thomas Sieverts called for the creation of unique spaces of experimentation, in which, for a limited period of time and within a limited area, regulations are suspended so that truly novel approaches can be tested (Ibid., 33). Such spaces of experimentation could help us to identify the regulations that matter and those that need further adjustment. According to Sieverts, social vividness, the power of self-organization, and the creative mentality of pioneers are needed to this end.

Zona Libre
This is the name of a group of activists, artists, and local residents in the Kreativquartier Munich who convey their desire for freedom, happiness, and their collective form of organization. Experimentation

already happens within the quarter and within the possibilities of existing regulations. Yet, it is precisely the framework of existing regulations that hinders the testing of new instruments. True spaces of experimentation would offer the freedom to create and choose between suitable rules and user roles. The goal should not be to reinvent existing rules, but to identify the necessary degree of regulation and to redefine the scope of their use.

Porosity cannot be planned. It is possible, however, to create urban structures and forms of organization that enable the production of porosity.

References:
Adams, T. 1936. *Outline of Town and City Planning.* New York. | Albers, G. 1965. *Städtebau zwischen Trend und Leitbild.* Dortmunder Vorträge 75. Dortmund. | Feldtkeller, A. 1995. *Die zweckentfremdete Stadt: Wider die Zerstörung des öffentlichen Raums.* Frankfurt am Main. | Feldtkeller, A. 2017. "Es wurde zu wenig experimentiert, Andreas Feldtkeller im Gespräch mit Christian Holl," *der architekt* 2: 64–69. | Habermas, J. 1985. "Moderne und postmoderne Architektur," *Kleine politische Schriften*, vol. 5, *Die neue Unübersichtlichkeit.* Frankfurt am Main. | Jaspers, K. 1932. *Die geistige Situation der Zeit.* Berlin, 1979. | Krautzberger, M. 2010. "Gesellschaftspolitischer Wandel und Städtebaugesetzgebung," in *Berliner Gespräche zum Städtebaurecht*, vol. 2, *Dokumentation Festveranstaltung/Materialien*, 37–56. Berlin. | Sennett, R. 2015. "The World Wants More 'Porous' Cities—So Why Don't We Build Them?" *The Guardian*, November 27, 2015. | Siebel, W. 2006. "Wandel, Rationalität und Dilemmata der Planung," *Planung neu denken*, vol. 1, *Zur räumlichen Entwicklung beitragen*, edited by K. Selle, 195–209. Dortmund. | Sieverts, T. 2017. "Experimente wagen, Thomas Sieverts im Gespräch mit Annette Rudolph-Cleff," *der architekt* 2: 28–33.

Cities in Suspension
Sofia Dona

The ancient Greek word *Πόρος* (*poros*), which is the etymological root of *porosity*, defines the shallow part of the river where one can cross. *Πόρος* makes *Πέρασμα* (*perasma*) possible, which is the passage from one side to the other, the crossing of a natural border. *Πόρος* is a natural condition that often allowed the creation of cities but also their conquest. If one characteristic of porosity is this definition of the passage, two urban stories narrate porosity today through the exact opposite characteristic, a nonpassage, a block in a process, a dysfunctional condition, which intentionally or unintentionally stifles potential and produces cities in suspension.

Urban Pheasants, Detroit
In the city of Detroit, nature has invaded and occupied the abandoned houses and plots, transforming the urban landscape into large fields of nature. Trees and wild plants grow between bricks and rocks, penetrate windows and ceilings, and overcome buildings replacing their roofs with a new natural green cover. Water enters through the holes of the buildings and freezes during wintertime, transforming the large surfaces of big buildings into informal ice rinks.

In the midst of this wild invasion by nature, a rare species of pheasant came and settled in Detroit. The pheasant managed to find a foothold in the city because of the large spaces that turned into meadows after houses had been demolished. One can encounter these birds on architectural elements of famous abandoned buildings such as the window ledges of the Free Press Building, built by Albert Kahn in 1925. Pheasants are able to adapt to almost every kind of environment, even the most inappropriate. What makes the arrival and settlement of these rare species in the city interesting, is their protection under environmental law.

Detroit, known as the Motor City, was one of the fastest-growing cities in the United States during the early twentieth century, which by combining human labor and technology became a symbol of capitalism. The city became the paradigm of a new type of metropolis and a modern society, until in 1956 the population reached its peak and subsequently began to shrink. Since the 1950s Detroit has lost nearly a million people and is still experiencing an ongoing urban crisis until today. According to Thomas J. Surgue, "Detroit's postwar urban crisis emerged by the consequence of two of the most important, interrelated, and unresolved problems in American history: that capitalism generates economic inequality and that African Americans have disproportionately borne the impact of inequality" (Surgue 1996, 5). More and more white people moved to the suburbs, the infrastructure of the city started decaying, and African American people "found themselves entrapped in rapidly expanding, yet persistently isolated, urban ghettos" (Ibid., 8). The residential segregation appeared with a depressed central city area of black people and a ring of white suburbs, to which black people were not allowed to move. Part of this segregation led to the construction of massive highways reconnecting the white suburbs to Detroit's center. These highway-passages, which aimed to bring the suburbanites quickly to the center while avoiding the black areas, completely destroyed African American neighborhoods, interrupting the social structure and urban tissue of the city.

The inhabitants of Detroit responded to the urban threat to their neighborhoods by recourse to the invasion of the pheasant in the city. Cities function under various laws that are connected to the land and the terrain. One example is a law that protects an area inhabited by species on the verge of extinction. In the larger area of Michigan and the Midwestern, where Constantinos Doxiades once imagined Megalopolis, the pheasant is in danger of extinction. There are different reasons for this, such as the use of pesticides on crops, or even the hunting of pheasants at the beginning of the twentieth century to protect the pigeon post, which led to the predicament of this bird. The inhabitants of Detroit try to approach and attract the birds, helping them to create nests in various parts of buildings or plots in order to claim their neighborhoods as protected areas under environmental law and prevent the expropriation and destruction of poor neighborhoods for the construction of highways. The inhabitants, together with the elements of nature, the trees, and the birds, reclaim their city, suggesting suspension as a different means of revival.

Akinito—Immobilie, Athens

The word *Ακίνητο* (Akinito) refers to the Greek legal term for real estate or landed property, highlighting its character as a fixed—or immobile—entity that is connected to the ground (in German: *Immobilie*, in Italian: *immobile*). The modern city of Athens was not created through large urban developments and planning but through an economic model based on exchange called antiparochi. This model made it possible to construct multiapartment buildings—the typical Athens polykatoikia—without monetary transactions between landowners and contractors. In the development process, the landowner provides the building plot, usually undeveloped or built over with a single-family dwelling, while the contractor constructs the apartment building. Depending on the ratio between land value and construction cost, the number of newly constructed apartments is split between owner and contractor, who may keep them for personal use or as an investment, or sell them on the market. Hence, antiparochi activated a whole economy of construction based on individual agreements and produced a city of multiownership properties.

Together with the model of antiparochi, two laws influenced the way the city and its buildings were constructed; the first was the law for individual horizontal properties, and the second the law for undivided shares. The law for individual horizontal properties regulates the division of a property into several discrete property rights, meaning that both the building and the land can be owned by many different entities and individuals. The second law also results in multiownership, but differs in that the property as such remains undivided. In this ownership arrangement, different people—usually family members—are able to own a share in the property, whereby the property rights are not assigned to specific units of space. In large family structures, which are fairly common in the Mediterrenean region, inheritance arrangements may result in more than forty relatives owning a single building.

Inside these multiowned buildings, which are a result of both Greek law on ownership and family structure, any common agreement is very difficult to arrive at. In the case of individual horizontal properties that form the polykatoikia, the owners select one of them as the manager of the building and a regular assembly is arranged to decide on issues that concern the maintenance and everyday use of the building. Either because of the large number of flats in one building, or because more tenants than owners inhabit the buildings and are not eligible to vote in the assembly, agreements on maintenance and use are less driven by practical considerations and are often difficult to achieve. In the case of undivided shares, a building that once belonged to one or two people ends up being owned by a large number of relatives, often the second or third generation of economic migrants, living in Greek diaspora communities in faraway places such as Melbourne or Astoria. Apart from the undefined shares that are also an obstacle to decisions about what each owner wants to do with their part, the geographical distance between shareholders makes it almost impossible for them to all meet and to take common decisions on the property. As a result, many buildings, predominantly beautiful historic houses built back in the 1900s, are left abandoned and begin to decay. Interestingly, this particular complexity that results by multiownership and seems problematic at first glance is being used strategically in antigentrification housing projects in many northern European cities. The Mietshäuser Syndikat approach means ownership rights for a single property are combined in a way that is meant to prevent a future agreement on the sale of the respective building, thus effectively taking the property out of the cycle of investment and capital gain. The goal is to keep rents and contributions affordable, to empower individuals and groups to collectively decide on and provide for their own housing needs without the pressure of the market, and to cofinance new projects of the same kind (Mietshäuser Syndikat 2017).

Looking closer into multiownership properties in Athens, one can find many family stories that reveal an emotional bond to flats or buildings, often related to the tradition of dowry and inheritance, an essential part of the life and economy of many Mediterranean cultures. Initially connected to the tradition of marriage and later to the parents' concern to secure a decent life for their children, those properties could be seen as emotional properties that are not destined for the anonymous market. Apart from the family peculiarity, Ioanna Theocharopoulou (2005) argues that, because construction was the mainstay of the economy of the country back in the 1950s, and through the model of antiparochi, everyone—both women and men—had a direct and personal connection to buildings and to their construction, either as owners, workers, constructors, or small businessmen providing building materials—another reason for the emotional investment in properties.

In the last few decades, the number of the empty flats in the center of Athens increased, reaching a peak of 30 percent during the crisis, as a result of many people leaving the city and the country. While all public property in Greece (ports, airports, train stations, public buildings) is being privatized and sold off to companies like Fraport or Cosco, the complexity and dysfunctionality of the private microproperties seem to resist the big real estate funds and property speculation. All these fragmented multiple-ownership cases in Athens, with their hidden family ties and dependencies, prevent the sale of whole buildings on the market, thus setting limits to the scale of redevelopment schemes. At the same time, it creates the many apartments that are currently left empty—a porous and resilient tissue of small holes in the homogenous fabric of the city.

References:
Mietshäuser Syndikat. 2017. "Self-organized Living—Solidarity-based Economy!," accessed October 30, 2017, https://www.syndikat.org/en/. | Surgue, T. J. 1996. *The Origins of the Urban Crisis: Race and Inequality in Postwar Detroit.* Princeton Studies in American Politics: Historical, International, and Comparative Perspectives. Princeton. | Theocharopoulou, I. 2005. "The Housewife, the Builder and the Desire for a Polykatoikia Apartment in Postwar Athens," in *Negotiating Domesticity: Spatial Productions of Gender in Modern Architecture*, edited by H. Heyen and G. Baydar, 65–82. London.

A City Is an Apple Tree
Alex Lehnerer

"The tree of my title is not a green tree with leaves." This is the introductory disclaimer to the title of Christopher Alexander's rejection of the city being a tree in 1965 (Alexander 1965). His tree represents an abstract structure of city organization, which he compares to another, more favorable structure: the semilattice.

The tree in my title, however, is meant to be a real tree with green leaves and full of delicious red apples. My tree is standing on my plot, however, right at the edge of my neighbor's yard. It is fall and the branches have started to hang low with all the heavy fruits on them. This is my tree since it is rooted on my property. I enjoy looking at it, but even more I enjoy the prospect of eating all these apples. One day my neighbor shows up, approaches the tree, and picks an apple. And eats it right in front of me. How can he? The idyllic moment is spoiled. It is only an apple, but here a topic much bigger than this particular scene emerges. It is one of the most fundamental questions of our collective idea of city. It is the question of what is mine and what is mine but could potentially be used by or affect the others around me, commonly known as my neighbors. And my tree is not an abstract thought but one of several elements in the city that frequently and literally transgress property lines and question our modern idea of landowner-ship and property, especially property that has one owner but more than one user, or at least others who are affected by it, positively and negatively.

Christopher Alexander's text belongs to the canonical texts on the city. But it is certainly of a very specific type, as it is exemplary for our discipline's endless quest to abstract the phenomenon of urbanity into conceivable analogues and metaphors. So, let's get back to me sitting at the window writing this text. Here, I do not see any semilattice, nor do I feel like belonging to one; I do not even see "the city." The only thing I am aware of is being surrounded by all my neighbors in the immediate vicinity—once my eyes manage to stop focusing on the neighbor eating my apples. I only know a few of them, many I don't. Still, my neighbors are my connection to the city. They are as tangible as the city can get. They embody and represent context. So let me talk a bit more about my neighbors and the elements that connect us with each other—or keep us apart.

The Hedge and Its Four Ideal Heights
An important element, indicative of complicated relationships between neighbors, is the inconspicuous perimeter hedge. "Fences, walls, or hedges shall not exceed eight feet (2.4 m) in height when located in a required side yard or rear yard. Fences, walls, or hedges shall not exceed forty-two inches (1 m) in height when located in a required front yard." (The City of Santa Monica 2007)

A site hedge has three sides, or three evaluative criteria: the owner plants a hedge in order to gain protection from undesired views onto his property, or to block views from it onto unattractive surround-ings. In most cases, as far as the owner is concerned, a hedge cannot be dense or high enough—the height limit is reached when the hedge casts an excessive amount of shadow. For the most part, a hedge is adapted in its dimensions and proportions to the size of the property it surrounds. Important for the owner, finally, are ecological or natural-aesthetic desiderata. Green areas should never be reduced! At the same time, however, the hedge adjoins a neighbor's property. And it affects that property in all the ways listed above, with one decisive difference: lacking the requisite property rights, a neighbor cannot con-trol or actively shape the hedge's growth. The resultant visual shield may not only be undesirable, it may even block views into the distance; due to its disadvantageous orientation, a hedge's shadow may darken an entire neighboring property, or it may be taller than that property is wide. Depending upon which side of the hedge the evaluator happens to occupy, evaluations of one and the same hedge can be diametrically opposed. Then too, there is the perspective of the public—the view from the street, as represented by the responsible authorities. In most cases, the community has a responsibility to shape the character of private gardens within a residential district. While individual residents may wish to close themselves off by means of hedges, the community may pursue the ideal of a light and air-flooded quarter featuring open view axes, maximum opportunities for "street and neighborhood watches" (Jacobs 1961, 29–54) and good visibility at intersections. And finally, there is the perspective of the natural rate of growth peculiar to the hedge itself.

In this way, a simple hedge quickly comes to possess four virtual and ideal dimensions. If these depart markedly from one another, conflict is inevitable, and a hierarchization of heights becomes necessary.

The law is the law! The more controversial the opposing claims are, the more horizontal neighborly relationships are supplemented or even supplanted by vertical, administrative regulatory instruments. Decentralized control is taken over by a central authority. If maximum and codified heights are in force, one need no longer come to an agreement with neighbors. Control sacrifices its "self" and neighborly relations become hygienic, that is to say, continuity vanishes while the context acquires a kind of care-free status. When two people quarrel, a third is needed to reconcile them. Usually this is done by introducing strict regulations. The ambivalence of the hedge is confronted by an absolute rule without any discretion. This qualitative incongruence between the real and the implementation of the desired is the perpetual dilemma of any attempt to actually steer the urban, by whatever means.

The Beauty of Shadows

... lies in their ephemeral power. Shadows do not care for property lines. They regularly transgress boundaries with ease. The city of Zürich understands this quite literally. It is one of several Swiss communities that have established the 2-h Shadow Rule, which specifies that neighboring buildings may not be substantially inconvenienced, in particular by the shadows cast by high-rises, particularly on residential buildings or those located in residential zones. A "substantial shadow inconvenience" is specified as a wintertime light blockage of the buildable surfaces of a neighboring site lasting more than two hours (Amt für Regionalplanung Kanton Zürich 1967).

An introduction taking the form of a leaflet explains how this magnitude of a two-hour-long shadow interval is to be determined and construed in relation to the site. The rule establishes close neighborly linkages in the form of an obligatory consideration. This rule's superficial utilitarianism is striking, yet at the same time it harbors enormous regulatory potential through its intimate interconnection of morphology, density, and program.

Remixed: Zurich's shadow rule applies exclusively to residential buildings, and thereby almost automatically becomes an instrument for mixing uses: In order to achieve a certain level of constructive density while at the same time complying with the rules, housing development is necessarily mixed in with other (less sensitive) programs including offices, service areas, shops, parking facilities, etc. A rule concerning lighting requirements thereby realizes the social dream of mixed-use urban quarters—and even makes these obligatory.

Rephrased: granted, this two-hour shadow rule is the sole valid standard, and has been introduced only on a trial basis, within existing urban quarters having the requisite density, and as a guiding principle for the development of hitherto undeveloped districts. In the first case, depending on the existing density of residential utilization, the rule is capable of impeding all new building activity and additional specification. In the second case, the rule means that whoever arrives first has the license to build as high as and large as he wants. For all subsequent buildings, the degree of consideration required rises, reducing size options correspondingly. The operational use of such a rule as a phasing instrument in planning comes close to generating a real and quasi-unguided temporal development: it is only the contingent sequence of project development that determines the degree of freedom or determination conditioning each. This occurs at the cost of a comprehensive planning perspective, one that would grant all protagonists equal opportunities, no matter how quickly they manage to build.

The rights and freedoms of first-comers is explicitly manifested in England's so-called Ancient Lights Doctrine. If an English building has enjoyed uninterrupted sunlight through its windows for a period of twenty years, then the owner has the right to enjoy such undisturbed sunshine in perpetuum (Town and Country Planning Prescription Act 1832)—and this holds true even if the sunlight must pass through another property in order to reach the owner's property, thereby restricting or altogether blocking its future development. Of course, an owner can enlarge his windows or insert new ones, but in such cases, his right to enjoy permanent and unobstructed sunlight through them comes into effect only after an additional period of twenty years following such modifications.

Things became difficult in British cities like London after the enormous destruction of World War II. New buildings wholly lacked these accumulated rights to light access. Of course, the building sites were still there, but the walls and windows laying claim to unobstructed sunlight, and hence capable of preventing adjacent development, no longer existed. In the short term, property owners were able to re-secure these rights by registering, while the effective waiting period was now extended from twenty to twenty-seven years.

In this comprehensive form, the English rule never traveled across the Atlantic. Not even in the 1980s, when Americans could quantify the loss of sunlight objectively in terms of the reduced performance of their solar panels. In 1980 the *New York Times* reported numerous cases in which the proud owners of solar panels were unable to take advantage of these devices because a nearby tree had grown too tall, or because a new, multistory apartment building cast an enormous shadow across it. It was in this period that many cities and communities began to consider their options for sensibly administering such solar access. Given the experiences of the last oil crisis and the explosive rise in oil prices, such considerations had become unavoidable.

But here too, the sequence of development is essential: already in the early 1980s, a number of North American states introduced solar access rules. New Mexico was among them. At the time, New Mexico guaranteed unrestricted and permanent access to sunshine to anyone with new solar paneling, provided no existing building blocked it already. But this preemptive legal move was open to misuse, as characterized vividly by David Engel of the US Department of Housing and Urban Development (HUD) in the *New York Times* article "Rights-to-light Legislation Can Lead to Absurdities." "Imagine: some developer plans a multimillion-dollar building and a guy buys a small lot next door, parks his mobile home, and puts up a solar collector. You've got a perfect setup for bribery." (Charle 1980)

Also cited was Melvin Eisenstadt, a solar power adviser to the state of New Mexico, who mentioned another unintended consequence of the first-come-first-serve rule: "A while back, we were all holding our breat. [...] A developer in Albuquerque wanted to put up a six- or seven-story hotel on land abutting a residential section. The residents tried to stop the project, but the zoning commission decided in favor of the developer. Really, all they needed to stop the project was to pass around the hat, get several thousand dollars, and install a solar collector on one of the homes that would be shaded by the hotel." (Ibid.)

On the model of New Mexico, residents of Zürich can bring about the downfall of any undesirable high-rise development—and not necessarily by rejecting it via referendum. All they have to do is to find a developer capable of erecting a residential building quickly and directly adjacent to the future high-rise, that is to say, falling somewhere within its true two-hour shadow (Lehnerer 2009). Here's to becoming good neighbors!

This little essay on apples, hedges, and shadows is written to emphasize that there is hardly a more powerful yet conflicted position in the city than that of being a neighbor. A neighbor-to-neighbor situation comprises the heart of the city. And it is ubiquitous. There is no one without neighbors. Moreover, these conditions of coexistence, charged with solid private interests, are better handled with a set of equally relative rules than with a strict plan. Establishing complete hygiene between neighbors damages the relations between them and eventually destroys our city. Now, my neighbor is finished with his apple.

References:
Alexander, C. 1965. "A City Is Not a Tree," *Architectural Forum* 122, no. 1: 58–62. | Amt für Regionalplanung Kanton Zürich, ed. 1967. *Anleitung Zur Bestimmung Des Schattenverlaufes Von Hohen Gebäuden: Die 2-Stunden-Schattenkurve.* Grundlagen zur Orts und Regionalplanung im Kt. Zürich. Zurich. | Charle, S. 1980. "New Laws Protect Rights to Unblocked Sunshine," *New York Times*, July 20, 1980. | Jacobs, J. 1961. "The Use of Sidewalks: Safety," in idem., *The Death and Life of Great American Cities*, 29–54. New York. | Lehnerer, A. 2009. *Grand Urban Rules*. Rotterdam, 2014. | The City of Santa Monica. 2007. *Planning and Zoning: Fence, Wall, Hedge, Flagpole*. Los Angeles. | Town and Country Planning Prescription Act. 1832. Section 3. United Kingdom.

Porosity—Is Munich a Porous City?
Elisabeth Merk

The notion of a city as an organism that not only allows for many layers of complexity but actively generates them, has been fascinating urbanists since Walter Benjamin published his famous essay. First and foremost, a city is the product of real-life interactions between its citizens, expressed in architecture, urbanism, and spatial concepts.

Among Germany's metropolises, Munich represents a European urban model which, despite the terrible destruction it suffered in World War II, mostly preserved the integrity of its prewar structures in reconstruction. Munich is perceived as a consolidated city, which has methodically and successfully navigated intermittent spurts of growth since the second half of the twentieth century. The social changes that have come with this growth, particularly since the 1972 Munich Olympics, have shaped a metropolitan, democratic ideal of urban community living. Recently, this facility to adapt quickly to social changes has been demonstrated once again in rising to the challenges presented by the refugee crisis.

Despite ever-higher real estate prices in Munich, large portions of the citizenry and an overwhelming majority of the Munich City Council support the use of legal instruments, such as socially equitable land use, to redistribute urban resources in an equitable fashion. For several decades now, Munich has been among the cities that place great value on diverse neighborhoods. By pursuing its strategy of openness, Munich is, in a sense, obeying the fascinating necessity of survival of urban society as defined by Walter Benjamin.

Munich Seen from the Outside
An outside observer would not immediately recognize Munich as a city with an aptitude for porosity—it functions too smoothly; in many ways, it seems too predetermined; it does not appear to offer enough free and undefined spaces. Its spatial setup, in particular, seems to suggest that Munich is a fully formed, "finished" city—well defined in its high quality of life as well as its stable residential environment and neighborhoods.

The Close-Up
An insider, however, will be aware of a far more complex picture. Munich is growing, not just at its peripheries, but also from the very center. The entire city is in a state of transformation: former industrial production sites are morphing into residential areas; downtown quarters that used to be predominantly residential are attracting new business formats because of their location; military compounds that were long off-limits are now connecting neighborhoods.

Munich is in a transition from large city to international metropolis. This means rising prosperity, but also stress; growth anxiety is taking the population to the limits of its psychological resilience. Conflicts over land use are being waged over ever-fewer available spaces. As a consequence, land prices and rents are skyrocketing; citizens in downtown neighborhoods are becoming increasingly hostile toward growth; and segregation is on the rise, which in the long run will threaten the sustainability of Munich's overall development.

Munich, a City in Transition: "La Città Soglia"
Munich is a city in transformation, searching for new ways to develop. The guiding notion of a porous city —*la città soglia* could provide some ideas for organizational principles to redefine spaces.

How do we design such forms of porosity, of permeability—both at a material, physical level that will impact urban structures, but also at a mental level, in the minds of the citizens? If we can speak to the city's emotional side and impact its self-conceptualization, can the positive aspects of growth amalgamate into a new quality of urban living? How does one unite all these various parameters and design principles to create a *Forma Urbis* that does justice to the notion of porosity as defined by Walter Benjamin and Richard Sennett?

To make this work for Munich, and to incorporate such considerations into a strategic reorientation of our urban planning, we must look at those aspects and situations where porosity is already a reality in the city today.

What can we learn from Munich's existing quarters? Fusing and layering different uses and lifestyles and interlacing various work environments creates great energy. What can we do to support and harness this energy for urban planning and ultimately, quality of life?

Where in Munich can we identify spatial settings or interactions that have clearly reached a threshold that either requires active intervention, or conversely, might find its quality if we allow for experimentation, unplanned and community-driven urban development?

The question of the *città soglia* also involves an analysis of the city's various paces. Urban development and planning moves along various timelines at different speeds.

These are the questions I would like to explore by analyzing spaces of encounter, integration, and porosity in Munich. From this analysis, I will derive ten theses.

Searching the City for Cues

Munich has a great tradition of public spaces that are interconnected by a system of courtyards, passages, and arcades. Some have been reinvented, such as the Fünf Höfe or the Hofstatt. Others are at risk, like the Arcades of the Alte Akademie, which connect the Alte Akademie building with the public space.

Thesis 1: Differentiating public and private spaces requires urban planning and architectural design.

In many ways, the annual Oktoberfest and its venue, the Wiesn, are a paradox. Once a year, this location hosts the highest density of live bodies per square meter and an enormous degree of diversity. Once Oktoberfest is over, however, strolling across this central space in the city gives you a sense of spaciousness and emptiness that you cannot find anywhere else in Munich.

Depending on the season, the Wiesn rhythm oscillates between extremely intense and utterly tranquil. It is almost a matter of course that the usual regulative practices, bidding procedures, and policing systems follow a different set of parameters here. For a brief moment, bureaucratic lethargy seems to go into zero-gravity mode, turning into a baroque feast. There has never been an official price index for a square meter of Wiesn; time is not a factor at this transitory, recurring event. Prices are as eye-watering at the Oktoberfest as they are anywhere else in Munich, and yet the city succeeds in finding the courage to regulate the Oktoberfest in such a way that it remains a festivity that is accessible to all, and to defend this strategy in public debate.

Thesis 2: A city needs spaces that allow for different qualities at different times. These spaces must be governed by flexible legal provisions.

The town hall of Munich and the large cultural center the Gasteig, which was built almost a century later and is home to the Philharmonic Orchestra, are located in completely different places in the city. Yet they both inhabit the urban maze as architectural metaphors of a rock with multiple openings. In fact, a visitor entering either of these two buildings will get a sense of being in a multilevel labyrinthine cavern. Both buildings were designed specifically for the citizens. There are no access controls, not even now in times of elevated terror alerts. The city authorities repeatedly emphasized that the value of accessibility for all is a tangible expression of democratic openness and therefore trumps any safety precautions. The sheer size of the two complexes and their large, porous structures almost automatically create a simultaneous, multilayered network of visitors and intentions. Many a tourist has lost their way in the town hall and ended up walking into a city council meeting on the upper floor, asking for directions to one attraction or the other. In the Gasteig, high culture and community college curricula merge with the liberal arts scene. The Olympic stadium and compound harness the symbolism of an Alpine landscape, which, despite its scale and majesty, communicates the idea of openness and porosity. The complex is the city's crystal crown of democracy.

Thesis 3: Projects for urban transformation also need iconic power.
Theodor Fischer's tiered building code provided a clear legal context and a creative framework for the growth of cherished Munich quarters such as Schwabing.

Thesis 4: Our urban planning for new quarters must start out from public spaces.
Many quarters already feature a mix of commercial and residential spaces, such as the Kreativquartier or the Werksviertel.

Thesis 5: Anchors in the present cityscape must be preserved and embedded in new concepts.
The Isar River is a massive natural space in the city. Its noncommercial public use serves as a unifying artery.

Thesis 6: Nature and open spaces are an integral conceptual element and play an important role in urban transformation.
The Petuelpark demonstrates that infrastructure projects can help connect quarters. New forms of mobility will redefine streets as communal spaces and the central hub of the quarter (according to Walter Benjamin).

Thesis 7: New mobility concepts can be an important element in urban porosity.
There is a lot of support among Munich's policymakers and citizens for a cooperative model. Co-ops like Wagnis Art (Dare Art) and others provide new value concepts for urbanism in the city's quarters.

Thesis 8: Neighborhood concepts and cooperative development in urban quarters are engines of progress.
Dialogue with the citizenry has been enriching urban planning processes in Munich for half a century. In the past, transparency and porosity in decision-making has made a great difference and has been tried

and tested in projects like the citizens' review of the Kunstareal or of regional development. The idea of an urban structure that is embedded in a regional urban development process in the sense of a *città soglia* defines the porosity of urban structures as an opportunity to overcome both internal boundaries and the outer city limits, sparking an open citizens' dialogue that is both material and metaphysical.

Thesis 9: In order to succeed, the community of citizens must be given various opportunities for participation.
The cityscape with its great wealth of resources and artistic expression was both preserved and reinvented in postwar modernism.

Thesis 10: To create a sense of identity, we need beauty in all its diversity and its different expressions over time.

Conclusion
Munich's city structure offers a variety of locations and use profiles that allow for porosity. Our task is therefore to preserve these places and their atmospheres as we transform these quarters and give them room to breathe. As we develop and build these new quarters, we must identify strategic, multiuse, communal places in order to create sustainable anchoring points and to successfully transition between the old and the new. What we need to achieve this is not more rules, but rather a common understanding of our city. Via the concept of the *città soglia*, we can create quality for our growing city and its metropolitan area.

Just *Design* It: Porosity as Leeway for Designing Urban Space
Nikolai Frhr. von Brandis

The term *porosity* may evoke various connotations but can also surely be described as an indispensable urban quality that can be considered tantamount to being an urban practice and a prerequisite for it at the same time.

Instead of rigid regulations for the practice of urban design and the spatial outcome of these design processes with imposed allocation of different realms, zones, and spaces, there is a need for more and better negotiation processes about how to design urban spaces. Here *porosity* can be understood as a metaphorical term, for using and creating internal gaps in the rigid, compact, and ubiquitous system of automatisms in urban design practice that literally open up the space to design The basic idea is the observation that frequently a higher degree of freedom of action and literally more room for maneuver is highly beneficial for achieving urban qualities. This is backed up by a performative conception of space which encourages an approach to designing space, rather than calculating it on the basis of fixed recipes thought to be based on scientific principles.

Design as defined by Rittel is a method for dealing with "ill-defined or wicked problems" (Rittel and Webber 1973). It is always the first choice whenever problems have to be tackled where other scientific methods do not lead to the desired results because a solution cannot be defined as true/untrue, right or wrong in advance. Design works instead with variations and different scenarios.

Many aspects of spatial structures can be described mathematically, but space is more complex. A mere geometrical conception of space turns out not to be sufficient. As shown by Lefebvre and others, space is not static; it has performative qualities that are enacted as well, being culturally induced to a high degree. Design has proven to be the most suitable method to deal with such a high complexity. As a matter of fact, most of the time we deal with wicked problems in urban planning. Thus design, as the most capable method in the realm of architecture, urbanism, and spatial planning, is the method of choice. If we follow this conclusion, the question arises, how the scientific method and cultural practice of designing are reflected in the everyday practice of urban planning? Where do we find the political and creative leeway and, last but not least, the required time to design?

More or less acknowledged attempts to negotiate urban space (and new forms of resistance) like E. Gündüz's widely acclaimed performance *Standing Man* in Gezi Park in Istanbul 2013, or critical mass flash mobs (for example, the campaigns by bicyclists in Munich), cannot hide the fact that the ability of urban stakeholders to negotiate on urban matters seems to be decreasing. Various factors seem to undermine this ability to negotiate on urban space in a constructive manner (or, in other words, undermine the ability to design), thus reducing room for maneuver and leaving ground to unspecific, schematic policies that often aim only at the mitigation of conflicts and—in the end—have the effect of segregating objects, emissions, and eventually, people. A porous city in this regard envisions a city where the ability to communicate and to negotiate on space is not only crucial but also a vibrant practice. It would be synonymous with a city where there is leeway to create spaces charged with specific characteristics rather than being filled with interchangeable schemes.

We are now in a position to refocus the question above: Can we identify the key factors leading to the current neglect of design?

In the first instance, it can appear quite surprising that after decades of development of the discipline from a self-conception as an engineering science with experts working for the benefit of society toward a self-image that shows a discipline at the edge of engineering and cultural sciences and, at the same time as a central facilitator between these and city inhabitants, has of all things a problem with this mediating role and its ability to negotiate on urban space. Generations of urbanists have worked on participation models and yet their current diagnosis is that the urbanistic discipline has lost its ability to manage design processes and has lost ground to legal experts and to an expansion of schematic regulations. How could this have happened?

First of all, it is important to realize that urban regulations have emerged to a large extent from regulations that addressed safety matters, along with infrastructure and ownership issues, and risk allocation arrangements. Here, in technical and legal matters, differences between the private realm and the res publica derive from. These regulations deal with private and public interests and the conflicts between them. Where will we route the high-voltage line? Where can we preserve recreation spaces? And can these considerations be reconciled? A workable combination was never ruled out of course, but it is crucial to understand that urban regulations have their origin in the aim to organize things and people in such a way that conflicts, harm, and risk are minimized, and therefore tend to favor arrangements where disparate things are juxtaposed rather than made compatible with each other..

The clash between different claims and demands is a constituent feature of urban space. Thus, conflict is pivotal when discussing urban space. In every design process there is a need to solve conflicts (for example, by making a decision that A is more important than B); a need to bring things together, to merge diverging interests. One's own interests and those of others have to be acknowledged, evaluated, and finally, if necessary, be fought out. Dealing with the other is inevitably incorporated in every design process. Acquiring scientific facts and calculable factors remains important in order to provide urban stakeholders with common ground for negotiations on space. Nevertheless, it is important to note that a jointly elaborated set of universally respected facts as well as legal guidelines and procedures cannot be a substitute for design processes and negotiations.

Dealing with the other—recognizing this as a central feature of urbanism gives us a crucial clue as to why the ability to negotiate on space is in decline. And it is not surprising that this aspect can be located in the cultural and sociological field: Max Weber fundamentally analyzed the term *city* and described trade as a key trait of a city and together with this a certain presence of foreignness, contrary to rural realms (Weber 1920, 67). Therefore, dealing with strangers, with newcomers or foreigners can be conceived as part of the definition of urbanity in sociology. But indeed, our relationship toward foreignness has undergone subtle, often overlooked changes recently. It often seems that these changes have not yet been taken into account and conclusions have been reached that do not stand up to closer inspection.

Byung-Chul Han's observations in his book *Die Austreibung des Anderen* (The Expulsion of the Other, 2016) may help us locate the problem. He takes a critical look at our contemporary means of communication. He argues that connections have become a substitute for relationships and that proximity has been replaced by a kind of "gaplessness" (Ibid., 52). In these spaces of "hypercommunication"—without binding commitment but with an inherent striving for total transparency—feelings of responsibility are gradually dissolved. Furthermore, secrecy (a precondition for politics, for example, but generally seen by Han as an indispensable *conditio humana* [Han 2012]), foreignness, and mystery are completely annihilated in transparent spaces. Han thus develops an explanatory model for the evolving echo chambers in digital spaces that in turn retroact upon real life. In such environments—that continuously move forward to ubiquitously interlock with our analog world—the other starts to fade away. Subsequently, he states that in the absence of counterparts—along with the absence of physical objects of resistance—our perception has withdrawn from these phenomena (Han 2016, 79–80). Vast realms are now beyond human perception and are no longer available as bodily experiences. Contrary to today's common sense, the scope for connecting up with anyone at any time and any place does not necessarily lead to being overwhelmed by the presence of others. Rather, digital environments with their digital objects offer no resistance. On the contrary, they solicit our attention and admiration. They want us to like them. The digital sphere does not present itself to us as reluctant, rebellious, or disturbing; devoid of divergence and deviation, the digital sphere invites our affection.

Taking Han's view into account, what does it tell us about the decreasing ability to design, to negotiate on urban space? The removal of any distance between places, people, and events as well as the exponential growth in communication technology has not necessarily lead to an intensification of conflicts, nor has it necessarily lead to an improved ability to deal with them. New means of communication have not necessarily improved our understanding of other people's interests, feelings, and objections, and obviously they have had even less of an impact on our understanding of their bodily limitations and experiences. Predicted correlations between the technological developments of the past decade and the rise of social media have failed to appear. Instead, we have evidence that other correlations can be observed: An increase in narcissistic self-reference fueled by congenial digital environments makes us deaf and blind to the needs of others—the voices of others fade away in a digital white noise and this leads to a paralysis of our ability to empathize. As Han puts it: "*Eros*, conceived of as the pursuit of the other, which can be seen as an integral part of thinking, is also paralyzed by the disappearance of the other in the form of counterparts and resistance of other people as well as objects" (Ibid., 71, author's translation). This other can be seen as synonymous with foreignness—as alien, discomforting, outside our comfort zone; but at the same time also as the source of desire for the unexpected, the event, and the ability to surprise.

In the final analysis it is the latter—and the pleasure that results from it—that emerges here only when we do not avoid conflicts but engage with them in a fruitful way. In other words, when we start dealing with conflicts we have already started designing. And design is the only method of provoking the new and the other; of systematically making the unexpected and surprising accessible. It is also probably the only method that can create affective ties that turn gaplessness into proximity and turn connections into stable relationships with a sense of responsibility for place.

Ultimately, this absence of the other and the lack of an ability to develop an understanding of physical limitations and resistance is, on the one hand, overcome by design; but on the other hand it is a pivotal reason for the decline of our ability to design: something of a chicken-and-egg-dilemma. A possible remedy here is perhaps to keep in mind the frequently quoted line attributed to philosopher Karl Friedrich von Weizsäcker: "Freedom is an commodity which increases with use, decreases with nonuse." ("Freiheit ist ein Gut, das durch Gebrauch wächst, durch Nichtgebrauch dahinschwindet.") The argument leads, in the end, to a very performative approach: *Just do it.* Just start and while doing it, let the normative force of the factual do its work and—metaphorically—keep the pores open, thus hindering schematic planning recipes and preventing the proliferation of dogma.

Design needs stakeholders with the competence to tackle conflict as a prerequisite just as much as it needs a legislative framework, scientifically backed-up facts and sufficient time. But the practice of design itself is a powerful tool, to a great extent capable of suspending the paralysis of digital soliloquies, establishing stronger ties to places and people, and thereby strengthening responsibility; and it is more effective in this way than schematic procedures and regulations can ever be. Openly structured design processes ideally offer immediate feedback to participating stakeholders, thus providing experiences of self-efficacy, while without this experience responsibility remains solely abstract.

At the same time it remains crucial that in the interaction of all stakeholders that produce urban space and compete as well as eventually collide with their interests, common citizens can act at eye level with the others. Activation, involvement and empowerment remain key issues for urbanists that need careful attention in the wake of the ever-changing conditions for negotiation processes in our society and their legal framework as well as cultural context. Only this will be able to regain leeway for design as understood here and in the context depicted. Carefully and specifically designed procedures and methods for common design processes for the development of the Esso-Häuser (PlanBude 2017a) in Hamburg, for example, show the potential as well as the need. It was initiated and developed in a bottom-up process by the PlanBude collective (PlanBude 2017b), mainly, it should be added, by urbanism-related activists, and was later officially funded by the senate. To a great extent this process managed to bypass paralyzing moments and even to take advantage of the specific force that design entails under the primacy of the digital which defines communication and perception in our era.

References:
Han, B. C. 2012. *Transparenzgesellschaft*. Berlin. | Han, B. C. 2016. *Die Austreibung des Anderen: Gesellschaft, Wahrnehmung und Kommunikation heute*, 2nd ed. Frankfurt am Main. | PlanBude. 2017a. "Schlagwort: Essohäuser," accessed September 10, 2017, http://planbude.de/tag/essohaeuser/. | PlanBude. 2017b. "PlanBude," accessed September 10, 2017, http://planbude.de/. | Rittel, H., and M. Webber. 1973. "Dilemmas in a General Theory of Planning," *Policy Sciences* 4: 155–69. | Weber, M. 1920. *The City*. Glencoe, 1958.

Cairo's Advanced Informality
Marc Angélil and Cary Siress

It is January 2008 and crowds are lined up in the poor Cairo neighborhood of Imbaba to buy baladi bread—the basic staple of the Egyptian diet also known as "the people's food." Customers elbow their way to the front of the line, thrusting money at the baker through the bars that separate him from an angry mob. There were even reports of breadline violence in other parts of the city, with people shooting at each other in order to get their share. Bread, in Egyptian Arabic *aish* meaning "life," has nurtured acts of desperation that have even resulted in deaths.

But how can something as common as daily bread be caught up in a ruthless game of life and death? Remember that 2008 was a watershed year in many respects, not least because it marked a new height in soaring food prices around the world, pushing even more millions into poverty in that year alone (United Nations 2011, 63). Risky speculation in agricultural commodities along with severe drought adversely affected all markets associated with food production that year. Egypt was particularly hard hit, given its reliance on grain imports. With scores of people unable to afford basic provisions, there was a run on bakeries like the one in Imbaba to secure cheap bread.

If baladi bread is the staple food of the poor in Egypt, then its spatial equivalent is the baladi neighborhood, home to a majority of the populace. Common wisdom would have it that one feeds the other: cheap bread sustains the masses. Yet, the ostensibly clear relation between urban core and the greenbelt beyond normally used for food production has been compromised in Egypt. Fertile land in the Nile Valley has been steadily decreasing due to the encroachment of settlements over time, with urbanization claiming ever more territory. Informal building densification on farmland in Egypt still follows the given subdivision of agricultural plots—small, rectangular, and separated by long straight irrigation channels, which now serve as access arteries for the ever-expanding districts. Here, form follows food, or at least this is the pattern of those properties on which it was formerly produced. This is the bitter truth of urban growth in Egypt: less and less territory is available for locally produced crops, and unavoidably the country becomes more and more reliant on foreign markets.

What makes the imbalance between arable and urban land here all the more complex is that the ongoing appropriation of farmland has been conducted primarily informally and extra-legally, despite government awareness of the accelerated rate at which agricultural land has been urbanized. Such encroachment stands in defiance of the law strictly prohibiting any construction on rural property. Illegality, it would seem, constitutes a hushed form of common law, a low-lying norm that not only determines behavior but also gives shape to urban development. Since achieving independence in the early 1950s, Egypt has faced an acute housing shortage, a condition exacerbated in the following decades by the state's inability to provide a sufficient number of low-cost dwellings. Without a formal solution to this problem, successive regimes have turned a blind eye to informal construction, as if simply wishing it away would absolve the government of any municipal responsibility. Government neglect vis-à-vis popular urbanization has not only jeopardized the nation's capacity to feed itself, but has also given rise to marginalized neighborhoods known as the ashwa'iyat—literally meaning "disordered," "haphazard," or "random"—that have become the most prevalent response from below to rampant population growth and lack of affordable housing. Insofar as these settlements are seen as spontaneous and unplanned, they are viewed as a possible threat to urban well-being and thus figure ominously in Egypt's imaginary.

According to economist David Sims, there were hardly any informal areas recognizable as such in the capital in the 1950s. He reports that half a century later "a full 63.6 percent of the population of

17.3 million inhabitants lived in informal areas" (Sims 2010, 96). With more than 10 million people reportedly living in marginalized areas of the city, it is difficult to imagine how such a multitude could be ignored, yet they were, and the consequences have proved unstoppable. The pace of informal construction in Cairo was further accelerated following the Arab Spring, due to an even more tenuous chain of command in urban governance brought about by the ensuing power vacuum. At that point, almost anything went.

Imbaba, home of the small bakery besieged by angry mobs in 2008, is one of the largest informal neighborhoods in Cairo, and has become the quintessential gauge of informality nationwide. But it began very modestly, given that urban expansion on farmland is a process that proceeds incrementally. Having begun as a small makeshift village in the 1950s, the following decades of Imbaba's evolution saw the construction of reinforced concrete frames and slabs with masonry infill, a technique most likely imported by Egyptian migrant workers returning from jobs abroad. Usually no more than five stories tall, the next generation of buildings went higher, in some cases reaching up to ten stories. By 2017 informal real estate speculation had taken off to such a degree that illicit developers were building tenements of up to fifteen stories tall. These structures seemed to go up almost overnight where space permitted, producing an almost seamless fabric that has since grown into a seemingly endless and homogeneous skyline of brick marking the fateful shift from greenbelt to "red belt" taking place in the capital.

It must be said that informal construction in Egypt is of a very different order than in other parts of the world due to its unusually high quality. In spite of being built outside the purview of official regulations, buildings in places like Imbaba adhere to strict rule-of-thumb standards and are executed by extra-legal construction crews using well-established technologies. Payoffs are made to inspectors to look the other way, and negotiations with suppliers are conducted at the margins of legality. What results is a parallel society nested within the city proper, built up beyond official norms and guided by its own systematized behavior. So the common perception that these agglomerations are unplanned, random, or haphazard is indeed a misconception. On the contrary, informality here is a highly organized physical and social condition that has matured to engender what would be better identified as "advanced informality," a self-processing phenomenon that is becoming ever more enmeshed with the formal city.

The complexity of the physical fabric is mirrored in that of social relations within the ashwa'iyat. Depending on where boundaries are drawn, the population of Imbaba is estimated to be between 850,000 and a million inhabitants, but no one knows for sure (Ibid., 115). Informal provenance notwithstanding, Imbaba has become a bona fide community in its own right, if not a city within the city. Entire industries have emerged to service the neighborhood's specific needs, providing all necessary trades of the building sector such as local laborers, building firms, contractors, developers, and real estate brokers. "Personal acquaintance and community-sanctioned trust are the main guarantees of sale transactions" (Ibid.,114). Local networking is key; word-of-mouth recommendation is the primary mode for securing commissions; who knows whom and who owes what to whom determines what gets built, sold, or rented. But areas like Imbaba are not just home to a multitude of people; they are also employment generators comprising a profusion of small enterprises that contribute to Cairo's overall economy. In sum, these informal agglomerations are essentially working-class neighborhoods, heterogeneous in their ethnic makeup and income levels, and tight-knit in their social structure. Those who dwell and work here have been brought together by circumstance, a chance convergence that has spawned an informal ecology for living and working that is part of the larger ecology of Cairo.

Though essentially overlooked for decades, informal communities gained media attention in the early 1990s. The turning point was a major coordinated assault led by the military in December 1992, specifically targeting Imbaba. Suddenly, "a nameless neighborhood became a symbol, a paradigm: Imbaba was besieged by 16,000 security forces, led by 2,000 officers, one of the biggest sweep operations ever undertaken in Cairo," wrote urban geographer Eric Denis in one of the first scholarly accounts of the event (Denis 1994, 121). This incident brought the society of informality into the limelight, and since then it has become impossible to ignore it. The sweep lasted six weeks, during which hundreds of residents were arbitrarily interrogated and many imprisoned, including a number of suspected militants, as part of a state operation to bring outlaw territory under control.

This intervention changed the fate of the district overnight, serving to brand it as even more deviant and treacherous, for most reports in the press used the so-called discovery of informality as an opportunity to criminalize the poor and their habitat. The Siege of Imbaba, as it came to be known, was a political spectacle, an "instrument of governance or a mechanism that attempted to shore up the ideological legitimacy and authority of the government and public support for its policies" (Singerman 2009, 117). The ensuing discourse took on a biopolitical dimension by equating an unwanted urban condition with disease for political gain. Imbaba was Cairo's cancer that needed to be cured; residents were animals to be tamed; informal settlements were depicted as pathological to distance them from the civilized city (Ibid., 118–25). Imbaba was portrayed as a literal blight on the land endangering the nation's capacity to sustain itself, with the problems and anxieties associated with food security having been projected onto this particular community. Stigmatization served as a political tool to construct an other for the sake of legitimizing the regime's repressive nature.

The smear campaign served an additional agenda as well, namely, that of discrediting militant religious movements and thereby reducing their power. With informality now linked to Islam, these settlements were branded as being not only uncivilized but also as a breeding ground for terrorism. Islamic fundamentalists had taken root in parts of Imbaba and had become quite influential as a local political force in recruiting new members from among the neighborhood's youth and fomenting dissent toward the government. One religious cell in particular, Gama'a Islamiya, a radical offshoot of the Muslim Brotherhood, is notorious, having been accused of numerous crimes against political figures, the most prominent being the assassination of President Anwar Sadat in 1981. This reputation notwithstanding, such groups have performed important social functions in dispossessed communities by providing much needed assistance in the face of government indifference. Having won popular support, members of the Muslim Brotherhood announced their plans in November 1992—just a month before the siege—to found an independent "Republic of Imbaba" right in the heart of Cairo, a plan obviously meant to incense a sluggish state (Ibid., 113–14).

The prospect of a fundamentalist city in the nation's capital was certainly one of the main motivations of the crackdown that aimed in one blow to clean up the scourge of society, secure the elite's ruling monopoly, and improve Egypt's image both domestically and abroad (Al-Sayyad 2011, 3–4). And this siege was just a prelude to other such bouts of government repression in Imbaba and other ashwa'iyat that would take place prior to and after the Arab Spring revolts, with residents being harassed, imprisoned, or shot. President Abdel Fattah el-Sisi, who came to power after the 2013 coup d'état, pursued state perse-cutions that were no doubt largely due to former President Mohamed Morsi's affiliation with the Muslim Brotherhood as one of its earlier leading members. As informal communities grew and came to occupy more and more agricultural land, and in the process gained strength as a constituent force, they were increasingly branded as a national threat and thus constituted a menacing political foe to be eliminated. Imbaba was singled out as dangerous territory, especially due its association with Gama'a Islamiya, which has since been designated a terrorist organization linked to the militant group Islamic State. All this said and irrespective of the attempts made to fix such neighborhoods, either by decree or force, a resilient sense of normality somehow still prevails in the ashwa'iyat.

Coming back to the relation between baladi bread and baladi neighborhoods, it is clear that the means of sustaining urban populations in Egypt are anything but secure, subject as they are here to increasingly crossbred socioeconomic constellations in which formal and informal sectors have become inextricably intertwined by the biopolitics driving urbanization along the Nile. The entanglement of food and power, evidenced all the way from the top down to the local bakery in Imbaba, becomes more complex in light of another entanglement of the food-power dynamic with urban informality. The polit-ical economy of food security is fundamentally related to the political economy determining land tenure security, even in contexts where the latter is not officially recognized or guaranteed. So what appears as down-to-earth as having a roof over your head is intimately tied to getting food on the table, with agri-cultural land giving way to an unregulated building frenzy, with the wheeling and dealing of farmers and developers eager to purchase land, with building inspectors bribed by local contractors to build on agricultural parcels, with displaced families given no choice but to migrate to urban margins, with the government casting a blind eye to blatant infractions of the law, with religious fundamentalists taking advantage of state indifference to establish their own bases of power, and with government crackdowns on poor neighborhoods given legitimacy by media stigmatization, it is no wonder that Egypt is facing the familiar refrain of revolution in its city streets. It is even less a wonder that in a country marked by habitual state indifference to the fate of its people, further advances of informality seem an inevitable course for the nation's development.

References:
Al-Sayyad, N. 2011. "The Fundamentalist City?" in *The Fundamentalist City? Religiosity and the Remaking of Urban Space*, edited by N. Al-Sayyad and M. Massoumi, 3–25. Abindgdon. | Denis, E. 1994. "La mise en scène des 'ashwaiyyât': Premier acte: Imbâba, Décembre 1992," *Égypte/Monde Arabe*, no. 20: 117–32. | Denis, E. 2012. "The Commodification of the Ashwa'iyyat: Urban Land, Housing Market Unification, and de Soto's Interventions in Egypt," in *Popular Housing and Urban Tenure in the Middle East: Case Studies from Egypt, Syrian, Jordan, Lebanon, and Turkey*, edited by M. Ababsa, B. Dupret, and E. Denis, 227–258. Cairo. | Sims, D. 2010. *Understanding Cairo: The Logic of a City Out of Control*. Cairo. | Singerman, D. 2009. "The Siege of Imbaba, Egypt's Internal 'Other' and the Criminalization of Politics," in *Cairo Contested: Governance, Urban Space, and Global Modernity*, edited by D. Singerman, 111–43. Cairo. | United Nations. 2011. *The Global Social Crisis: Report on the World Social Situation 2011*. New York.

p. 186: Figure-ground plans on the northwestern edge of
Imbaba along the ring road circumscribing Greater Cairo,
showing the extent of informal growth from the 1970s (left)
and 2010s (right)

p. 187: Informal construction accelerated
by informal speculation on property development following
the Arab Spring, Cairo

Cairo Episodes
Monique Jüttner

Cairo both challenges and absorbs the visitor in equal measure. Layers and patterns of the metropolis expose one and a half millennia of turbulent history. In the last few decades, Cairo has witnessed immense population growth, which has spiraled into a rapid, uncontrolled urban expansion. The city has undergone massive densification, and informal urban extensions have sprung up around its core. Extreme scarcity of space coupled with Arab urban tradition have perforated and molded urban structure and architecture. Negligence and the unique capability of humans to act in the porous network of the fragmented, granular city define a particular condition. Though often considered precarious, precisely this condition creates an outstanding beauty and quality that facilitates the coexistence of millions in close proximity. Cairo Episodes is an attempt to capture this condition.

Lovers' Retreat

Fishpark, Zamalek, Cairo. At the entrance of the park we pay a fee and deliver ourselves to the scrutiny of the guard. Inside, the noise of the city appears muted and a panorama of abundant green opens to us. Here and there, colorfully dressed couples blink through the dense vegetation, disappear into the cavities of an artificial grotto, or shyly sit next to each other on a bench. The park, a remnant of the Khedive's pleasure garden, today is the last resort for lovers of all ages and provenance—a fragile bubble amid an environment that rarely tolerates extramarital contact between men and women.

Urban Refuge

Al-Zahir Baybars Mosque, El-Zaher, Cairo. It was a courageous undertaking to cross the speedy road that separates the old mosque from the neighborhood. Immediately beyond the walls, we find silence in the blank space that remains unnoticed by the rampant metropolis. Massive apartment blocks crawl up the walls and peek inside where microcosms of different habitats silently unfold. Construction workers tinker in a corner, visitors pray in the shade, guard tents are scattered at distant angles, and street dogs doze in the sun. We move cautiously and cherish the forgotten place.

Expanded Shopping

Market Street, El-Gamaleya, Cairo. The night falls, buildings disappear into darkness, shop-fronts light the streets and illuminate the city from within. Seen from above, the scene reveals the transformative power of the market. Facades, furniture, merchandise, people, and vehicles spill out into the street, merging indistinguishably, leaving no spot idle for long: colored lights in motion, engines rattling, and sellers bargaining. We watch this wonderful spectacle of architecture, installation, improvisation, and appropriation in flux from above. Back on the street, the hustle either dazzles us or sends us into a total shopping frenzy.

Bounce Back

Sakakini Square, El-Zaher, Cairo. Having left the crowded metro at Ghamra station, a narrow street leads to a square where everything moves at a slower pace: kids passionately playing soccer in the street, families having a juice at the traveling stands and men smoking in the cafés. El Sakakini Palace, a lavish but crumbling rococo villa in the middle of the square, dominates the scene and reminds us of the grandeur of that area at the end of the nineteenth century. New building blocks in today's dense working-class area proudly adopt the baroque opulence of the palace. Bouncing in and out, the facades create spaces of withdrawal as well as exposure, embodying a principle that is crucial in Arab society in providing quality of life, especially for women.

Living Landscapes

El-Sayeda Zainab, Cairo. Ibn Tulun, one of Cairo's oldest mosques, once indistinguishably merged with the dense mass of buildings of El-Sayeda Zainab, was peeled away from the encroaching urban fabric of the neighborhood in the 1920s. Looking across from the roof of the mosque, we can trace how layers of brick, concrete, mortar, and light structures have accumulated and remodeled the buildings surrounding it many times. The pressing demand for space driving that process is palpable and still continues to defragment the roofscape in front of us. The sound of the buzzing city is dampened; the voice of the muezzin beckons the faithful to prayer.

The Apparent and the Concealed

Invisible Nile Banks, Zamalek, Cairo. Fences, walls, and buildings frame the Nile in many places. Limiting access to club members, class affiliates, or wealthy clientele, they steal the river away from the city. Impressive architecture, with multilayered facades, beautifully animated by the sunlight, tries to compensate for the obstructed view of the Nile. Caught by the glitzy scenery, we almost overlook an inconspicuously fenced site alongside the water. Invited by an unattended gate we find the most beautiful garden on the riverbanks in the midst of the city. Negotiations and a small tip convince the keeper of the mashtal (tree nursery) to share the place with us for a little while.

Living Landscapes

El-Darb El-Ahmar, Cairo . On the slope of Al-Azhar Park, the busy street life is out of sight. Ahead of us a panorama of massive brick masonry, cluttered with the evidence of human life, reveals itself. Clothes dry in the sun. Antennas, chairs, and cushions furnish the rough landscape. Platforms with climbing ladders lead to roof terraces and lonely pigeon houses rise up into the air. On the last floor of a building, a man is setting up his house and garden. Kids are playing hide and seek. Colorful balconies glow through the haze and in every space, crack, or cavity is life.

Urban Territoriality and Strategies

Moving from the Macro- to the Microscale in the Anthropocene
Sofia Dona

Unlike trees or their roots, the rhizome connects any point to any other point, and its traits are not necessarily linked to traits of the same nature; it brings into play very different regimes of signs, and even nonsign states. [...] It has neither beginning nor end, but always a middle (milieu) from which it grows and which it overspills. [...] In contrast to centered (even polycentric) systems with hierarchical modes of communication and preestablished paths, the rhizome is acentered, nonhierarchical, nonsignifying system without a general and without an organizing memory on central automaton, defined solely by a circulation of states. (Deleuze and Guattari 1980, 23)

This chapter analyzes porosity in connection with urban territoriality. Breaking through the hard surfaces of the modern city and moving from the large to the small scale, porosity is introduced in the various patterns of different scales, through design concepts such as the sponge city, constructed wetlands, and decentralized networks of canals, able to activate various architectural elements of the city, reconnect spaces, and improve urban microclimates. Working on the microscale of the city means working with what already exists, not only in terms of buildings but in terms of the already existing network of people connected to those buildings. Finding, for example, new ways to deal with water in the microscale of a building or neighborhood should become something more than bringing solutions to flood emergency, and should move in the direction of building new commons. Examples such as New York's Green Roof movement or Rotterdam's submerged water squares functioning as a network of retention basins are able to function in both formal and informal contexts (Redeker, 205). In the case of urban villages in Shenzen, a structural infiltration is suggested by transforming the concept of constructed wetlands into a decentralized network of canals that infiltrates the water and eventually structures and forms the space of the city. In one of China's fastest-growing megalopolises, the Tai Hu Basin, a new housing model is developed by using the waterfronts of canals as public spaces in attempting to deal with the continuous loss of the geophysical and historical landscape. In the case of Istanbul, where new boundaries of social exclusion are being created by urban renewal development, it is important to reconsider the niches as both valuable and vulnerable spaces in the city, able to bring different social milieus together and carefully preserve them (Bauer, Schaefer, Schoebel and Xie, 226).

Bringing together is a condition that porosity promises, but what does this mean in today's cities that have become large agglomerations and emerging polycentric structures? One of the suggestions is to reinterpret porosity today under the concept of the creation of knowledge in this polycentricity. Looking at connectivity in both the visible world of the city and the immaterial network of infrastructure that supports the exchange of information, one key to creating knowledge is being together and being connected. Translating Benjamin's "true laboratories" of the cafés in Naples into the coworking spaces of today suggests a contemporary concept of porosity redefined in the new urban reality and the polycentric city-regions (Thierstein, 222).

Zooming out from the microscale to the larger scale of defining the city in connection with the relationship between humans, nature, and space, the Anthropocene reminds us that the city as a "machine helping to overcome nature" (Giseke, 200) was an illusion. Claiming to be liberated from the forces of nature, the modern city created the space of the outside, where sewage translated as waste is hidden or camouflaged under the concept of making invisible. This imperceptibility has been spatially translated to the underground of the city or the countryside, and the hygienic city is able to make natural processes invisible. Since those borders have been defined to serve various economies such as the real estate or tourism industries, the time has come to look back to the undefined zones as the valuable ones. Areas like Java that combine a human-made urban fabric with the natural existence of forty-five volcanoes and the consistent threat of eruption, can help us gain a new understanding of nature in contradistinction to the artificially preserved and consumed landscape (Ursprung, 210). While the purified city defined by borders to the outside has come to an end, recognition of the Anthropocene exhorts us to look at the city via concepts such as urban metabolism, the zero landscape and the ergosphere, which are not only able to dissolve the borders between the inside and the outside but also to suggest a different perception of design in connection with its temporal and historical dimensions (Giseke, 200).

Going back to Gilles Deleuze and Félix Guattari, the philosophical concept of rhizome moves porosity from a metaphoric to a physical dimension. Either as a body of water that erodes what is in its way, or a ginger root that expands, resisting the organizational structure of the root-tree system, rhizomatic theory understands multiplicities rather than a hierarchical conception of knowledge. Under this concept, rethinking porosity from the perspective of urban territoriality opens up directions of finding new states of equilibrium between disturbances and infiltrations, repeatedly establishing a new but unpredictable smooth space. As Wendy Brown (2015) argues, we are living in times where neoliberalism extends into every sphere, even the ones that have never been connected to economic factors before (education, statecraft, culture), taking over all forms of human activity and transforming people into market actors. If the holes or cracks of the porous urban fabric open up to any kind of invasion, there is an urgent need to create spatial mechanisms of complexity and disfunctionality able to reproduce themselves in random ways and in every possible direction.

References:
Brown, W. 2015. *Undoing the Demos: Neoliberalism's Stealth Revolution.* New York. | Deleuze, G., and F. Guattari. 1980. *A Thousand Plateaus.* Translated by B. Massumi. London, 2004.

The City in the Anthropocene—Multiple Porosities
Undine Giseke

The Anthropocene, briefly put, views human activities as comparable to geological forces in the changes they effect in the Earth's systems. The emergence of agriculture and cities is undoubtedly closely linked with the profound planetary transformation in the Anthropocene (Renn 2015, 199). These processes throw a new light on the assumed separability of nature and culture and—as a consequence—on the concept of the European city. In his statements on the culture of the (European) city, Siebel emphasizes that "the city [...] [begins] as an act of liberation from the forces of nature. Urban life only becomes possible when the agricultural population produces more than it needs to survive." (Siebel 2015, 30) He underlines that the original term *culture*, coming from agriculture and derived from *cultivate*, was "expanded in the second half of the eighteenth century [...] to include everything that humans created in the process of emancipation from nature. [...] The city thereby becomes the epitome of culture." (Ibid., 29)

However, with the awareness of the Anthropocene, this notion begins to totter: "Human beings, who for a long time saw themselves as part of a process of civilization whose goal was to use the earth, nature, simply as a resource suddenly again realize that they are part of larger natural processes. The processes of freeing themselves from nature [...] were clearly in part an illusion." Humans "must realize that they are only part of a complex circulation of materials and energy" (Renn and Scherer 2015, 12–13).

The modern dream of the city as a machine helping to overcome nature seems to fade away. It had a strong, promise-filled period in the nineteenth century: modern urban development promoted the hygienic city and effected a consistent making-invisible of natural processes and their accompanying urban material flows, making this the norm. Gandy (2004) and Bernhardt (2005) explain, for example, how since the nineteenth century water was banished underground and inside houses and thus increasingly vanished from the cityscape. Hauser (1992) and Frank (2004) also refer to the development of urban sewer systems to illustrate how at this time sewage became categorized as waste, while the civilization and cultivation of the city progressed simultaneously in response to the middle-class need for cleanliness, order, and beauty and the "purification of nature" through industrial-technological means (Hauser 1992, 302). This touches not only on water but also on many urban metabolic processes.

Windmüller, for example, investigates the spatial distribution of waste. She shows that the areas reserved for waste disposal tend to be marginalized and stigmatized, and even subject to the paradoxical phenomenon of disappearance through exposure, when mountains of rubbish are dumped into the landscape over a long period of time and camouflaged through recultivation (Windmüller 2004, 224 and 231). Pothukuchi and Kaufmann identify first and foremost urban planners' blindness to the city food supply, which relies on the countryside as the component for production and the market for distribution (Pothukuchi and Kaufmann 1999).

The concept of the hygienic city became a driver to keep bodily functions and the city's metabolism under control. Adherence to the principles of rationality, reason, and morality was supposed to ensure bodily soundness, cleanliness, and health. Along with that, these functions were spatially relocated and rendered invisible. This making-invisible was accompanied by the establishment of infrastructure and control systems and the creation of new "cultural borders" (Hauser 1992). This was an extremely far-reaching process: "The civilization of the city, or *Kultivierung* as it is known in German, is the expulsion from the city of what today we still associate with the countryside. And that is—besides agriculture, the great vegetable gardens, the idyllic and bucolic—the dirt, the decay, the rot, the stink, the first processing of organic material. The systematic purification of the city means the establishment of new city limits, the border between the cultured area of industrial society and that which it evacuates to an Outside of its culture in a controlled manner" (Ibid., 294).

This process of making imperceptible was generated architecturally and technically and was tied to particular places, topographies, and spatial systems. In addition to the topos of the outside as the space far from the city that we connect with the countryside and agriculture, Susanne Frank emphasizes in her work the significance of the underground within these processes. Referring to Victor Hugo's novel *Les Misérables*, she shows that "mines, quarries, trenches, catacombs and sewage canals [...] [formed] *one great den of evil* from which the sewer rose." The latter represented for Hugo "the dark, fathomless, untamed belly and night of the surface civilization" (Frank 2004, 169).

Not only in Hugo's time did the sewer resist society's planning by threatening to overflow and besmirch the city with its "brazen sludge" (Ibid., 170). The sewer systems of today's large cities display an equal brazenness at a time of increasing severe precipitation events driven by climate change. The underground thus again interrupts the order that was established with the introduction of the sewer system in model cities like Paris and Berlin.

The Anthropocene discourse today questions the reasonableness of separating technological, cultural, and natural systems, and with it also the systems of knowledge that have supported this separation until now (Renn and Scherer 2015). The perception of the relationship between humans, nature, and space is radically transforming. The shine is fading from the ideal of the hygienic city as a pure technical solution, which in the past was a driver for the rendering invisible of material urban processes. Rather the perspectives are beginning to reverse. Questions are asked, research is conducted, visibility and transparency are demanded as to how the city is supplied, what goes in and what comes out, how the urban and the natural systems interact. This change in perception is not unambiguous, yet it clearly pursues a further expansion of the principles of rationality, mechanization, and control. The greatly elevated global metabolism and the rapidly growing demand for resources of a globally industrializing and urbanizing society make a more efficient use of urban resources indispensable. Digital technologies provide the necessary technological requirements. On the other hand, however, positions also emerge that are more fundamental in dissolving old categorical (and spatial) boundaries and question the drive to decouple modernity, city, and nature and therewith social and societal processes. Thus Swyngedouw (2006), for example, contrasts this understanding with the concept of the city as a nature-culture hybrid or cyborg and defines the city explicitly as the spatial manifestation of a local metabolic process.

In this context, it makes sense to take a brief look at the concepts of urban metabolism. One area dealing with urban metabolism is, of course, urban design. Its forerunner was the Japanese architectural movement of the 1960s, which linked the building of architectonic megastructures with biological growth. At about the same time the concept found its way into scientific and urban-planning contexts. Since then, it has evolved and diversified. Wolman (1965) focused predominantly on the model-based quantification of input and output flows in urban systems. Giradet (1990), an early pioneer of industrial ecology, placed the emphasis on the circulatory processes within the city and urban region. At the beginning of the twenty-first century, attention is directed more to how and where the material flows in the city are being transformed (Zhang 2013). Gandy (2004) and Swyngedouw (2006) view the urban metabolism more comprehensively from the perspective of political ecology. For them, it is not a matter of biological, technological, or modernistic concepts or of a metabolic system that exists independently of the other basic parameters of the city and its historical reality. The concrete design and organization of material flows then is a part of the city as a politically negotiated, socioecological process tied to a specific spatial context. Urban metabolism in this sense represents the city neither as a biological organism nor as a cybernetic system or efficiently run machine, but rather as specific socionatural assemblages. Emphasized here are the ways in which social and natural systems interact and how these interactions manifest themselves in space.

Consequently, the approaches taken to urban metabolism differ. They all pay attention to flows and exchange processes, and in so doing quite often overstep the boundaries of spatial categories. In the light of the Anthropocene, it will be useful to take a closer look at the ways the different approaches conceive of these assemblages. Not all, however, overcome the culture-nature dualism.

Even so, the once-clear categories of inside and outside are beginning to break apart. Inside formerly was city and culture, while outside was countryside, landscape, and nature. With these categories came a clear division of labor between production and reproduction. Yet, the construction of an outside that incorporates everything the city wants to dispose of and that provides everything the city needs, no longer holds. Flows, connections, and assemblages replace the concept of borders; and there is a growing interest in the type of connection, its components, its spatial expression, and the social and natural processes related to it. These shifts have a far-reaching influence not only on our culturally shaped perceptions of cities, nature, bodies, countryside and landscape, and their corresponding images but also on design approaches.

The dissolution of boundaries is found in the concept of the zero landscape as formulated by Morton. Morton urges us to stop viewing the landscape from a perspective that originated in Petrarch's climb of Mont Ventoux in the year 1336. According to Morton, the modern Western perception of the landscape is still based on the separation of subject and object, like the separation of the first- and third-person perspectives. Morton suggests "instead [to] seek out a zero-person perspective" (Morton 2011, 81). In his eyes, it is a matter of overcoming the aesthetic distance in favor of being "in the object." Pursuing this train of thought further, it ends up in questioning the concept of an external nature.

What form do spaces take when instead of representing distance they represent a new intimacy, a being-in-the-object, such as Morton puts forward with his concept of the zero landscape? What do the spatial concepts of assemblages look like, or the concepts of metabolic spaces? There are a number of examples from research as well as expert and social praxis, which express the changed spatial relationships and novel assemblages of spatial systems, material flows, and objects.

In 2014 the architecture biennale *Urban by Nature* in Rotterdam showed a series of projects making significant contributions to spatial design for the organization of urban material flows. The Rotterdam region itself became a laboratory (Brugmans and Strien 2014). Through the German research on future megacities, novel spatial, functional, and cultural assemblages between the urban and rural spheres were highlighted via a multiscale project for Casablanca's urban region—encompassing approaches from smaller neighborhoods to the entire region (Giseke et al. 2015). Further, increased usage of the concept of territories reflects an overcoming of previous spatial boundaries between city and countryside, reinforced by design strategies (see, for example, Schröder et al. 2016).

The numerous civic and social projects focused on food, such as urban gardening and regional food boards, spotlight the breakup of cultural borders and make urban food systems the subject of design.

On the urban scale, the city of Munich made urban metabolic processes, along with densification and deceleration, one of the three focal points in their long-term public open space development planning (Landeshauptstadt München 2015). And in the spring of 2017 the first residents of Hamburg's model district Jenfelder Au acquired a building featuring a novel drainage and energy system. Its innovation consists in its treatment of partial flows: black, gray, and rainwater drain separately, and are conserved on site, prepared, and partially used locally for the building's energy or water supply (Giese and Londong 2015). The WC, which received so much enthusiasm in the nineteenth century for magically making things disappear, is here suddenly no longer the place from which wastewater is invisibly sent out to a treatment plant far away out there.

Many of the projects mentioned follow a systemic approach. They link together a number of spaces, places, actors, and processes thus overcoming the focus on only one scale. Systemic design guides the connections between the various components and an elastic switching between scales. Nevertheless, many questions still remain: how can one sensually (and spatially) experience this simultaneity of scales beyond apps and social media? What knowledge is required for this?

The dynamics of the Anthropocene urge us to question the existing knowledge. Based on traditional classifications and separations between culture, nature, technology, humans, and nonhumans, it is too limited to tackle these challenges (Renn and Scherer 2015). Not least, the Anthropocene requires a different understanding of temporal dimensions. It brings the deep time of geochronological epochs to the perception, conception, and design of spaces and thus forces us to place design solutions in a larger temporal and historical context. Considering the enormous speed of global urbanization, however, this seems more than paradoxical. How, therefore, can not only spatial but also temporal scales overlap in the porous city of the Anthropocene? How can this take effect? Following Renn (2017), the concept of the ergosphere entails a "rule of invasive thinking." This says that we can use our cooperatively developed knowledge even in seemingly desperate situations to create change if we are familiar with its local possibilities for adaptation. So—question, explore, research, feel, design, cooperate, negotiate, and, finally, build to further shape the metabolic city.

References:
Bernhardt, C. 2005. "Die Vertreibung des Wassers aus der Stadt und der Planung," in *Geschichte der Planung des öffentlichen Raums*, edited by C. Bernhardt, G. Fehl, G. Kuhn, and U. von Petz, 71–83. Dortmunder Beiträge zur Raumplanung 122. Dortmund. | Brugmans, G., and J. Strien, eds. 2014. *IABR–2014 Urban by Nature: Catalogue of the 6th International Architecture Biennale Rotterdam*. Rotterdam. | Frank, S. 2004. "Die Disziplinierung der weiblichen Körper: Kanalisation und Prostitution in der Großstadtentwicklung des 19. Jahrhunderts," in *Vernunft—Entwicklung—Leben: Schlüsselbegriffe der Moderne*, edited by U. Bröckling, S. Kaufmann, and A. Paul, 167–83. Munich. | Gandy, M. 2004. "Rethinking Urban Metabolism: Water, Space and the Modern City," *City* 8, no. 3: 363–79. | Giese, T., and J. Londong, eds. 2015. *Kopplung von regenerativer Energie gewinnung mit innovativer Stadtentwässerung: Syntheseberichte zum Forschungsprojekt KREIS*. Schriften reihe des Bauhaus-Instituts für zukunftsweisende Infrastruktursysteme 30. Berlin. | Girardet, H. 1990. "The Metabolism of Cities," in *The Living City: Towards a Sustainable Future*, edited by D. Cadman and G. Payne, 170–80. London. | Giseke, U., et al., eds. 2015. *Urban Agriculture for Growing City Regions: Connecting Urban-Rural Spheres in Casablanca*. Abingdon. | Giseke, U., R. Keller, J. Rekittke, A. Stokman, and C. Werthmann. 2017. "Draußen," in *Draußen/Out There: Landschaftsarchitektur auf globalem Terrain*, edited by A. Lepik, 8–12. Exhibition catalogue, Pinakothek der Moderne, Munich. Berlin. | Hauser, S. 1992. "Reinlichkeit, Ordnung und Schönheit: Zur Diskussion über Kanalisation im 19. Jahrhundert," *Die alte Start* 19, no. 4: 292–312. | Landeshauptstadt München. 2015. "Konzeptgutachten Freiraum München 2030," https://www.muenchen.de/rathaus/dam/jcr:38cecb80-7c6a-46dc-a525-3669bb8b70e6/FRM2030_WEB.pdf. | Morton, T. 2011. "Zero Landscapes in den Zeiten der Hyperobjekte," *Grazer Architektur Magazin*, no. 7: 79–87. | Pothukuchi, K., and J. L. Kaufmann, J. L. 1999. "The Food System: A Stranger to the Planning Field," *Journal of the American Planning Association* 66, no. 2: 113–24. | Renn, J. 2015. "Was wir von Kuschim über die Evolution des

Wissens und die Ursprünge des Anthropozäns lernen können," in Renn and Scherer 2015, 184–209. | Renn, J. 2017. "On the Construction Sites of the Anthropocene," in *Out There: Landscape Architecture on the Global Terrain*, edited by A. Lepik, 16–19. Berlin. | Renn, J., and B. Scherer, eds. 2015. *Das Anthropozän: Zum Stand der Dinge.* Berlin. | Schröder, J., et al., eds. 2016. Territories: Rural-Urban Strategies. Berlin. | Siebel, W. 2015. *Die Kultur der Stadt.* Berlin. | Swyngedouw, E. 2006. "Metabolic Urbanization: The Making of Cyborg Cities," in *In the Nature of Cities: Urban Political Ecology and the Politics of Urban Metabolism*, edited by N. Heynen, M. Kaika, and E. Swyngedouw, 20–39. Abingdon. | Windmüller, S. 2004. *Die Kehrseite der Dinge: Müll, Abfall, Wegwerfen als kulturwissenschaftliches Phänomen.* Europäische Ethnologie 2. Münster. | Wolman, A. 1965. "The Metabolism of Cities," *Scientific American* 213, no. 3: 179–90. | Zhang, Y. 2013. "Urban Metabolism: A Review of Research Methodologies," *Environmental Pollution* 178: 463–73.

A New Water Metabolism: Porosity and Decentralization
Cornelia Redeker

We are surrounded by hard surfaces. Although the ideal modern city is embedded in green, the predominant materials of our urban environment remain concrete, asphalt, and brick. Reintroducing productive and regenerative landscapes can make our cities livable as our previous parks and gardens have only done to a certain extent. Increasing the porosity of our cities today by urgently needed green buffers can improve urban microclimates, mitigate flood impacts, create habitat, reduce energy consumption, and reintroduce a new layer of productivity while breaking with the existing concept of scale.

As we are confronted with new water-related urgencies as diverse as increasingly frequent flash floods, water scarcity, and substandard water quality, we are not only called to develop new urban models, but also to retrofit existing predominantly mixed-sewer systems that clearly do not accommodate current extreme weather frequencies and do not provide infrastructure for the predominantly off-grid informal urban realm. The ongoing paradigm change entails a shift from hard, static, and defensive structures toward mitigating green interventions which add a new buffer, a new permissiveness and softness to our networks of subsurface pipes, canals, dikes, and impermeable surfaces.

Interestingly, retaining water by means of green-blue infrastructure can provide benefits for both water excess and water scarcity. In this context the small-scale becomes an excellent resource for generating ecosystemic change accumulatively. In consequence, it also demands a new awareness of how to use not only resources, but also existing and new infrastructural systems with a return to more individual responsibility. The current fatberg clogging of London's outdated sewer system illustrates both all too vividly: our ignorance as users and a sewer system unable to accommodate change. Beyond consistently valid financial incentives to enable behavioral change, a new form of stewardship seems to be part of the equation to transform our infrastructure to become more interactive (Giseke 2017).

Many landscape architects and urban designers are currently involved in finding new, more tangible approaches to handling water on the building and neighborhood scale which not only mitigate the impacts of given urgencies, but which also create a new commons with the call for stewardship (Helfrich and Haas 2009). Many of these solutions are low-tech, low-cost, and low-maintenance and provide robust and, in contrast to previous systems, accessible infrastructure which is more than just that. They offer green urban spaces that may store and/or filter water, reduce dust, and produce all kinds of by-products such as food, fodder, building material, etc.

Inspiring examples are evolving in places where governments have realized that climate change needs to be embraced as a driver for new forms of development instead of as a mere threat. How we adapt this approach to most global urban development, which catapults us into the predominantly informal context whose inhabitants are also the most fragile group, remains to be defined. The intuitiveness and technical simplicity of green-blue infrastructure allows us to focus on the real challenge—how to communicate it. Increasing porosity to accommodate both excess and scarce water on site, also for filtration and thus for further use, offers a multitude of benefits but calls for new models of governance, knowledge exchange, and training to enable a return to a lost, sustainable, vernacular practice to arise in places most in need.

Water Urgencies—Between Too Much and Not (Good) Enough

With the UN sustainable development goals (SDGs) set for 2030 we still have a long way to go as facts and figures for the water and sanitation sector illustrate:

- 2.6 billion people have gained access to improved drinking water sources since 1990, but 663 million people are still without.
- At least 1.8 billion people globally use a source of drinking water that is fecally contaminated.
- Between 1990 and 2015, the proportion of the global population using an improved drinking water source has increased from 76 percent to 91 percent.
- But water scarcity affects more than 40 percent of the global population, and this figure is predicted to rise. More than 1.7 billion people are currently living in river basins where water use exceeds recharge.
- 2.4 billion people lack access to basic sanitation services, such as toilets or latrines.
- More than 80 percent of wastewater resulting from human activities is discharged into rivers or sea without any pollution treatment.
- Each day, nearly 1,000 children die due to preventable water- and sanitation-related diarrhoeal diseases.
- Hydropower is the most important and widely used renewable source of energy and, as of 2011, represented 16 percent of total electricity production worldwide.
- Approximately 70 percent of all water extracted from rivers, lakes, and aquifers is used for irrigation.
- Floods and other water-related disasters account for 70 percent of all deaths related to natural disasters. (United Nations 2017)

Formal vs. Informal Context

Our formal cities' subsurface water infrastructure is not necessarily laid out for change. This applies for medium- to long-term fluctuations in population numbers and density as well as acute peaks in the system during increasingly frequent heavy rains and flash floods as well as dry periods. At the same time many highly urbanized informal areas are to some degree off-grid and are facing existential struggles regarding water availability and quality. Both systems allow wastewater to mix with fresh water supply, putting the habitat and the food cycle at risk. Large parts of rural Egypt, for example, are still without improved sanitation—15–20 percent according to UNICEF estimates. Open septic tanks serve as sewage containers. These are then pumped empty with sludge being dumped in the desert, or even worse, into the Nile or onto the fields without further treatment. This system allows for wastewater to eventually enter our food cycle resulting in severe, often fatal health implications. With increasing informal urbanization the septic tanks are then built on, leading to structural instability of the buildings. Again, we are discussing largely invisible infrastructure, a subsurface system separate from the piping on the exterior of the facade and the shaft lid. Both formal and informal contexts call for a new integration of handling water storage and treatment on site. By taking an incremental and, ideally, incentivizing approach, we move away from large-scale new building projects, not only to avoid questions of ownership, consensus, and land availability on the communal scale, but to work with what is already there and with the people are who are already there: the dwellers, building owners, the company using the building, etc.

While climate change adaptation to cope with excess water in the visible urban realm seems to have become part of urban agendas in most of the world—with inspiring examples in Australia, Europe, China, Japan, and the US—recent and projected events reveal the race against our lack of preparedness when facing the complexities of extreme weather events. According to the reinsurer Munich Re, weather-related disasters are increasing. The number of weather-related disasters increased from 200 in 1980 to 600 in 2016. The World Heath Organisation (WHO) predicts a 6 percent increase of annual costs due to hurricanes. Flood damage in Europe is expected to increase five-fold by 2050. The UN estimates that storms and floods caused $1.75 trillion in damage over a period of twenty years until 2015 (Economist 2017, 9).

Water Scarcity—The Nile Basin

For many countries that will be affected existentially by water scarcity, awareness-building, strategic development, and the implementation of water harvesting and recycling plants are still missing. Damaging and uncontrolled discharge into deteriorating and diminishing water bodies, leakage, and lack of control, but also a lack of geopolitical coordination, define current realities for Nile basin countries that are still anticipating according strategies. In the meantime global corporations are privatizing the water sector. The Nile River provides the primary source of drinking water for almost 500 million people, around 40 percent of Africa's population (Akol et al. 2016). In addition to being severely threatened by the impacts of climate change, the river is about to get its second large hydro structure, the Grand Renaissance Dam in Ethiopia, and this without resolved coordination of water usage with the other Nile basin countries. Since the 1960s the Aswan High Dam in Egypt has already fully transformed the ecosystem of the Nile Valley and Delta, turning the once most prosperous agricultural nation in the world into one largely reliant on food imports. The Renaissance Dam will reduce the flow during its filling phase of around 2–5 years and produce evaporative losses once filled.There have also been reports of extended desert reclamation projects based on irrigation which may make further demands on the dam water. This supraregional reality is coupled with sea level rise and saltwater intrusion into diminishing aquifers that are further at risk due to planned large-scale desalination plants along the Mediterranean coast, which will require large quantities of brine to be pumped into the subsurface, thus eventually further polluting scarce groundwater. The effect of severe population increase means that the availability of drinking water for Egypt, most of which comes from the Nile, will decrease from 1000 m³ of fresh water in 2005 to less than 600 m³ per year per capita in 2025. Drinking water supply in arid regions with no rainfall could to some extent be provided if the water from increasingly frequent flash floods was harvested regionally. A study by TU Berlin El Gouna has shown that if the rainwater from the flash floods in the surrounding wadis of Hurgada on the Red Sea was collected, it would provide enough water to supply the city for a year. On a smaller scale, evaporation techniques may provide a viable water source. Low-tech, self-build solutions exist, such as the warka water tower with pilot projects in Ethiopia, which claims to harvest 50–100 liters per day, potentially enough to support a family. Until now, evaporative techniques have found limited implementation.

Buffering Flash Floods

Water storage during peak events can be partially accommodated in the urban fabric as new, highly diverse and context-driven approaches show. According to Climate Research at Columbia University (NPR 2016), New York's green roof movement has calculated that the capacity of roofs to function as a sponge, if applied on the scale of the city, could lead to storage of around 38 million cubic meters of runoff a year. At the same time, green roofs contribute to thermal comfort, reduce energy costs, and provide much-needed habitat while offering new urban gardens for the building's users. Rotterdam, simultaneously threatened by river floods and storm surges, has implemented submerged water squares to contain rainwater. Although the city is below sea level, the water squares work with a system of submerged public squares that become storage basins during heavy rainfalls. This network of retention basins has been in place since 2013, and we find similar approaches recently applied on a large scale in Copenhagen. Retaining water on site until the drainage system has regained capacity, creating cloudburst boulevards which offer emergency routes while large sections of the street are used to direct water to open water bodies during heavy rains, and expanding retention zones, has become the city's main strategy for coping with extreme events. Predictions of sea level rises and increases in the frequency of extreme rainfalls—where in 2011 and 2014 the actual frequency of extreme rainfalls, as well as prolonged dry periods, overturned statistical predictions of them as 100-year events—have led the city to reevaluate its approach. Large parks are being developed as storage basins while being used as sports fields during dry times. Connective gardens allow water to move from this central infrastructure to smaller gardens as it is filtered along the way. These new approaches also prove to be financially more sound. While the city expects to provide 1300 new jobs with these measures, the actual costs are expected to halve those of conventional gray infrastructure (Cathcart-Keays 2016). Costs are shared between the municipal budget and the inhabitants via their utility charges. Something that is also regarded as community involvement stands at the base of these projects. Tåsinge Plads, a square in Copenhagen's Saint Kjeld district, planned as the city's first climate-resilient neighborhood, is part of the city's plan to cope with the effects of climate change. It is one of 300 surface-based solutions to be implemented over the next twenty years. During heavy rains, the swale flowerbeds fill with water and suspend draining until the storm runoff subsides. Upside-down umbrellas harvest rainwater to later irrigate the plants, while storm water is directed into large underground water-storage tanks above a trampoline playground used to pump water through the pipes below.

Urban Regeneration through Constructed Wetlands

Plant-based water treatment through constructed wetlands increasingly finds application on multiple scales. These systems may offer viable solutions to the world's inability to provide sewage treatment comprehensively (Hoffmann 2014). Small- and medium-scale constructed wetland projects have been implemented and are under way around the world. Examples are a project to upgrade the highly polluted Baima Canal in Fozou, China, using a so-called Canal Restoration Device that utilizes a floating walkway planted with more than 12,000 native plants as a way of biologically treating the waste for the entire neighborhood; and in the free state of Friland, Denmark, a project where a restaurant together with Aarhus University is exploring the possibilities of certifying the irrigation of its greenhouse crops with its own wastewater treated by sand filtration and the capillary root system of the plants. In Samaha village near Mansoura in Egypt, a constructed wetland water-cleansing plant for a village of 10,000 inhabitants has been implemented, retrofitting its existing septic tank system. It filters domestic wastewater before discharging it to a private drain for irrigation (Eid 2014). In addition, the constructed wetland is planted with reeds and papyrus. The papyrus is harvested regularly and then cut and pressed to produce papyrus paper on site. As well as this, the project is experimenting with shredded car tires to replace the gravel bed to increase efficiency. Similar water-cleansing plants can be found in the Egyptian cities Ismailia, Beni Suef, and Fayoum and look likely to be repeated elsewhere as they offer low-cost, low-tech and low-maintenance solutions to the lack of sanitation in multiple contexts. So far the potential of constructed wetlands to become part of landscape designs has mainly been explored in China, where a number of regenerative parks have transformed former brownfields. These now provide new urban habitats and green public spaces. This may become the strategy for all blue-green infrastructure: to overcome the divide between a merely aesthetic perception of landscape and the rediscovery of its productive capacity—an approach that may also offer strategies to overcome the social divide.

Knowledge—Local Micromanagement, Expert Control, and "Learning from"

Strategies toward increasing urban resilience today are expert-led, research-based and are framed by the urban realm as a laboratory condition: All the referenced projects involve universities. For societies with high educational levels this may also enable new formats of participation. For other parts of the world struggling not only with illiteracy, but with the manifestation of a new vernacular in the informal, where any environmental knowledge has been lost in the course of modernization, and a formal context where a lack of willingness to embrace a sustainable practice prevails against all informed alternatives this remains a challenge. In both these cases, development is framed by the prevailing econometrics without any signs of awareness of detrimental consequences and by nostalgic belief in the necessity of economic growth as a prerequisite to addressing environmental urgencies. Not only do we need to continue to invest in awareness building, education, and training on the ground, but governments and municipalities also need to expand their position to include not only participation, but trial and error at a strategic level. Currently, these important links between local micromanagement and expert control and strategic "learning from" are still missing in the majority of the world. The few progressive countries that enable greater public involvement and include strategic feedback loops are for the most part wealthy Western countries. How comparable models in regard to much-needed societal porosity can be transferred to different socio-cultural contexts remains to be seen, but proves crucial when aiming to enable mitigation starting from the household and the neighborhood scale. Vocational training is a crucial layer in achieving these goals.

References:
Abdel-Gawad, Sh. 2007. "Actualizing the Right to Water: An Egyptian Perspective for an Action Plan," *International Journal of Water Resources Development*, vol. 23, 341–354, accessed April 30, 2012, https://doi.org/10.1080/07900620601181788. | Akol, P. J., et al. 2016. "Nile Basin Resources Atlas: Nile Basin," *Nile Information System*, accessed September 1, 2017, http://nileis.nilebasin.org/content/nile-basin-water-resources-atlas. | Cathcart-Keays, A. 2016. "Why Copenhagen Is Building Parks That Can Turn into Ponds," *Citiscope*, accessed September 28, 2017, http://citiscope.org/story/2016/why-copenhagen-building-parks-can-turn-ponds. | Economist. 2017. "Natural Disasters: How to Cope with Floods," *The Economist*, September 2–8, 2017. Eid, M. A. 2014. "Hydraulic Study of Drainage System 'Constructed Subsurface Wetlands,'" PhD diss., Mansoura University, Mansoura. | Giseke, U. 2017. "Productive Landscapes as Urban Infrastructure," presentation given at *Landscaping Egypt: Productive—Aesthetic* conference, German University in Cairo, May 5–6, 2017. | Helfrich, S., and J. Haas. 2009. "The Commons: A New Narrative for Our Times," *Global Commons Trust*, accessed January 5, 2018, http://commonstrust.global-negotiations.org/resources/Helfrich%20and%20Haas%20The_Commons_A_New_Narrative_for_Our_Times.pdf. | Hoffmann, S. 2014. *Technology Review of Constructed Wetlands*. Eschborn. | Ministry of Health and Population, Egypt. 2014. *Egypt Demographic And Health Survey* 2014, accessed September 1, 2017, https://www.unicef.org/egypt/wes.html. | NPR. 2016. "Do Cities Need More Green Roofs?" accessed September 1, 2017, https://youtu.be/FlJoBhLnqko. | United Nations. 2017. "Goal 6: Ensure access to water and sanitation for all," accessed October 15, 2017, http://www.un.org/sustainabledevelopment/water-and-sanitation/.

Project references:
Water Squares Rotterdam: http://www.urbanisten.nl/wp/?portfolio=waterplein-benthemplein | Regenerative Parks in China: https://landarchs.com/10-projects-that-show-how-turenscape-is-leading-the-way-in-ecological-design/ | Bayma Canal restoration, Fozou, China: expeditiongowanus.wordpress.com; http://toddecological.com/files/case-studies/china.pdf

Holes in the Future City: Java's Volcanoes
Philip Ursprung

With a population of 140 million in an area three times the size of Switzerland, the island of Java in the center of the Indonesian archipelago is one of the most densely populated areas and one of the fastest-growing economies of the world.* For an inquiry into urban phenomena, it is a special case. In fact, we can treat Java as the prototype of the future city. In addition to the metropolitan area of Jakarta and Bandung with forty million inhabitants, and the Surabaya area in the East with almost six million inhabitants, the island is covered by an urban fabric that can be defined as desakota, a juxtaposition of urban and agricultural dwelling (from Indonesian *desa*: village, and *kota*: city) (McGee 1991). This man-made fabric is interrupted by the island's forty-five volcanoes. A recent image from a NASA satellite shows the island of Java by night. The urban network that covers most of Java, and even spills beyond the contours of the island to the sea with its heavy shipping traffic, is interrupted by a chain of black holes—the areas left empty around the cones of the volcanoes. Geologists observe them carefully as the most active part in the Pacific Ring of Fire, because they mark the zone where three tectonic plates collide. But from the perspective of urbanism, they are quiet zones; they form a *terrain vague* in the midst of the rapidly densifying urban fabric, an area which is not cultivated and colonized. They allow us to locate the contours of what is not city.

The research project "Tourism and Cultural Heritage: A Case Study on the Explorer Franz Junghuhn," which I codirect with Alexander Lehnerer at Future Cities Laboratory in Singapore, aims to find new concepts and means of representation that can help revise and refine current research on urbanization. We work together with the artists Armin Linke, Bas Princen, and U5, an artist collective, as well as with the volcanologist Clive Oppenheimer, the designer Adrianne Joergensen, and the architect and historian Sebastian Linsin. The rule we have given ourselves is to follow the footsteps of the nineteenth century explorer Franz Junghuhn, who lived in Java between the 1830s and the 1860s. Junghuhn was both a celebrated botanist and one of the foremost volcanologists of his time, and is sometimes referred to as the "Humboldt of Java" (Goethe-Institut Jakarta 2009, Sternagel 2011). Junghuhn was not only the first to systematically explore the island's vegetation and volcanoes, he also produced the most accurate map of Java for that time. Instead of mapping the island's contours, as earlier British cartographers such as Stamford Raffles had done, he mapped it from within, from the viewpoint of its volcanoes. In addition to the map, he also published an elevation of the island. We were particularly struck by Junghuhn's elevation, with its many volcanoes in a row, because it seems to prefigure the skyline of a metropolis. It seems both to prefigure the modern metropolis with its skyscrapers and point to something else which is yet to come and which is not entirely man-made. We therefore decided to retrace Junghuhn's path and climb seventeen volcanoes in a series of expeditions.

Why are we doing this, and what is its relation to architecture, we are sometimes asked. One of the challenges that theoreticians face when reflecting on urbanization is the issue of concepts and the means of representation. They address immensely complex phenomena with only a handful of concepts and a rather narrow range of means of representation. For instance, the terms *built environment* and *urban* are commonly used as synonyms. The book *The Endless City* (Burdett and Sudjic 2007) exemplifies the continuing focus on the metropolitan city. The back cover of the book gives us the narrative of the growth of urbanization—"Ten percent of the world's population lived in cities in 1900, 50 percent live in cities in 2007, and 75 percent will be living in cities in 2050"—a narrative that we hear on every occasion. In short, the grand narrative of the urban has replaced the grand narrative of progress that dominated

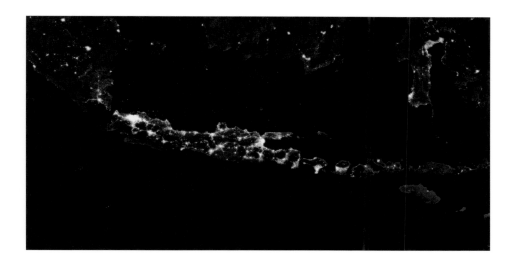

twentieth-century thought. Simultaneously, nature has reentered the picture. With its positive connotations, nature takes the form of sublime landscapes and beautiful places for retreat and recuperation.
With its negative connotations, nature takes the form of climate change and natural catastrophes such
as floods or desertification. Positively or negatively connoted, nature is assimilated to anthropogenic
phenomena, most notably as part of the concept of the man-made geological area created by the process
of industrialization—the Anthropocene.

    The question, however, is still open as to what is to be understood as urban or nature. I would
argue that neither the urban nor nature is appropriate anymore as an analytical term within architectural discourse. Each has lost its grip as an instrument of analysis, so to speak. One reason is that politics,
real estate and the tourism industry—one of the largest sectors of today's economy—have seized these
terms and instrumentalized them for their own purposes. Politics, real estate and the tourism industry
refine, if you like, the raw products of the urban into a "city"—in other words, into a controlled and
museum-like context that promises entertainment and offers optimum conditions for consumption.
The same raw material of the urban can also be marked as suburb, agglomeration, or informal housing
in order to be prepared and made available for improvement or gentrification. In parallel, the raw material of nature is domesticated as "landscape," made ready for preservation and for consumption—as
exemplified by the holiday island, the resort, or the natural park. Or it is marked as soiled, damaged, and
contaminated and as such is then primed for reclamation and development. Since the 1970s the most
influential example of assigning meaning in this way—and, naturally, also of increasing value—is
UNESCO's award of the World Cultural Heritage status to a site, be it urban or natural, material or
immaterial.

    Both the real estate and tourism industries and politics tend to present the urban and the rural as
divided, as a duality. The reason for this, I would argue, lies in the fact that the border between these
zones, the site of exposure of one to the other, is particularly valuable. A house in the countryside or a
sea-view flat is sought after and expensive. A nature reserve, a holiday resort, or a recreational island are
increased in value if they are easily accessed, that is, the nearer they are located to a metropolis or an

international airport. A wide-open view to the open sea, the untouched nature, or a skyline, in other words the unobstructed view of resources, raises a property's value. The more a city can offer borders of this kind, the more attractive it is in real estate terms. Accordingly, our appetite for new borders is becoming insatiable; for borders with a view of the other, independent of whether it is a natural or an industrial landscape, as in the case of the New York High Line, where, transformed into a park, the disused raised railway line has become a magnet for investment.

Miniature Theory

The notion of porosity that Sophie Wolfrum brings into play offers alternatives to the dualistic and teleological optic that prevails. It is well suited to the topic of the volcano that we are focusing on. I therefore propose to use the concept of porosity in an elastic way, both concrete and metaphorical, in the sense indicated by Mieke Bal in her book *Travelling Concepts in the Humanities: A Rough Guide.* Her definition of concepts as "miniature theories" can readily be transferred to our own research on urbanism and architecture: "Concepts are the tools of intersubjectivity: they facilitate discussion on the basis of a common language. Generally, they can be thought of as abstract representations of an object. But, like all representations, they are neither simple nor adequate in themselves. They distort, unfix, and inflect the object. To say something of an image, metaphor, story, or what have you—that is, to use concepts to label something—is not a very useful act. Nor can the language of equation—'is'—hide the interpretative choices being made. In fact, concepts are, or rather do, much more. If well thought through, they offer miniature theories, and in that guise, help in the analysis of objects, situations, states, and other theories." (Bal 2002, 22)

Porosity defines the amount of empty space in a solid environment. It is used in daily life and it is used in scientific disciplines such as earth science, pharmaceutics, chemistry, ceramics, engineering. For geologists, for instance, porosity is important as a measure of the capacity of matter to absorb water. For chemists, porosity is interesting because it defines a maximum of surfaces where interaction between substances can take place. If frontiers are a cherished quality for city planning, then porosity with its maximizing of frontiers and areas exposed to difference can work well as a tool. Wolfrum refers to the essay on Naples by Walter Benjamin and Asja Lacis in the collection *Denkbilder*, a series of short essays that were originally published in newspapers in the mid-1920s. In their essay, the authors evoke porosity as metaphor for the spatiality, life, and society of Naples. They evoke the grottoes and caves carved into the rock the city is built on and state: "As porous as this stone is the architecture" (Benjamin and Lacis 1925, 165). They perceive the city as a scenography for a performance that goes on night and day, merging the stage with the actors and spectators. The backdrop inspires the play, and the actors animate their environment. "Buildings are used as a popular stage. They are all divided into innumerable, simultaneously animated theaters. Balcony, courtyard, window, gateway, staircase, roof are at the same time stage and boxes," the authors write (Ibid., 167). They also conceive of porosity as a symbol for improvisation and as a law of life.

What strikes me in Benjamin and Lacis's essay is that they use porosity both in a concrete and in a metaphorical sense. Naples is built at the foot of Vesuvius, one of the most active volcanoes of the world. But it is not only built at the base of the volcano, it is also constructed with its material. Most buildings, streets, walls, and squares are made out of porous, volcanic stone. Benjamin and Lacis recall

that the city looks "gray" rather than colorful. And, in fact, this omnipresence of grayness is a result of the material used for the buildings. I therefore see the concept of porosity as an opportunity to discuss the relation between the city and the ground, between the built environment and the topography it is inscribed in. I find particularly fruitful the openings or holes in the city that reveal the ground on which it sits. In other words, I am interested in the connection between what is man-made and what is not.

Junghuhn collected a large number of geological samples, catalogued them, and sent them to Bandung or Leiden. During our expeditions to Java, in the plane, the bus, hiking, waiting, resting, we made innumerable images and videos, recorded interviews, and took extensive notes. But, of course, we also collected a lot of samples. We were inevitably attracted by the oddly shaped rocks from volcanoes, the traces of recent and more ancient eruptions, some of them pointed out to us by specialists, others just taken because of a certain form or color. Their porosity, in particular, fascinated us. Both hard and soft, heavy and light, full and empty, their variations are manifold. Like Chinese scholars' rocks they inspire one to imagine landscapes in the stone miniature. Collected as souvenirs they contain memories of traveling. The artist collective U5 chose a selection of these items for their video presentation *Collection of a Tourist.*

Mount Kelud

In June 2017 we made our final expedition to Java, visiting three volcanoes in a row. We climbed Mount Semeru, the highest volcano on Java and, after a short rest, drove on in our small bus to visit Mount Kelud. Kelud is one of the most dangerous volcanoes in Indonesia, because it erupts frequently. The latest euption, in 2014, killed three people and forced 100,000 to evacuate. Yet despite its danger, the mountain is a source of life, due to the fertile soil, and also an attractor for local tourism. It is an exemplary case for discussion of both the material and the metaphorical aspects of porosity, an area which reflects the relation between the man-made and the nonhuman. In this rugged landscape, urbanity and volcanism are juxtaposed. Different scales and temporalities collide. Only 90 kilometers from the metropolitan area of Surabaya, the volcano serves as a recreational area and weekend attraction. While people ascend the summit to take selfies, monitors surveil every movement on the ground, every rumble in the earth. Unlike mountains in Europe, the United States, or Japan, Kelud is still relatively unexploited. There are neither cable cars nor infrastructure for mass tourism. A journey to Kelud thus is also a journey in time, back to the early stages of tourism.

The access to this volcano led us through a vast, strange landscape, marked by the traces of a gigantic mud flow. Rivers had carved their way through the mud. The vegetation along the creeks was abundant, mostly bananas, pineapples, and coconuts, but no rice fields. The land had obviously been shaped recently by the many lahars (mud flows) following the 1990 eruption. Earlier eruptions had occurred in 1966 and 1919. The lahars can travel long distances, some more than twenty kilometers. They are the result of an eruption under a crater lake, but secondary flows can also be induced by rainfall, when the porous stone layers on the volcano's slopes start to glide. A concrete road had recently been built over the muddy ground. Because of the cost of long bridges, but probably also because the entire region is unstable, the roads were inclined toward the river. Boys with flags directed the traffic and warned drivers to drive at a slow pace. The bus could only move forward slowly, and we were able to take a close look at the topography.

While we traveled slowly, still in the comfort of an air-conditioned bus, Junghuhn's book in our pocket, Junghuhn himself had approached Kelud in September 1844 on horseback and on foot with a group of local porters who carried his instruments and food. He was fascinated, as we were, by the valleys carved into the sand and eager to find out more about the mud flows. He carefully described the scenery: "One stands at the entrance of a wild picturesque landscape; deep clearing of the clefts; gray walls of sand emerging between the grove; rugged rocky peaks; the whole mountain range is irregular; huge boulders, which are wildly stacked in the river beds: these are the phenomena surrounding the traveler, and are witnesses to the turbulent, volcanic forces whose scenery one now enters" (Junghuhn 1854, 471–72). He was particularly interested in the loose material covering the entire area: "This sand is gray, very fine, and a result of the destruction of trachyte and various lavas, from which it contains many small, often pumice-like fragments. It is undoubtedly a product of the recent activity of the volcano. [...] It seems to have been mixed with water as sludge, and, after the evaporation of the water, without other binding materials, has attained a slight coherence which is particular to it." (Ibid., 473) The description of the gray environment recalls Benjamin and Lacis's description of Naples, and although Junghuhn used the notion of porosity only in regard to individual stones, the "slight coherence" indicates the quality of a terrain that is basically unstable because of the loose sedimentations.

At the foot of the volcano, we left our bus and changed to a smaller vehicle that could drive up the steep road. Some twenty minutes later, we changed again, now to the back of motorcycles, to reach the summit. Since 2014, the crater has been closed to the public. The eruption destroyed the access road and pathways for visitors. Quite literally, the entire crater area is now under repair. In fact, among all the craters we had visited, Kelud had the grimmest aspect. The rugged crater rim speaks of many devastating eruptions. The road we took was porous from the impacts of lava-fragments, as if it had been bombed. The thick concrete roof of a shelter near the summit was riddled with holes.

For us, again, it was an effortless climb, but for Junghuhn it had been highly strenuous. On the other hand, he did see the sublime crater lake, which has today disappeared. He describes how he approached the rim of the crater and was confronted with the frightening aspect of a large, blue-green lake several hundred meters below. The lake, which was inaccessible due to the steep crater walls, filled his soul with "the feeling of trepidation, as if treason and danger were hidden behind its smile" (Ibid., 482). His feet, he wrote, "are burning at this uncanny site" and he retreated all the more rapidly, because he realized "with horror" how fragile the walls are (Ibid., 482): "No volcano has made such a frightening impression on me as this G. Kelut did by his gruesome wildness. The prospect which one enjoyed from this crag was terrible-picturesque, and, in fact, dizzying-sublime. On all sides the rock fell down to several hundred feet in vertical depths; shady-gritty gaps, the bottom of which barely reached the eye, yawned from their abysses. [...] Between these peaks, there lay deep down in the crater the fatal lake, whose bosom had already pillaged and destroyed the country more than once, and surrounded a 300 to 500 feet high wall of loose sand, which threatened to collapse at any moment."(Ibid., 483)

What can we learn from Mount Kelud? Already in the early twentieth century, the crater lake was partially drained by a tunnel to diminish the risk of mud flows. Today, the crater area continues to be a construction site with a view to both taming the forces of nature and easing access for visitors. Kelud, like most of the forty-five volcanoes on Java, is a point of orientation within the fabric of the desakota. It is a topographic, cultural, religious marker. It is neither landscape, nor city, neither dead nor alive. People do not use it as they would use parks in a metropolis. Families might visit Kelud on a weekend, because it is easy to access, but no one goes there regularly. Several visitors I met confessed that they were here for the first time, although they lived nearby. Most other volcanoes are visited much more rarely, perhaps once in a lifetime, mainly by small groups of young students. But wherever we went in Java, the volcanoes were a common ground for discussion, an issue of shared interest. Their sheer existence and presence is a basic precondition for the urbanity of Java. They are the entry points that provide access to the something that lays beneath the urban fabric, that was there before it started and will be there after it ends. Just as Benjamin and Lacis were attracted by the tiny church spaces that opened up between the dwellings as a "secret gate for the initiate" (Benjamin and Lacis 1925, 166), so we, like Junghuhn and many others before us, felt magnetically attracted by the openings of the volcanoes. In most contemporary cities, such holes have been plugged and homogenized. But wherever they appear, even momentarily, such as the La Brea Tar Pits in Los Angeles, the solid rocks of Central Park in New York, the sand in a building pit in Berlin, they animate the urban fabric. In the near future, the growing tourist industry might transform the volcanoes and colonize them with infrastructure. But in their current state, the volcanoes in Java show how precious an undefined zone is for the coherence of the entire urban fabric.

References:

Bal, M. 2002. *Travelling Concepts in the Humanities: A Rough Guide*. Toronto. | Benjamin, W., and A. Lacis. 1925. "Naples," in *Reflections: Essays, Aphorisms, Autobiographical Writings*, edited by P. Demetz, 163–73. New York, 1978. | Burdett, R., and D. Sudjic. 2007. *The Endless City*. London. | Goethe-Institut Jakarta, ed. 2009. *Forschen—vermessen—streiten: Eine Ausstellung zum 200. Geburtstag des Java-Erforschers Franz Wilhelm Junghuhn (1809–1864)*. Exhibition catalogue, Goethe-Institut. Jakarta. Junghuhn, F. W. 1854. *Java, seine Gestalt, Pflanzendecke und innere Bauart*, translated by J. K. Hasskarl. Leipzig. | McGee, T. 1991. "The Emergence of Desakota Regions in Asia," in *The Extended Metropolis: Settlement Transition in Asia*, edited by N. Ginsburg, B. Koppel, and T. McGee, 3–25. Honolulu. | Sternagel, R. 2011. *Der Humboldt von Java: Leben und Werk des Naturforschers Franz Wilhelm Junghuhn 1809–1864*. Halle.

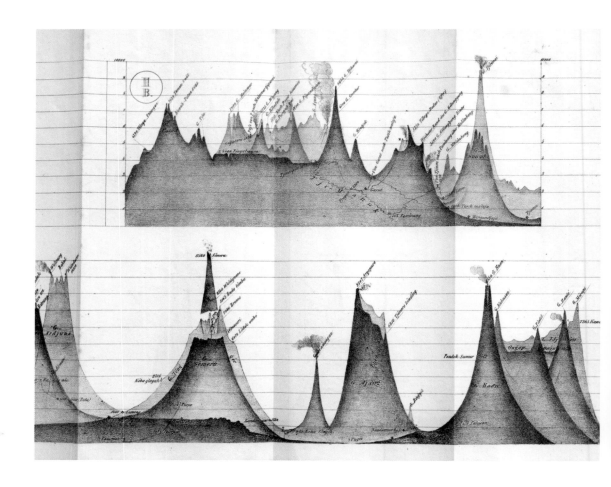

Porous or Porridge City?

Kees Christiaanse

Today's renaissance of the city seems to be the final acknowledgment that a high-density, compact, walkable, and diverse urban environment served by public transport is the most sustainable and livable solution for the world's still fast-growing population. The city of Jane Jacobs (1961) and the adaptive perimeter blocks of the nineteenth-century neighborhoods with slightly varying typologies, ranging from the Meat Packing District in Manhattan to Prenzlauer Berg in Berlin, even seem to be able to accommodate clean-tech research and microindustrial ecosystems. The atomization of households and entrepreneurship finds a fertile seedbed in the porous urban structures in which permeability by a multidirectional street pattern with transformable street profiles, adaptive ground floors, semipublic courtyards with occupiable zones, and diverse uses in upper floors and courtyard buildings constitutes its DNA.

In Shanghai's French concession, the rich and diverse early twentieth-century typologies, like the red brick Lilongs, the accumulation of small-scale business with microeconomic activity, and its central location, triggered the emergence of an urban renewal culture in which heritage and creative industry policies coincided (Zhou 2017).

In the HafenCity quarter in Hamburg, one of Europe's largest and state-of-the-art waterfront projects, an open city, designed and developed with the abovementioned DNA, seems to have successfully developed in an incremental way, despite the fact that almost the entire neighborhood is newly constructed (www.hafencity.com). The project also adapts during its development to changing insights concerning district infrastructure and electric mobility, for instance by reducing parking places and preparing the residual ones for car-sharing and charging boxes.

In the urban design for the Olympic City in Hamburg, opposite HafenCity on the south bank of the Elbe, where planning for the long-term post-Olympic conditions dictated the short-term Olympic specifications, the urban perimeter blocks have been designed to be partly raised in order to allow large-scale logistics and other port-related uses at ground level, with overhead greening.

However, these inner-city neighborhoods in larger metropolitan cities also represent the less challenging part of the Open City project (Sennett 2011; Rieniets, Sigler, Christiaanse 2009). Most examples are in the affluent West or in enclaves where Western expatriates are numerous. They are generally inhabited by a well-educated majority and most of the time situated in a more or less liberal social-democratic context. In addition, they are under constant threat of overgentrification, causing land values to soar.

The flip side to the success stories above are the numerous more or less informal settlements in developing countries variously known as favela, slum, kampong, and urban village. Some of these neighborhoods are highly open and adaptive, some are under the control of criminal networks. They often have an emancipatory function in enabling families from the country to climb the social ladder within two or three generations (Saunders 2011). The combination of high-density populations, low-rise buildings, and fine-meshed pedestrian systems in these neighborhoods allows people to use their space as an economic unit for commerce and other activities. Despite the deprived state of facilities relating to pollution and waste, health and environment, the individual ecological footprint per person paradoxically is far lower than in affluent neighborhoods in the West, simply because the people living in them have less money to spend on consumption. These neighborhoods are often more diverse and vibrant than the official centers of their cities. In Shenzhen, many former industrial plants have been taken over by semilegal residents and used for a variety of different purposes. The buildings have been divided into small-scale units or extended or rebuilt. They now form vibrant and porous urban centers in contrast with the official (sub-)centers planned and built by the government (Ting 2017).

The greatest urbanistic challenge for the physical realization of an open society (and its enemies) (Popper 1945), however, lies in what I used to call *plankton urbanism*, what McGee called *desakota* (1991), Neutelings *carpet metropolis* (1990), Garreau *edge city* (1990), Conolly *landscape urbanism* (1994), Sieverts *Zwischenstadt* (1997), Brenner and Schmid *extended urbanization* (2012), Topalovic *the architecture of territory* (2015), Viganò *horizontal metropolis* (2013), and Cairns *archipelago cities* (2017).

218
219

If we compare a UN (undated) map of the world's population density with one for rice production per hectare by the University of Minnesota, we notice that they are almost identical. It becomes apparent that the areas with the highest population, mainly along rivers and their deltas, for instance along the Ganges, the Jangstse, the Mekong, the north side of Java, the Po, and the Rhine Delta also have the highest agricultural output. This means that the widely repeated statement that half the world's population lives in cities may not be entirely true and should be amended: at least half the world's population lives in urbanized landscapes, in desakota (Indonesian for "village-city").

The explanation for this form of development is clear: the low-lying flatlands along rivers and deltas historically were both fertile and easily accessible by boat. Roads were also easy to build. These conditions spurred the development of intricate networks of roads and waterways, villages in close proximity, and a specialized economy serving the agricultural and fishing culture. It is not surprising that the same conditions also promoted the development of industry and logistics. The result was a dense mix of different applications, a productive landscape, with a high degree of connectivity and porosity. Today it also supports essential large-scale functions, amenities, and infrastructures like power plants and airports.

It is clear that we should recognize desakota as a permanent, nonerasable type of urbanization which may house the majority of the world's population. However, all over the world, desakota regions are suffering from increasing inefficiency, due to scaling distances and extensive density, a mobility gridlock which clogs roads, rail- and waterways, and the high cost of technical infrastructure and large-scale monofunctional development. In addition, it generally suffers from ground and water pollution, uncontrolled depositing of waste, sinking groundwater and soil from excessive freshwater pumping, and consequent flooding problems, also due to hard surfaces and eutrophication from the overuse of fertilizers.

Specifically, decreasing accessibility and congestion in the road network from lorries, cars, and—in Southeast Asia—motorcycles and scooters is paradoxical. The emancipation of mobility as a result of increased wealth and the greater availability of means of transport paralyzes itself. It is a huge problem on the island of Java, and also, though taking a different form, in the Randstad in Holland. The greatest threat the gridlock brings is the compartmentalization of the landscape by motorways, railroads, high-speed canals, noise-protection screens, and large gated compounds like airports, military installations, data and logistics centers, plants, sports complexes, and gated communities. Whereas most elements of desakota regions in the past could be easily crossed by foot, bike, or horse, allowing for a high degree of openness and porosity in the human environment, these new elements force desakota into a jigsaw puzzle of impenetrable fragments, once more frustrating connectivity and accessibility and consequently communication.

Apart from the fact that further deterioration of the landscape should be prevented, desakota contain essential infrastructures complementary to those of the city. Desakota and the city are, of course, reciprocal. This is the reason why working on the decongestion of desakota regions is of utmost urgency. If we do not find solutions for the problems described, the process will continue, turning the porous into porridge, and become a real threat to the planet's habitability.

On the other hand, there is hope. In some developed liberal social democracies like Switzerland, the physical and administrative constraints form a set of "braking factors" which to a certain degree protect desakota against uncontrolled large-scale sprawl.

Among these braking factors the Forest Law prohibits timber harvesting in designated forest land; the Landscape Initiative protects landscape preservation areas; the Crop Rotation Area (*Fruchtfolgefläche*) defines the minimum area of agricultural land required to feed the population in times of disaster or war; the Regional Zoning Plan restricts municipal development on unbuilt land; fragmented property challenges expropriation of buildable land; topography impedes construction in higher areas; noise protection and emission laws impede construction in exposed zones; water regulations restrict construction; not least because of stakeholders in the Swiss direct democracy are powerful and, public transport is highly efficient and provides excellent accessibility, reducing motorized individual traffic.

We propose these protective mechanisms against expedited urbanization as a positive brief for an urban design approach of inversion and substraction.

For instance, the noise contours around Amsterdam Schiphol Airport region have impeded the conglomeration of the cities of Amsterdam, Haarlem, and Leiden. If the airport had not been there, the area today would have become one massive porridgeification of heterogenous developments. Instead, the airport forms a large green heartland where the surrounding areas are intelligently exploited for recreational facilities such as sports fields, golf courses, a park with noise-dispersing dykes and elevations. In addition, the airport clearly defines the border between the cities of Amsterdam and Haarlem (Boucsein et al. 2017).

Other examples are the strategic creation of forests in sensitive areas to prevent future zoning changes and the designation of flood-retention areas as natural reservations, two inverse design interventions we introduced in the Montpellier TGV station quarter. Such an approach to urban design contributes to the desakota's resilience and secures a shift in the prevailing paradigm (KCAP 2014).

Urban design is like skiing, it is the art of braking elegantly.

References:

Boucsein, B., et al. 2017. *The Noise Landscape.* Rotterdam. | Brenner, N., and C. Schmid. 2012. "Planetary Urbanization," in *Urban Constellations*, edited by M. Gandy, 10–13. Berlin. | Cairns, S., et al. 2017. "Archipelago Cities," *Future Cities Laboratory*, accessed January 5, 2018, http://www.fcl.ethz.ch/research/archipelago-cities.html. | Conolly, P. 1994. "An Affirmative Open Systems Conception of How to Design Landscape," PhD diss., RMIT, Melbourne. | Garreau, J. 1991. *Edge City: Life on the New Frontier.* New York. | Jacobs, J. 1961. *The Death and Life of Great American Cities.* New York. | KCAP. 2014. "Montpellier Oz," accessed January 5, 2018, http://www.kcap.eu/en/projects/v/oz_nature_urbaine/. | McGee, T. 1991. "The Emergence of Desakota Regions in Asia," in *The Extended Metropolis: Settlement Transition in Asia*, edited by N. Ginsburg, B. Koppel, and T. McGee, 3–25. Honolulu. | Neutelings, W. J. 1990. "Tapijtmetropool," *Archis*, no. 3: 16–21. | Popper, K. 1945. *The Open Society and Its Enemies.* London. | Rieniets, T., J. Sigler, and K. Christiaanse. 2009. *Open City: Designing Coexistence.* Amsterdam. | Saunders, D. 2011. *Arrival City: How the Largest Migration in History Is Reshaping Our World.* Toronto. | Sennett, R. 2013. "The Open City," accessed January 4, 2018, https://www.richardsennett.com/site/senn/UploadedResources/The%20Open%20City.pdf. | Sieverts, T. 1997. *Cities without Cities: An interpretation of the Zwischenstadt.* Translated by D. de Lough. London, 2003. | Ting, C. 2017. *A State Beyond the State: Shenzhen and the Transformation of Urban China.* Rotterdam. | Topalovic, M. 2015. "The Architecture of Territory: Beyond the Limits of the City," inaugural lecture given November 30, 2015, at ETH Zürich. | NASA. Undated. "World Map of Population Density," available at: https://eoimages.gsfc.nasa.gov/images/imagerecords/53000/53005/population_density.tif. | University of Minnesota Institute on the Environment. Undated. "Map of Rice Production across the World," compiled with data from C. Monfreda, N. Ramankutty, and J. A. Foley. 2008. "Farming the planet: 2. Geographic distribution of crop areas, yields, physiological types, and net primary production in the year 2000," *Global Biogeochemical Cycles*, vol. 22, GB1022. | Viganò, P. 2013. "The Horizontal Metropolis and Gloeden's Diagrams: Two Parallel Stories," *OASE*, no. 89: 94–103. | Zhou, Y. 2017. *Urban Loopholes: Creative Alliances of Spatial Production in Shanghai's City Center.* Basel.

The Connected and Multiscalar City: Porosity in the Twenty-first Century
Alain Thierstein

Porosity is not a common term in urban development. The source of origin gives us only a flavor of the potential stimulus this term might give to the ever-pertinent question of how does a city of today function? Benjamin and Lacis who described the peculiarities of a number of European cities, characterize the Italian city of Naples as follows: "Porosity is the inexhaustible law of life of this city, reappearing everywhere" (Benjamin and Lacis 1925, 168). European cities of today have been largely transformed, in part due to massive damage during World War II, the subsequent automobilization of inner cities, and suburbanization in general. Thus, porosity needs reinterpretation against the backdrop of the challenges which European cities face in the twenty-first century. Just as the transformation and festivalization of inner cities have become a key topic for urban planners and politicians, so has the upscaling process of urban interactions into emerging city-regional spaces been a top priority for scholars in urban development. Since contributors to this edited book come from different academic perspectives using different concepts and methodologies, let us identify a number of ways of reading these new urban structures: (1) morphologically, (2) functionally, (3) socially, (4) in terms of governance, (5) relationally, (6) intertemporally (Thierstein 2015, 254–55). This contribution will introduce a relational perspective along with the concept of knowledge creation in order to understand how these ideas interact across time and space and what porosity may offer the debate.

Cities, since their beginnings, have developed through interaction with other cities, through exchange of people, goods, services, and ideas. Offering spaces for efficient, effective interaction—which at the same time are able to generate some agreeable atmosphere and pleasant surroundings for the users—indicates the urge for a wider and more contemporary interpretation of the idea of porosity. The Naples of today, like all larger European cities, has long since become agglomeration or city-region, which exhibits some sort of emerging polycentric structure. Polycentricity has a morphological, a functional as well as scalar aspect. "The morphological dimension, referred to as morphological polycentricity, basically addresses the size and territorial distribution of the urban centers across the territory and equates more balanced distributions with polycentricity. The relational dimension, referred to as functional polycentricity, takes the functional connections between the settlements into account and considers a balanced, multidirectional set of relations to be more polycentric." (Burger and Meijers 2012, 1133) We can now view city regions as nodes in the global economy, which have specific functions that are connected with particular urban qualities. These city regions are morphing into polycentric "mega-city regions" (MCRs), characterized by a "series of cities and towns physically separated but functionally networked, and drawing enormous economic strength from a new functional division of labor" (Hall and Pain 2006, 3).

The contemporary academic debate raises fundamental questions about how we conceptualize spatial development and interpret functional urban hierarchies (Taylor, Hoyler, and Verbruggen 2010). The entry point for this multiscalar dynamics is the fact that the interrelationship between the functional and the spatial logic of the knowledge economy is the main driver in the emergence of polycentric MCRs and the change in urban hierarchies. Recent empirical work underlines the need to investigate the interconnectedness of knowledge-intensive economic activities across different geographical scales (Hoyler 2011; Lüthi, Thierstein, and Bentlage 2011; Derudder and Taylor 2016).

Scott and Storper state "that throughout the course of history, urbanization has been fundamentally engendered by a complex interaction between economic development, divisions of labor, agglomeration, specialization and external commerce [...] the most basic raison d'être for cities, certainly in the modern era, resides in their role as centers of economic production and exchange within wider systems of regional, national, and international trade" (Scott and Storper 2014, 6). The two authors concede that cities are always much more than this, and continue: "however, it is only by means of an analysis that begins with the complex spatial dynamics of economic activity that we can arrive at an account of the agglomeration dynamics common to all cities" (Ibid.).

Thus, agglomeration can be generally understood as a mechanism of sharing, matching and learning (Duranton and Puga 2004, 2066). Scott and Storper refer *sharing* to dense local interlinkages within production systems as well as to indivisibilities that make it necessary to supply some kinds of urban services as public goods; *matching* refers to the process of pairing people and jobs, a process that is greatly facilitated where large local pools of firms and workers exist; *learning* refers to the dense formal and informal information flows (which tend to stimulate innovation) that are made possible by agglomeration and that in turn reinforce agglomeration (Scott and Storper 2014, 6).

There is widespread agreement in the academic literature today that knowledge and the process of generating knowledge has become the main source of urban development in advanced economies. Based on the requirements for knowledge creation, most firms in the knowledge economy develop their location network as part of their overall business strategy, whereby highly specific human resources and core competencies are flexibly combined in order to create differentiation and competitive advantage. The locational strategy of a firm must consider both where a firm's internal functions should be placed and where suppliers and customers should be located. These internal and external linkages are woven across physical space, not only connecting firms and parts of firms but also connecting more or less dispersed cities and towns. As the increase in the overall number of such high-quality locations is limited, a functional urban hierarchy takes shape based on the activities and relations of the knowledge economy. Already here, we begin to sense how porosity may enter our discussion as a boundary object that connects and mediates between seemingly disconnected functional and spatial considerations.

Vibrant life and personal interaction in city centers and urban subcenters are still the core ideas of urban planners and city officials alike. These ideas have but morphed into functional city regions that organize their inhabitants' daily lives within a very different spatial reach and functional division of activities. The original idea of porosity can be applied exactly at these interfaces, where linkages intersect and generate dense interactions, but with a multiscalar perspective in lieu of an exclusively urban design or architectural scale. These spatially identifiable interactions are at the same time fostered by and dependent on certain locational requirements. A contemporary interpretation is offered by Bernardo Secchi and Paola Viganò, who use the term *porous city* for their reurbanization scenarios for the city of Antwerp—referring to the original interpretation given by Benjamin and Lacis. Interestingly enough, Secchi first starts the analysis from a top-down perspective, stating that Antwerp is undergoing modernization, as the city and its territory are evolving rapidly and radically into a metropolis within a large megalopolis known as the Northwest Metropolitan Area (Secchi 2007, 9). Focusing then on the city scale, Secchi/Viganò find that the "abandoned industrial sites and buildings within the urban fabric have turned Antwerp into a porous city. This porosity offers the opportunity to create a new constructed landscape within the urban region." (Ibid., 10) Secchi even refers to the dense rail connectivity between Antwerp, Brussels, Ghent, and Leuven, indirectly introducing a relational perspective to understanding the transformation of spaces. This urban design work by Secchi/Viganò perfectly illustrates the multi-scalarity of today's development in emerging polycentric large-scale urban areas. The supraregional level is connected to the supralocal and refers again to the subcity and the microlocal level, thus forming an intricate relatedness of nested and nonnested urban hierarchies of interaction between people, firms, infrastructure, and urban atmospheres.

Finally, after a roller-coaster ride between multiple spatial scales, morphological, functional, and relational perspectives, we eventually get back to where Benjamin and Lacis situated their narrative: the microurban scale, where even today proximity, density, and connectivity are key to understanding the smooth functioning of urban structures: "Urban density creates a constant flow of new information that comes from observing others' successes and failures" (Glaeser 2011, 247). Today, data is generated through sensors, user interaction, or user transactions, which then is aggregated into information. It is knowledge that finally matters, since it shows a double-face as product and as process: formalized knowledge as codified information and implicit or tacit knowledge, which is the product of personal interaction between people—very much in the sense Glaeser intends—that comes about through a process of being physically close and being connected at the same time. Thus, being close but also being connected is a key feature of knowledge creation, which in turn is fundamentally linked to Benjamin and Lacis's idea of how porosity works in a city: "Building and action interpenetrate in the courtyards, arcades, and stairways. In everything they preserve the scope to become a theater of new, unforeseen constellations." (Benjamin and Lacis 1925, 166–67) Surprisingly or not, we here find a link to a very recent topic in urban design: the debate on entrepreneurship and urban transformation with its concepts of coworking spaces and start-up ecosystems. Such contemporary coworking spaces strongly resemble Benjamin's and Lacis's description of the role of meeting places in Naples: "True laboratories of this great process of intermingling are the cafés. Life is unable to sit down and stagnate in them." (Ibid., 172) Coworking today is highly demanding, since this way of organizing work is a new and complex social phenomenon that includes multiple aspects: economic, spatial, and physical, along with social and communal dimensions and the interactions between them. Coworking spaces may be these true laboratories in which implicit knowledge is being created through personal interaction and face-to-face contact. These urban situations require adequate spaces, flexible and inviting, close to where people live, and which are proximate to other urban amenities and institutions.

In summary: the competitiveness of locations today relies heavily on a combination of agglomeration economies, which translates into spatial proximity, and network economies, which circle around relational proximity. The related and well-established empirical findings can be intimately linked to the Benjamin and Lacis descriptions of Naples, since they talk about the city of Naples and use the term *porosity* for their cultural and social perspective on the intertwining of urban spaces and the urban texture. The concept of porosity, however, needs reinterpretation. As with most reapplied concepts, literal transfer or propagation does not much help, and could even turn into its opposite if porosity is not adequately readapted to today's urban challenges as well as to the multiscalar character of urbanized polycentric city regions. Thus, the metaphor of the porous city might enable a variety of disciplines clustered around the key topic of urban transformation to deal productively with typical urban ambivalences: distance and proximity, physical and nonphysical, exclusion and integration, heterogeneity and homogeneity, anonymity and community.

References:

Benjamin, W., and A. Lacis. 1925. "Naples," in *Reflections: Essays, Aphorisms, Autobiographical Writings*, edited by P. Demetz, 163–73. New York, 1978. | Burger, M., and E. Meijers. 2012. "Form Follows Function? Linking Morphological and Functional Polycentricity," *Urban Studies* 49, no. 5: 1127–49. | Derudder, B., and P. Taylor. 2016. "Change in the World City Network, 2000–2012," *The Professional Geographer* 68, no. 4: 1–14. | Duranton, G., and D. Puga. 2004. "Microfoundations of Urban Agglomeration Economies," in *The Handbook of Regional and Urban Economics*, vol. 4, *Cities and Geography*, edited by J. V. Henderson and J. F. Thisse, 2063–118. Amsterdam. | Glaeser, E. 2011. *Triumph of the City: How Our Greatest Invention Makes Us Richer, Smarter, Greener, Healthier, and Happier.* New York. | Hall, P., and K. Pain. 2006. *The Polycentric Metropolis: Learning from Mega-City Regions in Europe.* London. | Hoyler, M. 2011. "External Relations of German Cities through Intrafirm Networks: A Global Perspective," *Raumforschung und Raumordnung* 69, no. 3: 147–59. | Lüthi, S., A. Thierstein, and M. Bentlage. 2011. "Interlocking Firm Networks in the German Knowledge Economy: On Local Networks and Global Connectivity," *Raumforschung und Raumordnung* 69, no. 3: 161–74. | Scott, A. J., and M. Storper. 2014. "The Nature of Cities: The Scope and Limits of Urban Theory," *International Journal of Urban and Regional Research* 39, no. 1: 1–15. | Secchi, B. 2007. "Rethinking and Redesigning the Urban Landscape," *Places* 19, no. 1: 6–11. | Taylor, P. J., M. Hoyler, and R. Verbruggen. 2010. "External Urban Relational Process: Introducing Central Flow Theory to Complement Central Place Theory," *Urban Studies* 47, no. 13: 2803–18. | Thierstein, A. 2015. "Metropolitan Regions: Functional Relations between the Core and the Periphery," *Planning Theory & Practice* 16, no. 2: 254–58.

Urban Landscape Infiltrations
Alexandra Bauer, Julian Schaefer, Soeren Schoebel, Yuting Xie

The typical format of the traditional city which, in every way, is so much the inverse of the city of modern architecture [...] the one is almost all white, the other almost all black; the one an accumulation of solids in largely unmanipulated void, the other an accumulation of voids in largely unmanipulated solid. (Rowe and Koetter 1978, 62)

Following *Collage City*, and the description of the urban texture as an "ambiguous figure-ground pattern" (Janson 2016) with its black built-up and white intermediate spaces, the idea of open space as blank volume oscillates between emptiness and hollowness—hospitable, ready to be filled with citizens' presence, perception, action, interaction, and confrontation. But the description of figure-ground patterns at the architectural and the urban scale can only partially explain the dramatic difference in the feeling of and in space, between premodern urban spaces, incrementally evolved over time, and postmodern urban spaces that spring up overnight, between animacy and resuscitation. There are many more patterns at the same and other scales that structure the urban space, creating a delicate, touch-sensitive surface, continuing the never-ceasing repetition of figure-ground ambiguousness of all that has been evolved. The most efficacious of these patterns are blue; they consist of pave and moss, bridge and water, flood waves at the quay wall, and the plague of jellyfish at the river bank—together forming a nature-absorbing porosity of the city.

Istanbul—Mediating Milieus through Spatial Permeability
Istanbul is one of the culturally richest and most diverse but at the same time often totally segregated cites—both porosity and tightness characterize this ancient megacity. But nowadays, informal and historical neighborhoods are razed to the ground. These urban renewal developments establish insurmountable boundaries, followed by exclusion of social and cultural groups by reducing the spatial and social porosity of the urban texture. While hermetic boundaries lead to the death of urban diversity and difference (Jacobs 1961, Sennett 2011, 325), porous borders like edges and niches have the opposite effect: they enable the mixture of different cultures and social groups living together and are therefore spatial origins of metacultures (see Ipsen 2000, 248–49).

Without any doubt, the Bosporus is the most prominent boundary and edge in Istanbul. Though it may seem to fragment the city, the waterfront in fact brings different social milieus together. As the only city in the world located on two continents—more than 1.2 million people have to cross the Bosporus every day (Casiroli and Sudjic 2009, 4)—the blue manifests itself as one of the most decisive qualities of Istanbul. It is precisely the traffic hubs such as ferry terminals connected to tram terminuses and road intersections ending at bridge heads, quays, and piers, in making contact with the waterfront, that bring people and cultures together and turn the Bosporus's strong boundary into a porous edge, far more than the generic designed and paved-over parks, parade squares, campuses, and clubhouses along the Bosporus can ever do.

Adjacent to the prominent waterfronts of the Bosporus, on the way to the dry tributary erosion valleys, small fishing villages such as Kanlica, Ortaköy, or Anadolu Kavaği, as traditionally cosmopolitan places, host a wide range of different cultures and origins, namely Muslims, Jews, Armenians, Greeks, and other Christians. Surrounded by the megalopolis, these old coastal villages with their small markets still give direct access to the water. Narrow alleys and pathways run between rows of houses at the water's edge, hosting endless varieties of shops and bars. Like the waves that lap perpetually on the stone steps and fishing boat hulls, these remnants have retained their ability to act as melting pots, as though the overall gentrification processes had never taken place (Bauer 2015). These niches are far more vulnerable than the prominent Bosporus waterfronts and should be preserved carefully. At very different scales—from the molecular to the regional—such urban qualities of blue are global phenomena and a matter of sustainability and survivability for megacities worldwide.

Shenzhen—Breaking through the Walls

Situated in the Pearl River Delta, the metropolitan area of Shenzhen is strongly influenced by water. To expand the city, large areas of the land were leveled and canals and drains were built. Although Shenzhen was founded less than forty years ago, today's redensification and postindustrial transforming process has created problems in the interaction between the city's social and water spaces.

The true core areas of Shenzhen are urban village districts which originated from farming villages. As a particular historical case of urban construction that "have a sense of place, the elements of true urbanity—and social and ecological diversity and resiliency" (Yu 2014, 4), they are being demolished and replaced by isolated gated communities. In between them, congested and polluted roadways appear as borders. Yu writes that "Shenzhen has lanes of traffic, not streets, and this makes the city blocks almost walled off. That does not create urbanity, it only creates island-like blocks where people live or work, isolated and disconnected." (Ibid.) Following Detlev Ipsen, these structural trends can be described as centralization, peripherialization, islandization, liquefaction, and placelessness (Ipsen 2004). In the remaining public open spaces, cookshops and hairdressers share the space with communal TV viewing, private laundry washing, and people sleeping on the pavement, leading to a blurring of the public and private spheres (see Hassenpflug 2010, 26). On top of this, the high degree of surface sealing and the conventional concrete-based river regulation in this predominantly monsoon climate results in flooding, especially in the poorer quarters. Water's destructive power has a serious impact on populations of high vulnerability and affects the daily routine of the whole urban society.

In our research project, we have tried to turn these weaknesses and threats into positive opportunities (Hoss and Schaefer 2015), taking the concept of the sponge city (Yu 2014) as a model. In the sponge city model, rainwater and storm water are collected and stored and then used to recharge the city's groundwater.

Water collected in this way is polluted by the air and the surfaces it crosses. So it needs to be cleaned before it can be used to infiltrate the groundwater. In contrast to conventional solutions, which involve expensive plants with mechanical and chemical filtration systems, the concept of constructed urban wetlands provides a simple solution with low complexity and costs. They absorb sediments and remove pollutants while also retaining the water. But since space is one of the scarcest resources of Shenzhen, we need to move from the molecular to the city scale, to a structural infiltration.

This now opens up additional urban social opportunities: instead of a central system, a decentralized network of canals and drainage spaces infiltrates water throughout the city. Green canals running parallel in the wide streets, small ponds in the communal spaces of urban villages, porous pools as centerpieces of newly built residential complexes, rainwater parks alongside riverbeds with filter gardens and green rooftops on high-rise and industrial buildings—such constructed urban wetlands can be integrated into any existing structure, linear or plane, in-between or on top. These artificial wetlands do more than just provide ecosystem services: they can stimulate and structure the public space. By following the rain to the canal, the canal to the river, and the river to the mountain, city and landscape will be connected. The wetlands provide access to rooftops, traverse walls, open up and connect gated communities, valorize historical village space, prestructure postindustrial conversions. They disrupt the islandization of disconnected settlements, reinterpret spatial liquefaction by redirecting floods, and thus create space.

Taihu Basin—Permanence of Hydraulic Structures in Metropolitan Regions

In China, as in Europe, cultural landscapes are aesthetically appreciated but are undergoing a loss of diversity, coherence, and identity, a chaotic fragmentation of traditional urban or rural structures.

In the Taihu Basin, a landscape in the Yangtze River Delta, all forms of cultural landscapes are the result of transformations, driven by the developments of land reclamation and hydraulic technologies, water conservancy, land-use systems, urbanization, and industrialization. The Yangtze River Delta has a unique hierarchical water system, which is a crisscrossed water network comprised of dense but short canals. Its basic structure dates back to the eighth century BC and continued to be developed until the middle of the third century AD. Continuous land reclamation, poldering, and the paddy-fish-silk farming system created stable and permanent structures and character in the delta lowlands that endured for thousands of years. Two substantial transformations can be identified: polder systems went from small to large and then back to small; and fragmented polder systems were replaced by more rational systems.

However, since the reform era (post-1978), this formerly highly productive agricultural region has been transformed into the fastest-growing megalopolis in China. Historical site-specific elements and structures have been gradually swallowed by unrestrained development, while new cultural but generic mixed urban and industrial landscape elements have become prevalent. The urbanization of polders can be seen as a third fundamental transformation, in which urban and industrial landscapes have superimposed on the historical polder landscapes rather than changing the polder systems themselves. This transformation has made these urbanizing polders more vulnerable to flooding.

All remaining water elements and structures are particularly fragile and vulnerable to structural and functional changes in ongoing new town and urban developments. The current development model of urban housing in this area, like most new town development in China, simply imposes new residential blocks without considering the geophysical or historical landscape of the site. These new residential blocks are normally developed as gated communities with private green space. In these areas, historical settlements have been gradually demolished, and historical rural road systems have been replaced by new grids of urban road systems. The main structures of the remaining historical canal systems have now been turned into channelized frames around the residential blocks; the waterfronts of these canals have lost their spatial quality and ecological function.

As a counterproject, we propose a new urban development model, which will utilize the canals and their waterfronts as public spaces by reconsidering the spatial relations of the water system with both built-up areas and road systems. Starting from the riversides and lakesides, which are valued as attractive locations by both investors and prospective buyers, the network of historical canals will be to a large extent preserved as permanent elements. Reconfigured as green-blue infrastructure, the canal system valorizes the historical settlements as borders or even open space hubs of high-rise and densely populated neighborhoods. The density, enclosure, and textures of historical settlements, created by the hydraulic system, can also be a reference for the planning of new housing. In this model, faceless and homogeneous new urban housing could acquire their own site-specific identities through integration with historical hydraulic, road, and settlement structures as permanent elements and forms. In China as a global phenomenon, where waterfront locations are highly prized and in great demand, in many places the preservation of irrigation and drainage canals could improve the social quality of residential and urban space.

Even though the architecture of the city fills porous space "with energy" (Rowe and Koetter 1978, 62), only these natural and man-made infiltrations—as well as those arising from human failure—can breath life into the city. Both are preconditions for the social production of space. Their figure-ground relations expose more between the masses than emptiness or hollowness—inhabited, animated, and decomposed by organisms and fluids. Situated between the white and the black, the porous city catalyzes blue-green as additional patterns that are essential to read and to collage the urban texture.

References:
Bauer, A. 2015. "Zwischenraum und -zeit: Entwicklung und Untersuchung des öffentlichen Raumes in den Rändern und Nischen Istanbuls," master's thesis, Technical University of Munich. | Casiroli, F., and D. Sudjic. 2009. "The City Too Big to Fail," in *Istanbul: City of Intersections*, edited by R. Burdett and W. Nowak, 3–4. London. | Hassenpflug, D. 2010. *The Urban Code of China.* Basel. | Hoss, P., and J. Schaefer. 2015. "Wasserintegration und Ortsbildung: Stadtumbau für die Ankunftsgeneration in Longhua/Longgang in der südchinesischen Metropole Shenzhen," master's thesis, Technical University of Munich. | Ipsen, D. 2004. "High Speed-Urbanismus," *ARCH+* 168: 28–29. | Jacobs, J. 1961. *The Death and Life of Great American Cities.* New York. Janson, A. 2016. "Porosity: Ambiguous Figure and Cloud," Cloud-Cuckoo-Land 21, no. 35: 35–46. | Rowe, C., and F. Koetter. 1978. *Collage City.* Cambridge, MA. | Sennett, R. 2013. "The Open City," accessed January 4, 2018, https://www.richardsennett.com/site/senn/UploadedResources/The%20Open%20City.pdf. | Yu, K. 2014. "Global Schindler Award: Interview with Professor Dr. Kongjian Yu," accessed January 4, 2018, www.turenscape.com/en/news/detail/319.html.

Porosity as a Structural Principle of Urban Landscapes
Udo Weilacher

Löwental. From a distance, viewed from Joseph Effner's Badenburg, the edge of the forest appears impenetrable and borders the wide, southward-facing meadow valley. The dense leafy treetops, mainly oak, beech, lime tree, and maple, reach almost to the ground and do not allow a view into the shady forest interior. A curved path leading toward the edge of the forest invites you to approach the periphery, and as you approach it, turns out to be much more open and permeable than initially expected. Walking through the forest, the periphery is experienced as a space-containing zone, in which outside and inside, light and shade penetrate each other. Once the eye has become accustomed to the light in the forest, a cavernous space of impressive dimensions reveals itself under the green canopy. Viewed from here, the edge of the forest looks like a "fenêtre en longueur" as Le Corbusier preferred it, a floor-deep long window that frames the panoramic view of the sunny meadow valley and allows light to penetrate the interior of the forest.

The garden designer Friedrich Ludwig von Sckell, who from 1799 onward was responsible for the transformation of the Nymphenburg Palace gardens from the baroque to the landscape style, well understood the attraction of the spatial experience in the permeable peripheral zones of the 180-hectare park. He knew that people need orientation in the landscape and therefore appreciate spatial boundaries as guidelines. On the other hand, spatial boundaries in the landscape, especially if they are formed from vegetation, are never completely impenetrable and should not be so. Whether on a macro or micro level, life can only evolve in nature if the dynamic exchange of light, air, and water between the subspaces is not completely inhibited. In the twentieth century, landscape ecology scientifically verified these interrelationships in environmental planning and demonstrated that spatial boundaries in the landscape must permit both material exchange and interaction between organisms in their respective habitats and biotopes.

The fact that permeable peripheral zones are also aesthetically appealing is basic knowledge in landscape architecture, already firmly established in Roman antiquity, when the garden gradually developed into an independent work of art. Not only garden designers but also architects have generated this awareness over the centuries from the observation and direct experience of landscape. In his inaugural lecture of 1893 on "The Essence of Architectural Creation" at the University of Leipzig, the art historian August Schmarsow insisted: "The wide hollow of a valley or a narrow gorge in the mountains, an accidentally created cave or a rock crevice are spatial impressions that reality offers to man, and inspiration for his spatial imagination; but the reproduction in his own creations regulates all lines and cleanses all forms according to the ordering of our minds" (Schmarsow 1894, 13). The forest in its manifold manifestations, divided by aisles or clearings, shaped like halls by old trees or dense young growth, has always offered a wealth of ideas for architectural "spatial imagination." Columned halls and arcades bear witness to this, as do plazas in the city, which can be seen as an urban counterpart to the forest clearing. As an archetype, it has always played a central role in garden design and landscape architecture. The fact that in architecture such constructions reveal permeable spatial boundaries, inspired by observation of the landscape, lies literally in the nature of things.

Porosity is therefore an essential property of spatial boundaries, which is always present in nature and landscape, and ensures that separate landscape units are connected to each other and to the environment. Geologists refer to open porosity as opposed to closed porosity, which is also known as dead-end porosity (Lever D. A. et al. 1985). In landscape architecture, open porosity does not have to be an extra demand because it is just as natural as it is inevitable when working with nature. It is one of the fundamental structural principles of living landscape. Walter Benjamin's dictum "Porosity is the inexhaustible law of the life of this city" (Benjamin and Lacis 1925, 168) is thus easily transferable to landscape. From the perspective of landscape architecture, this law applies not only to urban green spaces, but also to all the spaces in a city—exterior and interior. This view is due to a profound change in the understanding of the landscape that has taken place over the past century.

In the Anthropocene, landscape can no longer be understood as a phenomenon that is exclusively shaped by nature, no longer as "nature that is aesthetically present in the sight of a perceiving and feeling observer" as the German philosopher Joachim Ritter once put it (Ritter 1963, 150–51). Today, landscape architecture is much more in line with the view of John Brinckerhoff Jackson, one of the founding fathers of American landscape studies, who stated: "A landscape is not a natural feature of the environment but a synthetic space, a man-made system of spaces superimposed on the face of the land, functioning and evolving not according to natural laws but to serve a community" (Jackson 1984, 8). Permeability and porosity of spatial boundaries are essential for the city in an open society (Sennett 2015), both spatially and socially, but more about this later on.

A special character of landscape, which can be described as "deep-porous" or "spongy", is currently of particular relevance in the development of strategies to prevent urban drought and flood catastrophes. Chinese megacities, for example, as a result of global climate change and their rapid, unsustainable growth, are severely affected by these environmental catastrophes. In the city of Beijing, a metropolis with a population of twenty million, floods have claimed the lives of many people in recent years. "The rate of flooding is a national scandal," says Chinese landscape architect Kongjian Yu. "We have poured more than enough concrete. It's time to invest in a new type of green infrastructure." (O'Meara 2015) "Natural water systems are the blood vessels of the earth and the main infrastructure of the landscape's ecosystem.[...] The natural wetlands alongside a river act like a sponge, which can modify the water quantity to mitigate drought or flood." (Yu 2012, 152)

Kongjian Yu, who grew up as the son of a farmer and is familiar with the sophisticated methods of water management in traditional Chinese agriculture (Weilacher 2017), developed the idea of a sponge city. In 2010 he successfully realized one of his first storm water parks, which play an important role in the green structure of the Chinese city of Harbin. "Using the landscape as a sponge is a good alternative solution for urban storm water management. An example of this approach is demonstrated in Turenscapes storm water park in Harbin, which integrates large-scale urban storm water management with the protection of native habitats, aquifer recharge, recreational use, and aesthetic experience, in all these ways fostering urban development." (Yu 2012, 152)

Since 2014, the sponge city construction initiative has been implemented in China at considerable cost. The aim is not only to combat floods effectively, but also to ensure more sustainable water management. Similar programs for urban water management had already been launched decades earlier in other countries. The porosity of landscape has always played a decisive role in this process, whether in water-sensitive urban design (WSUD) in Australia, low-impact development (LID) in the USA or the sustainable drainage systems (SuDS) program in Great Britain. In German landscape architecture and planning, research on sustainable rainwater management was started in the 1980s of last century, and has learned to value the particular absorption capacity of green spaces in the urban open space network. In the context of global climate change, the topic is now being revisited and *sponge city* has become a popular buzzword all over the world (Harmsen 2017).

The city as a sponge, which with its porous green fabric can react very flexibly to fluctuating environmental influences, is a vivid image that can be conveyed to the public and politicians in order to help achieve environmentally relevant development goals. However, the importance of the stability of spatial structures must not be overlooked. "Porosity in the condition of finest atomization and mixing of smallest physical and spatial particles," also designated a *cloud* by the architectural theorist Alban Janson (Janson 2016, 45), is not a desirable state for landscape because clouds are largely unstructured. Landscape architects such as Kongjian Yu know that a functioning water system must not be completely porous and permeable in all directions, as the image of the sponge might erroneously suggest. Rather, such landscape systems require a structure that ensures both the flexibility and stability of living tissue. This basically also applies to all urban infrastructures. Even sponges, which in the scientific systematics of multicellular animals are called *porifera*, are by no means completely permeable and unstructured living beings. When Yu speaks of a new type of infrastructure in connection with the sponge city concept, he is deliberately referring to basic principles of structuralism. This theoretical approach has been of central importance in landscape architecture since at least the early 1980s, and its methodical application has led to the development of trail-blazing open space projects, which are characterized by broad readability, flexible utility, site-specific historical references, and high social permeability.

Although structuralism emerged in linguistics at the beginning of the twentieth century, it was not until around 1960 that it established itself as an important avant-garde trend in architecture. Until the seventeenth or eighteenth century, the use of the term *structure* was confined to architecture and was used exclusively in the sense of construction. However, this view changed in the wake of criticism of modernist functionalism. At that time, according to Swiss architectural theorist Arnulf Lüchinger, another definition was established among the structuralists in architecture. Structure was described as "a complete set of relationships, in which the elements can change, but in such a way that these remain independent on the whole and retain their meaning. The whole is independent of its relationship to the elements. The relationships between the elements are more important than the elements themselves. The elements are interchangeable, but not the relationships." (Lüchinger 1981, 16)

Functionalism had always demanded specific spaces for specific functions, which led to the emergence of rigidly ordered spatial structures with many fixed boundaries. The Dutchman Herman Hertzberger, one of the protagonists of the structuralist architectural movement, called for the creation of versatile and adaptable spatial systems, which man should be able to acquire freely. Research results from anthropology also indicated that man can only orient himself within new structures if they are linked to familiar, culturally inherited basic patterns. "Every solution at a different place or time is an interpretation of archetypical. [...] We cannot make anything new, but only revaluate already existing images, in order to make them more suitable for our circumstances. [...] Design cannot do other than convert the underlying, and the idea of ever being able to start off with a clean slate is absurd, and moreover, disastrous when, under the pretext of its being necessary to start completely from the beginning, what already exists is destroyed, so that the naked space can be filled up with impracticable and sterile constructions." (Hertzberger 1976, 23)

Structuralism became the focus of interest in landscape architecture when, in the mid-1980s, the ecology movement became increasingly strong and ways were sought to improve the ability to change, develop, and transform designed open spaces. "We are faced with the necessity of evolving structures and forms which can develop in time; which can remain a unity and maintain the coherence of the components at all stages of their growth. The absence of this must lead to self-destruction." (Lüchinger 1981, 42) This warning by architect and structuralist Willem van Bodegraven in 1952 defined the nub of the problem at the time and in landscape architecture today is still regarded as pioneering. A living landscape must be able to change its face without losing face. Open structures, it was recognized, are perfectly suited to developing growth-enabling integration that can change dynamically without losing their identity and inner cohesion.

In landscape analysis, which deals with the examination of complex landscape systems, structuralist methods are regularly used to identify multiple superimposed structural layers. Common analytical methods such as three-dimensional layering or so-called destratification are based on this basic principle. Watercourse systems, transportation route systems, open space systems, urban structures, and other relevant networks that make up a landscape are considered and examined separately for analytical purposes. The underlying construction principles of the respective structural layers, that is, the rules according to which the different networks are built up, are thus easier to decipher. Many of these rules in landscape and environmental design, for example those according to which a functioning water system in the sponge city must be built, are based on fundamental principles that have been valid at all times in all cultures worldwide.

"Design cannot do other than convert the underlying" (Hertzberger 1976, 23). This view is particularly important in landscape architecture for conversion projects, where the genius loci, the identity of the place, is to be preserved without restricting the future ability of the landscape to change and enrich itself. Landscape architect Peter Latz used structural analysis and design methods in well-known projects such as the Landschaftspark Duisburg-Nord in 1990 or the Hafeninsel Saarbrücken in 1985. He did not force the former Saarbrücken coal port's derelict landscape to be redesigned with a new identity, but recognized that "a new syntax had to be developed for the city's center, which would reassemble the torn-up urban structures, bind the variety of manifestations, but would not spill memories, and would rather crystallize the buried out of the rubble; the 'syntactic design' for an urban open space was created" (Latz 1987, 42). The design expression of the public park on Saarbrücken's harbor island was therefore not the result of the implementation of a planned garden design, but rather developed within an open and at the same time stabilizing network of overlaid structures.

In Saarbrücken, three further levels were selected from the multitude of fragmented, buried or forgotten structural layers in addition to the uncovered industrial remains: the urban development network with sight lines to the surrounding area, the spontaneously emerging flora, and some public gardens that were integrated into the new spatial structure. The aim of the project was to revitalize and secure the character of the place. For the new park, a permeable spatial structure has been created, which, in keeping with Herman Herzberger's philosophy, offers a wide range of polyvalent spaces which the most diverse user groups and people of different cultural backgrounds can value in their own way. In the words of the sociologist Richard Sennett: "Currently, we make cities into closed systems. To make them better, we should make them into open systems." (Sennett 2013) He demands and propagates a higher level of social permeability, and parks such as the harbor island of Saarbrücken, designed according to structuralist principles, exactly meet this requirement.

"The city of the future will be an infinite series of landscapes: psychological and physical, urban and rural, flowing apart and together," wrote the London landscape architect and landscape urbanist Tom Turner, concluding, "Christopher Alexander was right: a city is not a tree. It is a landscape" (Turner 1996, v). Whether one explicitly shares this viewpoint or not, landscape will be of decisive importance for the future development of the city. On the one hand, for the reasons described above, interwoven green spaces are indispensable in the urban space network to guarantee a porosity that is more far-reaching and deeper than is possible by architectural means alone. In addition, if one looks at landscape not only as an important part of the city but also as a model for the entire urban spatial structure—based on Colin Rowe and Fred Koetter's thesis of the "garden as a critique of the city and therefore as a model of the city" (Rowe and Koetter 1997, 255)—one inevitably acts on the basis of laws and structural principles that apply to all open, dynamic systems (of space) and secure their long-lasting existence.

References:
Benjamin, W., and A. Lacis. 1925. "Naples," in *Reflections: Essays, Aphorisms, Autobiographical Writings*, edited by P. Demetz, 163–73. New York, 1978. | Harmsen, T. 2017. "Unwetter und Starkregen: Berlin soll zur 'Schwammstadt' werden," *Berliner Zeitung*, June 30, 2017. | Hertzberger, H. 1976. "Strukturalismus-Ideologie," *Bauen + Wohnen* 30: 21–24. | Jackson, J. B. 1984. *Discovering the Vernacular Landscape*. New Haven. | Janson, A. 2016. "Porosity: Ambiguous Figure and Cloud," *Cloud-Cuckoo-Land* 21, no. 35: 35–46. | Latz, P. 1987. "Die Hafeninsel in Saarbrücken," *Garten + Landschaft* 11: 42–48. | Lever, D. A., et. al. 1985. "The Effect of Dead-end Porosity on Rock-Matrix Diffusion," *Journal of Hydrology* 80: 45–76. | Lüchinger, A. 1981. *Strukturalismus in Architektur und Städtebau*. Stuttgart. | O'Meara, S. 2015. "Why China Wants to Build Something Called 'Sponge Cities,'" *City Lab*, accessed September 15, 2017, https://www.citylab.com/design/2015/11/why-china-wants-to-build-sponge-cities/417114/. | Ritter, J. 1963. "Landschaft: Zur Funktion des Ästhetischen in der modernen Gesellschaft," in idem., *Subjektivität*, 6th ed., 150–51. Frankfurt am Main. | Rowe, C., and F. Koetter. 1997. *Collage City*. Basel. | Schmarsow, A. 1894. *Das Wesen der architektonischen Schöpfung: Antrittsvorlesung, gehalten in der Aula der K. Universität Leipzig am 8. November 1893*. Leipzig. Sennett, R. 2013. "The Open City," accessed September 15, 2017, https://www.richardsennett.com/site/senn/Uploaded-Resources/The%20Open%20City.pdf. | Sennett, R. 2015. "The World Wants More 'Porous' Cities—So Why Don't We Build Them?" *The Guardian*, November 27, 2015. | Turner, T. 1996. *City as Landscape: A Post Post-Modern View of Design and Planning*. London. | Weilacher, U. 2017. "Experiencing Landscape Is the Root of Landscape Design: Udo Weilacher Interviews Landscape Architect Kongjian Yu from Beijing, October 2016," *nodium: Zeitschrift des Alumni-Clubs Landschaft der TU München* 9: 4–9. | Yu, K. 2012. "The Big Foot Revolution," in *Designed Ecologies: The Landscape Architecture of Kongjian Yu*, edited by W. S. Saunders, 42–49. Basel.

Detecting Porosity

Site-based architectural and artistic urban intervention share with urban ethnography the problem of working within field-constellations. The field emerged as a concept in the social sciences when ethnographers and anthropologists began to observe social phenomena directly, which eventually also included research in cities. In this research tradition the field is "where the action is" (Goffman 1967). It is the site for making firsthand observations, for applying techniques of immersion and intersubjective participation, for "hanging around" (Shaffir, Dietz, and Stebbins 1994, 40).

The complexity of the urban field is mirrored by the range of definitions and ideas about the field. Correspondingly, there are different ways of hanging around, of doing research in the field (Schwanhäußer 2016). This is illustrated by the variety of instances in which the term *field* is used in this chapter. In the texts accompanying the series of photos by Candida Höfer about spaces of migration, the author Ela Kaçel suggests that "from the late 1960s on, the migratory conditions of living in postwar cities had captured the attention of photographers in Germany and offered them a new field of visual investigation" (Kaçel, 241). In the St. Louis project, the question is raised as to how to make "a field of deserted ruins [...] into bustling fields of experimentation for a better city" (Foerster-Baldenius et al., 254)? In the study on commoning in Berlin, Max Ott states that "by [...] using my fieldwork as an example of a critical reflection of the practice of porosity through commoning, I am able to illustrate not only the potential but also the conflicts that both influence porosity and result from it" (Ott, 251). In the analysis by Shan Yang and Jie Sun, the field is seen as "a complex entity" that is shaped by "interactions and transactions" (Yang and Sun, 272). Observations in the field may have the quality of thick descriptions (Geertz 1973), be they graphically or photographically explored, or based on field notes of participant observation. The observation of how situations change over time, showing the spatial effects of different interests and actions in the field, adds further thickness to an analysis.

The authors in this chapter, whether they explicitly use the term *field* or simply work in the field and with the field, seem to share the view that the urban field is not a neutral research territory, nor that there is a privileged, external, and neutral point from which it can be observed. The field is understood as being permeated by competing power relations, discourses, interests, and desires. In the analysis of Dalston in London, the urban condition is seen as a "contradictory field of enquiry" (Kling and Jungfer, 260). The study of kampungs in Kuala Lumpur traces a development "from counterinsurgency to urban quality" (Eisenmann, 280), while the authors of the study on Mexico city speak of a "network of relationships that weave plots into a territory" (Göbel and Espinosa Dorantes, 284). Hence, research work undertaken in the urban field is not limited to making observations on the micro level, to the world of face-to-face interaction and immediate perception. If the urban is understood as a condition of planetary scale, field investigation is inevitably confronted with questions relating to the "context of context" (Brenner 2014, 187). Field researchers, however, do not have to shift their empirical, artistic, or theoretical focus away from the actual field, for, if we follow Adele Clarke, there are no conditions, once identified as being connected to the research problem, that do not somehow appear in the situation under study itself—even if located at a great distance from the actual problem (Clarke and Keller 2014). Exploring this capacity by means of photography and narrative writing, Markus Lanz refers to "the relationships and the context beyond the picture frame," suggesting that "space can be read as a complex situation" (Lanz, 288).

Hanging around in the urban field is not an easy task. But the work in this book shows that it is never boring. In some field constellations, new personal relationships are established. Ela Kaçel draws our attention to the fleeting relationship established between the photographer Candida Höfer and the shop owner—a brief encounter mediated by the window, an everyday situation which is nevertheless unique and cannot be repeated. It is a situative task which requires researchers, participants, and actors to respond to changes in the field and to develop a sensibility for different situations. Everydayness and specificity mix with each other in the street scene observations of Florian Kurbasik and Sofia Dona. Researchers, artists, or whoever engages directly with the urban problematic are inevitably immersed in the field. Despite all the difficulties this entails, there is one big advantage in this: research and observation in the field take place as things happen. The unfolding and flow within situations, their instability during movements, make them accessible to spatial intervention and critical urban practice. Action research, artistic and architectural intervention, if applied to the urban field, is a form of research in which research–actors–space constellations are changed during the research process. Here, detecting and acting are realized collectively in the process, as in the appropriation of the boundary wall of a park in Karachi (The Tentative Collective). Likewise, the St. Louis project concludes with an open invitation to think about future alternatives and change.

In the editorial meetings, it was clear that the porous city cannot quite be reduced to distinct categories, or for the purpose of this publication, in chapters. Detecting, in one way or another, is a basic interest of most research projects. Researchers and researching artists have an interest in pushing the limits of what we can learn from the field, but the limits will remain; moreover, we could say that the presence of limits to what we can detect in the field is part of the porous condition; it is a key urban quality. The point we wish to make here, together with the authors in this chapter, is that the urban is not out there, as a distant research object, but rather all around us.

References:
Brenner, N. 2014. "Theses on Urbanization," in *Implosions/Explosions: Towards a Study of Planetary Urbanization*, edited by N. Brenner, 181–202. Berlin. | Clarke, A., and R. Keller. 2014. "Engaging Complexities: Working Against Simplification as an Agenda for Qualitative Research Today," *Forum Qualitative Social Research* 15, no. 2, accessed January 3, 2018, http://www. qualitative-research.net/index.php/fqs/article/view/2186/3667. | Geertz, C. 1973. "Thick Description: Toward an Interpretive Theory of Culture," in idem., *The Interpretation of Cultures: Selected Essays*. New York. | Goffman, E. 1967. "Where the Action Is," in idem., Interaction Ritual, 149–270. New York. | Schwanhäußer, A., ed. 2016. *Sensing the City: A Companion to Urban Anthropology*. Bauwelt Fundamente 155. Basel. | Shaffir, W., M. L. Dietz, and R. Stebbins. 1994. "Field Research as a Social Experience: Learning to Do Ethnography," in *Doing Everyday Life: Ethnography as Human Lived Experience*, edited by M. L. Dietz, R. Prus, and W. Shaffir, 30–54. Toronto.

Porosity in Public Spaces of Migration
Ela Kaçel

From the late 1960s on, the migratory conditions of living in postwar cities had captured the attention of photographers in Germany and offered them a new field of visual investigation, observation, and study of the processes of place-making, urbanism, and migration simultaneously. Daily encounters between photographers and migrants took place in public spaces—in train stations, urban squares, workplaces, stores, restaurants, and parks.

In her photography series *Türken in Deutschland* (1973–78), Candida Höfer presents a visual genealogy of porosity regarding the simultaneous (re-)making of identities of places and people (Höfer 1980). The urban experiences of migrant dwellers as newcomers varied from alienation to the appropriation of space, from socially predetermined boundaries to individually penetrable porosity in cities. This essay aims to expand the brief titles of Höfer's photographs given after a street and a city, while focusing on the porous qualities of spaces of migration.

References:
Engelbach, B. 2014. "Candida Höfer: Türken in Deutschland 1973–78," in *Unbeugsam und ungebändigt: Dokumentarische Fotografie um 1979*, edited by B. Engelbach, 79–81. Cologne. | Heinzelmann, M., and D. Mende, eds. 2009. *Candida Höfer Projects: Done*. Cologne. | Höfer, C., E. Kentner, H. Özerturgut, and G. Wasmuth. 1980. *Türken in Deutschland*. Cologne. | Kaçel, E. 2016. "Framing Migrants as City-dwellers: Identity, Space, and Photography," in *Migration, Stadt und Urbanität: Perspektiven auf die Heterogenität migrantischer Lebenswelten*, edited by T. Geisen, C. Riegel, and E. Yildiz, 403–21. Wiesbaden. | Sennett, R. 2015. "The World Wants More 'Porous' Cities—So Why Don't We Build Them?" *The Guardian*, November 27, 2015. | Wolfrum, S., and N. von Brandis, eds. 2015. *Performative Urbanism*. Berlin.

Lindenstraße Hamburg 1978, Candida Höfer

While conveying the new place-identities of urban migration, the shop windows of Turkish grocery stores, coffee shops, and music clubs underline the physical transitions between the store and the street, the private and the public, the foreign and the familiar. While trying to create a visual appeal to passersby, some of these stores do not reveal the semiprivate atmosphere of the interior through the sheer curtain behind the windows.

All of these commercial activities in these newly founded public spaces of migration occur between their initiators and users, who are predominantly men. The presence of a woman in such spaces is a rarity. Next to the only woman figure, the vocalist Nedret Baran whose portrait is posted outside on the side of the window, Candida Höfer places herself right at the center of the image holding her camera and looking down while her reflected figure penetrates the Turkish *Tanz Bar*, merging the regularities of the street facades behind her with the unpredicted, unfamiliar attributes of this public interior.

Weidengasse Köln 1975, Candida Höfer

Documenting transitional zones between the private and the public, between order and disorder, Höfer's main interest in public spaces of migration focused on the layout of public interior spaces and the arrangement of furniture, artifacts, and goods. While studying the materiality of space, she tends to eliminate people as *sujet* from the photographic frame and highlights the porous qualities of public spaces.

   The front view of a grocery store on Weidengasse in Cologne reflects just such a dynamic moment, in which her camera itself finds a way to permeate through the shop window into the architectural layout of the store. As reflected on the photograph, there is an arch on the building located across the street that is depicted, becoming the central focal point of the image. The shopkeeper is skillfully positioned in the complex conglomeration of objects on display inside and outside making the viewer aware of the photographer's porous identity—as the shopkeeper's gaze meets Höfer's as well as the viewer's.

Lokal Rotterdam 1975, Candida Höfer

In the photographs taken in public interiors, Candida Höfer becomes engaged with her subjects whenever people look directly at her camera. In that way, her own presence in the spaces of migration is also reflected in these photographs. Whenever she can avoid the gaze of the *sujet*, her presence in a certain place and her relation to the *sujet* becomes more ambiguous. In those cases, I would suggest that porous qualities of both spaces and people reveal themselves.

In the scene captured at a Turkish restaurant in Rotterdam, Höfer enters the space as if she is a regular customer without getting the attention of the customers sitting and eating there. There is a certain cinematographic quality in this scene, unlike the other photographs she made of coffee shops—mainly because, as viewers, we can sense the atmosphere of this unfamiliar interior and perceive how the photographer naturally permeates through the door confirming Richard Sennett's statement (2015) that "urban identities are porous in the sense that we are going in and out of lots of different experiences, in different places, with people we don't know, in the course of a day."

Eifelstraße Köln 1973, Candida Höfer

The presence and visibility of Turkish migrant women in public spaces is very limited in comparison to migrant men, whose public image is identified mostly with lingering on streets, squares, or in stores. This scene captured by Höfer on Eifelstraße in Cologne illustrates a very rare situation in which the cultural codes of social status, gender, and family structure are concurrently in play with the appropriation of space on a public street. The object of photographic attention is both the car and the woman busy washing it. To be part of this performative action, the private household moved from inside to outside, treating the public sidewalk almost as their private front yard. The man sitting and waiting at the wheel is rather passive; yet he is still able to symbolically reproduce the public image of migrant men and reflect his power in the scene.

Pulverteich Hamburg 1978, Candida Höfer

Having begun as an artistic documentation of her daily encounters with new migrant dwellers in the streets of Hamburg, Berlin, Düsseldorf, and Cologne, Höfer's photography of public spaces of migration is a reflection of urban qualities that are in flux, mostly obscure, and ambivalent both in definition and use. While continuously observing the changing human landscape and its visual imprint in several postwar cities, Höfer developed a photographic interest in studying precisely the urban qualities that were obscure, transitory, and unfamiliar—for instance, clusters of men gathered randomly at odd places yet always near the main train stations. While standing around in public is the simplest act of socializing migrants can indulge in their free time, it is essentially the embodiment of a self-conscious statement of place-making that has generated a radical redefinition of the public sphere in postwar German cities through the migrants' appropriation and inhabitation of urban space.

Volksgarten Köln 1974, Candida Höfer

In Volksgarten, one of the public parks in Cologne, Höfer frequently documented the migrant communities and their use of space. Only in such photographs can women freely expose their urban identities as men do in public space; yet they are mostly bound to a certain group made up either of relatives or friends. The formation of clusters is a recurring theme in Höfer's photographs, one which reflects the gender relations between men and women. Nowhere else in cities do the boundaries between places and people become irrelevant other than in parks.

When Commons Become Common
Max Ott

Ethnographic notes on the ethics of porosity and the practice of porous space

Fade-in

For a few years now new forms of collaborative gardens have been evolving in numerous cities. These urban community gardens are an experimental space for a good city life. Together we [...] transform fallow land into meeting places, experiment with various types of composting, and exercise ourselves in preserving produce. We advocate a city worth living in and an urbanity that is future-oriented. A public space without access limitation or the obligation to consume is very important for a democratic and plural urban society. (Urban Gardening Manifest 2014)

If you want someone to outline a network of physical and social space produced by spatial practice and thus define porosity in the most trivializing words, here you are. If you want to get a glimpse of the ethics of a porous city, with words like *collaborative, experimental, worth living*, or *plural urban society*, here you are again. Such catchphrases are common in both urbanism and city marketing. Maybe depictions of porosity are only inspiring if we leave them to Benjamin and Lacis. At least they know how to trigger our nostalgia for ancient Italian cities (Benjamin and Lacis 1925). But to be honest, I only put these sentences at the beginning to invite conflict and contradiction to lead into the following.

Fieldwork

I read the abovementioned introductory words of the Urban Gardening Manifest while I'm standing in front of a thick wooden pillar. Someone has attached a printed version there with several strips of tape. The pillar bears the load of an open structure of accessible platforms on three levels. Its facade is partly covered with plants. The lowest platform covers a stage, thus creating a place to assemble even when it rains. This architecture provides space for the Neighborhood Academy, a "platform for knowledge exchange, cultural practice and urban-rural activism" (Nachbarschaftsakademie 2017). The Pergola—the official name of the wooden construction—was built with the help of students of architecture and is meant to be accessible and usable by everyone. It stands on the grounds of the Prinzessinnengärten at Moritzplatz, in the district of Kreuzberg, Berlin. Since 2009, a nonprofit initiative has run this participatory urban garden, where, in addition to growing vegetables, educational opportunities and training places are provided along with a beer garden. Until recently, Moritzplatz was typically referred to as a space "in the middle of nowhere," a periphery: "project housing from the 1960s, a gas station, discount shops, a cheap hostel, prefab buildings, firebreak walls; finally a roundabout" (Thomma 2011). But with the transformation of a former urban void into a public urban garden, its surrounding area has visibly changed. Prinzessinnengärten has become a frequently publicized and often visited prime example of the creative change of Berlin's former inner-city peripheries through a self-initiated collaborative use of urban voids (Ring and SenStadt 2013) and practices of urban commoning (Ferguson 2014). Nowadays, Prinzessinnengärten can be found in nearly every Berlin travel guide. Thus, it does not only exist as a fixed physical space, but also as a place where the hopes and aspirations of those producing it could become true. And it seems to be not only the contents, but also the atmosphere and the aesthetic of a self-made urban garden like this which appeals to people and thereby allows it to become appropriated for various and sometimes quite different purposes.

That is the reason several urban gardening activists come together under the roof of the Pergola one evening in August. They want to discuss the potentials and contradictions of urban gardens. We are sitting in a circle that allows for better interaction, as Steve Hall explains. Hall has been working in urban gardening projects for about ten years; at first only practically, but then he started to investigate urban gardens from a scientific perspective as well. Today, he is doing action research: he aims to look more critically at the often positively framed subject of urban gardening and hopes for some feedback. Together with three other gardeners he has listed some contradictions, which will be talked about in the following two hours.

The four participants agree that urban gardens are places where questions of environmental justice are negotiated and practically answered. And they are also sure that urban gardening is becoming increasingly coopted by strategies of city marketing. Furthermore, they observe that many corporations pick up their ideas to "greenwash" and obscure interests that would in fact oppose the very principles of an urban gardening movement. At this point, the debate begins to turn into a critical self-reflection, as two participants talk about their own cooperation with private companies: Martin Launer of Prinzessinnengärten brings up a small amount of funding from a cosmetics company. He calls it a "situational" decision, based on both the observation that the methods of the company did at least not collide with the ethics of the gardeners, and the relative insignificance of the financial amount meant that unpredictable dependencies would not occur. Andrew Follinger got into a somewhat bigger dilemma with his collective garden project in Cologne: after heated debate, his initiative decided to accept funding from the energy company Rheinenergie; a five-digit sum of money that was indispensable for the coordination of the project in its initial phase. The gardeners only agreed to this because the company guaranteed it would not attempt to influence the distribution of the money. But without this funding, the garden would never have come into being.

"We have to watch the clock because there are some contradictions left" Steve Hall interrupts. And now, ideas about urbanity and the urban condition, so far more or less disregarded by the participants in the discussion begin to be developed. The organizers of that evening conceptualize their urban gardening projects as places of social diversity and understand them as a spatial practice to help put into practice Henri Lefebvre's famous claim for a right to the city (Lefebvre 1968). But concurrently, they ask to what extent these urban gardens might be places of exclusion and sites of gentrification. Martin Launer describes how such questions are becoming discussed more and more frequently, sometimes even fiercely, as processes of social segregation in Berlin's inner-city districts have been increasing in the last few years. As he recalls, nobody was interested in the neighborhood around Moritzplatz when he moved from Prenzlauer Berg to Kreuzberg in the early 2000s. And even when Prinzessinnengärten started in 2009, he could not have foreseen either the prominence that the project would gain in such a short period or the rapid increase in private real estate investments and how that would reinforce the pressure of valorization on inner-city properties. Back then the annual renewal of an agreement with the Berlin state, which regulates the temporary use of the property, seemed to be just a formality. Now, Launer says, the garden initiative even has to be grateful to have negotiated its tenure until 2018. And this again would only be the result of a broad and successful protest they organized in 2012 against the intentions of the Berlin state to privatize their property. The Urban Gardening Manifesto and the Neighborhood Academy should also be understood against this backdrop, as they both took up a position opposing the processes of gentrification and tried to make it clear that Prinzessinnengärten is much more than just a place to grow vegetables. In fact, Launer says, it creates an accessible space to collectively produce and share knowledge about ecological and social sustainability and is thus an open network for a good life in the city.

But commoning is not easy. Andrew Follinger points out how the very attempt to design an urban garden as a space for all did produce a particular form of exclusion. Driven by the intention to establish urban commons beyond any form of individual property, the urban gardeners in Cologne created only one continuous raised garden bed without any partitions. This was meant as a materialization of collective ownership and was based on the idea that nobody has exclusive legal property rights in the garden and nobody, as someone in the circle explains, "can question the rights of others to use and in this sense 'own' the same commons as well" (see also Kratzwald 2015). But the expected collective appropriation of the raised bed could not be activated and the initial group of participants was not diverse in terms of social or cultural background. This situation did not change until readjustments had been made and more individual raised garden beds had been built. "I don't want to use any clichés," Follinger says, but only then did heterogeneity among the participants increase and more elderly people and people with "migrant backgrounds" start to use the garden on a regular basis. Follinger is convinced that one could learn from this experience in many respects: On the one hand, it shows that establishing a project of spatial commons according to its fundamental principles requires hard work from its commoners and the willingness to constantly negotiate and intervene. On the other hand, it reveals the existence of specific sociocultural boundaries, mostly unwanted and often invisible at first sight. Follinger looks around and states that today's group of participants would also more or less consist of white German middle-class males, who would probably deal with urban commons from an academic perspective. Although he might be right concerning his middle-class argument, he exaggerates in regard to gender and nationality. Among the participants there are more women than men, and throughout the evening people speak Spanish, French, English, and Italian. But nonetheless, for Follinger this much is clear: the challenge is to create a productive connection between those who are most of the time writing about urban commons in academic terms, but are relatively inexperienced in commoning, and those who are long time commoners, but are not used to theorizing about the broader social context of urban commons and its contradictions, or have other needs and wishes with a higher priority.

During the discussion about urban commons, social diversity, and exclusion, someone has raised his hand. He is also participating in an urban gardening project in Berlin and he wants to talk about another issue he is concerned with. He says all the effort that people put into collective urban gardens in inner-city districts like this one will be useless unless processes of gentrification come to an end: if they do not, urban gardens will then only be available for "yuppies" who can still afford to live in Kreuzberg. "It's nice" to talk about gardens, but he would be troubled much more by rising rents and he sees the ongoing evictions in his neighborhood as the real threat. Toward the end of the event under the roof of the Pergola, the participants address the connection between urban gardening and gentrification. An activist criticizes the fact that many bottom-up initiatives are dedicated to transforming urban voids into new public spaces—completely unpaid and therefore in perfect accordance with the austerity policies of Berlin's city government, which promotes self-reliant creative action. And furthermore, it would be exactly this practice that actively contributes to the valorization of urban space and increases the risk of such initiatives becoming gentrification's next victims.

For the last time this evening, Martin Launer stands up. He picks up the argument of the previous speaker that a valorization of space in terms of atmosphere and cultural practice would eventually increase its financial value. Launer does not deny this connection but neither does he want collaborative urban gardens or other forms of community-oriented temporary use of urban space to take the blame for processes of gentrification. Instead he passes responsibility to others and supports his argument with the words of a high-profile researcher: Of course, it is necessary to critically reflect on one's own contribution to an economic valorization of urban space, Launer says, but he remembers a recent lecture by Saskia Sassen, where the American sociologist and economist pointed out that in 2015 alone an amount of several billions was invested in Berlin's housing market by private real estate funds. For him, this shows who is really influencing the spatial transformation in districts like Kreuzberg, even though these processes take place almost invisibly. He points to an apartment house at Moritzplatz to illustrate his words: "Many of its mostly migrant inhabitants do not know that they are living there only temporarily [*auf Abruf*]," he says. The building—since 2005 owned by Goldman Sachs—was purchased by the real estate company Deutsche Wohnen after the financial crisis. Launer is convinced: "Affordable housing or mixed neighborhoods are not at the top of their agenda." Against this backdrop, the critique of temporary uses as fuel for gentrification could be really annoying—everyone should just try to imagine for one moment what will happen to the property of Prinzessinnengärten once it becomes traded on the free market as a valuable future building site.

Fade-out

Do we still agree on the notion of porous space as a relation of physical and social space? If we do, then I suggest we have to focus on this very relation to prevent our observations becoming superficial and our theories essentialist. And if we want to investigate relatedness, we need to be aware of the fact that we are not dealing with a fixed objectivity of space where the material is only a result of the social (as many sociologists explicitly argue) or the social is determined and thus bound by the material (as many architects implicitly argue). If space is a product (Lefebvre 1974), then it is never one-way. In fact we have to investigate a contradictory sociomaterial assemblage, which is always shaping and being shaped by conflicting spatial practices. Society is not a realm of harmony and overall consensus, but is defined by diverging interests, moralities, or ethics, by opposing rationalities and by manifold contradictions and contestations.

I discussed Prinzessinnengärten to shed at least some light on these assumptions that I regard to be crucial whenever we start to think about porosity. By addressing the urban garden as a project of porosity through urban commons and by using my fieldwork as an example of a critical reflection of the practice of porosity through commoning, I am able to illustrate not only the potential but also the conflicts that both influence porosity and result from it.

On the one hand, the specific design for a once informal parking lot in Berlin's former border territory and its appropriation as Prinzessinnengärten since the year 2009 can be considered an inspiring example for the practice of porosity. An urban void, vanished from public notice and utility, has been transformed into a place. A fence, which was previously meant to keep people away, is now defining territory as an urban common for everyone, which celebrates the very idea of porosity. A three-dimensional wooden construction is a result of collective efforts and creates space to interact, to communicate or just to sit, watch and catch one's breath. The garden in the heart of the city does far more than just material-ize an ideal of sustainable ecourbanism. It is meant to be urban because of its potential and capability to gather together different people with different backgrounds and different purposes.

On the other hand, the evening discussion provided an insight into how this porous project is intertwined with broader questions of spatial transformation, urban governance, gentrification, or social diversity, which define a specific scope of action and produce particular conflicts and contradictions. Prinzessinnengärten as a creative and accessible use of abandoned property transformed the perception of the area around Moritzplatz and increased its attraction as a desirable neighborhood to live in with great potential for future development. Against the backdrop of the increasing pressure of growth on Berlin's inner-city districts and in the light of austerity politics, where property is mostly privatized according to the speculative and competitive principles of a market-based economy, the spatial practice of Prinzessinnengärten might therefore be understood as a pioneering driver of gentrification (Holm 2010; Bauer 2012). At the same time, and I would argue even more so, the urban garden could become the next victim of a financial valorization of urban space. Thus, the whole concept of a space for everyone, which represents a socially mixed neighborhood community, is considered to be at stake. But it is not only this threatened porous space that has become a subject of critical inquiry, it is also the everyday practice of producing it. The participants realize that a specific spatial design does not necessarily result in an appropriation by a diverse group of participants. There is a gap between those—for one thing—who promote and conceptualize urban space according to ideals of urban diversity, and—for another thing—all the different wishes, needs, and desires of those being addressed by such ideals (Roskamm 2013). This gap has to be taken seriously as it reveals the diverse realities of sociomaterial space and spatial practice.

What does that mean for attempts to move from an epistemological understanding of porosity toward a perspective that regards it as a category for urban design concepts and thus seeks to strengthen its ontological dimension? I suggest there are at least two important matters of concern: first, the given political economy within (or against?) which porosity has to be negotiated as a spatial concept with spe-cific values that cannot be expressed in the pseudo logic of numbers and second, all the frictions, fractions and distinctions (Bourdieu 1984) that represent and reproduce the heterogeneity of an urban society whose members differ in terms of age, class, gender, nationality, religious and political beliefs, or cultural background. They will, no matter whether we like it or not, contest our understanding of porosity and in doing so reveal our implicit preconceptions and orientations.

References:

Bauer, P. 2012. "Die Hipster, die ich rief," *Süddeutsche Zeitung*, January 13, 2012, 13. | Benjamin, W., and A. Lacis. 1925. "Naples," in *Reflections: Essays, Aphorisms, Autobiographical Writings*, edited by P. Demetz, 163–73. New York, 1978. | Bourdieu, P. 1984. *Distinction: A Social Critique of the Judgement of Taste*. Translated by R. Nice. London, 2010. | Ferguson, F., ed. 2014. *Make-Shift City: Renegotiating the Urban Commons*. Berlin. | Holm, A. 2010. *Wir Bleiben Alle! Gentrifizierung: Städtische Konflikte um Aufwertung und Verdrängung*. Hamburg. | Kratzwald, B. 2015. "Urban Commons—Dissident Practices in Emancipatory Spaces," in *Urban Commons: Moving Beyond State and Market*, edited by M. Dellenbaugh et al., 26–41. Basel. | Lefebvre, H. 1968. *Le Droit à la ville*. Paris. | Lefebvre, H. 1974. *The Production of Space*. Translated by D. Nicholson-Smith. Malden, 1991. | Nachbarschaftsakademie. 2017. "About," accessed September 16, 2017, www.nachbarschaftsakademie.org/about/. | Ring, K., and Senatsverwaltung für Stadtentwicklung und Umwelt Berlin, eds. 2013. *Self-Made City Berlin: Stadtgestaltung und Wohnprojekte in Eigeninitiative*. Berlin. | Roskamm, N. 2013. *Das Leitbild von der "Urbanen Mischung": Geschichte, Stand der Forschung, Einund Ausblicke*. Berlin. | Thomma, N. 2011. "Robert Shaw: Früher Regisseur und Videokünstler, heute Gärtner," *Süddeutsche Zeitung Magazin*, no. 48, accessed September 16, 2017, http://sz-magazin.sueddeutsche.de/texte/anzeigen/36669/1/1. | Urban Gardening Manifest. 2014. Accessed September 16, 2017, http://urbangardeningmanifest.de/mitmachen.

252
253

Participant observation:

The empirical data of the meeting in Prinzessinnengärten was collected during a participant observation on August 3, 2016. I use assumed names to ensure the anonymity of those quoted, and I put direct quotes, written down during the discussion, in quotation marks.

St. Louis
METROPOLIS OF THE MISSISSIPPI VALLEY
DRAWN IN PERSPECTIVE A.D.
1875
CAMILLE N. DRY
DESIGNED & EDITED BY
Rich. J. Co...

FEAT. SPACEBUSTER

raumlaborberlin

Here you can see the city of churches, breweries, brickyards, bureaucracy and almost a million people in bloom. One hundred years after St. Louis was bought by the US President/Architect Jefferson, St. Louis held a World Fair and the Olympic Games. Now world-famous, the city gr... like a mushroom.
St. Louis was composed of the same sort of mix we had in Ber... at that time. Maybe this is why many Germans settled here. An... as in Berlin the growth stopped i... the 1950s, though the city´s declin... started twenty years earlier...

St. Louis 1875
One hundred years after its foundation.
The funny thing is: in the year when Camille N. Dry made these axonometric drawings the city looked in large parts the same way it does today:
some dense areas, but mostly blocks with a lonely house here and there. As if it had never been otherwise.
But it wasn´t always like that...

a report on 150 years of urban practice:
drawn by Yü Chen & C. Dry
concept + text: Sabine Zahn + Benjamin Foerster-Baldenius

St. Louis St. Louis, Big City once a dream but everything in Gateway City ain't always what it seems ♪ you might b...

urban practice :
° = movement
* = places

1° urban horse riding
2° drinking in public
3° building houses

4° walking
5° praying
6° private gardening

7* **Lewis Place** – originally a "white" neighborhood—after one black doctor managed to buy a home, property value decreased heavily and turned the neighborhood "black" in just a few years. Home on Enright Avenue 4562.

...onsed when you come out of town, but racial divide is no more common ground ... ♪♫♪ So little just little people is better...

8° Pruitt-Igoe – 1955 first American social housing complex. Famously destroyed in 1975 (designed by the same architect as the World Trade Center).

9° Pulitzer Arts Foundation – a public building designed by Tadao Ando owned by a private foundation with an engaged staff strongly involved in community projects.

10° driving the car

Dividing the city

During Roosevelt's New Deal policy in the 1930s, when state and city politicians drew a red line through St. Louis—One side would get subsidies, the other wouldn't. People living north of the dividing line on Delmar Blvd. are 98 percent African American, and people living in the south are 73 percent white. Even today this line remains visible: the median home values are $73,000 north versus $335,000 south, median incomes $18,000 versus $50,000 and the percentage of residents with bachelor's degrees are 10 percent, versus 70 percent.

7* **Lewis Place** in the past 60 years many houses were demolished here. In 2016 raumlabor disassembled number 4562 Enright Ave and brought it across Delmar to the Pulitzer.
12* **College School** – a private "experiential" primary school in Webster Grove. Great campus—cool teachers—super classes—nice kids—but almost no African-Americans.

13* **Barbara C. Jordans public elementary school** in University City. Okay campus—they have teachers, regular classes, and we saw one white kid. The area is full of Asian restaurants—where are the Asian-American kids?
14* **WashU** – Best of all unis in Missouri. Situated in (mostly black) University City: guess the color of the students!

15* **Cherokee Street** – on Cherokee Street—Mexican food and stores domain—finally Hispanics on the street!
16* **Lovebank Park** – ambitious basketball field—neighborhood project run by Anne from across the road and the owner of the pizza joint next door. Black kids playing basketball.
17* sitting on porches

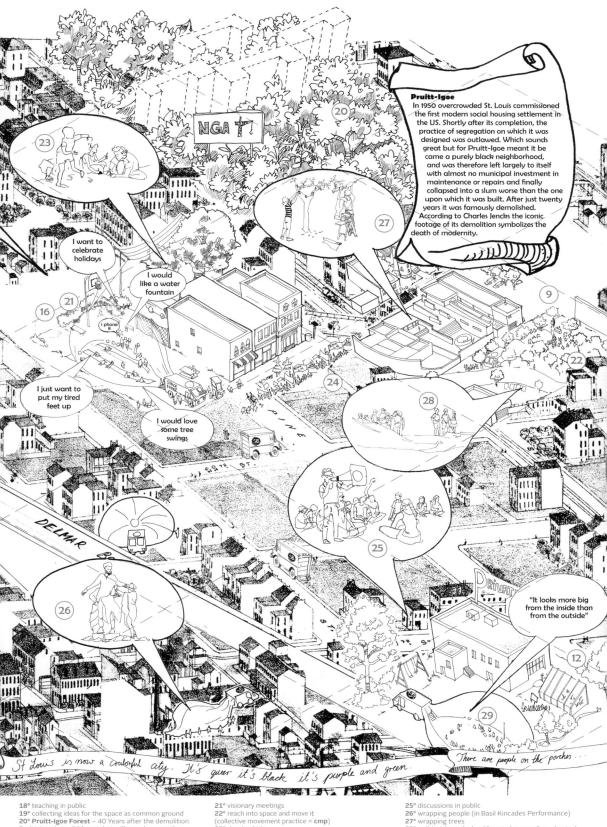

18° teaching in public
19° collecting ideas for the space as common ground
20° **Pruitt-Igoe Forest** – 40 Years after the demolition
Pruitt-Igoe is a wild forest, but will soon become the
National Geographic Agency (NGA) (same same like NSA).

21° visionary meetings
22° reach into space and move it
(collective movement practice = **cmp**)
23° dancing kids
24° protest

25° discussions in public
26° wrapping people (in Basil Kincades Performance)
27° wrapping trees
28° walking through cloud forests (cmp on Spacebuster)
29° learning in public

14* Spacebuster @ WashU
30° revival of drinking in public
7* Spacebuster @ 4562 Enright
31° public voting for questions
32° planting questions
33° making gardens with coffeebags and landscape staples

34* Butterfly Garden @ 4562 Enright
35* Public College School
36° listen to the feet—lie down on the street
37° water fountain chats
38° dipping into pools (like the Pulitzers?)
39° sitting in the corner watching people

40° cmp all over
41° visionary thinking on horseback
42* Pulitzer Acropolis – temples of art for everyone
43° hanging out and over public furniture
44° smartphone-free zone
45° crossing ephemeral borders

The landscape of potentialities

Is it possible to create a colorful new city only with the fantastic people we met as protagonists? A city that is not ruled by prejudice, a city of diversity, a city of trust and experimentation? It would still need a whole new set of urban practices not only in schools and universities, but also for the police, the administration and on the streets (not to mention the gun laws). We found some cool initiatives in these pockets of a new common ground such as Lovebank Park, the Lewis Place Neighborhood, and the Pulitzer Arts Foundation. These are places with an alternative economy, new discourses, and habits.

What if these places started to spread their values like the old city did a century ago and converted the remains of St. Louis into bustling fields of experimentation for a better city?

So little, too little People - no Cash! AH AH AH AH AH ... !!! ♪ ♫ ♬ ♩ So little Too little People .... AH AH AH AH by B. F. Baldenius

46° looking at the city upside down
47° leaning against objects in the city, resting
48° walking! down the street to meet friends
49° Lovebank (+ Basketball and Dancing Park)

50° Mississippi River – making the river into a public space
51° St. Louis Brick Festival – all the things that can be done with old bricks: brickfitti

52° Cahokia – center of the Mississippian culture 700–1400 AD with est. peak population of 40,000

Contested Porosities
Norbert Kling and Carsten Jungfer

A Spatial Inquiry into Urban Conflicts in Dalston, East London

Engaging porosity from an urban perspective means working with notions that are difficult to grasp. Drawing from the writings of Henri Lefebvre, we understand the urban condition as an open and contradictory field of inquiry which is defined by movements between appropriation and domination on the one hand, and by movements between dispersion and accumulation on the other hand (Lefebvre 1974, 343, 386–87; Brenner 2014, 194; Schmid 2012, 56). For the purpose of this study, we distinguish between space as a territorial unit, which we refer to as site, and space as a relational arrangement (Löw 2001) which is socially produced and which recursively acts upon its constituent process. Urban territories and spatial arrangements are seen as being continuously negotiated and reproduced, and therefore as being in a state of constant change.

Obsolescence or creative destruction, in combination with economic recession, political inactivity or conditions of uncertainty, produce spaces that fall out of the cycle of hegemonic spatial (re-)production for extended periods of time. They become available to alternative modes of space production, to experiment, to other ways of doing architecture (Awan, Schneider, and Till 2011). If we think of porous spaces as the residues of the urban (Lefebvre 1970, 55–56 and 87), and in that sense as destabilizers of established routines, we acknowledge that porosity could be a major factor in processes of urban change. In terms of their capacity to define and accommodate differences, porous spaces seem to resemble the heterotopias conceptualized by Michel Foucault (1967). But while heterotopias are planned spaces of otherness, conceived as stabilizing and reaffirming hegemonic modes of space production through containment (Löw 2001, 140), porous spaces challenge the urban condition and its mechanisms of domination. Porous spaces have agency in that they may be configured to serve different goals. Some spaces are the result of countercultural movements and act as highly visible exponents of an urban other, some are more concerned with alternative practices of the everyday or community life. It is through processes of individual and collective appropriation, through generating the unexpected and disorderly, through making new connections, that these spaces reproduce their specific qualities. Porous spaces could be seen as accommodating and supporting processes that are concerned with changing how the world is. This distinguishes them from spaces that are established through institutionalized routines. Hence, on the one hand we have the promise of porous spaces to make a difference in the city, which, ultimately, could be seen as making a difference in how we change ourselves (Harvey 2008); on the other hand there is the looming commercial interest to reactivate them as sites of accumulation and valorization, and to revert them to the cycle of institutionalized spatial (re-)production. This basic conflict defines porous spaces as a contested zone in the city. They are sites where multiple problems and conflicting desires meet. They are prime targets in the politics of space.

To focus our inquiry we take a closer look at the area around Ashwin Street in Dalston, which has been the home to our London practice for almost ten years. Dalston is a ward in the London Borough of Hackney (LBH) in East London. Decades of gradual economic decline and the relocation of light industry have freed up spaces for low-revenue and creative uses that have developed and been adapted over time. A diverse mix of groups and organizations, including many nonprofit organizations, cooperatives, and charities, are located in or near Ashwin Street and provide their services to the local and wider community. Since the turn of the millennium, Dalston experienced substantial change through urban restructuring and investment in new public transport infrastructure. The area became more accessible and widely known, not least because Hackney was one of four hosting boroughs for the Olympic Games in 2012. Dalston is now seen as a bustling hub for creative businesses, social enterprises, and cultural activities. But it is also the home to minority populations, migrants, and households with low incomes; it is a place of radical spatial transformation, of rapidly rising rents, of persistent inequality and urban struggle (LBH 2017, 19).

The transformation process in Dalston bears the characteristics of two distinct patterns of change. On the one hand are the multiple, small-scale adaptations of incremental change initiated by different actors. On the other hand we see the construction of urban infrastructure, large housing schemes, and new commercial developments procured in public-private partnership and funded by what Jane Jacobs terms "cataclysmic money" (Jacobs 1961, 291ff). Invested to initiate rapid and far-reaching modifications of the urban environment, cataclysmic money is linked to processes of centralized decision-making and follows the dominant and institutionalized model of space production. If, from the perspective of dominant space production, porous spaces are primarily seen as resources that are best exploited through reintegrating them in systems of accumulation and valorization, any failure to do so must appear as challenging the dominant system and as a destabilizing condition. Conversely, any attempt to reintegrate porous spaces into the dominant system must appear as a threat to the activities that unfold within them. Due to the asymmetry in terms of access to knowledge and resources, the stakeholders use different strategies to act in the situation. The local authorities and commercial stakeholders have an interest in channeling the process toward established routes of procurement. Their actions are underpinned by existing property rights, planning legislation, long-term investment plans, and the requirements of public-private partnership arrangements. These processes are optimized to the interests of the dominant mode of space production. Conversely, the actors in porous spaces make use of the potential of their spaces to create network connections, to assemble initiatives, and to generate social power, with the intention to keep the urban arena of change open to multiple interests and to resist domination. The current Dalston Area Action Plan (Dalston AAP), which is part of the Council's Local Development Framework, is based on the idea that there could be a resolution to the ensuing tensions—through establishing a Dalston Quarter which integrates porous spaces with conventional modes of space production (LBH 2015). However, the plan conceals the basic urban conflict and fails to recognize that, in the sense of an urban agonistics proposed by Chantal Mouffe (2013), the conflicting modes of space production must be understood as incompatible with each other. It could well be, as has happened in other areas of London before, that the pressure on porous spaces in Dalston will be further increased, and that some of them may disappear as a result of the landmark Council scheme (LBH 2015) being realized. Their future seems to depend on the preparedness of actors in the dominant mode of production to tolerate, and maybe even value, the copresence of a different and latently destabilizing mode of space production, without forcing upon them the logics of dominant space. However, if the actors whose primary concern is the market value of their urban developments support a politics of porosity friendliness only as long as it has no adverse effects on their own goals (Stratis 2015, 1042), the limits of wishful thinking become apparent. The actors would need to accept the idea of persisting conditions of conflict. It would require them to invest time and energy in a continuous effort to negotiate the relations of different modes of space production. Both long-term community activities and long-term investment initiatives would need to deal with conditions of uncertainty in a new way. In relation to the future of porous spaces, the problem of how actors working within porous spaces manage to relate to dominant modes of space production without losing their multiple identities and their capacity to generate urban otherness will be a core issue.

Based on the outlined condition of the basic urban conflict, we will now shift the focus to the physical and material constituents of space—to architectural arrangements—and the conflicts we find in their relatedness to social processes. The proposition we put forward is that conflicts are not limited to the obvious and well-understood conflicts that occur between sites of porous spaces and development sites—overshadowing, questions of access and control, emissions, rising rents—but that we also find them as contradictions within the porous domain itself. We have argued that it is characteristic of porous spaces that they connect to multiple groups, that they generate different ideas of the urban, and that they are in a state of movement and change. If closure implies immobility (Lefebvre 1970, 174), porous urban spaces must be conceived as open spaces. Urbanist Socrates Stratis suggests that "establishing urban porosities means increasing the degree of coexistence in open spaces and the degree of sharing of infrastructures" (Stratis 2015, 1042).

If coexistence, open spaces, and ideas of sharing are at the core of porous spaces, it is not self-evident that there is a strong presence of physical enclosures in and around Ashwin Street and that much attention is paid to their articulation. They define an inside and an outside and are consequential for both domains. They could be seen as negotiating access to and control of spaces, and therefore as instruments of power, but also as devices in the construction of identities and in the organization of everyday lives. According to sociologist Helmuth Berking et al., "the struggle for control of urban spaces is an ambivalent mode of sociation, one that cuts systematically across the whole of everyday life: in and by producing themselves, groups produce exclusive spaces and then, in turn, use the boundaries they have created to define themselves" (Berking et al. 2006, 9; see also Löw 2001, 191). The ensuing conflict between inclusion/exclusion raises specific problems and could explain why the architectural articulation of the enclosing structures is far more than an engineering exercise. For Richard Sennett the porous border is not so much a line of demarcation but rather an interface and meeting zone, "an edge where different groups interact" (Sennett 2007). The wall and porous border create "a liminal space; that is, space at the limits of control, limits which permit the appearance of things, acts, and persons unforeseen, yet focused and sited" (Ibid.). This proposition implies that both inside and outside, porous space and hegemonic space, engage in a mutual relationship with each other, in particular at their boundaries. Porous boundaries do bidirectional work. The enclosure around artist Leandro Erlich's *Dalston House* makes sense only because there are people from the outside who pass through it so that they can interact with the installation; the ground-floor lobby of Print House and the staircase leading up to Dalston Roof Park are liminal spaces in which inside/outside encounters are not only possible, but likely to occur. The inflatable structure on the roof, which provided a sheltered environment for a multitude of events for a few years, enabled the users to completely transform the space, define a unique inside, and to signal a strong message of otherness to the outside. The gateway to The Eastern Curve community garden project acts in its opened state as a three-dimensional structure that can be occupied in different ways. The boundaries are situated within and influenced by the same contradictory movements as the spaces they help to define. In this sense, porous boundaries and porous spaces are messengers and producers of otherness in the contested arena of urban change.

References:

Awan, N., T. Schneider, and J. Till. 2011. *Spatial Agency: Other Ways of Doing Architecture*. Abingdon. | Berking, H., et al., eds. 2006. *Negotiating Urban Conflicts: Interaction, Space and Control*. Bielefeld. | Brenner, N. 2014. "Theses on Urbanization," in idem., *Implosions/Explosions: Towards a Study of Planetary Urbanization*, 181–202. Berlin. | Foucault, M. 1967. "Of Other Spaces: Heterotopias," translated by J. Miskowiec, *Diacritics* 16, no. 1 (1986): 22–27. | Harvey, D. 2008. "The Right to the City," *New Left Review* 53: 23–53. | Jacobs, J. 1961. *The Death and Life of Great American Cities*. New York. | Lefebvre, H. 1970. *The Urban Revolution*. Translated by R. Bononno. Minneapolis, 2003. | Lefebvre, H. 1974. *The Production of Space*. Translated by D. Nicholson-Smith. Malden, 1991. | London Borough of Hackney (LBH). 2015. *Forward Strategy for the Delivery of the Dalston Quarter*, accessed August 12, 2017, https://www.hackney.gov.uk/media/3259/Dalston-Quarter-cabinet-report/pdf/Dalston_Quarter_Cabinet_Report_Nov_2015. | London Borough of Hackney (LBH). 2017. *A Profile of Hackney, Its People and Place*, accessed August 12, 2017, https://www.hackney.gov.uk/media/2665/Hackneyprofile/pdf/HackneyProfile2. | Löw, M. 2001. *The Sociology of Space: Materiality, Social Structures, and Action*. Translated by D. Goodwin. New York, 2016. | Mouffe, C. 2013. *Agonistics: Thinking the World Politically*. London. | Schmid, C. 2012. "Henri Lefebvre, the Right to the City, and the New Metropolitan Mainstream," in *Cities for People, Not for Profit: Critical Urban Theory and the Right to the City*, edited by N. Brenner, P. Marcuse, and M. Mayer, 42–62. New York. | Sennett, R. 2007. "The Open City," in *The Endless City*, edited by R. Burdett and D. Sudjic, 290–97. London. | Stratis, S. 2015. "Urban Porosity Patterns for Exchange in the City: The Case of Europan," in *Proceedings of the 29th Annual AESOP 2015 Congress, Definite Space—Fuzzy Responsibility*, edited by M. Macoun and K. Maier, 1027–45. Prague.

p. 264: Contested porosities: the changing urban situation in and around Ashwin Street in Dalston, East London. Sites 1–4, owned by the council, and the site to the east of Eastern Curve are earmarked for development.

p. 265: Setting up—and fencing in—of *Dalston House* by artist Leandro Erlich in 2013. A large mirror makes an accessible platform appear as facade. The installation is an invitation to participate in the distortion and subversion of spatial reality.

p. 265: The former car park at the rear of the Bootstrap Company's Print House and Fitzroy House is currently occupied by the Dusty Knuckle social project bakery, 40FT Brewery, and other micro-enterprises and activities. The Local Area Plan defines this space as development site 4.

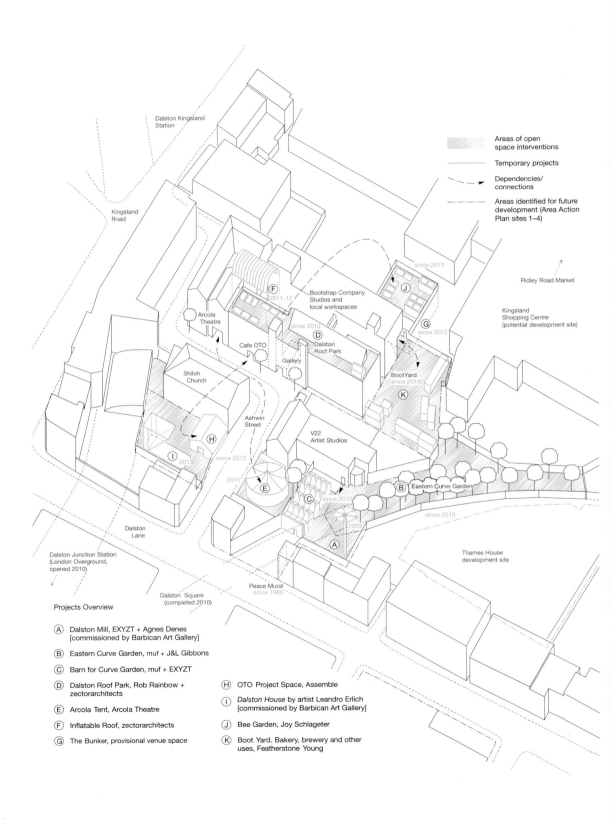

Dalston Kingsland
Station

Kingsland
Road

Areas of open
space interventions

Temporary projects

Dependencies/
connections

Areas identified for future
development (Area Action
Plan sites 1–4)

Ridley Road Market

Kingsland
Shopping Centre
(potential development site)

since 2013

F 2011–12

Arcola
Theatre

Cafe OTO

Gallery

Bootstrap Company
Studios and
local workspaces

J

G since 2012

since 2010

D

Dalston
Roof Park

BootYard
since 2015

K

Shiloh
Church

H

I 2013

since 2013

2011

E

Ashwin
Street

V22
Artist Studios

C

since 2010

B

Eastern Curve Garden

A

3
2009

since 2010

Thames House
development site

Dalston
Lane

Dalston Junction Station
(London Overground,
opened 2010)

Dalston Square
(completed 2010)

Peace Mural
since 1985

Projects Overview

A Dalston Mill, EXYZT + Agnes Denes
   [commissioned by Barbican Art Gallery]

B Eastern Curve Garden, muf + J&L Gibbons

C Barn for Curve Garden, muf + EXYZT

D Dalston Roof Park, Rob Rainbow +
   zectorarchitects

E Arcola Tent, Arcola Theatre

F Inflatable Roof, zectorarchitects

G The Bunker, provisional venue space

H OTO Project Space, Assemble

I Dalston House by artist Leandro Erlich
   [commissioned by Barbican Art Gallery]

J Bee Garden, Joy Schlageter

K Boot Yard. Bakery, brewery and other
   uses, Featherstone Young

Bahnhofsviertel
Florian Kurbasik

A ladies' wear store was established in a former diner. Goethestraße, Munich

Goods for a butcher's shop are delivered through a window. Landwehrstraße, Munich

A converted bank branch now serves as a hairdresser's. Schwanthalerstraße, Munich

The loading area of a grocery store extends to the street. Goethestraße, Munich

Overripe fruits are sold in a passageway. Landwehrstraße, Munich

Flatbread is produced in a former garage. Landwehrstraße, Munich

From Diversity to Porosity
Shan Yang and Jie Sun

A Spatial Investigation into a Chinese University and Its Neighborhoods

Porosity is often treated as meaning a boundary's ambiguity and permeability. Accordingly, considerable attention is paid to intervention in boundaries as an effective way to generate porosity. Yet porosity is not determined by one single factor. As a complex entity of the urban environment, it results from the interwoven layers of sociospatial components that vary from place to place. Linked by the general relationship of affiliation and analogy, porosity and such concepts as diversity, urbanity, publicness, etc., can be subsumed under a "familienähnliche" (Wittgenstein 1953, 36) category of urban quality, wherein the closest relation is between porosity and diversity.

Referring commonly to the mixture of components, porosity and diversity are two poles on the spectrum of the mixture. Whereas the defining characteristics of diversity are a multiplicity or variety of components, porosity features their interpenetration and integration. Although the two qualities are closely interrelated, diversity does not necessarily convert into porosity, or vice versa. A staged diversity may be only the cliché of programmatic juxtaposition, thereby hardly tolerating a jumble of uses and triggering unpredictable interpenetration, while an undue porosity may grow into overpermeability so as to assimilate the other through complete integration. Between the extremes, there is a continuous range of intermediate levels embodied by different urban situations carrying traits of both qualities.

To understand this ambiguity, we could sketch the place-making process of a Chinese university, Nanjing University (NJU), and show how the intrinsic connections between diversity and porosity were built up. The campus and its surroundings, located in Gulou District, represent the most vital and idiosyncratic area in Nanjing and are animated by Jacobs's "generators of diversity" (Jacobs 1961, 150–51), but are also entwined with a complex mélange of factors including history, topography and institution.

Mixed-use

According to Jacobs, mixed primary uses are a necessary condition for diversity. "By primary uses she means residential and major employment or service function—any land use that generates a large number of people moving through an area" (Hoppenbrouwer and Louw 2005, 970). Obviously, the campus with its 10,000 students and employees undertakes a primary use. Another one is the residential neighborhoods next to the campus's west flank with almost 14,000 inhabitants. The two primary uses further produce the demand for secondary uses such as restaurants, bars, and other small-scale facilities. In addition, the degree of mixing is secured through the urban texture, for example, density, grain, and permeability. Firstly, with nearly 327 people per hectare, the population density surpasses the threshold density of 250 people per hectare defined as "in-between" density by Jacobs (Jacobs 1961, 210–11). Secondly, the west section of the area is subdivided into many small parcels by narrow streets. None of the lots exceeds 3 ha. Roads, lanes, and paths cut across and connect the campus and neighborhoods, providing democratic choices for changing direction and chances to encounter others. Paralleling the textural features, certain uses with transactional ingredients also enhance the spatial capacity for interpenetrating. Such land use types as the playground or the streets, shops, and bars offer an intense series of interactions and transactions between the university and the neighborhood.

Of course, mixed-use is not an automatic panacea for stimulating diversity and porosity. The evolving process of urban quality always goes beyond the extent to which people and factors outside the planners' immediate sphere of influence condition what is built and its quality (Rowley 1996).

History

Most Chinese elitist universities grew out of a Christian college. One of NJU's precursors was the University of Nanking, founded in 1910 and sponsored by the Methodist Church; another was National Central University, established by the Nationalist Government. The current university is located at the former church university's campus.

Its place memory has been preserved through the sequential layering of the landscapes and buildings in the different eras, particularly the building cluster built between 1910 and 1921, which forms the east axis. Along with the visual memory stimulated by the architectural heritage, the social and public memory is reactivated through cultural events, academic communication, and even periodic cosplaying. By wearing the old 1920s uniform, many seniors nearing graduation seek to preserve their campus memories, fusing them with the place memory. Besides, as it is different to the mainstream, the Christian background always fuels heterogeneous idiosyncrasy on the campus. As the church university was founded in 1910, its location was far from the bustling central zone, in an area of unpaved roads, interspersed with farmland, hills, ponds, and some mansions for early missionaries. One of their famous owners was the 1938 Nobel Laureate in literature, Pearl S. Buck. By 1949, the Communist government had started to evict all missionaries and foreign experts, and shortly afterward, the church university ended up being merged into NJU in 1952. However, its heterotypic flavor never disappeared. Since the Center for Chinese and American Studies of NJU was established in 1986, restaurants, cafés and bars catering to overseas students and scholars (most from the USA) have mushroomed. By 2010, the northwest corner had won its reputation as a place of discovery, vitality, and a wide range of social and economic exchanges. Hence the municipality had to reward it with an appellation "exotically youth-cultural quarter" (Board of Gulou Chronicle 2012) to officially admit its status.

Topography

Nanjing is a hilly city with lakes and rivers. The complex topography impeded the overrapid formation of the built-up environment. The topographic differences, such as terrains, revêtements, and slopes, create rich spatiality as backdrops, shelter, edges, and thresholds to encourage energetic urban scenes in daily life, which are full of surprises. Over a hundred years, different human patterns have been impressed onto the contours of the natural environment, which produces a heterogeneous surface through the superimposition of various fabrics, structures, and layers. For instance, there is a group of firefighters stationed beside the playground, under its west steeply sloping stand caused by the abrupt change of the elevation.

Institution

Since the early 1980s, the socialist *danwei* (work-unit compound), once the predominant sociospatial pattern in urban China, has gradually disintegrated. Despite its innate antithesis to porosity and diversity, its residual impact instead converted into a prerequisite of diversity along with the parcelization of the quarter. In the 72 ha site, there are almost 10 *danweis*. None of them can ensure overall control of the whole area, even NJU with its 43 ha area as the biggest one. Once the housing reform was launched nationwide in 1988, the dispersion of landownership, along with the small lot sizes, guaranteed various actors' involvement in real estate development. Some cracks then emerged for the inhabitants to open their house walls and renovate the rooms as small cafés, shops, and restaurants. Work, teaching, leisure, and socializing merge with one another in a synergistic interrelationship.

As a rule, housing privatization aggravates housing inequality and residential segregation in urban China. But once again, something special has happened here. With a certain degree of freedom in terms of residential mobility and housing choice, the consolidated social stratum of the university has been broken up without the occurrence of serious gated communities or gentrification over the last three decades. To some extent, it is still multiownership and the residual *danwei* impact that has mitigated overcommercialization and curbed large-scale redevelopment, and thus maintained the affordability of the dwellings. With its central location and low rental rate it meets the financial capacity of the youth and migrants. What remains is its social mix as the ultimate basis of uncertainty, unpredictability, and also of creativity, tolerance, and stability.

Incomplete Integration

In relation to the dynamics of sociospatial development, both diversity and porosity are elusive, hard to be reproduced or planned under a single condition. The two are codependent and share most necessary prerequisites. NJU, as such, combines and embodies the features of the two at the level of neighborhood. There is a blend of various types of people (elderly, students, tourists, foreigners, etc.), of building forms (high-rise, low-rise, building heritage, open space, etc.), of uses (sport, teaching, residence, hospital, restaurant), with intensive interactions and transactions everywhere—students hanging out along the ground-floor frontage after classes, the neighbor's appropriation of open spaces for their morning and evening exercise, and tourists sightseeing around the architectural relics. Fortunately, the quarter succeeds in keeping out of a state of eutrophication, which means either a staged diversity attracting accusation of inauthenticity, or only convergent components circulating due to profound integration with solidarity. After all, incomplete integration is the prerequisite of publicness (Bahrdt 1998, 86–89). As a self-contained public institution, NJU has an innate proclivity for segregating in the sense that its members share similar lifestyles, common representations, or sets of beliefs. The logic of belonging and similarity sets a glimmering boundary to distinguish NJU from other communities. However, it is the boundary that keeps the momentum to interact by protecting different identities, as long as the boundary remains blurred and its segregation is not so sheer as to exclude strangers and outsiders completely.

References:
Bahrdt, H. P. 1998. *Die Moderne Großstadt.* Opladen. | Board of Gulou Chronicle. 2012. *2012 Yearbook of Gulou District.* Nanjing. Hoppenbrouwer, E., and E. Louw. 2005. "Mixed-use Development," *European Planning Studies* 7, no. 13: 967–83. | Jacobs, J. 1961. *The Death and Life of Great American Cities.* New York. | Rowley, A. 1996. "Mixed-use Development," *Planning Practice & Research* 1, no. 11: 85–98. | Wittgenstein, L. 1953. *Philosophical Investigations.* Translated by G. E. M. Anscombe, P. M. S. Hacker, and J. Schulte. London, 2009.

Porous Boundary Spaces in the Beijing Old City
Tianyu Zhu

Since 2013, I have been investigating in Beijing's residential neighborhoods for my dissertation "Boundary Spaces of Communities in Urban Beijing." A boundary space is the space perceived between private or communal realms and city spaces. It is, on the one hand, signified by physical divisions with static material forms, and on the other hand recognized through social thresholds according to dynamic mutual identifications. Due to various perceptions of spatial transitions, multiple interpretations of boundaries may occur, integrating and fluctuating the solidity of physical divisions and the fluidity of social thresholds. Boundary spaces as such can be described as porous, since there is always an ambiguity of ownership, relation, accessibility, identity, and belonging waiting to be defined through human performatives in spatial situations.

Dating back to 1407 AD, residential areas in the Beijing Old City originally consisted of courtyard houses and hutongs (narrow lanes in northern Chinese cities). Since the early twentieth century, as the population of the city rose, overlayering changes have taken place in the area. After the establishment of the P. R. China in 1949, the number of hutongs was doubled. In the 1960s, most of the courtyard houses were turned from single-family houses into shared tenement houses, where each family occupied only one or two rooms. Extensions and outdoor living appeared in both courtyards and streets. Starting in the 1970s, courtyards were torn down to make spaces for apartment buildings. By 1990, when the protection of the Old City started, its building density had risen 1.5 times. According to the 1994 statistics, two-thirds of the 33,000,000-square-meter floor space in the Old City was new build. The area today is a mixture of penthouses, shared or single-family courtyards, small retail establishments, gentrifying enterprises, gated communities, and work-unit compounds. The changes not only undermined the rigid physical boundaries structured by courtyard walls and street networks, but also generated a mixture of identities with different origins, length of residence, former work-units, residence proximity, social classes, and tourists that expanded their realms beyond walls and streets. Therefore, in the Beijing Old City, ambiguous boundaries are ceaselessly configured by people, and each spatial situation may bring about particular understandings of the place.

To illustrate this vividness of boundary spaces, I took photos of same places at different times of the day and year. The following are two series of them. The first photos were taken in summer 2014 and spring 2017. A household grows from a wall of a neighborhood with apartment buildings and encloses a garden on the pedestrian road with flowerpots made of Styrofoam boxes prevalent in markets. With changes in the flowerpots, hanging clothes, and plants on the window, different levels of the household's attachment to the street can be perceived. The other series shows a shoe-mending stand at a crossroad of a hutong and a city street. The stand owner is an immigrant who has been living in the area for decades. His chairs are an invitation that provide possibilities to reveal various identities and participate in making an entrance to the hutong with the simple action of sitting down. Unfortunately, these scenes will disappear soon due to a government initiative to remove informal retails and "recover" the walls of residential buildings in Beijing, which started in early 2017. However, whether the power of such informal activities to create porous boundary spaces via performative incidents will also disappear, remains to be seen.

p. 277: The house in the wall, Beijing
pp. 278–79: The shoe mender's shop, Beijing

From Counterinsurgency to Urban Quality
Frank Eisenmann

A Case Study of Kampung Air Panas, a Chinese New Village in Kuala Lumpur, Malaysia

Air Panas is a typical kampung in Kuala Lumpur. It is located 5 kilometers from the Petronas Twin Towers, the busy commercial heart of the Malaysian capital. A kampung is a residential quarter with a village-like structural pattern. In Malay language, *kampung* means "village" as physical and administrative entity as well as community in a social sense. However, many kampungs have evolved over time into residential quarters that demonstrate urban rather than rural characteristics. Consequently, the closely related term *village* is often misleading in today's context. At first sight, Air Panas is not easy to identify as a distinct neighborhood. It is like any other place made up of small houses in the midst of traffic arteries, high-rise buildings, patches of tropical rain forest, and omnipresent commercial and industrial areas. Yet Air Panas contains all the ingredients of the iridescent Asian city—it is chaotic, heated, crowded, loud, mysterious, and therefore urban.

What are the qualities synonymous with this kind of urbanity? Can the concept of urban porosity help us evaluate these qualities? Today, the fate of kampungs in Kuala Lumpur is often at stake. The Malaysian capital finds itself in an accelerated global competition that puts pressure on everything that is not in line with its commercial, economic, and administrative philosophy. How do the residents of Air Panas deal with an ambivalent mix of commercial competition, real estate development, and administrative arbitrariness?

First, one needs to understand the origin of the neighborhood and trace the specific history of the Chinese New Villages in Malaysia of which Air Panas is a key example. This history is surprising yet disturbing because it is rooted in the military counterinsurgency campaigns of the past (Nyce 1973). During World War II, Japanese forces occupied Malaya and caused all European, especially British, settlers to leave. After the surrender of Japan, Malaya fell into a power vacuum. An already established Communist guerrilla movement used this situation to eventually gain control over the country, which had been traumatized by the occupation. Their aim was to oppose by force any colonial or imperial power, and it was the Chinese population that was targeted by the Communists as potential support, mainly for two reasons: exchange of information and supply of food (Aun 1966). After the British colonialists returned to Malaya, they saw a growing problem in this Communist infiltration. The situation grew violent, and after a series of assassinations, the British military started a large resettlement program all over Malaya to prevent any interaction between Chinese peasants and members of the Communist guerrilla force (Harper 1999). This so-called Emergency Period lasted from 1948 to 1960 and kampung Air Panas is a result of the resettlement program. It is a village that was specifically designed and built to keep the Chinese peasants in control. Standardized houses were built around a simple layout including a market area, sheds for animal livestock, a central cooking area, a community hall, and a school. Equally simple is the infrastructure, which consists of a central water supply and a barricaded access street. The relocation of only Chinese families resulted in a homogeneous population. The entire village was spatially separated from the surrounding rain forest by a barbed-wire fence. Access was granted only during daylight and after passing a military checkpoint. The aim and result of this effort was a non-porous environment of absolute control.

Surprisingly, and sixty years later, this rigid scheme has led to its opposite. Today, kampung Air Panas is a predominantly Chinese residential neighborhood with a lively market hall at a busy street intersection. A row of congested shop premises provides everything for daily use. Busy street stalls complete the already opulent offerings of a couple of open-air restaurants. And small repair workshops do anything from steel welding to carpentry to motorcycle repair. Mixed with this Chinese lifestyle is a strong Indian and, to a lesser extent, Malay influence. Heavy traffic can be observed, especially at peak hours, whereas the back streets are much less frequented. Many residents, mainly older Chinese men and women, use the bicycle for their daily routine. Others travel on foot, especially to the market hall that, together with the adjacent shops, houses, restaurants and hawker stalls, forms the commercial and, more importantly, social center of the neighborhood. The location of this small urban nucleus is at the intersection of two main streets that run through the kampung in east-west and north-south directions. Most residents have jobs outside the kampung; some nearby in factories, some further away in offices downtown. But a sizeable fraction of the residents work in the neighborhood; the workshops and restaurants are very much a local affair. Over the years, new residents, of Indian and Malay descent, have moved into the neighborhood, along with their religious and cultural traditions. The building plots are owned by the government and leased on a 99-year basis. None of the former facilities of the New Village, for example, sheds for animal livestock, central cooking area, or community hall, have survived. There are still a few wooden first-generation houses from the Emergency Period in Air Panas, but they have been altered significantly over time.

In summary, the history of the village as an internment camp is in no way obvious in the present day. But the original spatial layout of the New Village is clearly visible in the characteristic distribution of open space, street grid, and residential areas. Looking at the overall urban condition, one has to conclude that the neighborhood has a spatial quality that is worth further investigation. To describe the porous characteristics of the spatial quality, I will use the terms *proportion*, *density*, and *coincidence*.

Proportion—The structural backbone of the kampung is two main streets meeting at an offset intersection. Here, traffic is heavy and the noise level is high. Most commercial activity is located on these two roads, allowing small businesses to prosper by attracting customers. This basic urban layout divides the kampung into four similar-sized residential areas. These areas, with their smaller streets, remain less frequented and therefore less obstructed. In combination, this balanced proportion forms a simple and accessible network of streets and residential areas that allows the residents to walk or bicycle through the entire neighborhood. In addition, the layout of the building plots plays an important role. Their relatively small size prevents inconsiderate extension of businesses or workshops. Most of them do not have larger footprints than the residential houses adjacent to them. The proportions of the main architectural elements are equally balanced. The popular market hall, where fresh produce, fish, and meat are sold fulfills the daily needs of local residents and customers from outside alike. The building is clearly visible from the street but is not oversized. The school has been altered and extended over the years and serves pupils from surrounding neighborhoods as well. It has grown to several buildings and its location is at the edge of the kampung. It is therefore not a dominant or distracting element in the neighborhood. The same is true for the main Chinese temple and the Indian temple. They are of modest size and not centrally placed or set apart but slightly hidden at the fringes of the residential areas. Historically, they were built to serve the needs of a small and limited community, not the needs of utter representation. Of course, the architectural features described are distinct and recognizable, but they do not dominate or overshadow any other features. In summary, the balanced proportion of urban and architectural elements and the kampung's porous character are clearly responsible for the positive urban quality. This quality is reflected at the human scale, which is difficult to measure but easy to notice.

Density—Air Panas is made up of single- and double-story detached houses. The residential plots and the footprint of the houses are the same size and the overall density is modest. The standardized urban layout conforms to grids of repetitive rows. Despite this simplistic arrangement, the houses are far from uniform and are home to a variety of different social groups. Old, wooden houses stand side by side with modern brick buildings. Many of the older buildings are divided into several individual parts to accommodate a large number of residents, typically occupied by marginalized city dwellers or groups with lower incomes. Many work as household maids, street sellers, or unskilled workers in businesses nearby. Economically, they play an important and active role in the neighborhood and the city. At the same time, many of the houses have been modernized and are inhabited by middle-class families. It seems especially easy for wealthier private owners to upgrade a building over time, for example by adding another floor or replacing the old wooden construction with a modern one. This partly explains why well-established middle-class families still live in the kampung. They own businesses or work in regular white-collar jobs in the city. In Air Panas, residents of very different economic and social status live side by side in individual houses. The porosity of the residential structure contributes to the acceptance of in- and out-migration. The advantages of this dynamic social mobility cannot be denied. This is in clear contrast to governmental high-rise buildings or the exclusive private housing compounds nearby. The kampung, however, is able to absorb and integrate residents of very different backgrounds. This also influences lines of communication in daily life—the residents seem to know the whereabouts of their immediate neighborhood and therefore take an active part in the life of the kampung. This seems possible only in neighborhoods where manageable quantities of residents live and work. The modest density in combination with the porous and heterogeneous residential structure is a clear and positive contribution to this.

Coincidence—Being able to occupy the same space in different ways over time shapes the daily routine of kampung life. Residents make use of this simultaneity in various ways and with different degrees of involvement. There is no unused space and no overused space. On almost every street, small businesses are integrated with residential houses. Sometimes, private, residential houses are used as the premises for small shops or family businesses. One example is the shop of an Indian family. A small convenience store occupies the entrance space and is run by the male members of the family. A workspace for the wife's tailoring business is in the middle part and bedrooms are located in the back of the house. The family makes use of their house in the most efficient way. This porous setting can be adapted to changing circumstances. Open space in Air Panas is treated in a similar fashion. Additional market stands are temporarily extended into the surrounding streets if necessary. Residents tolerate this practice as long as the flow of circulation is not completely disturbed and the "occupation" is not permanent. The Padang, a former parade ground, is used as communal open space for public events or as an informal sports field during the week. Most surprisingly, with the addition of a simple covered walkway at its northern end, the Padang has become a transitional space between the secondary school and the bus stop on the main road. The covered pathway allows children to safely walk to the bus stop and further to their home. The additional benefit is that school buses do not have to drive through residential streets to pick up the children. The Padang is not reserved for a single use. It is a communal space that contributes to the overall spatial quality of the kampung. The open and therefore porous character of urban and architectural elements allow for the communal uses described. Of course, this is supported by the general acceptance of the local residents and authorities alike. It is silently understood that the resulting quality outweighs its drawbacks.

Daily urban life in Air Panas is closely related to its qualities in terms of proportion, density and coincidence. Obviously, external forces such as commercial, economic, and administrative pressures on the neighborhood and its residents cannot be ignored. Over the years, many kampungs had to make way for large-scale infrastructure or commercial projects. In other cases, the existing neighborhoods are squeezed between projects of this kind. Urban development, especially in Asia, is very often synonymous with new development. It is therefore fascinating to witness the transformation of a former resettlement into a mature neighborhood with exemplary spatial qualities. We can conclude that the porous characteristics of Air Panas make for a framework of urban stability and spatial quality.

References:
Aun, G. H. 1966. *The Emergency in Malaya.* Penang. | Harper, T. N. 1999. *The End of Empire and the Making of Malaya.* Cambridge. Nyce, R. 1973. *Chinese New Villages in Malaya.* Singapore.

Flows, Processes, and Weak Urbanization in Mexico City
Christof Göbel and Elizabeth Espinosa Dorantes

Ferrocarril de Cuernavaca Street

In the urban fabric that defines the area of study, there coexist several infrastructures that run through it, limiting and contrasting it: bridges, industries, cycling paths, avenues, museums, low- and high-density housing, and metropolitan equipment. This zone has as its antecedent an important transformation of its original industrial function into a service area, retaining as its main feature the tracks of the Cuernavaca Railroad, which originally connected the preexisting industrial area with the industrial area in the northern part of Mexico City. This analysis focuses on the zone that brings together the most representative architectural elements of this transformation, such as the Soumaya and Jumex museums, the Carso Shopping Mall, and the Inbursa Aquarium.

Porous City

In order to define the concept of the porous city, it is necessary to assume the existence of an organizational city model characterized by flows and productive processes, where the form is disconnected from the physical construction without neglecting it (Martínez Capdevila 2014). The latter generates morphological regions that, in addition, distinguish social and cultural variations, promoting another type of urban environment based on the configuration of a network of centralities, with functional vagueness, constructed with fluid, permeable, and interconnected perimeters.

That means that the delimitation of urban space and architecture is supported as a network of relationships that weave plots into a territory, integrating spaces that do not always possess physical continuity. These networks can represent different flow intensities in each section of their mesh, resulting in complex spaces with an apparent loss of unity and homogeneity, with urban and architectural fragmentation, and a loss of obvious borders.

The concept of limit is central to the formulation of a porous city, although it must be understood as membranous and selective, in which exchange mechanisms are produced and move from a culture that discerns linear, continuous, therefore limited development, as distinct from one that assumes the existence of both physical limits and the limits of other systems. This approach seeks to define the limits based on the relationships among objects, between objects and people, and among people who inhabit and use the urban space, in that the environment is not only a physical fact but also a symbolic one (Ibid.). In summary, the porous city is the city understood in relational terms, where places are characterized by their relation with other places, with dissolution of the inner and outer limits of the urban space (Pujadas 2012). In this manner, the city is a mosaic of heterogeneous places that appear to have no contact with each other.

Microcosm of the Museum Area: Scenery of Flows and Processes

In the porous city, the importance of definition of limits is very relevant. Thus, to initiate the analysis of the microcosm of the museum area, it is necessary to define its physical limits. The area is bordered on the east by Prolongación Moliere Street, on the north by Río San Joaquín Avenue, on the west by Press Falcón Street, and on the south by Boulevard Miguel de Cervantes Saavedra. This polygon is crossed by the Ferrocarril de Cuernavaca Street, where the railway sporadically continues to circulate.

Although there are relevant architectural typologies in the area, such as the Soumaya and Jumex Museums, an architecture of forms detached from function predominates, where large cubes, as generic and neutral forms lacking in urban, architectural, and aesthetic personality coexist with small, autonomous architectural elements. This setting, which in appearance generates fragmented spaces, constitutes a structure of networks that support diverse flows and productive processes and uses.

By analyzing the relations among the objects, although there is a functional relationship between the museums and the aquarium that conforms to a flow that we could also term cultural, we see that other types of relationships are more intense. This is because, through their relation with other fragments of the space (shopping malls, houses, small restaurants, offices, parking lots, etc.), the people of the area satisfy other needs, although the space is apparently fragmented by a physical limit defined by the railroad tracks.

This means, if permeability also implies mobility, that it is necessary to overcome the physical limits, not only of the urban space, but also of the building. For example, in physical terms, the concept of porosity is unclear, in that the construction of the buildings is definitive and immutable. Only the Jumex Museum displays, timidly, the rupture between the inner and outer borders of space, by means of two small terraces that allow for interaction between public and private space. The other architectural objects (office buildings and neutral services) function only as a backdrop that gives primacy to an isolated architectural piece, for example, the Soumaya Museum.

The relationship between objects and people generates a network of relationships in which there is interaction among urban spaces that determine places with opportunity for improvisation (Gendrault 2009). Here we find, for example, Cerrado Lago Andrómaco Street, where spontaneously emerging typologies become a space of networks, of services, of relationships. They are always available for transformation, where a passage of the communication among various homes is transformed into a corridor specializing in home-cooked meals, which coexists with the intimate activities of residential living. In these spaces, what matters are the elasticity and, especially, the secondary role and the ephemeral character of the architecture (Martínez Capdevila 2014).

The limits defined by the relationships among people are determined by the space, whose external image does not correspond to the activities taking place within it. Thus, in the buildings, we find activities that are independent and separate from the architectural typology characteristic of offices. Here, internal flows are created by the people who circulate in the space, communicating by mobile phones, absent from the physical space that surrounds them, and abstracting themselves from the urban context, generating an immaterial network of communication with other scenarios.

Model of Weak Urbanization

The architecture of the city, considered as one of its elements, has lost its specificity, its autonomy, and its purity. This is because accelerated technological innovation contributes means and arguments in favor of discontinuity, becoming a disjointed setting that undermines the ability to generate urban fabric. Architectural forms have dissolved or diversified excessively, creating a barrier between the architecture and the urban space surrounding and shaping it (Chaves 2005).

Therefore, the city comprises a setting of contradictory elements and logics, the result of the separation between technology and form, between function and form, and above all, a consequence of a lack of unity and the absence of a symbolic and integrating apparatus. Andrea Branzi, from an eminently architectural view, argues that the context is also part of architectural work (Martínez Capdevila 2016).

In addition, he denies the uniqueness and harmony of the set of elements that make up the urban space, which are responsible for creating an identity that he calls weak, but one that is flexible, open to change, differentiated, and reflective. Based on these ideas, Branzi establishes a model of weak urbanization in which the role of architecture is diminished. The latter is reformulated in terms of a closed and stable object, whose envelope only summarizes the representative and symbolic burden of the space, perceiving the facades as the background of a scenario. This is where flows and interactions between urban and private spaces, between architectural elements and urban elements, are produced, configuring the space of the city, the urban texture, and the porosity of space (Martínez Capdevila 2014).

So, to speak of the porous city is to speak of weak urbanization, in the sense of a noncompositional urbanization, but as just one of a set of relations and employing an architecture directed toward surpassing the physical limits of the building: a permeable and evolutionary architecture that reevaluates the relationships of everyday life.

Conclusions

If in the urban space boundaries disappear and juxtapose the tangible with the intangible, beyond the visual characteristics of each of the spaces and of their territorial discontinuity, we must identify the relationships of affinity among the physically separated areas and create a world in which the category of the infinite is the only possible symbolic form. We must create a porous space, extremely flexible and movable, that adapts automatically, implying the creation of an urbanism of indeterminacy.

Models of weak urbanization can be seen as structures that deny all uniqueness, models that project a partial and incomplete character, models that are fragmented, heterogeneous, chaotic, and devoid of historical object. Nonetheless, the architecture may be the main fragment through which the relations that define different boundaries and relationships are delimited.

References:
Chaves, N. 2005. *El diseño invisible: Siete lecciones sobre la intervención culta en el hábitat humano.* Buenos Aires. | Gendrault, C. 2009. "Naples: Repenser la ville à partir de la qualité des frontières internes," *ERES* 138: 85–97. | Martínez Capdevila, P. 2014. "Andrea Branzi y la Cittá Senza Architettura de la No-Stop City a los modelos de urbanización débil," PhD diss., Polytechnic University, Madrid. | Martínez Capdevila, P. 2016. "Hacia una arquitectura débil: Andrea Branzi y Gianni Vattimo," *Cuadernos de Proyectos Arquitectónicos*, no. 6: 82–89. | Pujadas, J. J. 2012. "Itinerarios metropolitanos: Policentrismo, movilidad y trayectorias personales en la ciudad porosa," *Biblio 3 W* 17, no. 968, http://www.ub.edu/geocrit/b3w-968.htm.

Situation
Markus Lanz

She can borrow her mother's monthly pass on their days off on Sundays. She mostly comes here. She travels an hour through the city to reach the metro station at the beginning of the avenue and then walks the last part. Even when it's raining. The only time she doesn't come is when the flea market is on under the wide roof of the museum's large exhibition space. To skate she uses the other side of the street. The surface in front of the park is smooth. She never knows exactly why she comes here but something always happens. On the water basins. Or on the surrounding bank, at the front of the terrace with a far-reaching view of the city. This is where she learned to play chess—from a boy she often met here. Everyone meets here. They come for the music or to perform, or to ride their bike through the city or to protest. Thousands have come here recently to do just that.

Open space (and thus also the open picture of the space) encourages speculation to act. This reveals the architecture of Lina Bo Bardi. In the process-oriented manner of design, the conceptional complexity and also the direct simplicity of its implementation, her architecture opens up manifold possibilities of appropriation.

He was already on his way. That's when they called him. The flight was delayed, which meant he still had two hours. He turned around, moving away from the terrace to the next corner and, after passing the narrow passage, down well-worn stone slabs overlooking the fenced excavation site. The park was just behind it. Past the shop windows and display stands. Traders on the steps of doorways. In front of the metro station, turning right onto the square. He passed through the deep shadows of the arcades. Street furniture of the homeless in front of closed shopfronts, even here. He carried on behind the detached church toward the market storerooms in the light-flooded halls. Meat followed by fish. He continued to the other side and through the closed-off street, pushing past the protesting crowds. He went down the ten steps at the corner in front of the string of Chinese businesses and entered the refreshingly cool underground restaurant with the two doors. He had to be back at the meeting point in one and a half hours to show the group the mass burial site dating from 700 BC before dusk.

Lasting distinctness in its figure, yet at the same time offering a wealth of experience due to the openness of use. This is where the quality of architectural space becomes visible; in the diversity and possibilities of relationships. Among things, creatures, and people. Between the open space and individual space.

As usual, she came from up there across the wide meadow. Jumped onto the terrace, under the pilotis of one wing. The open ramps back and forth, up to his office. She picked up her diploma. It started raining. Before leaving town, she sat in the garden under the roof for a while. To assure herself of the place where she had stayed for the last few years. At this moment. To recognize the entire exterior from the inside. In an all-encompassing mashrabiya. Without the pressure of history. Without tradition. Wind through the house. The rough concrete still warm. Murmurs behind the windows of the hanging hall. Raindrops in the fold at the hem of her greatcoat. Water in the deep basins under the falling spouts. Trickles on the leaves of hanging and climbing plants. A Sabiá through the grid. Dense clouds moving above. She will soon see the same moon in her grandma's home. She tore a page out of her book. Folded it into a boat and put it on the stones on the ground. He was still standing there by the railing behind the open glass. She opened the hood of her tightly woven Djellaba. And left. Over the bridge. Through the rain. Nearly limitless periphery.

The monolith dissolves into a constellation of heterogeneous bodies that are rearranged according to spatial criteria of relationship and transparency. Multidimensional. Architecture is the separation of spheres. My clothing is my closest own space. The initial perception of space is the reception of an atmosphere, followed by understanding and describing constellation and materiality.

He can remember the day in great detail. They both tried it again. They took the yellow line from the northeast via the motorway ring road into the center. This time they had even bought fashion pieces. They got in the queue. They waited. He had never seen so many important people here. He recognized them all. From the TV. Everyone who had a finger in every pie. They didn't get inside. Insults were hurled at them. The usual clobber. But this time… he had tried to hold his friend back. In vain. At first they had escaped, over the trenches. They had mustered up the courage on the boulevard and turned back. There was nobody there now. They took a car for the journey home. It was standing there on the roadside. Open. They had continued on to the sea. At sunrise. The first time getting to where he once had arrived. He can now no longer become a driving instructor, somebody told him. He had tried.

The concreteness of space and the possibilities of interaction relate to and involve each other. Visible. A variety of inter-action and relationship do not develop causally from a specific spatial urban typology.

Now they have to leave the workshop behind, almost exactly three years after abandoning the shop. At the time they were given an offer to buy the small workshop in the backyard. Now the whole area is going to be redeveloped. All that remains now are two of the small workshop buildings and the chimney in the former brickyard. The chimney is protected due to its local construction method. A few of the rooms are used by artists in the run-up to demolition. The original idea has now been abandoned. An expert demonstrated that the buildings are not suitable for housing refugees. The new landowners want to target a young, creative clientele with their big project. According to them, they are going to develop an urban quarter, a mix of functions. Apartments with large balconies and roof terraces. Shops and offices. A lifestyle company has already expressed interest in taking over all the commercial space. The soil excavation for the subway expansion has uncovered all sorts of things: oil from an old petrol station, an aircraft bomb and the remains of a wall, probably of Moorish origin. Work has been temporarily stopped.

A photograph depicts the visible areas of space. Relationships of certain times past become evident in the appearance of the concrete. Homogenous spaces offer fewer relationships. Homogenous spaces create clear pictures.

He was looking forward to all that. His company offered him the possibility of getting away. Away from there. Away from family. Finally, his own apartment, his own room, a door. In the city, in a neighborhood he liked. Just him. No daily routine, no conversations, no prayers, no music of other people. He bought himself a sofa. He sometimes went for a beer with his work friends in the evening. Before long he was moved from the Game department to the Animation department. The game manufacturer, for whom they were making the mods and add-ons, was now producing games elsewhere. The new team is flexible and encourages working from home. He generates animal hair and fur for animation films. He sometimes goes to the zoo for study purposes. He uses the company equipment at home to stream all sorts of things. Unfortunately, the important football matches are pay-per-view. This prompts him to go outside, on the streets. He keeps in contact with his family via a group chat.

You can't photograph space for itself. People in the picture, however, illustrate the features of space. Interactions in architectural space, visible in depth, point to the urban fabric, the relationships, and the context beyond the picture frame. Here, space can be read as a complex situation.

Accentuate the Positive…
Karl Detering and Simon Beesley

Porosity, like other nominalizations in the urbanist lexicon—hybridity, performativity, inbetweenness—is not a word that charms the ear. What porosity lacks in phonological elegance, however, it more than makes up for in theoretical versatility and potency. It incorporates both space and substance, thereby ensuring that however snugly it sits alongside other modish terms in postmodern discourse, it does not dissolve into mere relativism and theoretical ineffectuality.

We argue that it is a robust and useful term in the field of urbanism but that its application to architectural design and urban planning is problematic. However, in our view, this does not diminish its conceptual-theoretical value. For us, the concept of porosity is immensely useful in illuminating the multiple ways in which the built environment affects—determines, structures, shapes—our interactions with each other.

In what follows, we distinguish between porosity as a tool of analysis and porosity as applied to practice. We begin with a brief discussion of the former and then go on to make some critical observations on the latter and, in passing, draw a further distinction between positive porosity and negative porosity.

1. The Naples essay might best be categorized as a piece of literary journalism. In her introduction to *Illuminations*, Hannah Arendt comments that Benjamin's use of figurative language enabled him to "write a prose of [...] singularly enchanting and enchanted closeness to reality" (Arendt 1968, 16). This alerts us to the fact that there is a distinction between critical-theoretical use of figurative language and literary use of metaphor, particularly in poetry. The word *porosity* and Benjamin's inspired application of it did not emerge from nowhere or simply from the coils of his literary genius. It was the result of a very happy coincidence—Naples as a city of abundant porosity, rich in porosity, is built on volcanic rock. This suggested the term *porosity*, which then took on a new life, not purely metaphorical or literary but closer to a new theoretical-descriptive concept, one which organizes the phenomena in a new frame. One can imagine him writing about other cities equally as porous (in this new sense) and not hitting on this supremely effective term.

Of course, Benjamin and Lacis were not concerned to make a theoretical statement but the use of porosity establishes it as a powerful concept that could be applied to any set of seemingly diverse phenomena to which its figurative use relates and organizes as an objective property. Almost immediately in "Naples", porosity loses its metaphorical character and goes to work as an abstract concept. Tie this to the distinction between literary uses of metaphor and figurative language and literary criticism and, more generally, the uses of figuration intrinsic to all theoretical discourse, and we can begin to understand porosity not just as a metaphor but as a conceptual-theoretical tool with which to grasp otherwise elusive phenomena, such as those described in the following passage from Wolfrum's "Still Here while Being There":

"All these spaces are superimposed upon one another; their borders are in a state of instability and have the tendency to drift. In many instances they are not articulated in an architectural sense, even though their delicate traces might have materialized, over time, as engravings in the urban fabric." (Wolfrum, 60)

Porosity illuminates, makes it possible to see and reflect on these objective phenomena. Hence the significance of Wolfrum's remark in "Urbanes Gebiet" that the ingredients of porosity were already there—as it were, in themselves, as objective facts in the cultural dimension of cities—before the word *porosity* or the concept became currency. (Wolfrum, 158) This makes a crucial distinction between the term *porosity* and the concept of porosity.

We can draw an analogy here with Pierre Bourdieu's use of the term *capital*. In his 1986 paper "The Forms of Capital," Bourdieu introduced the notions of cultural capital and social capital (Bourdieu 1982, 241–58). Later works extended the categories of capital to symbolic capital, intellectual capital, and academic capital. The movement from the original economic meaning of the term *capital* to other spheres parallels the semantic passage of *porosity* from its technical sense as a property of physical materials to its use as a technical-theoretical term in urbanism. However, the figurative extension of capital does not start with a material term. Money, of course, exists in a material or literal form as currency but the concept of money is located in the symbolic, cultural realm. Money is a cultural object. By contrast, many of the general concepts of urbanism are drawn from the vocabulary used for material objects and man-made structures; among them, *urban fabric*, *threshold*, *texture*, and *material* itself in a nonliteral sense, and the various nonmaterial uses of *space*, *edge*, *border*, and *boundary*. *Porosity* belongs with these, but it may also be regarded as more versatile and flexible and, more significantly, existing at a higher level of generality. Porosity is thus a superordinate concept in the sense that terms and concepts such as *urban fabric, threshold, space*, etc., are its ingredients.

2. In "Naples," porosity is animated by chance. Indeed, the element of chance is an integral part of Naples life. Coupled to the public spectacle of private lives, the disruptive and unpredictable intrusion of chance produces a state of affairs that is fundamentally un-German—if we grant that not only is the private sphere culturally and legally sacrosanct in Germany, but one of the most deeply rooted of German cultural traits is the adherence to rule and order. Except in a narrowly literal (neutralizing) sense, porosity is resistant to rule and order. Planned porosity is an oxymoron on a par with planned spontaneity. By extension, porosity is representative of a set of qualities antithetical to enclosure, confinement, regulation, and plan.

Benjamin was not alone in noticing the preeminence of chance in Naples life. Sartre also remarks on it in his poisonous observations on the city's populace, written nearly ten years after Benjamin and Lacis: "Everywhere in Naples, chance is master" (Sartre 1936, 56). The descriptions in "Naples" are hardly comparable to Sartre's diary but the contrast is noteworthy. It forces one to ask whether "Naples" sentimentalizes the life of the Neapolitan poor, reducing it to the quaint or exotic, precisely because Naples (particularly in the sociocultural sense but also in the architectural) is exotic for the affluent Northern European (perhaps none more than the enculturated German). The authors themselves make the point explicitly: "To exist, for the Northern European the most private of affairs, is here, as in the kraal, a collective matter" (Benjamin and Lacis 1925, 171). Where they appear to see poverty almost as a precondition of porosity—"Poverty has brought about a stretching of frontiers that mirrors the most radiant freedom of thought" (Ibid.)—Sartre sees only squalor, sloth, and stupidity. We may dismiss Sartre's remarks as excessively jaundiced but we are still left with the troubling question of whether the ingredients of porosity are not in a profound sense the products of urban poverty.

Since it is always those environments where the urban poor cluster that seem to offer the richest real-world examples of porosity, one could be forgiven for thinking that porosity studies are little more than sociotheoretical poverty porn—researchers' field trips to the Dharavi in Mumbai, the Canada Real in Madrid, the favelas of Rio de Janeiro, and so on, do nothing to allay this suspicion. The conditions of poorer urban landscapes—where these are not the product of centralized planning—seem to be constitutive of the architectural and social permeability porosity articulates.

This brings us to the question of gentrification. The processes of gentrification are in play where the extempore elements of porosity (spontaneously repurposed interstitial spaces—such as the impromptu vendors' stalls on empty corners and gardens that extend into the street, for example, those pictured in this book by Tianyu Zhu in the hutongs of old Beijing [Zhu, 276] become victims of their own success and are stifled by external capital interests in the course of gentrifying. Highly porous urban environments are prey to speculators, as in the expropriation of grass-roots community initiatives in formerly poorer neighborhoods of big cities (see Stengel, 108).

Broadly speaking, gentrification is an example of what we term *negative porosity*, to the extent that negative porosity is destructive of porous features of the urban landscape conducive to unregulated human interactivity. We define negative porosity as comprising the forces hostile to *positive porosity*. These forces are usually concomitant with capital interests. Modernist housing projects of the twentieth century, where the emphasis on order, efficiency, hygiene, etc., which signally failed to take account of (or simply ignored) the importance of social interaction, fall into this category. Negative porosity effects of this kind are endemic in the urban planning regimes of Robert Moses. The consequences of this top-down approach—among them the deracination and hollowing out of inner-cities areas as described by Foerster-Baldenius and Zahn (254)—are still painfully apparent.

To negative porosity we would add the subcategory *pseudo porosity*. Gentrification, for example, produces certain short-term porosity effects in the form of social mixing (or permeability), but its long-term effects are the opposite of porous. So-called trickle-down economics is another instance of pseudo porosity (that is, negative porosity masquerading as positive porosity) in that its premises are porous (it is speciously suggestive of economic porosity) but its effects are demonstrably not. Examples on the design dimension would include the open-plan office, hybrid café-bookshops, interactive museum installations, and similarly pseudo-porous, constructed environments, although this begs the question of how we define porosity.

Some ingenious ways of resisting gentrification by taking advantage of the porous character of regulations are suggested by Dona (Dona, 167), for example, by applying the system of multiple ownership of apartment houses in Athens, or the exploitation of a loopholes in the law in Detroit. However, these suggestions, splendidly creative though they are, depend on very particular configurations of local conditions. One has only to look at how environmental protection and building construction legislation is currently being rescinded in the US to conclude that the porosity inherent in regulations is scant defense against deregulation. At the same time, as Mumm makes clear (Mumm, 162), it is difficult to see how porous social and spatial planning can avoid falling foul of planning regulations or, at the same time, how it can do without them.

Among suggestions for reducing unnecessary regulative interference is the creation of regulation-free zones where the need for regulations or not can be tested. This sounds interesting on paper but what is the likely outcome in practice? Christiania redux perhaps, a now irretrievably gentrified zone. Which is not to say that gentrification is the inevitable or necessary outcome of such experiments, but positive porosity is clearly vulnerable to the destructive forces of negative porosity via misappropriation and misconstrual. Which invites a further caveat: an antiregulatory stance might actually suggest an overlap or synonymy with deregulation. Removal or relaxation of regulations in building standards and norms comes uncomfortably close to sounding like a recipe for exactly the kinds of slums so eloquently depicted in "Naples." Kees Christiaanse draws attention to the possible association between porosity and "porridge-ification" (Christiaanse, 218). The processes leading to the emergence of urban porridge represents a degenerate form of porosity, a form of clogging, which we would also categorize as negative porosity.

We should be equally wary, as Michael Koch points out in his essay "News from Naples?", of misconstruing "the Naples of Walter Benjamin as the prototype of a pioneering urban design" (Koch, 21). Where much postmodern theory discourse tends to the abstruse and palliative, porosity offers itself as a powerful antidote to the ills of modernism, gentrification, gated communities, and so on. But this puts practitioners in a bind. Regardless of how well-intentioned, inclusive, or communitarian initiatives to nurture porosity may be, how does one design or plan for porosity, or rather the conditions conducive to porosity, without repeating the very prescriptivism one wishes to undo?

Heinemann (Heinemann, 64) suggests various forms of provocative architectural intervention based on space of negotiation, where the specific uses of space are determined bottom-up (that is, user-led). To what extent creative design along these lines succeeds in shaking off the *tu quoque* of prescriptivism is perhaps itself negotiable. Porosity by design, as we have already indicated, is something of a contradiction in terms, and as Heinemann himself notes, no proof against misappropriation: "porosity [...] doesn't prevent grandiosity" (Heinemann, 66).

In short, defining and disambiguating the vexed relationship between design, planning, regulation, and porosity is not only a matter of theoretical nicety. The question of how to create the conditions in which porosity might flourish appears to us to be less one of planning or architectural design than of politics, capital, and regulation. As Koch puts it: "To what extent the [...] emancipative use of the provided non-predetermined spaces is realized, depends on the financial resources and to a large measure on the legally granted scope of appropriation" (Koch, 23).

3. None of these considerations need detract from the value of porosity as a general conceptual-theoretical term in urbanism. It makes perfect sense that the theoretical concepts of urbanism should be grounded in figurative extensions of material terms. We can see the logic of this natural affinity—porosity finds its most congenial home in urbanism—since it concerns the way the city interacts with people. As such, the term *porosity* stands for a set of phenomena central to urbanism; that is, those elements conveyed by the notion of urbanity, "the condition of life in a city" (Forty 2004, 113). Porosity need not wear its metaphorical or figurative character on its sleeve. It can instead be treated as an indispensable addition to the terminology of urbanism. The phenomena have always been there, for as long as people have lived in built urban environments, but were waiting, as it were, for recognition under a general concept before they could properly become objects of serious study.

Enthusiasts for porosity often seem to take the Naples essay for a contribution to a series on the theory of urbanism, a manifesto for a communitarian view of urban space. Skeptical voices also appear to regard "Naples" as a treatise on urbanism, but one which is undone by poeticism, a failure in its overly metaphoric use of the idea of the porous (see, for example, Erben, 26). As we see it, once one is disabused of reading *porosity* as a metaphorical term alone—and understands it as a theoretical concept and general term for real urban material-cultural phenomena—one can begin to recognize its semantic potency.

Although negative porosity (the forces hostile to positive porosity) is covalent with political and economic forces, positive porosity is not confined exclusively to desakotas, favelas, or hutongs. Nor, we contend, is porosity predominantly a feature of Southern cultures. Where in Benjamin's superporous Naples, "families interpenetrate in relationships that can resemble adoption" (Benjamin and Lacis 1925, 172), similar if less dramatic examples of social porosity are to be found everywhere.

In the process of proofreading the contributions collected in this volume, we underwent a conversion, a road-to-Damascus moment, brought about by recognizing the supreme usefulness of porosity as a general descriptor for a range of familiar ways in which the city interacts with its inhabitants. Moreover, porosity seems to us characteristic not only of Benjamin's way of thinking in terms of the indivisibility of material and immaterial phenomena, but his sensitivity to the particularity of the German language: combining the ethereal and earthy, porosity is self-instantiating, marrying thought and object as *Denkbild* ("thought picture")—itself a linguistic blend of the abstract and the concrete—thus making it especially germane to urbanist theory. Just as "architecture is the most binding part of the communal rhythm" (Ibid., 165) in "Naples," so porosity pulls the seemingly disparate phenomena of urban life and landscape together under a single organizing concept. As a micro example of such phenomena, we conclude with a passage from an email exchange between the authors of this article:

"Yesterday John took me out the front of his house [in a residential street off the Uxbridge Road in West London] to show me the work done on the two houses next to his, both bought by people who work in the City [the financial district of London]. What really shook me were the gates and front garden fences—at least six feet high, two wrought iron gates with a semicircle top per house (like mini versions of the iron gates to large houses in horror films), and wrought iron railings with spikes on top (in contrast to the low wall or hedge in almost all the other houses in the street). You could hardly have a more concrete and vivid example of the deleterious, negatively porous effects of gentrification. The thing that most struck me was that this was a very concrete example of what the urbanists mean with their figurative-theoretical extension of the word *threshold*; here was a case of threshold destruction. For in many of the streets running between the Uxbridge Road and Goldhawk Road, there is quite a considerable mix [of inhabitants]. And with this social composition goes a surprisingly high degree of porosity. What's more, most of it takes place in this threshold space, with people standing half in, half out, at their gate or talking over the low walls.

Seeing this small-scale destruction of porosity made this abstract urbanist concept very solid for me and put the seal on my conversion from porosity skeptic to porosity enthusiast."

References:
Arendt, H. 1968. Introduction to W. Benjamin, Illuminations, 1–60. Translated by H. Zorn. New York. | Benjamin, W., and A. Lacis. 1925. "Naples," in Reflections: Essays, Aphorisms, Autobiographical Writings, edited by P. Demetz, 163–73. New York, 1978. | Bourdieu, P. 1986. "The Forms of Capital," in Handbook of Theory and Research for the Sociology of Education, edited by J. Richardson, 241–58. New York. | Forty, A. 2004. Words and Buildings: A Vocabulary of Modern Architecture. London. Sartre, J-P. 1936. "1936," in Witness to My Life: The Letters of Jean-Paul Sartre to Simone de Beauvoir 1926–39, edited by S. de Beauvoir, translated by L. Fahnestock and N. MacAffe, 51–72. New York, 1992.

Contributors | Authors

Marc Angélil is an architect and professor of architecture and design at ETH Zurich.

Giorgia Aquilar is an architect and Alexander von Humboldt Fellow at the Technical University of Munich.

Stephen Bates is an architect and professor of urban design and housing at the Technical University of Munich.

Alexandra Bauer is a landscape architect, research associate, and a PhD candidate at the Technical University of Munich.

Simon Beesley is a journalist, author, and reviewer for the *Times Literary Supplement.*

Nikolai Frhr. von Brandis is an architect and urban planner at the Landesbaudirektion in Nürnberg.

Eduard Bru is an architect and professor of architectural design at the Universitat Politècnica de Catalunya in Barcelona.

Margitta Buchert is an architectural theorist and historian, and professor of architecture and art of the twentieth and twenty-first centuries at Leibniz Universität Hannover.

Yü Chen is an architect from Belgium.

Kees Christiaanse is an architect and urban planner, and professor of architecture and urban design at ETH Zurich.

Christopher Dell is an urban theorist, musician and composer, and professor at the Urban Design Program at HafenCity University Hamburg.

Karl Detering teaches English at the Technical University of Munich.

Alissa Diesch is an architect, research associate, and lecturer at Universidad La Gran Colombia in Bogota and a PhD candidate at the Technical University of Munich.

Sofia Dona is an architect and artist, and research associate at the Technical University of Munich, and a PhD candidate at the University of Thessaly.

Frank Eisenmann is an architect and urban designer, lecturer in urban design at the Technical University of Munich.

Dietrich Erben is an art historian and professor of theory and history of art, architecture and design at the Technical University of Munich.

Elisabeth Espinosa Dorantes is an architect and professor of urban design at the Universidad Autónoma Metropolitana Azcapotzalco in Mexico City.

Angelika Fitz is a cultural theorist and director of the Architekturzentrum (AZW) in Vienna.

Benjamin Foerster-Baldenius is a performing architect and member of the raumlabor collective in Berlin.

Francesca Fornasier is an architect from Munich.

Undine Giseke is a landscape architect and professor of landscape design at the Technical University of Berlin.

Christof Göbel is an architect and professor of urban design at the Universidad Autónoma Metropolitana Azcapotzalco in Mexico City.

Uta Graff is an architect and professor of architectural design and conception at the Technical University of Munich.

Maren Harnack is an architect and urban planner, and professor of urbanism and urban design at the University of Applied Science in Frankfurt / Main.

Christoph Heinemann is an architect and urbanist, and professor of *Architektur und Stadt* at HafenCity University in Hamburg.

Florian Hertweck is an architect and professor of architecture at the University of Luxembourg.

Candida Höfer is a photographer from Cologne.

Alban Janson is an architect, architectural theorist, and artist from Munich.

Carsten Jungfer is an architect and urban designer, and senior lecturer at the University of East London.

Monique Jüttner is an architect, research associate, and a PhD candidate at Brandenburgische Technische Universität Cottbus–Senftenberg.

Ela Kaçel is an architect and architectural historian, assistant professor at Bahçeşehir University Istanbul, and Alexander von Humboldt Fellow at RWTH Aachen.

Norbert Kling is an architect, urban designer, and research associate at the Technical University of Munich.

Bernd Kniess is an architect and urban planner, and professor of urban design at HafenCity Universität Hamburg.

Michael Koch is an architect, urban planner, and professor of urban design and *Quartierplanung* at HafenCity University Hamburg.

Bruno Krucker is an architect and professor of urban design and housing at the Technical University of Munich.

Florian Kurbasik is an architect and research associate in urban design at the Technical University of Munich.

Markus Lanz is an architect, urban researcher, and photographer from Brasilia.

Gunter Laux is an architect and urban designer, and professor of urban design and planning at Hochschule für Technik Stuttgart.

Alexander Lehnerer is an architect and urban designer, and assistant professor of architecture and urban design at ETH Zurich.

Ton Matton is an urban planner and designer, and professor of space and design at University of Art and Design Linz.

Elisabeth Merk is an architect and urban planner. She is the head of Municipal Planning and Building Control Office of Munich.

Imke Mumm is Regierungsbaumeister, research associate, and PhD candidate at the Technical University of Munich.

Max Ott is an architect, urban researcher and PhD candidate at the Technical University of Munich.

Dominique Peck is an urban designer and a research associate in urban design at HafenCity University Hamburg.

Rita Pinto de Freitas is an architect and professor of architecture and urban design at GUC Cairo.

Cornelia Redeker is an architect and urban planner, and professor of architecture and urban design at GUC Cairo.

Anna Richter is a sociologist and a research associate in urban design at HafenCity University Hamburg.

Alex Römer is an architect and the founder of the collaborative construction practice ConstructLab.

Hanne Rung is an urban designer and curator from Munich.

Julian Schäfer is a landscape architect, and a research associate in landscape architecture and regional urban space at the Technical University of Munich.

Sören Schöbel-Rutschmann is a landscape architect and professor for landscape architecture and regional urban space at the Technical University of Munich.

Cary Siress is an architect and a senior researcher in territorial organization at ETH Zurich.

Stavros Stavrides is an architect, activist, and professor of architectural design – space – culture at the National Technical University of Athens.

Heiner Stengel is an architect, urban designer and research associate in urban design at the Technical University of Munich.

Jie Sun is an urban planner and a PhD candidate at Nanjing University.

Alain Thierstein is an economist and professor of urban development at the Technical University of Munich.

Dimitris Theodoropoulos is an architect, cofounder of the Errands group in Athens, and research associate at the University of Patras.

Philip Ursprung is an art historian and professor of history of art and architecture at ETH Zurich.

Paola Viganò is an architect and urbanist, and professor at the Laboratory of Urbanism at the Ecole polytechnique fédérale de Lausanne.

Udo Weilacher is a landscape architect and professor of landscape architecture and industrial landscape at the Technical University of Munich.

Sophie Wolfrum is an urban designer and professor of urban design and regional planning at the Technical University of Munich.

Yuting Xie is a landscape architect and research associate in landscape architecture and regional urban space at the Technical University of Munich.

Shan Yang is an architect and urban designer, and associate researcher at Nanjing University.

Sabine Zahn is a choreographer from Berlin.

Tianyu Zhu is an architect and PhD candidate in urban design at the Technical University of Munich.

Christian Zöhrer is an architect and research associate in urban design at the Technical University of Munich.

Doris Zoller is an architect and urban planner, and head of project development and maintenance at GEWOFAG München.

Picture Credits

p. 72 © Tabea Bähr, Camila Beccar Varela,
  Julia Mäckler 2016
p. 73 © Matteo Pelagatti, Peter Prey, Simon Rott 2016
p. 74 © Myrthe Geelen, Tanja Schmidt,
  Sonja Schneider 2017
p. 75 © Louis Saint Germain, Byeongcheol Kim,
  Daria Rath 2017
p. 83 © Uta Graff 2017,
above left to right:
  Armin Aschenbrenner, Jakob Defnner, FelixSchröder
  Theresa Borngräber, Anna-Maria Hahn, Luisa Holm
  Sophie Lausch, Derik Steichele-Frieder Wilk, CC
center left to right:
  Magdalena Bauer, Nina Welte
  Anela Dumonjic, Sophie Gerland, Marie Stockmaier
  Luise Hansetin, Josefin Orlovsky, Gisela Reis
bottom left to right:
  Deniz Lâl Genç, Karoline Altgelt, Sandra Draheim;
  Antonia Beltinger, Samuel Blaschke, Maike Steidler;
  Elisa Huber, Rebecca Kranner, Lena Zintl
pp. 91–95 © Doris Zoller 2014
pp. 96–99 © Markus Lanz 2012
p. 105 © Alban Janson 2016
p. 125 © Rebecca Wall, Beyza Gürdogan
p. 133 © Errands 2012
p. 133 below © Errands 2008
p. 135 © Errands 2011
p. 135 below © Errands 2009
p. 143 © Sofia Dona 2009
p. 148 © Shalalae Jamil 2011
p. 149 © Babar Sheikh and Usman Malkani 2011
p. 186 left, p. 186 right © Charlotte Malterre-Barthes
p. 187 © Lorenz Bürgi 2015
pp. 189–95 © Monique Jüttner 2017
p. 211 © NASA
p. 213 © U5 2017
p. 216 © Franz Junghuhn 1854
p. 217 © Bas Princen 2017
pp. 242–47 © Candida Höfer, Köln; VG Bild-Kunst,
  Bonn 2017
pp. 254–59 © raumlaborberlin 2017; drawn by Yü Chen,
  idea / text by Benjamin Förster-Baldenius, Sabine Zahn
pp. 264–65 © Norbert Kling and Carsten Jungfer
pp. 266–71 © Florian Kurbasik 2017
p. 275 © Shan Yang 2017
pp. 276–79 © Tianyu Zhu 2014
pp. 284–85 © Frank Eisenmann 2015
pp. 290–95 © Markus Lanz

Impressum

This book was created at the Chair of Urban Design
and Regional Planning, Prof. Sophie Wolfrum, Department
of Architecture at Technical University of Munich.

Editors: Sophie Wolfrum, Heiner Stengel, Florian Kurbasik,
Norbert Kling, Sofia Dona, Imke Mumm, Christian Zöhrer

Copyediting: Karl Detering, Simon Beesley

Proofreading: Keonaona Peterson

Translation: Karl Detering: Dietrich Erben p. 26,
Udo Weilacher p. 230, Angelika Fitz p. 110, Norbert Kling:
Imke Mumm p. 162, Francesca Fornasier p. 79, Maren
Harnack p. 38, Florian Hertweck p. 154, Michael Koch p. 20,
Gunther Laux p. 88, Sophie Wolfrum p. 60

Graphic Design: Heinz Hiltbrunner, Munich

Typesetting: Daniel Sieber, das formt, Munich

Project management: Annette Gref, Regina Herr

Production: Heike Strempel

Paper: 135 g/m² Magno volume

Printing: Beltz Bad Langensalza GmbH

Library of Congress Cataloging-in-Publication data
A CIP catalog record for this book has been applied for
at the Library of Congress.

Bibliographic information published by the
German National Library
The German National Library lists this publication in the
Deutsche Nationalbibliografie; detailed bibliographic data
are available on the Internet at http://dnb.dnb.de.

This publication is also available as an e-book
(ISBN PDF 978-3-0356-1578-4).

© 2018 Birkhäuser Verlag GmbH, Basel
P.O. Box 44, 4009 Basel, Switzerland
Part of Walter de Gruyter GmbH, Berlin/Boston

Printed on acid-free paper produced from chlorine-free
pulp. TCF ∞

Printed in Germany
ISBN 978-3-0356-1601-9

9 8 7 6 5 4 3 2 1
www.birkhauser.com